The Pecking Order

The Pecking Order

SOCIAL HIERARCHY AS A PHILOSOPHICAL PROBLEM

Niko Kolodny

HARVARD UNIVERSITY PRESS
Cambridge, Massachusetts, and London, England · 2023

Printed in the United States of America

FIRST PRINTING

Library of Congress Cataloging-in-Publication Data

Names: Kolodny, Niko, author.
Title: The pecking order : social hierarchy as a philosophical problem / Niko Kolodny.
Description: Cambridge, Massachusetts : Harvard University Press, 2023. | Includes bibliographical references and index.
Identifiers: LCCN 2022032807 | ISBN 9780674248151 (cloth)
Subjects: LCSH: Social stratification—Philosophy. | Political science—Philosophy. | Philosophy and social sciences.
Classification: LCC HM821 .K65 2023 | DDC 305.01—dc23/eng/20220804
LC record available at https://lccn.loc.gov/2022032807

For Jessica,
In theory, with equal,
in practice, with none

Contents

The Pecking Order

Introduction: A Negative Observation and a Positive Conjecture

Much in our interior mental lives and in our exterior social structures presupposes that we, human beings, are conscious of social hierarchy, of differences in rank and status. We are "conscious" of hierarchy in both senses of the word: "aware" of and "anxious" about (Anderson et al. 2015). This consciousness appears to be rooted in our natural history (Van Vugt and Tybur 2016). Many social animals are likewise preoccupied with "pecking order." These animals include not only chickens, who literally peck, but also our closest primate relatives (de Waal 2007). And this consciousness of hierarchy, transformed by our species' special bent for symbol and self-reflection, has driven much of our nonnatural history. The main chapters of the human story might be defined by the prevailing answers to the questions of who among us, if anyone, would be above, and who, if anyone, would be below. For most of the career of *Homo sapiens*, we appear to have lived in societies that were predominantly and often vigilantly egalitarian, at least for adult men (Boehm 2001; Flannery and Marcus 2012).[1] At various times and places, this was eventually upended, with the great many being subordinated, in enduring ways, to the very few. Modernity, albeit not without precedents, is in large part the tale—at times inspiring, at times cautionary—of our experiments with reconciling the equality of individuals with the differentiation of roles and concentrations of power and authority of large-scale, complex societies—with, in one sense of the word, civilization.

Suppose this is all true. What question does it raise for philosophy, as opposed to social science? First, there is the analytical question of what we mean by "hierarchy." This book answers that it consists of asymmetries of power and authority, as well as disparities of regard. Second, there is the normative question of why, if at all, we should care. Perhaps hierarchy matters only insofar it breeds other evils: an unfair division of material goods or heightened cortisol levels for those on the bottom rung. Nevertheless, this book asks what might follow if hierarchy should matter in its own right: if hierarchy—not in all forms, but at least when not appropriately tamed or managed—should itself be something to avoid or regret.

This book gets to these questions eventually. But it begins with a broader question: What, in the most basic and general terms, may we ask of others? At a minimum, it would seem, we may ask that others respect the boundaries of our persons. We may ask, for example, that others not subject us to gratuitous violence. Beyond that, we may ask that, where it does not burden them too much, they make things better for us. We may ask, for example, that others help us secure clean drinking water. That others respect the boundaries of our persons, and make things better for us, at least when it does not cost them too much, is already a tall order. It is an order so tall that perhaps no society has ever filled it for each of its members—or ever will. Indeed, it is an order so tall that one might be forgiven for stopping there and so overlooking that we also ask for something further and distinct. However, I doubt that we can fully understand our own moral sentiments unless we recognize that we do ask for something further and distinct. We ask that others not make us their inferiors or anyone else's.

It is early, I know, to resort to terms of art. But some settled labels may provide steady orientation, which we will need when we plunge headlong into the thicket of detail. So, let me restate what I have just said, with some admittedly ungainly regimentation. This book considers a number of "commonplace claims": moral ideas that recur either in high theory or in ordinary discourse about society and politics. These moral ideas are of the general form that individuals have claims to certain social institutions and forms of treatment. Put in negative terms, individuals have a complaint if they are denied those institutions or not treated in those ways. For example, the public has a complaint against officials who abuse their offices corruptly, members of a racial minority have a complaint against discrimination in public accommodation, and citizens have a complaint when they are denied an equal say over their government.

With respect to each of these commonplace claims, the book then tries to substantiate a "negative observation." This is that the commonplace claim can't be fully explained by appeal to "rights against invasion"—that others respect the boundaries of our person—or by appeal to "interests in improvement"—that others make things better for us. Nor can the commonplace claim be explained by a combination of rights against invasion and interests in improvement. There is a stubborn residue left unaccounted for.

The book then makes, with respect to each commonplace claim at issue, a "positive conjecture." This is that the commonplace claim, or some part of it left unexplained by rights against invasion and interests in improvement, can be seen to represent a "claim against inferiority"—that we not be set beneath another in a social hierarchy. The book then proceeds to the next commonplace claim and follows the same pattern. In other words, the basic rhythm of book is (with apologies to Hegelian dialectic and the waltz as an artform) a triplet: commonplace claim, negative observation, positive conjecture. If the reader ever feels out of time, that's the drumbeat to listen for.

This project would be of little interest, of course, if these allegedly commonplace claims were themselves peripheral or idiosyncratic. But, on the contrary, they underlie the most central and widely shared theoretical commitments of contemporary political philosophers: for instance, that the state somehow needs to be "justified" or "legitimated." And these claims fuel some of the most powerful and least controversial protests in ordinary public discourse: for instance, that governments should not be corrupt or undemocratic, that they should follow the rule of law and treat like cases alike. Everyone within the liberal democratic West, and often beyond, is expected to agree on at least these precepts—whether or not they agree, say, that "every billionaire is a policy failure."

This project would also be of little interest if interests in improvement and rights against invasion were peripheral or idiosyncratic moral ideas. Little wonder if two notions chosen at hazard do not account for everything! However, to say that people have interests in improvement is to say, more or less, that society should be organized so as to situate people to live better lives, in a way that is fair to all. John Rawls's *A Theory of Justice*, for instance, puts forward one version of this very general idea (Rawls 1971). It calls for a "basic structure" that distributes "social primary goods," understood as "all-purpose means" to advance "life plans," according to the "two principles" of "justice as fairness." And to say that people have "rights against invasion" is to say, more or less, that agents—whether individual or collective, natural or artificial—should not violate "individual rights," even to make individuals' lives better. Robert Nozick's *Anarchy, State, and Utopia* puts forward one version of this idea (Nozick 1974). It forbids more than a "minimal" state on the grounds that it would violate individual rights. In sum, the negative observation amounts to saying that, even if we help ourselves to whatever resources we like from Rawls and Nozick, we will still find ourselves at a loss to explain the commonplace claims.[2] Moreover, we will also, from time to time, consider other possible resources, such as an interest in the satisfaction of preferences for policy. And we will find that they don't provide the needed supplement.

This book would, finally, be of less interest if we already had a settled understanding of the content of the positive conjecture: a settled understanding of what complaints against inferiority are and what they can and can't explain. To be sure, my account of complaints against inferiority owes much to the discussions of relating as equals by relational egalitarians, such as Elizabeth Anderson and Samuel Scheffler; to the discussions of nondomination by neo-Roman republicans, such as Phillip Pettit and Quentin Skinner; and to the discussions of independence by scholars of Kant's political and legal philosophy, such as Arthur Ripstein. But illuminating and suggestive though these discussions are, they still leave much unsettled. In particular, I worry that they do not clearly distinguish objections to social hierarchy from objections of other kinds. This makes it hard for us to keep our focus on what is distinctive of social hierarchy and what it distinctively contributes to our moral thinking. Moreover, these discussions do not fully register how many and varied the phenomena are that claims against inferiority can be, and need to be, invoked to explain. Claims against inferiority animate a broader range of political commitments—namely, our various commonplace claims—than has been appreciated.

Let me now describe the structure of the book. Part I aims to substantiate the negative observation with respect to a first commonplace claim: a claim against the state's "coercion" of those subject to it—or against, at any rate, something about how the state relates to those subject to it—that requires the state to clear a special bar of "justification" or "legitimacy." Chapter 1 spells out the received materials for the negative observation: interests in improvement and rights against invasion. The remaining chapters of Part I set forth the case for the negative observation: that these materials are insufficient to account for the felt claim against the state. Put another way, we find that whatever it is that the state has to answer for, it is not one of the usual charges: that it uses force or violence, that it threatens or coerces, that it binds us against our will, or that it expropriates what we own.

Part II presents the materials for the positive conjecture: that the commonplace claim just shown not to be explained in terms of interests in improvement or rights against invasion might be instead explained in terms of claims against inferiority. These are claims against standing in a "relation of inferiority" to another individual—against being set beneath them in a social hierarchy. Such relations consist, I suggest, in asymmetries in power and authority, as well as in disparities of regard. To be sure, such asymmetries and disparities are not always and everywhere objectionable. Asymmetries of power and authority and disparities of regard constitute objectionable relations of inferiority where they are not limited or contextualized by what I call "the tempering factors." Having presented the materials, I then propose the positive conjecture with respect to the claim against the state. I suggest that the claim against the state, which imposes a special burden of justification or legitimation, is a claim against its hierarchical structure.

Part III follows this template with respect to further commonplace claims. Chapters 11 and 12 consider claims against corrupt uses of office. Chapter 13 considers claims against discrimination on the basis of, say, gender or race. Chapter 14 considers claims to equal treatment—of the sort that are violated when the state or an official plays favorites. Chapter 15 explains how the earlier discussion already accounts for claims to the rule of law. Chapter 16 addresses claims to equal liberty, in part by trying to come to terms with the powerful, Marxist idea that a lack of money is as much a lack of liberty as a legal prohibition. Chapter 17 considers claims to equal opportunity, especially in employment. Chapter 18 considers claims against poverty. And Chapters 19 and 20 consider claims against "illiberal" interference, such as fines, in choices of certain kinds, such as religion. If the reader takes away nothing else from Part III, I hope they will at least share a sense of surprise that so many seemingly disparate concerns can be seen as linked by a concern about hierarchy. One of the main aims of the book is to uncover these underappreciated systemic connections.

Part IV distinguishes the positive conjecture from similar ideas, such as those of the relational egalitarians, republicans, and Kantians noted earlier. I explain why I believe that claims against inferiority offer the better interpretation of the intuitions that all of us fellow travelers are trying to articulate. I also contrast the positive conjecture with "luck" or "telic" egalitarianism, which agrees that there is an egalitarian idea distinct from interests in improvement and rights against invasion but views it as a matter of the cosmic unfairness of being worse off than someone else. I believe these neighboring ideas have, at times, both obscured and borrowed their appeal from claims against inferiority.

Parts V and VI comprise a book-length treatment of one final commonplace claim regarding democratic structures of decision-making, which give each person, at some appropriate level, if not at all levels, an equal say. Part V tries to identify the basic values at stake, arguing that they are not accounted for by interests in improvement, rights against invasion, or, as is often presupposed in democratic theory, interests in the satisfaction of policy preferences. Instead, if there is a case for democracy, it is that it answers to claims against inferiority by making the decisions of the collective no more the decisions of any other individual than one's own decisions. Democracy is not so much a matter of being self-governing as a matter of not being governed by another. Part VI then asks what these identified values would imply. What sort of democracy would address claims against inferiority? The upshot is a certain kind of democratic pessimism. On the one hand, what is required of formal institutions is often very weak, perhaps deflatingly so. There is no simple argument against supermajority requirements or for "responsive" institutions, as "responsive" is usually understood. I present, as a case study, the elusiveness of objections to gerrymandering. On the other hand, what is required of informal conditions may seem very demanding, perhaps unrealistically so. Inequalities in time, money, and information are, in certain respects, like inequalities in the vote itself.

The conclusion reviews the main ideas of the book by drawing out some central themes. In retrospect, we can see the book as suggesting, in the first instance, that what drives much of our political thought and feeling is less a jealousy for individual freedom, as it may first appear, and more an apprehension about interpersonal inequality. That is, one might view the book as a kind of slow-motion, anti-libertarian judo. Press hard enough on some complaints of unfreedom and you end up in a posture not so much of defense of personal liberty as opposition to social hierarchy.[3]

Or, perhaps a better way of putting the point is that the opposition to social hierarchy can be understood as a claim to liberty of a different kind.

On one understanding of liberty, one is free insofar as one has the opportunity to live a worthwhile life. If so, then claims to liberty are just claims to improvement. On another understanding, one is free insofar as one is not invaded, whether or not invasion might improve one's condition. If so, then claims to liberty are just rights against invasion. Noninferiority represents a further conception of liberty. The sort of freedom pressed by claims against inferiority isn't freedom understood as being resourced to chart a life according to your choices or being insulated from invasion by others. Instead, it is freedom understood as having no other individual as master, of being subordinate to no one.

So understood, the book can be seen as distinguishing different conceptions of freedom and identifying what they explain and demand. In fact, the book considers still other conceptions of freedom besides the three just mentioned—claims to improvement, rights against invasion, and claims against inferiority. There is the republican's conception of nondomination, which I suggest is an unstable amalgam of rights against invasion and claims against inferiority. And there is the idea of freedom as positive self-rule, which one enjoys when the decisions under which one lives are one's own decisions. The aim of freedom as self-rule, I observe, is strictly harder to achieve than the aim of freedom as noninferiority. For while all inferiority, at least where asymmetries of power and authority are concerned, is rule by a will other than one's own, not all rule by a will other than one's own is inferiority. This is because the ruling need not be that of another natural individual, to whom one can stand in a relation of inferiority, but might instead be that of, say, a democratic collective. Thus, if we seek self-rule, and not simply noninferiority, there is more to put us at odds with our social world, and there are fewer routes to reconciling us to it.

All the same, noninferiority, as I understand it, may already seem an impossible ideal. Can noninferiority really be reconciled with civilization, with its characteristic division of labor and institutional hierarchies? Perhaps seeing the commonplace claims and the social structures that address them as animated by claims against inferiority helps explain them. And perhaps the various tempering factors that I list temper asymmetries of power and authority and disparities of regard to some extent. But do they temper them adequately so that we no longer have complaints against inferiority? I confess that I do not know. Something is left to the reader's judgment.

If civilization itself would make claims against inferiority impossible to adequately address, however, then the reader might take this as a reason to doubt, among other reasons to doubt, that there are claims against inferiority in the first place. Even if we grant that supposed claims against inferiority lie at the root of commonplace claims such as claims to democracy and equal treatment, perhaps those commonplace claims themselves are without merit. Perhaps, as so often happens with anxieties, once we name their source, once we dredge them up from the murk and into the light of day, we find nothing left to trouble us. In this case, the upshot would be more confident skepticism of the commonplace claims and greater assurance that we can dismiss them with a clear conscience. At best, concerns about undemocratic government, corruption, discrimination, unequal treatment, and the like, as such, are overgeneralizations, or vestiges of associative reasoning, borne of the fact that undemocratic government, corruption, discrimination, unequal treatment, and the like tend to travel with a failure to satisfy claims to improvement or with the invasion of rights. This would be a more deflating finding. But it would still be a finding that only an exploration of claims against inferiority—and of the support that they lend commonplace claims to democracy, nondiscrimination, and the like—helped us see.

How should you read this book? Perhaps not straight through at first, unless you have angelic patience or a thing for endurance events. If you want only a feel for the basic approach of the book, read just Chapters 1, 2, 5, and 8, as well as the conclusion. Chapter 1 lays out the received materials: interests in improvement and rights against invasion. Chapter 2 gives you an instance of a commonplace claim and the associated negative observation. Chapter 5 lays out the materials for the positive conjecture. Chapter 8 gives one instance of the positive conjecture. That would be one measure of the triplet of commonplace claim, negative observation, and positive conjecture. I would urge you, then, to read the conclusion, which draws broader lessons.

So long as you have read Chapter 1 and Part II, you can dip into the topics that most interest you. If you are interested in corruption, for example, then you can read Chapters 11 and 12. If you are interested in discrimination, then you can read Chapter 13. And so forth. One exception is the discussion of illiberal interventions in Chapters 19 and 20. This does require reading Chapters 2 and 3 on justifying the state. (And people who are interested in justifying the state might wish to read Chapters 19 and 20.)

Part IV is mostly for those who are interested in how claims against inferiority differ from other ideas in the conceptual neighborhood. How does the positive conjecture differ from republicanism, or relational egalitarianism, or luck egalitarianism? I do think the contrasts help sharpen the positive conjecture, but then I would think that. Perhaps a more objective observer would caution about a narcissism of small differences and, as can happen with narcissism, a risk of drowning.

If you are interested in democracy, then there's a lot of additional material. But you don't need to read it all. So long as you have read Chapter 24, you don't need to read all the negative discussion of Chapters 25 and 26. If you are interested in high theory, then you can skip or skim Part VI, which is about institutional details. If you are interested in institutional details but not much interested in gerrymandering, which is a uniquely American problem, then skip Chapter 30. More generally, while I devote a lot of space to democracy, and while the central ideas in this book first saw the light of day in a pair of articles on democratic theory, I don't view this book as solely, or even primarily, a contribution to democratic theory. In many ways, the democratic implications of noninferiority are what I feel most diffident about. As so often happens, volubility is sometimes a sign of the opposite of confidence.

I

A First Instance of the Negative Observation

Justifying the State

This part presents the case for the negative observation with respect to the commonplace claim against the state: that the commonplace claim cannot be explained by interests in improvement or rights against invasion.

1

The Received Materials

Improvement and Invasion

In this first chapter, I lay the groundwork for the case for the negative observation with respect to the commonplace claim against the state: that that claim cannot be explained by interests in improvement or rights against invasion. I do so by defining the basic terms: "claim," "interest in improvement," and "right against invasion."

1.1 Claims

Our moral thinking, I believe, is largely organized around the concept of a person's having a claim on an agent (Scanlon 1998; Wallace 2019). I won't try to defend this belief here. But this belief will inform just about everything else I do try to defend. So let me begin by saying what I take claims, in general, to be.

First, claims are held by natural, individual persons. Second, claims are on other agents, whether individual or collective, natural or artificial, to act in certain ways. Third, claims are grounded in the interests of these natural, individual persons, or, as Scanlon (1998) puts it, in the reasons that these natural, individual persons "have on their own behalf." These include, but are not necessarily exhausted by, interests in living a worthwhile life, controlling how others use one's body, and being treated fairly. Fourth, when an individual, Indy, has a claim on a potential benefactor or malefactor, Benny, to act in a certain way, that is a reason of a special stringency or priority for Benny to act in that way. Finally, if Benny does not act in that way, and so does not meet Indy's claim, because of a lack of due concern for the interests that ground that claim, then Indy has a complaint against Benny. Benny thereby wronged Indy. Indy has this as a reason to resent Benny. "Lack of due concern" is to be understood broadly to include malice, indifference, recklessness, negligence, and, perhaps, ignorance of certain general normative truths.

This view of morality, as organized around the claims that individuals have on agents, may seem so natural as not to be worth making explicit. However, it contrasts with a view of morality as organized around the impersonal goodness of states of affairs, which agents have reasons to promote. And it contrasts with a view of morality as organized around an ideal of agency—such as coherence or proper functioning—which agents have reasons to live up to. Neither of these alternative views of morality assigns the same importance to the place of a claimant (Wallace 2019).

It is worth highlighting an ambiguity in the use of "claim." When we ask, "What claim, if any, does Indy have on Benny?" we ask it with three different foci. With the "grounding" focus, we look to an interest of Indy's that might ground a claim on Benny. With the "guiding" focus, we look to what we would advise Benny to do in light of that interest. With the "reactive" focus, we look to whether Indy has grounds to resent Benny for what Benny does.

There are two broad kinds of case where the grounding and guiding foci, on the one hand, and the reactive focus, on the other, suggest different answers to the question of "What claim, if any, does Indy have on Benny?" First, there are cases of "failing to meet a claim, despite acting for the right reason." In such cases, when we take the grounding or guiding focus, we are apt to say that Benny has due concern for Indy's claim but nonetheless fails to meet it. The clearest instances, and perhaps the only instances, are where Benny is nonnegligently ignorant of some relevant, particular, nonnormative fact. Benny has taken Indy's coat, thinking that it is his, while Indy shivers from the chill. With the grounding focus, we onlookers, who know better, see that what Benny is doing does not, in fact, serve the interest for which Benny has due concern. And with the guiding focus, we onlookers, who know better, see that Benny in fact has reason, in light of that interest, to do something other than what he is doing. He should return the coat. We would advise him accordingly, if we could. So, with the grounding or guiding focus, we are apt to say that Indy has a claim on Benny to do otherwise. However, with the reactive focus, we may think that Indy nonetheless has no unmet claim against Benny, since Benny is acting with due concern (Wallace 2019, 10–11).

Second, there are cases of "meeting a claim for the wrong reason." In such cases, when we take the grounding or guiding focus, we are apt to say that

Benny does not fail to meet Indy's claim, although this is in spite of Benny's lack of due concern for it.[1] Suppose that Benny believes that Indy needs medication; that Benny, from malice, refuses to give it to him; and that unbeknownst to Benny, Indy's health is best served by not giving it to him. If we take either the grounding or guiding focus, we may wish to say that Benny is not failing to meet a claim that Indy has on him. Benny has not wronged Indy. But if we take the reactive focus, we may wish to say that Indy has an unmet claim. Benny has wronged Indy. At least, Indy has grounds to resent Benny.

With respect to cases of "meeting a claim for the wrong reason," it is perhaps too general to say that Benny has wronged Indy merely by lacking due concern. At least it sounds odd to say that Benny has wronged Indy if Benny's lack of due concern is completely inert: that is, if Benny's lack of due concern is never expressed in an action or omission because no opportunity, real or apparent, to harm Indy, transgress against Indy, or aid Indy ever presents itself. It is a good question, however, whether it sounds odd only because "wronging Indy" conveys doing something to Indy. In any event, it seems less odd to say something narrower: that Benny wrongs Indy by an action or omission that expresses a lack of due concern for the interests that underlie Indy's claims, even if, as it happens, that action or omission serves those interests.

In light of cases of failing to meet a claim, despite acting for the right reason and meeting a claim for the wrong reason, we might, perhaps somewhat artificially, regiment our use of "claim," on the one hand, and "complaint" and "wronging," on the other. We might say that Indy has a complaint against Benny for some action or omission, or that Benny wrongs Indy by it, just when that action or omission expresses—that is, is an outward manifestation of—Benny's lack of due concern for the interests that underlie Indy's claims, where "claims" are understood in the way that seems natural when we take the grounding or guiding focus.

1.2 Interests in Improvement

So far we have described only the structure of claims. What of their content? To begin with, I assume that among the claims an individual, Indy, has on other agents are claims grounded in Indy's interests in improvement. Indy has interests in being better situated to lead a fulfilling life, and these interests can support the conclusion that Indy has a claim on a potential benefactor, Benny, to act so as to better situate Indy to lead a fulfilling life. Since, in general, Indy is better situated to lead a fulfilling life when Indy knows that he is, Indy can have a derivative interest in being able to confidently predict that Benny will satisfy some improvement claim, such as a claim to potable water, that Indy has on Benny. So Indy can have a further improvement claim on Benny to put Indy in a position to confidently predict that Benny will satisfy his improvement claim to potable water: a claim on Benny not to leave it in doubt whether Benny will grant Indy access to the well. For Indy's interest in improvement to support, in this way, a claim on Benny, I assume Benny need not have any special relationship to Indy, other than that Benny can improve Indy's situation. Indy might have an improvement claim on Benny, for example, even though Benny belongs to the present generation, while Indy belongs to distant posterity.

"Improvement" is meant broadly. First, improvement is relative not to how things were or are but instead to how things could have been or could be. Not making Indy's situation worse than it is counts as improving Indy's situation if Benny had the option of making it worse. Second, improvement is not restricted to the provision of material goods. Benny's protecting Indy from physical harm at the hands of a third person, Altra, or, indeed, Benny's refraining from physically harming Indy himself, counts as improving Indy's situation. This is so even though Benny's refraining may, in addition, respect Indy's right against invasion, which we will discuss in Section 1.6.

To say that Indy's interest in improvement tends to support the conclusion that Indy has a claim on Benny to improve Indy's situation is not necessarily to say that whenever Indy has an interest in an improvement that Benny might provide, Indy has a claim on Benny to provide that improvement. First, there is the question of how the improvement to Indy's situation compares against the burdens that Benny, who has his own life to live, would have to bear to provide it (or even to be subject to providing it). Second, there is the question of how the improvement to Indy compares with the improvements to others, such as Altra, that Benny might make if he forwent the improvement to Indy—as it were, the moral opportunity cost of improving things for Indy. Indy might lack a claim on Benny because improving Indy's situation would prevent Benny from improving Altra's situation, in a way that trades off Altra's interests in improvement at an unfairly low rate against Indy's.[2]

In this way, Indy's claim to improvement on Benny will often be comparative, in the sense that whether Indy has such a claim depends on comparing the improvement to Indy with a foregone improvement to Altra and on trading off their interests fairly. Had the improvement to Altra been comparatively more significant, Indy might lack that claim. However, Indy's interest in improvement, by contrast with his claim to improvement, is not an interest in something comparative, such as getting from Benny what Altra got from Benny or not being worse off than Altra. Indy's interest in improvement is simply an interest in Indy's situation being better in absolute terms. What happens with Altra is neither here nor there.

This means that, insofar as interests in improvement are concerned, the fact that improving Indy's situation would increase inequality between Indy and Altra has no bearing, in itself, on what Benny should do. This is easiest to see in cases in which Indy and Altra are equally well situated and Benny can costlessly improve Indy's situation further but cannot improve Altra's situation further. In such cases, improving Indy's situation would indeed increase inequality. However, it would not come at the cost of forgoing an improvement to Altra's situation. So, as far as interests in improvement are concerned, there is nothing to weigh against Indy's interest in improvement. It is as though Altra wasn't there. Suppose Benny faces a choice between an outcome in which Altra is as well off as Benny can make her and Indy is at least as well off as Altra and a second outcome in which Altra is no worse off but Indy is even better off. Then we can say that Benny's choosing the second outcome is, relative to the first outcome, an inequality-increasing weak Pareto improvement. Interests in improvement support and do not oppose such inequality-increasing weak Pareto improvements.

1.3 Fair Trade-Offs

In the previous section, I said that how a benefactor, Benny, trades off Indy's improvement interests against Altra's improvement interests can be fair or unfair. How is fairness to be understood in this context? I will assume that what counts as a fair trade-off is, to some degree, prioritarian. That is, in evaluating whether a trade-off is fair, we give greater, but not necessarily absolute, weight to improving the situation of those worse situated. Thus, if Altra is worse off than Indy overall, it can be fair to improve her situation by a lesser increment, even if we must thereby forgo improving the better-off Indy's situation by a greater increment.

Some might suggest an alternative, or at least a supplement, to this. What counts as a fairer (or, at any rate, better) trade-off, they might say, should be sensitive to what Indy and Altra deserve. If Altra is more deserving, due to her character or past actions, than Indy, then, even if Altra is no worse off overall, it can be fairer to improve her situation by a lesser increment, even if we must thereby forgo improving Indy's situation by a greater increment. I will assume, however, that Indy's and Altra's improvement claims do not depend on desert. This is because I don't believe in desert, at least not of the relevant kind. This is just an explanation, not a justification. And it is also because it won't matter to the discussion, except in a few places, which I will note.

As I have described them, considerations of "priority" play the following role. They triage the interests in improvement of different people, such as Indy and Altra, in determining which, if either, has a claim on Benny (compare Munoz-Dardé 2005, 275, 277; Anderson 2010a, 2). However, many moral philosophers see considerations of priority (and, for that matter, considerations of desert) as playing a different role. Considerations of priority determine whether one state of affairs is impersonally better than another. If the fact that one state of affairs is impersonally better than another affects Benny's reasons for action, on such views, it is only via a further principle to the effect that one has greater reason to bring about a better state of affairs or that it is wrong to fail to bring about the best state of affairs one can (unless, perhaps, one is exercising a personal prerogative or running up against a deontological constraint).

Indeed, many moral philosophers believe that a moral theory must rank states of affairs as impersonally better or worse in order to guide action (or to guide some other response, such as hope or regret). But I don't see why. To be sure, a sane moral theory needs to say when, because of the properties of the outcomes of the actions open to Benny, it might be wrong for Benny to take a certain action or when Benny might wrong someone by taking a certain action. Among the relevant properties of outcomes, for example, might be that Indy's situation would be better to this or that extent. But to do this, a moral theory need not say anything about whether one outcome is better than another. Indeed, talk of better outcomes seems at best an unnecessary and at worst a distorting intermediate layer. Why say that producing this outcome is wrong because (i) it is wrong to produce a worse outcome, (ii) this outcome is worse, and (iii) it is worse because of its properties and the properties of alternative outcomes? Why not cut out the middleman and just say that this choice is wrong because of the properties of the outcome it would produce and the properties of alternative outcomes?

That said, it can be helpful, at times, to view a certain agent (such as the state) as aiming at a certain state of affairs: namely, the state of affairs that is constituted by that agent's fairly meeting the improvement claims of each person of some relevant group (such as those within the state's jurisdiction). I use the phrase "the public interest" as a compact expression for this aim: that is, a situation in which no one in the relevant group has an improvement complaint against the relevant agent.

This expression, "the public interest," must be treated with caution. First, it is not as though there is some collective entity, "the public," that has this interest. Instead, there are just the claims of individuals to have their situations improved, compatibly with fairness to others. Second, while it is true enough to say that the public interest is a state of affairs that the relevant agent has reason to promote, the agent does not have reason to serve the public interest, in the first instance, because it is a better state of affairs. Again, the agent has reason to promote the public interest instead because, first, individuals have claims on that agent to improve their situations, compatibly with fairness to others, and, second, meeting those claims just is what promoting the public interest comes to. Finally, keep in mind that the public interest involves only interests in improvement. Individuals have other interests, such as those that underlie rights against invasion and claims against inferiority.

1.4 Chances

I have described Indy's improvement interests as interests in being better situated to lead a fulfilling life. Put in more general terms, Indy's improvement interests support claims on others to a better choice situation, in which Indy's chances of leading a fulfilling life, in one or another respect, depend in certain ways on how Indy chooses. In a way, this is merely terminological. Whatever Indy has a claim to might be described as a "choice situation." That is, if Indy has a claim on others that they bring it about that he enjoys certain goods, period, then we can describe that as a claim to a "degenerate" choice situation, in which Indy enjoys those goods for sure and no matter how Indy chooses. It becomes more than merely terminological if we grant, as I think we should, that Indy sometimes has claims to choice situations in which Indy has a better or worse chance of enjoying certain goods if Indy chooses accordingly. In this section, I say something about how to understand chances in this context. In the next section, I say something about how to understand choices in this context.

In many cases, the most that Benny can do for Indy is to give Indy a better chance at a given good, rather than give it to Indy for certain. In such cases, Indy has a claim on Benny, therefore, not for certain possession but instead for a better chance—or, rather, as high a chance as Benny can give Indy, without unfairness to others or undue cost to himself. Why might Benny be able to distribute only chances, not certain possession? Sometimes it is simply because the world is an uncertain place. Benny physically can't distribute certain possession. The best he can do is to raise the chances.

At other times, however, it is because Benny morally can't distribute certain possession to Indy. Fairness to Altra requires that Benny distribute to Indy only a chance of possession. Suppose that Benny controls some indivisible good that would improve Indy's and Altra's situations in the same way. Intuition suggests that fairness requires Benny to distribute the good by a lottery that gives each a 0.5 chance. What explains the intuition? Well, consider any other distribution of chances: for example, that Benny were to give Indy a 0.6 chance and Altra a 0.4 chance. Altra might then complain that Benny could have improved her chances by giving her a 0.5 chance. This would not have been unfair to Indy. After all, Indy, who is relevantly similar, would have had just as high a chance: namely, 0.5. In such cases, the justification for a fair lottery is that it gives each potential recipient the highest chance at the good—the greatest improvement—that is compatible with fairness to other potential recipients. We might call lotteries justified in this way "highest fair chance lotteries."

1.5 Choice Situations

We turn now from how to understand chances to how to understand choices. The basic question is this: What does Indy have a claim on Benny to do going forward from some time, *t*? Is it that Benny take steps to ensure, going forward from *t*, that Indy has a better chance of enjoying certain goods if Indy chooses accordingly—a proper choice situation? Or is Indy's claim on Benny to take steps to ensure, going forward from *t*, that Indy enjoys certain goods no matter how Indy chooses—a degenerate choice situation? Although this question may seem, at this point, to be a digression, the answer bears on a number of the topics that will be later discussed. Most immediately, the answer will bear on what we will call the "Distributive Complaint" in Section 2.3: the thesis that the state requires justification because its imposition of deterrent penalties is distributively unfair to those who suffer the penalties.

For several reasons, Indy may have a claim on Benny to a proper, rather than a degenerate, choice situation: to a situation that leaves something to Indy's choice. The first reason is simple impossibility. It may be impossible for Benny to provide the goods to Indy without leaving something to Indy's choice. In other words, in many cases, there simply are no steps that Benny can take to give Indy a degenerate choice situation. Whatever Benny might do, Indy will enjoy the relevant goods, or better chances for them, only if Indy himself pitches in and makes a certain choice. Granted, sometimes Benny can give Indy a degenerate choice situation. For example, Benny might supply Indy with an environment free of a pathogen, no matter what Indy chooses. But many cases are not like this. In some of these cases, in which Benny cannot give Indy a degenerate choice situation, Benny's incapacity is technical. Lead Indy to water as you will, you can't make him drink. In some of these cases, in which Benny cannot give Indy a degenerate choice situation, Benny's incapacity is constitutive. Some of the activities that make for a fulfilling life are what we might call "choice dependent." They are possible or valuable only insofar as they flow from Indy's own, autonomous choices or judgments. These choice-dependent activities include expression, religious observance, association, or—as Raz (1986) understands "autonomy"—being the author of his life as a whole. Benny can arrange a marriage for Indy, for example, but not a love match. Similarly, Benny cannot choose a gift for Indy's husband that will convey Indy's judgment about what best expresses the significance of their marriage and the occasion. (This is Scanlon's [1998] example of what he calls the "representative" value of choice.)

A second reason why Indy may have a claim on Benny to a proper, rather than a degenerate, choice situation is inefficiency, whose cost Indy bears. Even if it is possible for Benny to provide goods without asking Indy to pitch in, those goods, or the chances of obtaining them, will be worse for Indy. Leaving something to Indy's choice more efficiently divides the informational or physical labor between Indy and Benny, and Indy reaps some of the benefits of that efficiency. This may be, first, because Indy's choice is a more reliable indicator of which goods suit Indy than any other indicator available to Benny. (This is what Scanlon [1998] calls the "predictive" value of choice.) If Indy is a diner, and Benny is the kitchen, then Indy usually will know best which item on the menu Indy will enjoy. Or, even if Indy's choice is no more reliable an indicator than the alternatives, Indy's choice may still be a cheaper indicator than the alternatives. For example, if a state authority had to do all the work of identifying who among millions might benefit from a given program, this work of information gathering might all but exhaust its budget, with the result that the authority couldn't offer much to the recipients it succeeded in identifying. A system that asks prospective recipients to do the work of identifying themselves by enrolling or applying might offer them more. Finally, setting information aside, there are logistical considerations. Perhaps Benny can make Indy drink, after all. Benny can pry open Indy's lips and pour. It's just that the added expense of prying and pouring will leave Benny with only half a draught. Force quenching is labor intensive. Indy may have more reason to want the full draught set before him, for him to drink or spill himself.

I have just listed a number of factors that make a degenerate choice situation a less efficient division of labor, where the inefficiency comes at Indy's expense. Of course, the same loss in efficiency might come at someone else's expense. Benny, for one, might have to bear the costs. Force quenching is exhausting work. So, even if Indy has reason to prefer a degenerate choice situation, it might ask too much of Benny to take steps to provide it going forward from *t*, in which case Indy might have a claim only to a proper choice situation. Similarly, the same loss in efficiency might be borne by Altra. So, even if Indy has reason to prefer a degenerate choice situation, it might come unfairly at Altra's expense for Benny to take steps to provide it going forward from *t*. If so, then Indy might have a claim only to a proper choice situation.

My suggestion, then, is that improvement claims are, in general, to improved proper choice situations. This explains, in turn, why, often when Indy has made some choice—for example, to consume, invest, gamble, neglect, forgo, etc. some resource or opportunity that Benny has made available to him—Indy lacks a further claim on Benny. The explanation is that Benny already gave Indy what Indy had a claim to: the choice situation from which

Indy made that choice. That is, what Indy had a claim on Benny to do was to provide Indy with a proper choice situation, namely one in which Indy could make certain choices with certain results. And Benny has already provided Indy with that choice situation. Consequently, Benny has met the claim Indy had on him. Therefore, Indy has no further claim on Benny (compare Vallentyne 2002).

Note that the fact that Indy makes a particular choice within the relevant choice situation doesn't itself have any further effect on Indy's claims on Benny or on whether Benny has met those claims. Again, this is because Benny providing Indy with the choice situation already settled accounts prior to Indy making a particular choice within it. It is easier to see this when Benny doesn't have to do anything in response to Indy's choice in order to ensure he has, in fact, given Indy the choice situation to which Indy has a claim: that Indy's choices have the relevant consequences. In such cases, Benny just sets up the choices for Indy and then lets the chips lie where they fall. It is harder to see this, by contrast, when Benny does have to "do something"—to take some active, positive step, *X*—in response to Indy's particular choice in order to ensure he has, in fact, given Indy the choice situation to which Indy has a claim: that Indy's choices have the relevant consequences. In such cases, we may be tempted to say that Indy's particular choice creates a claim on Benny to do *X*. But we see things more clearly, I think, if we say instead that by doing *X*, Benny sees to it that he indeed gave Indy what Indy already had a claim to. That was a choice situation in which, among other things, if Indy made that choice, the relevant consequence—namely, the consequence constituted or brought about by Benny's *X*-ing—would occur.

Note that the choice that Indy makes and to which Benny responds by *X*-ing need not be an active, positive, conscious, capital *C* Choice to accept the associated results, as such. It depends on the case. Indy might only have a claim to be clearly informed that, in order to avoid bad results *B*, he must avoid behavior *A*. If Indy is informed of this but then engages in *A* and so suffers *B*, Indy's claim has been met, even if, when Indy engaged in *A*, he did not choose to accept *B* or did not even remember that engaging in *A* would bring down *B* (Scanlon 1998). In other cases, however, Indy's reason to want protection from bad results *C* might be so strong in comparison to the reasons others have to want not to provide that protection that Indy has a claim to avoid *C* unless Indy expressly, in no uncertain terms, chooses, there and then, to accept *C*.

Again, I have been proposing an answer to the question of why, intuitively, it is often the case that when Indy has made some choice, Indy lacks a further claim on Benny. The proposed answer is that Benny has already provided Indy with what he has a claim to: namely, the choice situation in which Indy made that choice. This proposed answer is perhaps best clarified by contrasting it with some alternatives. So consider three different accounts of why it is often the case that when Indy has made some choice, Indy lacks a further claim on Benny. The first account is that what Indy really has a claim to is some "final stuff," realized by consummated enjoyment, such as pleasure or satisfied final desire. Since Indy's choice produces this final stuff, Indy's choice satisfies his claim to the final stuff. Suppose that Benny gives Indy and Altra each an apple. Indy chooses to eat his, whereas Altra waits to eat hers. As a result, Indy has no claim on Benny for an additional apple, even though, in some sense, it's now the case that Altra has an apple whereas Indy has none. The reason, according to this answer, is that Indy's apple has been converted into the final stuff by Indy's consuming it (G. Cohen 2009, 18–19, 25). What matters, on this account, is not, strictly speaking, that Indy made a choice. It is instead that the final stuff was produced. Indy's choice just happens to be, in this case, what initiated the final stage of the production process.

The first difficulty with this account is that Indy's claims on Benny are not only to final stuff. There are other features of choice situations, besides a tendency to produce final stuff, that Indy has reason to want, such as the ability to pursue choice-dependent activities. The second difficulty with this account is that in some cases, when Indy has made a choice, Indy can lack a claim on Benny, even though the choice does not produce any final stuff. Not all the relevant choices are choices to consume. There are also choices to gamble, invest, and dither. Suppose, for example, that Benny gives everyone an apple. Altra eats her apple, but Indy makes a gamble that his apple will keep another day. Or he buries the apple, betting on the start of an orchard. The apple spoils, or never takes root, and so he loses the consumption of an apple that Altra had. Indy does not, in this case, convert the apple into final stuff. But still it seems, at least if the rest of the scenario is suitably described, that he does not have a claim on Benny for more.

The second alternative account of why it is often the case that when Indy has made some choice, Indy lacks a further claim on Benny is that Indy does not deserve more. On this account, Indy's choice weakens the claims he can make on others by, as it were, making him a less compelling claimant. As I noted in Section 1.3, I set aside desert. In any event, even if one considers desert, the choices that leave Indy with no further claim on Benny need not be "bad" choices, of a kind to make Indy less deserving. One needn't believe that letting an apple go bad is a sin in order to believe that if Benny gives Indy an apple, and Indy lets it go bad, Indy has no claim on Benny for anything more. Or suppose that Indy makes a gamble with Altra for an extra half an apple. Each deposits half an apple with Benny. Indy loses. So, if Benny is to honor the gamble, Benny must give Indy's half to Altra. In this case, Indy hasn't done anything that Altra hasn't also done. So, if Indy doesn't deserve an apple, then neither does Altra. So, if the reason why Benny shouldn't return Indy's half to Indy is that Indy does not deserve a half, then that is equally a reason why Benny shouldn't give Indy's half to Altra. But if one generalizes this conclusion, then it follows, implausibly, that, once and for all, all bets are off.

The final alternative account of why it is often the case that when Indy makes a choice, Indy lacks a further claim on Benny is that in making the choice, Indy somehow waives or forfeits a further claim on Benny. On this account, Indy's choice about what to do with the apple matters because it is additionally the exercise of a normative power with respect to Benny: a power to waive or forfeit further claims on him. One problem is that, in many relevant cases, there is no obvious candidate for the further claim on Benny that is supposedly waived by Indy's choice. When Indy chooses to let his one allotted apple spoil, for example, what further claim on Benny is Indy thereby supposed to waive? It can't be a claim on Benny to give Indy the apple that Indy let spoil, since Benny already satisfied that claim. And it isn't a claim on Benny to give Indy another apple, because Indy never had a claim to a second apple. But the deeper problem is that the power to waive or forfeit claims itself calls for explanation. Why should Indy's claims on Benny depend in that way on Indy's choice? I suspect the answer will appeal to reasons that Indy has to prefer that choice situation—that is, a choice situation in which Indy's claims on Benny can be waived in that way by choice—over the alternatives. But then the appeal to waived or forfeited claims is not an alternative to our proposal. It is instead a special case of it.

Our suggestion, then, is that when Indy makes a choice, he often lacks a further claim on Benny because Benny already gave Indy what Indy had a claim to: namely, the situation in which he made that choice. But one might still wonder why Indy does not have a further claim on Benny. After all, even if Indy had reason at *t* to want that Benny, going forward from *t*, take steps to give him a proper choice situation, Indy may have reason, at a later time, *t'*, to prefer, retrospectively, that, going forward from *t*, Benny had instead given Indy some degenerate choice situation, which left nothing to Indy's choice. Perhaps Indy suffers a slip 'twixt cup and lip, spilling the whole draught, and now at *t'* wishes that Benny had force-quenched him. Why doesn't Indy now have a claim on Benny to give him what he would have had from the degenerate choice situation?

One answer is that Benny cannot give Indy what he would have gotten from the degenerate choice situation. The steps that Benny had to take going forward from *t* in order to give Indy the proper choice situation can't be undone. The draught has been spilled. Another answer is that it would be too burdensome for Benny, especially in light of burdens that Benny has already borne, to provide Indy with the proper choice situation. Yet another answer is that giving Indy what Indy would have had from the degenerate choice situation would come unfairly at Altra's expense. This is because it would retroactively make it the case that Altra's choice situation was unfairly worse. Benny might say: "The only way to improve your situation now, Indy, would be to take some of the potable from Altra to give to you. But that would retroactively deprive Altra of the choice situation that, at *t*, it was fair to give her. It would retroactively make it the case that the choice situation that I gave Altra, at *t*, was that whatever Altra chose, Altra would get at most half a cup, whereas the choice situation that I gave you, at *t*, was better: namely, either a whole draught if there was no spill or half a draught if there was a spill. That would have been unfair to Altra."

If, on the other hand, Benny can now do something more for Indy, without this being unduly burdensome and without its coming unfairly at Altra's expense, then that just means Benny in fact could have given (and perhaps can now still give) Indy a better choice situation: namely, one with the insurance policy that Benny would do the additional something in this eventuality. In recognizing that Indy may have a claim on Benny to a choice situation with such an insurance policy, the view I have been advancing differs from the "luckist" position that Indy has no claim on others to mitigate (absolute or comparative) bads that result from his choices: to ameliorate bad "option luck" (compare Vallentyne 2002).[3]

Return to the case in which Altra eats her apple but Indy delays and his apple spoils. That Indy does not eat his apple, it would seem, is due to his own choice. It is his own bad option luck. Had he chosen, as Altra did, to eat the apple without delay, he would have eaten it, just as Altra did. So, according to this luckist view, he has no further claim on others. On our account, by contrast, whether Indy has a claim on others depends on whether they have done what they needed to do to give him the choice situation he had a claim on them to give. Suppose the best choice situation that Indy and Altra each could have been given, without unfairness to the other, was one in which, even if they postponed eating their apple, they were partially indemnified if it went bad. In that case, Indy does have a claim against others. Perhaps he has a claim against Altra for eating her whole apple and thereby depleting the store of funds against which Indy's insurance claim could be filed. That deprived Indy of a better choice situation to which he was entitled. This is so even though Indy could have had what Altra had if he had made a different choice. It is so even though his being left without an apple is just bad option luck.

This is not to say that the best choice situation that Indy and Altra each could have been given, without unfairness to the other, will always be one in which they are so indemnified. Perhaps the best choice situation was one in which postponing eating the apple was entirely at their own risk, which allowed each to eat their full apple without having to hold some in reserve to cover the potential losses of others. In this case, Indy does not have a claim against others because others gave him the choice situation to which he was entitled: namely, the one without insurance.

What then makes one choice situation better than another? It is a difficult question, and I don't have a full answer (see Vallentyne 2002; Olsaretti 2009). As a negative point, though, I do reject the following proposal for a full answer: that one choice situation is better than another just when it has a higher "expectation," where the "expectation" of a choice situation is something like the sum of the values of the outcomes of the specific choices open to Indy discounted by the probabilities that Indy will actually make those choices. I agree that the values of the outcomes of the specific choices, as well as the probabilities that Indy will make those choices, can bear on the value of his choice situation. But other factors also bear on its value. In lieu of a full answer to the question of what makes a choice situation better, I offer instead, in Section 3.5, a list of factors that, other things equal, tend to make a choice situation better or worse. This list of factors is partial, of course, since it says nothing about when other things are not equal. However, this list may be enough for our purposes.

1.6 Rights against Invasion

We have been suggesting that Indy has interests in improvement, which can support claims on Benny that he improve Indy's choice situation when this would not be unfair to others or unduly burdensome. Indy also has claims—or, here it seems more natural to say, "rights"—against invasion. If Indy's interests in improvement present themselves (or rather their satisfaction) to Benny as goals, Indy's rights against invasion present themselves to Benny as constraints, even on the pursuit of such goals. Even if Benny could thereby improve the situation of Altra or even Indy himself in a fair way—even if Benny could bring about a greater good—Benny may not invade Indy to do so.

At a minimum, Indy has rights against others that they not dispose of his body, at least absent certain conditions, such as Indy's consent. Indy may also have rights against others that they put him in a position to confidently predict that they will not so dispose of his body. Perhaps Indy also has rights against invasion of things other than his body. Perhaps Indy has rights that other agents not invade his external property (at least such property as is not itself a creature of social institutions). Or perhaps Indy has rights that others not invade his choice situation—although, as I argue in Chapter 3, I find this hard to make sense of.

Our discussion of rights against invasion will focus, specifically, on the:

> "Force Constraint": Indy has a claim on others that they not invade his body when this does not produce a greater good or as a means to, or a foreseeable side effect of a means to, a greater good (compare Kamm 2006), barring something, such as consent, that "lifts" this constraint.

One might worry, however, that this focus on the Force Constraint is too narrow. First, one might say, the Force Constraint is only a part or implication of some more extensive right over one's body. Kantians may call this more extensive right "equal external freedom." Libertarians may call it "self-ownership." These labels typically invoke more than merely the Force Constraint. For example, self-ownership may imply that one is morally permitted to do whatever one likes with one's body; that one can permit, by consent, anything to be done to one's body (whether or not it achieves a greater good); or that one can transfer such rights over one's body to someone else. However, I doubt that these more extensive rights over one's body will help explain the commonplace claims where the Force Constraint doesn't.

Second, one might say that the focus on the Force Constraint is too narrow because, as noted earlier, there may be rights against invasions of things other than one's body. In Section 4.2, I suggest that rights against invasion of one's external property do not help explain the commonplace claims where rights against invasion of one's body don't. And in Chapter 3, I argue that there are no plausible rights against invasion of one's choice situation.

1.7 Appendix: Natural Injustice, Structural Injustice, and Claims against No One

Our political philosophy is organized around complaints held against agents (whether individual or collective) for an action (or omission). Some might question this. They may insist there can be injustices—or, at any rate, ills of a kind that a political philosophy ought to concern itself with—even when no one has a complaint against any agent for any action: that is, even when no agent has wronged anyone. There are, it may be said, natural injustices. Or there are structural injustices. Indeed, it might be said, among such structural injustices are often those involving what I go on to describe as "relations of inferiority." Much sexism and racism, it will be said, are structural. In sum, the objection runs, a philosophy of social hierarchy that is organized around complaints is ill suited to its subject matter.

Let me begin with the most concessive response. Suppose that, in the case of many of these ills, Indy should have no complaint. Nevertheless, there may still be reasons Indy has on his own behalf that would have grounded a complaint about what happens to him had there been a relevant agent. Granted, those reasons cannot support resentment. But they can support regret that things were not otherwise. Indy's interests in improvement may support regret about improvements that might have been. And Indy's interest in not standing in a relation of inferiority to another may also support regret, even if no agent could do anything about it.[4] Thus, my analysis of relations of inferiority and the positive conjecture that it is a bad to stand in them is still of interest, even with regard to cases where, because there is no relevant agent, one has no complaint about them.

Must we concede so much, however? Must we abandon a framework of complaint in order to make sense of, say, structural injustice? On the contrary, one might think it is central to the idea and experience of injustice that victims of the injustice have a complaint against it. Granted, Rawls, who held that the "basic structure" was the primary subject of justice, said little about complaints. But, by the same token, he never, to my knowledge, claimed that there can be injustice without grounds for complaint. Young's (2011) instructive account of responsibility for structural injustice might seem to suggest that there can be injustice without complaint. But I don't think she goes so far. It is true that she rejects a "liability" conception of responsibility for structural injustice. But what is Young rejecting in rejecting the liability model? First, she seems to be rejecting the thought that in contributing to structural injustice, agents must be violating "the law and . . . accepted norms and rules" (46). Her central example of contributing to structural injustice is participating in a housing market that results in many people being vulnerable to homelessness. But you might have a complaint against me for an action that does not violate the law or accepted norms and rules. (Suppose you are attempting to escape legal slavery and I turn you in.) Second, Young seems to be rejecting the thought that in contributing to structural injustice, agents are doing so intentionally (63), "with adequate knowledge of the situation" (97), "with explicit reflection and deliberation on the wider implications" (107). But you might have a complaint against me for negligent or habitual actions or for omissions. Finally, she is rejecting the idea that agents who contribute to structural injustice can be held responsible for some specific harm to specific people that is "traceable to specific individual actions or policies" (44), in a way that would ground claims to specific redress or compensation (as with a tort) and would not similarly apply to other agents who contribute to the system in the same way (105). But you might have a complaint against me for contributing to a system that can be expected to result in harms to people like you, even if no specific harm to any specific person can be traceable to my actions in particular and even if you have the same complaint against everyone else who contributes to the system in the same way.

Moreover, Young's positive "social-connection" model of responsibility grants that we, as individuals, have forward-looking responsibilities—by which she seems to mean duties—to work with others to change the system. Presumably, others have complaints against us for failing to discharge those responsibilities. In the face of structural racism, the statement that "White silence is violence" would seem to suggest that when individual Whites are silent, they are failing to meet a claim that Blacks have against them to speak out. So even if no one has a complaint against me for contributing to the system, people do have complaints against my failing to discharge my responsibility to work with others to reform the system. And it may be hard to maintain the distinction between contributing and failing to reform in any event. After all, to contribute to the system is itself to fail to take steps to reform it.

Some might agree that where there is injustice, or an ill of the sort that concerns political philosophy, certain people will have a complaint against it. However, they might deny that these complaints are always against some agent for some action. Some complaints are not complaints against an agent. There are, they say, claims against no one. One view of this kind is the Theory of Cosmic Fairness, which I discuss in greater depth in Section 21.1.

Another view of this kind arises from collective-action cases of the sort described by Estlund (2019). In these cases, we are given a set of all the relevant agents and all the various combinations of actions that might be realized by those agents acting in the ways open to them. There is a best combination and a second-best combination such that (i) had it been up to some agent to choose whether to bring about the best combination or the second-best combination, that agent would thereby have wronged a person, Vic, by bringing about the second-best combination but also such that (ii) no agent wrongs anyone by performing their act in the second-best combination, given that the other agents will perform their actions in the second-best combination. Estlund's (2019, 33) toy example is "Slice and Patch Go Golfing": "Suppose that unless a patient ["Vic," as we will call him] is cut and stitched he will worsen and die (though not painfully). Surgery and stitching would save his life. If there is surgery without stitching, the death will be agonizing. . . . Slice and Patch are each going golfing whether the other attends to the patient or not." In the best combination, Slice and Patch perform the surgery. In the second-best combination, Slice does not slice and Patch does not patch. Slice doesn't wrong Vic by not slicing, given that Patch won't patch. After all, slicing would only cause Vic pain. While this toy example might seem silly, the same pattern might be expected to recur with respect to Young's forward-looking responsibilities to work with others to reform the system. The value of what we do as individuals may turn on what others will do. As Young writes, "It is not false . . . for [someone] to believe, considered in isolation from the ways he might cooperate with others in the structures to change the way they constrain, and even though he is in a position of relative privilege in those structural processes, that he faces a limited set of options that are objectively given" (2011, 56).

While Estlund's probing treatment deserves more discussion than I can give it here, it seems to me that cases of this kind come in two varieties. In the bad-motive varietals, the second-best combination occurs because some agent, such as Slice, is not motivated to do their part in the best combination even if others would do their parts. Here it seems intuitive that Vic has a complaint against such agents (although Estlund's positive theory of "plural requirement" seems not to explain this). This is because, I would suggest, such agents meet Vic's claim for the wrong reason. In the good-motive varietals, the second-best combination occurs even though no agent lacks due concern for Vic. Presumably, these are cases in which each agent would do their part if only they knew that the other would, but they nonnegligently, falsely believe that the other agent won't do their part. In such cases I don't find it intuitive to think that Vic has any complaint at all. To be sure, Vic has reason to regret that fate has left the agents in a state of ignorance that keeps them from bringing about the best combination. But that fate set the agents up for failure is just bad luck, no different from a natural disaster.

2

Is the Claim against the State's Force?

The previous chapter introduced interests in improvement, which one might think of as the basic building block of Rawls's theory of justice: what is pressed by the parties in the "original position." And the previous chapter also introduced rights against invasion, which one might think of as the basic building block of Nozick's theory: the natural rights any agent—individual or corporate, natural or artificial—must respect.

The point of introducing these materials was to set the stage for our negative observation. In general form, the negative observation is that even with these materials, we still can't account for many commonplace claims in political discourse. By considering specific commonplace claims, we get specific instances of the negative observation. The rest of Part I pursues a first, specific instance of the negative observation with respect to the following commonplace claim. This is a supposed claim against the state, which is supposed to make justifying the state, or establishing its legitimacy, a problem.

2.1 The Ubiquitous Presupposition: A Claim against the State

The state, it is said, stands in certain relations of rule to its subjects. It wields authority or power over its subjects. It obligates, coerces, threatens, or uses force or violence against them so as to compel them to comply with its commands. It claims a monopoly or exclusive right to issue and enforce these commands. And so forth. Those who are subject to such relations of rule are thought to have, in most cases, a complaint against such relations. To justify the state, or to establish its legitimacy, is to answer this complaint: to show that those subject to the state lack such a complaint against the state.

This complaint against the state is not an improvement complaint. For it is supposed to persist even if we stipulate, for the sake of argument, that the state realizes the public interest: that it improves the choice situation of each person subject to it as much as it can, subject only to the constraint that it trades off among their choice situations fairly.

The standard view is that what answers the complaint, if anything does, is one of two things. Either it is a "legitimating condition" that the state satisfies—for example, that those subject to the relation of rule consent to it or find it acceptable—or it is a "limit of legitimacy" that the state respects in what it does—for example, that the state is "minimal" or that it respects the "Harm Principle" of Mill (1859). The state goes only so far, but no further.

A claim of this kind is patent in libertarian opposition to the state. A more extreme libertarian position says that the state, like any other agent, may enforce natural rights, but nothing more, unless the state satisfies the legitimating condition of actual consent (Simmons 1979, 2000, 2005). A more moderate libertarian position says that, absent consent, the state may enforce natural rights, or contributions to schemes that enforce natural rights, but nothing more. That is, the state may "enforce" its directives that people contribute to "negative" protection from invasion by others, but the state may not "enforce" directives to contribute to improving people's situations by providing "positive" goods, such as nutrition and medical care. Absent consent, the state must be "minimal" (Nozick 1974).

Why not a more extensive state, which requires contributions to schemes that provide opportunities beyond freedom from rights violations, such as greater literacy or protection from infectious disease? Few libertarians feel compelled to deny the truism that people's lives are improved if they enjoy greater literacy or protection from infectious disease. After all, the same libertarians may support private charities, or harbor personal hopes for the victims of command economies or markets stifled by excessive regulation, that are predicated on precisely that truism (Narveson 2010, 263). Instead, most libertarians will first answer: "Even if the state improves people's situations, that doesn't answer the complaint against the relations of rule that the state involves. For instance, it doesn't license the state to coerce people, without their consent, to improve their situation. The ends don't justify the means."

But it's not just libertarians. Liberals also insist on limits of legitimacy. Many accept some child or cousin of Mill's Harm Principle: roughly, that the state may "coerce" people only to prevent harm to others (Feinberg 1984). Hence, the state cannot "coerce" people to avoid choices that are bad for themselves alone, even if that would improve their situation.

And many liberals insist on a legitimating condition. Rawls, and the many theorists of "public reason" who have followed him, argue, very roughly, that the state's actions, or a special class of the state's actions, must meet the legitimating condition of having a "public justification," which does not rest on sectarian premises. Rawls's "liberal principle of legitimacy" says that because the state "exercises political power," it must meet the legitimating condition of being (as I put it) "reasonably acceptable" to those subject to it: roughly, justifiable to them in terms that do not presuppose any particular religion or philosophy of life (Rawls 1993, 136–137). Those subject to such "political power," it would seem, have some claim against it that must be addressed, if not by their consenting to it then by its being reasonably acceptable to them. The claim isn't answered simply by showing that the state meets claims to improvement. If it did, *A Theory of Justice* would not have needed a sequel.

To take another example, R. Dworkin agrees that there is a crucial "puzzle of legitimacy": "How can anything" supply a general "justification for coercion in ordinary politics?" (1986, 191). The legitimating condition that must be met, he argues there, is that those subject to such coercion comprise a community of a special and demanding kind—a "community of principle"—that goes beyond merely having a state that promotes the common good. And the later Dworkin (2011) is sown with thoughts of a similar form: the government "has no moral title to coerce, unless . . ." (372), "coercive political organizations undermine the dignity of their members unless . . ." (319–320), and so on. Even Raz (2001), otherwise so wary of liberal pieties, holds that state coercion, at least beyond a limit of legitimacy roughly modeled on the Harm Principle, requires a legitimating condition of "trust." And Williams (2005, 23), even warier perhaps of liberal pieties, grants that "the first necessary truth, one of few, about the nature of right" says at least that "coercion requires legitimation."

Finally, consider the idea that "economic" justice is more urgent within borders than across them. Certain relations of rule, such as coercion, are thought to obtain distinctively within borders. And these relations are thought to provoke a complaint, which is answered only by the legitimating condition of economic justice beyond mere humanitarianism. No doubt a minimal state improves people's situations beyond what they were in a state of nature. But despite these improvements, the minimal state's relations of rule provoke a new demand for justification, which no one faced in the state of nature. This claim must be met by this further legitimating condition: that it become more than minimal (Blake 2001; Nagel 2005). Others argue that since those outside a state's borders are exposed to its coercion, a further legitimating condition must be met with respect to them (Abizadeh 2008).

In sum, it takes searching to find a contemporary political philosopher who doesn't presuppose some such complaint against the state. But we should find this more puzzling than we do. After all, it's hardly true, in general, that measures to improve people's circumstances must meet legitimating conditions or respect limits of legitimacy. If I drain a stagnant pool in my own backyard, protecting my neighbors from mosquito-borne disease, I don't need the legitimating condition of their consent, or a public justification, or economic justice, or a relationship of trust. Nor do I if I urge them not to embark on some self-destructive course of action. Yet neither the drainage nor the advice respects any familiar limit of legitimacy. Neither aims solely to prevent invasions of rights. And the advice is manifestly an attempt to influence a self-regarding choice. So why, then, when the state improves people's situations, does it face some complaint that can be answered only by a legitimating condition or limit of legitimacy?

2.2 Enforcement

Some preliminaries before we begin our search for the complaint against the state: our search both for the relation of rule targeted by the complaint and for what it is about that relation of rule that provokes the complaint. To sharpen our focus, let us idealize the state in two ways. First, the state is an "ideal enforcer": it enforces its directives against all and only violations, either by foiling attempted violations or responding appropriately to successful violations. Its police, courts, and so on make no mistakes. Second, the state is "ideally directive": there is no alternative system of directives and enforcement that the state could implement that would better serve the public interest or meet claims to improvement—although, importantly, there will usually be many alternative sets that do equally well. Granted, this ideal state may automatically meet one of the legitimating conditions proposed in the previous section: namely, economic justice beyond humanitarianism. But it does not, unless more is said, satisfy the other legitimating conditions, such as consent or acceptability. Nor does it respect the limits of legitimacy of the minimal state; it aims to improve choice situations beyond simply protecting rights.

As we review the usual suspects for the complaint against the state, we will perform two tests to see whether we have identified the complaint against the state. The "Subtraction Test" asks whether removing the relation of rule quiets the complaint. That is, if we subtract, in imagination, the relation of rule that is supposed to provoke the complaint, are we still left, intuitively, with a complaint of the kind we are trying to make sense of? If not, then the candidate target cannot be the thing, or at least not the only thing, that provokes the complaint. The "Spare-Justification Test" asks whether we can answer the complaint, at least by the lights of those who insist there is a complaint, even without any significant legitimating condition or limit of legitimacy, let alone the legitimating conditions and limits of legitimacy they customarily invoke. Can we answer the complaint with a "sparer" justification? If so, then the relation of rule that has been proposed as the target cannot be the thing that provokes the complaint, which is supposed to be answered only with the help of legitimating conditions or limits of legitimacy.

So what might be the relation of rule that provokes the complaint against the state? Most often, perhaps, it is said to be the state's enforcing our compliance with its directives. Indeed, it is very often said that it is the state's use of force, violence, threat of punishment, or coercion that calls for special legitimating conditions or limits of legitimacy.[1]

What then does "enforcing" mean? It divides into three categories that call for quite different treatment. First, to enforce a directive, *D*, may be to threaten: to prevent the agent's violation of *D* by telling him that he will suffer some unwelcome consequence if he violates *D*. Second, to enforce *D* may be to defend: to prevent the agent's violation of *D* by more direct, physical means. Note that "defense" covers a wider range of cases than it might seem at first. Restitution "after the fact"—such as returning stolen goods—is often described as a response to a past violation. But often such responses are a forward-looking defense; they aim to prevent the future violation that would take place if, say, the thief were to remain in control of the stolen goods.[2] Finally, to enforce *D* may be to impose a deterrent: to follow through on the threat (whether or not the threat itself was permissibly issued) by visiting those unwelcome consequences on someone who violates *D*, not with the aim of preventing the violation of *D* itself (which has already occurred) but instead to sustain the potency of future threats to deter the agent or others from violating instances of the same sort of directive. I use the phrase "impose a deterrent" instead of (the admittedly less cumbersome) "punish" to stress that it does not involve condemnation—as punishment, perhaps by definition, does. The purpose of following through on deterrent threats is simply to induce cooperation, and that needn't involve condemnation.

For reasons that will become clearer as we proceed, I start by looking for a complaint against the state imposing deterrents for violations of its directives. Suppose that some subject, Violet, has violated a state directive. May the state impose a deterrent on her? Let us assume that the deterrent, following contemporary practice, is imprisonment. Imprisoning her would deter future violations, which sustains cooperation and, in turn, promotes the public interest. So what's the problem?

2.3 The Distributive Complaint

Needless to say, in order to be effective, the deterrent may need to curtail radically the opportunities Violet enjoys, not least her freedom of movement. But this is not enough for a complaint. For, by hypothesis, the deterrent improves the situations of others. By analogy, suppose we don't save one person, Uno, from a one-month-long entrapment in a pit in order to save Duo and Trio from two-month-long entrapments in similar pits. We do indeed leave the freedom of movement of Uno worse than we could have left it. But this is in order to avoid leaving the freedom of movement of Duo and Trio worse to a far greater degree. If Uno has a complaint, it seems straightforwardly answered by observing that we are triaging their claims to improvement in a fair way. We are serving the public interest.

It might be replied, however, that Violet's case is not like this. It isn't as though, if Violet isn't imprisoned, two others will be imprisoned in similar cells for twice the time. Instead, not imprisoning Violet will affect each other person far more modestly. By hypothesis, not imprisoning Violet will weaken deterrence. But the effect of this weakened deterrence will be to leave each other person only a little more exposed to property crime or with only a little less in the way of public services. In sum, Violet bears great losses in order to provide others with much smaller benefits. This is to say that imposing the deterrent on Violet does not promote the public interest and does not fairly triage improvement claims, since the trade-offs between Violet and others are unfair to Violet.

How, if at all, can this "Distributive Complaint" be answered? Section 1.5 suggested an answer. There I argued that Indy's claims to improvement should be understood not as claims to, say, the consummated enjoyment of final stuff but instead as claims to choice situations: to chances of enjoying goods, if Indy chooses appropriately. Recall an example from Section 1.5 that had nothing to do with imposing deterrents. Suppose that there is some publicly provided benefit to be distributed. In order to know how to distribute it, the state asks people to apply for it. Imagine that if the state had to gather the relevant information on its own, it would be too costly to provide the benefit. Dithers chooses not to apply before the deadline, whereas others do apply. As a result, shares of the benefit are distributed to those others but not to Dithers. Dithers protests: "Since I have just as much of a claim to the benefit as others, it is unfair that they have more than I." The state's reply is: "What you had an equal claim to was not the benefit but the opportunity to receive it if you applied. And your claim has been honored as fully as the claims of those who applied and received it."

Applying the same logic to Violet, she has the Distributive Complaint only if the state could provide her with a better choice situation without unfairness to others. But the state does not provide her with a worse choice situation than it could provide her without unfairness to others. Turn the clock back to before Violet's violation of the state's directive. At that point, the state offered her exactly the same choice situation that it offered everyone else. It was part of that choice situation that if Violet complied with a certain directive, she would not be imprisoned, and if she violated this directive, she would be. In imposing the deterrent on Violet, it might be said, the state isn't depriving her of this choice situation. What it does is consistent with her having it.

Violet might protest: "Yes, I grant that my choice situation was no worse than anyone else's actually was, but it was worse than anyone's needed to be.

The state could have provided everyone a clearly better choice situation in which, whether or not one complies with the directive, one does not suffer the deterrent. Surely it is better to have a choice situation in which one does not suffer the deterrent no matter what one does than one in which one runs the risk of suffering it! (Such a choice situation would not, for instance, foreclose any valuable 'choice-dependent' activities.)" However, Violet would be mistaken. Viewed in isolation, Violet's proposed revision might seem to make the choice situation better for each individual. But it would make the overall choice situation worse for each individual in other respects, which depend on the goods provided by the deterrence—the deterrence that Violet's proposed revision would undermine.

Observe that this answer to the Distributive Complaint has two welcome implications. First, it puts pressure on the severity of any deterrent to be necessary. If a less severe deterrent would have the same deterrent effect, then a better overall choice situation for each person is possible: namely, one with the less severe deterrent. Second, it puts pressure on the severity of any deterrent to be proportional to the violation. If the only deterrent that will deter a given violation is very severe, and such violations have only small effects, then that deterrent may well make the overall choice situation worse.

2.4 The Deontological Complaint

So much for the Distributive Complaint. Another complaint against the state's imposition of deterrents, however, seems to be staring us in the face. Grant that imposing the deterrent improves individuals' choice situations in a fair way. It promotes the public interest and so realizes a greater good. Still, there are certain things we may not do to a person even to produce a greater good. Granted, we may leave Uno in a pit in order to rescue Duo and Trio. But surely we may not push Uno into the pit as a means of rescuing Duo and Trio. It's not quite Thomson's (1985) paradigm of fatally pushing someone off a footbridge to stop a trolley that would otherwise kill five, since the numbers and stakes for each are lower and (arguably) since we are only removing, not using, the one. But it still runs up against similar deontological resistance. Likewise, one might protest on Violet's behalf that imposing a deterrent on her violates a right of hers against invasion, a deontological constraint on what may be done to a person even to produce a greater good. More specifically, it might violate the Force Constraint, which was introduced in Section 1.6. Recall that the Force Constraint says that a person has a claim on others that they not invade his body when this does not produce a greater good or as a means to, or a foreseeable side effect of a means to, a greater good, barring something, such as consent, that lifts this constraint. And, it might be said, imprisoning Violet subjects her to force as a means to, or a foreseeable side effect of a means to, a greater good. In sum, imposing the deterrent on Violet violates a right of hers against invasion. This, then, is the "Deontological Complaint."

As we will see in the rest of this chapter, however, we cannot pin the Deontological Complaint against the state. This is not to deny that there is something in the vicinity of the state's use of force that gives rise to a special burden of justification or legitimation. It is to observe, instead, that it is difficult to say what it is and that an answer eludes us, so long as we look for it in a complaint one private person might have against another, in abstraction from the hierarchical structure the state involves.

2.5 The Myth of the Omittites

Having now identified a possible complaint against the state, we perform the first of our two tests, the Subtraction Test. We remove the alleged target of the complaint, the thing that is supposed to provoke it, and see whether the complaint remains. One might wonder how we can remove the target in this case: namely, the force used in the imposition of deterrent imprisonment. How can a state impose deterrent imprisonment without force (Huemer 2013, 10)? It only takes a little imagination, however. The state might build a cage around Violet, while she sleeps in a public park, using materials she does not own, without laying hands on her directly or with the use of implements.

Now, it might be said that building a prison around Violet still "actively confines" her, even if it doesn't use force. And "active confinement" is a close cousin to force, subject to similar deontological constraints. But I wonder. After all, building walls and fences anywhere "actively confines" people to some extent. Granted, if the confinement is unfairly costly, if it does not improve the choice situations of others sufficiently to justify the impairment of the choice situations of those whom it confines, then the latter have an improvement complaint. Such confinement does not serve the public interest. But it isn't clear how a deontological line is to be drawn here. Where is the frontier to be chalked? Is it, say, at least a one-hundred-foot radius of unobstructed movement in two cardinal directions for sixteen hours per day? How are we to say that you can actively confine people this far but no farther, even to serve the public interest by improving people's choice situations in a fair way? By contrast, where force, or action on the body, is at issue, then it is clearer how a deontological line is drawn. The deontological boundary more or less traces the contours of the outer membranes of the corporeal person.

In any event, we can, for the sake of argument, imagine deterrents that consist not even in actively confining someone but instead in simply passively letting someone be confined. So, consider, for good measure, the Omittite Empire. The emperor, the Guardian of the Ladder, does not put violators of his directives in prison or build prisons around them. He doesn't need to. This is because each Omittite, to survive the elements, must descend into his naturally carved hole each night. Every morning, the Guardian drops the Ladder into each hole to enable its occupant to climb back up. His deterrent is simply to withhold the Ladder, confining the occupant there for a fixed period. Suppose an Omittite, Holton, violates some directive, and the Guardian, as announced, does not drop the Ladder into Holton's hole for several months. This isn't a use of force or even an "active confinement." It's simply a failure to aid.

It might be replied, however, that there are deontological constraints on refusals to aid, even for the greater good. We may refuse to give life-saving medication to the one in order to have it to give to the five. But we may not refuse to give life-saving medication to the one in order to learn from the progress of his disease how to save the five from it (Foot 2002, 28). I take it that this is explained by something like:

> "Withholding Aid": If one is otherwise required to aid someone, it is not sufficient to release one from this requirement that one can use, as a means to a greater good, not the withholding of aid but rather what happens to that person as a result of withholding aid.

But is the Guardian withholding the Ladder so as to use, as a means to a greater good, what then happens to Holton as a result of withholding the

Ladder? If we examine the situation more closely, we find that the answer is no. So Withholding Aid does not apply.

The Guardian is withholding the Ladder from Holton so that others, among them Dieter, will be deterred from violating the directive. Dieter is deterred by the combination of two beliefs. First, the "Belief in Credibility": Dieter's belief that the Guardian won't drop the Ladder to Dieter if Dieter violates. Second, the "Belief in Consequence": Dieter's belief that this is something for Dieter to avoid. Now, if the Guardian were withholding the Ladder from Holton so as to be able to make a spectacle of his confinement, so as to sustain Dieter's Belief in Consequence—as if to say, "Obey, lest ye suffer as, lo, this wretch suffers"—then he would be refusing aid so as to use what then happens to Holton as a means. But the Guardian doesn't need to sustain Dieter's Belief in Consequence and indeed probably can't have much effect on it. It's obvious to Dieter that it will be a bad thing for Dieter if the Ladder isn't dropped to him. He doesn't need to be "scared straight." The Guardian needs to sustain only Dieter's Belief in Credibility. And the means to sustaining that belief is simply not dropping the Ladder into Holton's hole, as if to say to Dieter: "Look, I mean business. The same will be done in your case." Nothing that happens to Holton as a result of withholding the Ladder is part of the Guardian's means to the greater good. Put another way, the Guardian's deterrent aim would not be thwarted if (contrary to fact) confinement were a benefit to Holton (if he needed and wanted more than anything quiet respite without the temptation of escape) or if refusing to drop the Ladder to Holton did not confine or otherwise involve him (if he, exceptionally, could survive the elements outside or climb out on his own). Suppose the Guardian's intelligence officers bring him two complete and fully accurate dossiers: one on how Holton would be affected by withholding the Ladder, the other on how Dieter (as he believes) would. It seems the Guardian has no reason to read Holton's but every reason to read Dieter's. If Dieter believes confinement would benefit him or he would not be confined, then the Guardian's deterrent aims will be thwarted. But what will happen to Holton—the contents of his dossier—is neither here nor there. So, in refusing to drop the Ladder, the Guardian does not use what happens to Holton as a result as a means to a greater good. So the Guardian does not violate Withholding Aid.

I conclude, then, that the Deontological Complaint cannot so much as be raised in Holton's case. And yet, intuitively, the Omittites' forceless system of deterrents seems not very different in its moral character from more familiar, forcible systems. I suppose a libertarian might reply: "Whether there is an objection to the regime all comes down to whether the Guardian owns the Ladder. If he wove it from his own hair (and happened upon the design by chance inspiration and not from any scarce genetic advantage, etc.), then all's hunky-dory. He's just a private citizen going about his business. But if he wove it from plant fibers (or did so without leaving enough and as good for others, etc.), well, then, he's an enslaving tyrant." However, if the libertarian's concern turns on such subtleties about the provenance of the physical instruments of deterrence, then it seems to me a long way off from any traditional or commonsense concern about relations of rule. It's doubtful that this could be the complaint against the state that so many have in mind.

2.6 The Natural Duty Argument

Suppose, however, that the state does not have the Guardian's luxury. It must use force in its deterrents. Might the complaint against the state then be the Deontological Complaint: that the state uses force in imposing deterrents, thereby violating the Force Constraint? This brings us to our second test of candidate complaints against the state. This Spare-Justification Test, recall, asks whether we can answer the candidate complaint without appealing to a special legitimating condition (such as consent or reasonable acceptability) or a special limit on legitimacy (such as the Harm Principle or the minimal state) by using only sparer resources, resources to which those who allege such a complaint are anyway committed. If so, then the candidate cannot be our sought-after complaint against the state, for that complaint is said to call for some special legitimating condition or limit of legitimacy.

I think we can answer the Deontological Complaint with sparer resources. That is, those who press a complaint against the state cannot, consistent with their other commitments, take there to be a complaint against the state's deterrent use of force, even when the state does not meet any legitimating condition or respect any limit on legitimacy. In the following sections, I explain why this is so. In this section, however, I consider a different proposed spare justification, the "Natural Duty Argument," which I believe fails. Roughly, the Natural Duty Argument says, "It's OK for the state to use force because the state is just enforcing duties that those subject to it have."

If, as I believe, this argument fails, why do I propose we study it? First, many resort to the argument, even if they aren't explicit, perhaps even to themselves, that they do resort to it.[3] Second, how the Natural Duty Argument fails is instructive. In particular, the Natural Duty Argument not only fails but also backfires. The principal reason why the Natural Duty Argument fails is that there are state directives to which there is no natural duty to conform. And this can make the Deontological Complaint look harder, rather than easier, to answer. For if one thinks the state's use of force is permissible only if Violet has a duty to conform to its directives, then one will think state force is permissible only if there are political obligations: duties to comply with the state's directives as such. And yet one might well doubt that there are political obligations. Indeed, as we will revisit in Section 4.1, I suspect that much of the philosophical interest in political obligation stems from an assumption, rarely made explicit, that state enforcement is impermissible unless we have political obligations. That is, what is thought to be at stake in the debate over whether there are political obligations, or a duty to obey the law, is not simply, or even principally, whether we, as agents, are obligated to do what the state tells us to do. What is thought to be at stake is also whether it is permissible that we, as patients, suffer certain forms of treatment at the hands of the state, on the assumption that such treatment is permissible only if we have political obligations.

The Natural Duty Argument runs as follows: Even would-be proponents of the Deontological Complaint, who believe that state force violates the Force Constraint, must accept that:

1. Each individual has a natural "Duty to Improve": to help meet others' claims to improvement, i.e., to promote the public interest.

We're assuming that the state is ideally directive—that is, that:

2. No alternative set of directives that the state could issue and enforce would better promote the public interest.

So, it follows that:

3. The uniquely best way for any individual to help promote the public interest is to comply with state directives.

So, it follows that:

4. Each individual's Duty to Improve is extensionally equivalent to a duty to conform to state directives, so that if an individual does not conform to state directives, then that individual violates their Duty to Improve.

Now, assume:

5. "Duty Permits Force": The Force Constraint is lifted, for purposes of deterrence, when the target violates a duty.

Then it follows that:

6. "State Imposition": The Force Constraint is lifted, for purposes of deterrence, when the target violates a state directive.

Therefore, the state's use of force does not violate the Force Constraint, even if the state does not meet a legitimating condition or respect a limit on legitimacy.

Even if the Natural Duty Argument were sound, it would have limited dialectical reach. First, some might deny Duty Permits Force.[4] In particular, they might say that the Force Constraint is lifted for enforcement of duties not to invade but not lifted for enforcement of other duties. Would they thereby draw an arbitrary distinction? Perhaps, but in advance of hearing some explanation of Duty Permits Force, how can we know? Second, some might deny that there is a natural Duty to Improve with application in the relevant cases. Libertarians, for example, may accept only that there is a natural duty to respect rights—or, at most, to provide aid in extreme circumstances.[5] And even nonlibertarians, so long as they are not maximizing consequentialists, may have reservations about too demanding a Duty to Improve.

But set aside these reservations. Even granting those premises of the Natural Duty Argument, it is invalid. Premise (2)—that the state is ideally directive—does not imply (3)—that the uniquely best way for one to meet claims to improvement is to conform to state directives.[6] Simmons's (1979, chap. 6; 2005, sec. 7) well-known "particularity problem" supplies one reason for this "Directive/Duty Gap": this divergence between what the Duty to Improve requires and what an ideally directive state directs. Suppose that individuals' Duties to Improve are "global": to contribute to meeting the improvement claims of all people without respect to national boundaries. And suppose that an individual can contribute to meeting the improvement claims of all people at least as well by complying with the directives of a foreign state as by complying with the directives of his own state. For example, a Swede, Gustavus, might contribute just as well by paying Danish taxes instead of Swedish taxes. Gustavus's Duty to Improve does not imply a duty to comply with the directives of the Swedish state to pay Swedish taxes, only a more permissive duty to pay Swedish or Danish taxes.

But the Directive/Duty Gap does not depend on particularity, so understood. Even if we assumed a single world-state, the Gap would still be there, for reasons familiar from discussions of rule utilitarianism. There is often no way for the state to carve out an exception for benign individual actions without worse consequences overall. To put it schematically: Although it serves the public interest at least as well for those in condition *C* to *X*, it detracts from the public interest for those not in *C* to *X*. And there might be no way for the state to deter the latter without a blanket prohibition of *X*-ing, whether or not one is in *C*. Myriad examples fit this schema. (A) In the case of coordination problems, it might promote the public interest at least as well for those in a condition in which enough others will coordinate to promote the public interest in some other way, although it detracts from the public interest for those in a condition in which not enough others will coordinate to do so. (B) Similarly, it might promote the public interest at least as well for those in a condition in which they can act competently without official authorization to act without official authorization, although it detracts from the public interest for those who cannot act competently without official authorization to act without official authorization. Examples would be the skilled and responsible operation of a motor vehicle or the practice of medicine without a license, entry into a secured space without proper identification, or the revelation of state secrets in the public interest. (C) Similarly, it might promote the public interest at least as well for those for whom it is known that their attempts at harmful acts will be futile (such as the subjects of an undercover "sting" operation) to attempt those acts, although it detracts from the public interest for those whose attempts will succeed to attempt those acts.

In sum, an ideally directive state will have to impose deterrents for the violation of directives to act in ways that are not required by the natural Duty to Improve. Because of the Directive/Duty Gap, even if Duty Permits Force is true, the state may still violate the Force Constraint in imposing deterrents for the violation of such directives. Of course, one might try to bridge the Directive/Duty Gap with political obligations: moral requirements to follow state directives. Again, much of the interest in political obligations, I believe, stems from the implicit thought that unless political obligations are there to bridge the Directive/Duty Gap, enforcing directives is impermissible. But it is not clear that there are political obligations, a point to which I return in Section 4.1.

In fact, instead of dispatching the Deontological Complaint, the Natural Duty Argument seems only to make it appear more formidable. Suppose we accept (i) "Force Requires Duty": that the only thing that can lift the Force Constraint, absent consent, is the violation of a duty. And suppose that we accept (ii) that there are not, in general, political obligations. Then we must accept that, in light of the Directive/Duty Gap, even an ideal state (unless it is, like the Omittite Empire, forceless) will routinely violate the Force Constraint in imposing deterrents for violations of its directives. That is a simple and powerful complaint against a relation of rule.[7]

To illustrate, consider how Raz (1986) is committed to this anarchistic consequence. On the one hand, Raz seems to accept (ii) that there are not, in general, political obligations. On the other hand, Raz seems to accept (i) Force Requires Duty. According to his version of the Harm Principle, "coercion," if not force, is permissible (absent a legitimating condition of "trust") only to prevent someone from violating a duty of autonomy.[8] However, by Raz's own lights, the state enforces many directives to do things that people have no independent reason, let alone duty of autonomy, to do. For example, people with specialized skills or knowledge in a given area, he observes, will often not have reason to follow the state's directives in that area (which is why, according to his "Normal Justification Thesis," those directives will not have authority over them) (74). These are just the (B) cases described a few paragraphs back. So, Raz appears to be committed to the anarchistic conclusion that such routine enforcement is wrong, in virtue of being a violation of his version of the Harm Principle.

2.7 The Avoidance Principle

The unmet ambition of the Natural Duty Argument was to provide a spare justification: to show, by appealing to resources anyway accepted by those who press the complaint against the state, that, even if the state does not meet a legitimating condition or a limit of legitimacy, its use of force in imposing deterrents does not violate the Force Constraint.

In this section, I propose an alternative spare justification, which avoids the objections raised in the previous section. Even if the state does not meet a legitimating condition or limit of legitimacy, its use of force in imposing deterrents does not violate the Force Constraint so long as it is at least permissible, as Locke would have put it, to enforce the "law of nature."

I take it that most who press a complaint against the state would accept at least this elementary, Lockean idea. Let us express the idea as:

> "Natural Imposition": The Force Constraint is lifted, for purposes of deterrence, when the target has violated the Force Constraint itself.

If we assume Natural Imposition, I argue, then the best explanation of Natural Imposition will also imply:

> "State Imposition": The Force Constraint is lifted, for purposes of deterrence, when the target has violated a state directive.

Put another way, there is no relevant moral difference between imposing deterrents for the violation of natural rights and imposing deterrents for the violation of state directives. This is so even though, as we saw in the previous section, the ideally directive state's directives go way beyond prohibiting the violation of natural rights against the use of force. Again, the ideally directive state's directives include directives to cooperate to help meet claims to improvement in many other ways: for example, to contribute to police protection and public education in the specific manner the state has decided. The point is that these differences between natural rights against the use of force and state directives simply don't matter to the permissibility of imposing deterrents for their violation. This line of argument does not assume Duty Permits Force, or political obligations, or even a natural Duty to Improve. Again, it assumes only Natural Imposition.

This argument begins with the point that if we accept Natural Imposition, then we need some explanation of it. Why is it that if some "state of naturalist," Flintstone, violates a natural right against the use of force, then the Force Constraint is lifted for the purposes of imposing a deterrent on him? It doesn't help to say that by punishing Flintstone we bring about the good of apportioning suffering to desert. Even if there is such a good, and even if punishing Flintstone brings it about, it isn't goods brought about by punishment that we need to find. We already have a greater good to be brought about by imposing a deterrent on Flintstone: namely, protection from force. In our list of pros and cons for imposing a deterrent on Flintstone, the pro column is already drenched in ink. What we don't have is an explanation of why the Force Constraint, which usually prevents us from using force even to bring about the greater good, should be lifted in this case. How do we overcome that con?

What lifts the Force Constraint in this case, I suggest, may be captured by the:

> "Avoidance Principle": The Force Constraint is lifted when the target of the force has or had adequate opportunity to avoid the use of force (Hart 1968; Scanlon 1998, 1999; Otsuka 2003, chap. 3).

"Adequate" is determined by fairly balancing the two main things at stake. On the one hand, there is the interest underlying the Force Constraint. This, I would argue, is the target's interest in not being subject to force by others that she does not control.[9] On the other hand, there are the burdens that others may have to bear in order to provide her with such control.

In some circumstances, the only control that would count as adequate is the target's present consent. In other circumstances, however, weaker control is adequate, given that the burdens others would have to bear to provide stronger control would be too great. In particular, it would burden others severely to require Flintstone's present consent, after he has violated a natural right, in order to impose a deterrent. This would make the deterrent empty, since one could always escape its imposition by refusing to consent to it. And others rely on the deterrent to sustain the credibility of a threat that induces behavior that meets their claims to improvement in a fair way: in particular, their claim to a choice situation in which they are left free from force under a wide range of choices. Hence, a weaker form of control seems adequate in Flintstone's case: the control exercised in not violating natural rights. Flintstone's adequate opportunity to avoid force was his opportunity not to violate natural rights.

Why think, as the Avoidance Principle claims, that adequate opportunity to avoid the use of force is what does the work in lifting the Force Constraint? In particular, why not just appeal to the glaring fact that Flintstone has a duty? This is the line of thought that seems to lie behind Duty Permits Force and Force Requires Duty. Let us first notice a point so straightforward that it is apt to be overlooked. The fact that Flintstone has a duty to refrain from force, by itself, is scarcely sufficient to impose a deterrent on Flintstone so as to induce others to refrain from force. After all, if Flintstone had complied with his duty to refrain from force, then it would be wrong to make him a scapegoat, even if this would be an effective deterrent. Why? Because he did not have adequate opportunity to avoid the force: even complying with his duty did not protect him from it.

Second is another point so straightforward that it is apt to be overlooked. It's uncontroversial that, even when someone has no relevant duty, the mere fact that he consents can lift the Force Constraint. The Avoidance Principle explains this straightaway. Withholding consent to force, when one had opportunity to withhold consent, is just a special case of exercising an opportunity to avoid force.

Third, even when someone has no relevant duty, the fact that they were given control weaker than consent can, in the right circumstances, intuitively lift the Force Constraint. Imagine (suppressing yet again a healthy sense of embarrassment about casuistry-of-bonking examples of this kind) that we are rushing to save two people from two-month-long entrapments in pits. In order to get there in time, we have to forcibly knock Block, who is in our way, into a pit for a month's stay. If Block's just stuck there in our way, then, as noted before, it seems we can't do it. The mere appeal to the emergency of saving others from longer entrapments is not enough. But if he could easily step aside, and we make him fully aware of the situation, and he still refuses, then I think we may knock him into the pit. Suppose, further, that it makes no difference to the success or cost of the mission whether he is in the way. If he isn't in the way, then we don't need to knock him. If he is in the way, then we do need to knock him, but doing so is completely effortless. Then Block has no duty to step aside (at least as far as the rescue mission is concerned). To repeat: his presence there makes no difference to the success or cost of the mission. It's not that he has a duty to step aside but rather that he cannot complain (at least not on grounds of the Force Constraint) if, when he doesn't step aside, we push him in. This is because he had adequate opportunity to avoid.[10]

Finally, I offer two theories of error for Duty Permits Force and Force Requires Duty: reasons why Duty Permits Force and Force Requires Duty might seem true, even if they are, in fact, false.[11] First, we may confuse Force Requires Duty with the:

> "Condemnation Principle": It is unfitting to condemn someone for wronging others when they haven't, in fact, violated a duty owed to others.

The Condemnation Principle, however, does not imply Force Requires Duty. So long as the state, when it imposes its deterrent on Violet for violating its directive, succeeds in "subtracting" any expression of thereby condemning Violet for wronging others, it would not be, as far as the Condemnation Principle is concerned, unfitting (let alone impermissible) for the state to impose its deterrent on Violet for violating that directive, even if Violet had no duty to comply with it.

Second, we may confuse Duty Permits Force and Force Requires Duty with the:

> "Wrongful Benefit Principle": The fact that someone had a duty to *X* can itself contribute to making it the case that their opportunity to avoid force by *X*-ing was adequate.

Violet cannot cite having to forgo the benefits of violating a duty to *X*—"ill-gotten gains"—as a reason why her opportunity to avoid force by *X*-ing was inadequate. Thus, the fact that Violet has a duty to *X* can be part of what explains why Violet's opportunity to avoid force by *X*-ing was adequate and so why, according to the Avoidance Principle, it is permissible to impose a deterrent on Violet for not *X*-ing. Still, the Wrongful Benefit Principle does not, even in combination with the Avoidance Principle, imply Force Requires Duty. Violet's having a duty to *X* is just one factor among others that can help explain why her opportunity to avoid force by *X*-ing was adequate. When other factors are present, her opportunity to avoid force by *X*-ing can be adequate even though she did not have a duty to *X*. In that case, the state's imposition of the deterrent would be, as far as the Avoidance Principle is concerned, permissible.

The Avoidance Principle, however, might seem vulnerable to counterexample. First, why think that Flintstone's opportunity to avoid was adequate? Suppose that the cost of compliance, of refraining from using force, was death. Flintstone would have died from organ failure had he not harvested the vital organs of his victim, Vic. The Wrongful Benefit Principle provides the reply. Flintstone may not cite, as a "cost" of exercising an opportunity to avoid force, that he thereby had to forgo the benefits of wrongful conduct.

Second, suppose Coldfoot consented yesterday, with the best possible opportunity to withhold consent, in the freest and most informed conditions, to our pushing him off a footbridge to stop the (slow but inexorable) trolley. Today, without anyone having materially relied on his consent, he says: "I no longer consent to being pushed." Arguably, we may not push Coldfoot. (This suggests that even once-off, historical consent, of the kind Locke envisioned, may not suffice to answer the Deontological Complaint; Huemer 2013, 21n3.) Or suppose that Hefty, with the best possible opportunity to avoid doing so, in the freest and most informed conditions, intentionally, knowingly, etc. steps onto an overpass, despite the sign that reads, "If you are heavy enough, you may be pushed off to stop runaway trolleys." However, mounting the overpass, Hefty clearly announces, "I do not consent to being pushed." Again, many will deny that we may push Hefty. We can't set up deontology-free zones simply by erecting signage. In other words, the opportunity to avoid that is intuitively adequate for Flintstone—namely, the opportunity to refrain from violation—is weaker than the opportunity to avoid that is intuitively adequate for Coldfoot or Hefty—namely, the opportunity to withdraw or withhold present consent. Why is this?

Our point of departure is that others are not overly burdened by a principle that grants Coldfoot (or Hefty) freedom from force provided he didn't consent yesterday (or doesn't mount the overpass). Given that, how much more are others burdened by a principle that grants Coldfoot (or Hefty) more extensive control: that insists, as it were, on a waiting period on Coldfoot's gift (or further conditions on Hefty's)? Not much, it would seem. By contrast, while others may not be overly burdened by a principle that grants Flintstone freedom from force provided he does not violate the Force Constraint, it seems they are significantly more burdened by a principle that grants Flintstone freedom from force even if he does violate it. That extension of Flintstone's control deprives them of the deterrent and its protection. It asks a great deal of others.

Let us take stock. In the face of the Deontological Complaint, we have been searching for a spare justification: that is, we have been trying to show, by appealing to resources anyway accepted by those who press the complaint against the state, that, even if the state does not meet a legitimating condition or a limit of legitimacy, its use of force in imposing deterrents does not violate the Force Constraint. Those who press the complaint against the state anyway accept Natural Imposition: that the Force Constraint is lifted, for purposes of deterrence, when the target has violated the Force Constraint itself. The best explanation of Natural Imposition, we have suggested, is the Avoidance Principle. And the Avoidance Principle also implies State Imposition. So we have our spare justification.

The crux is that there is no relevant difference between Flintstone's situation and Violet's. The state's use of force in imposing deterrents on Violet no more violates the Force Constraint than Flintstone's neighbors' use of force in imposing deterrents on Flintstone violates the Force Constraint. Just as Flintstone had opportunity to avoid the deterrent by complying with the natural prohibitions on force, so too Violet had opportunity to avoid the deterrent by complying with the state's directives. And just as to provide Flintstone with even greater opportunity (e.g., to require his present consent) in order to impose a deterrent would burden others severely, so too to provide Violet with even greater opportunity (e.g., to require her present consent) in order to impose a deterrent would burden others severely. Just as others rely on the deterrent in Flintstone's case to sustain the credibility of a threat that induces behavior that improves their situation by protecting them from invasion, so too they rely on the deterrent in Violet's case to sustain the credibility of a threat that induces behavior that improves their situation, either by protecting them from invasion or in some other way.[12]

To disrupt this spare justification and so rehabilitate the Deontological Complaint, therefore, one needs somehow to drive a wedge between Natural and State Imposition so that State Imposition, but not Natural Imposition, is ruled out. Somehow it has to be permissible to impose a deterrent on Flintstone but impermissible to impose a deterrent on Violet. The next two sections, which are the final sections of this chapter, consider and reject two possible wedges. The first, taken up in Section 2.8, is simply that Flintstone had better opportunity than Violet had to avoid the imposition of the deterrent. The second, taken up in Section 2.9, is the libertarian thought that force can be used on a person only in the service of certain kinds of goods: either protection from that person's force or protection from anyone's force. Whereas the force used on Flintstone serves such goods, the force used on Violet need not.

2.8 Avoiding State Imposition

To salvage the Deontological Complaint, then, one needs somehow to drive a wedge between Natural and State Imposition so that State Imposition, but not Natural Imposition, is ruled out. One might reply that we can do this even while granting the Avoidance Principle. While Flintstone's opportunity to comply with natural prohibitions is adequate, Violet's opportunity to comply with state deterrents is not adequate. So, the Avoidance Principle explains why the Force Constraint is lifted in Flintstone's case but not Violet's. Indeed, there are grounds for such a reply. Recall the Wrongful Benefit Principle: that one cannot cite as costs of exercising one's opportunity to avoid that one had to forgo benefits of wrongful conduct. Since Flintstone has a duty to exercise his opportunity to avoid—that is, to respect natural rights—it seems fairly easy to explain why his opportunity counts as adequate. But if Violet does not have a duty to exercise her opportunity to avoid by complying—that is, a political obligation to comply with the state's directive—it may be more difficult to show that her opportunity was adequate.

But, first, if we can assume a Duty to Improve, then this is less likely to present a problem—although, admittedly, this assumption somewhat limits the Avoidance Principle's range of application. For the situation will often be as follows. Violet can satisfy the Duty to Improve in way *X* or way *Y*. Neither is markedly more burdensome than the other, but either is markedly more burdensome than refusing to comply with the Duty to Improve. The state directive, however, is, specifically, to *X*. Can Violet complain, if a deterrent is imposed for not *X*-ing, that she did not have adequate opportunity to avoid? The main costs of *X*-ing were forgoing the benefits of refusing to comply with the Duty to Improve. But, since Violet has a Duty to Improve, she cannot cite these costs. The only costs of *X*-ing that Violet could potentially cite are forgoing the benefits of *Y*-ing. But since *Y*-ing is about as burdensome as *X*-ing, there are no significant benefits of this kind. Although Violet has no duty to *X*, Violet cannot claim that she did not have adequate opportunity to avoid because all the other things she might have permissibly done would have had the same cost.

Second, even if there is no Duty to Improve, complying with many state directives, such as the state's ban on private enforcement, carries little cost. Finally, if certain familiar features of the rule of law are respected, then there will be better opportunity to avoid state imposition than natural imposition. Deterrents will be imposed only if they are specifically announced in advance. At best, then, this line of reply enjoys piecemeal success. In some cases, under certain assumptions, there may be worse opportunity to avoid state imposition than there is to avoid natural imposition. And so, in those cases, it is less clear that the Avoidance Principle will support State Imposition as it supports Natural Imposition. Yet the Deontological Complaint, one might have thought, was supposed to be more categorical.

2.9 Two Libertarian Principles

So how else are we to drive a wedge between Natural Imposition and State Imposition? Perhaps by rejecting, or imposing a further constraint on, the Avoidance Principle in such a way that Natural Imposition remains standing but State Imposition does not. But how to do this? "Easy," a libertarian might reply. "Force can be used only to provide certain goods but not others. Force can be used to provide protection from force, sure. But force can't be used to provide, say, food or shelter or education." This reply, I think, might take a stronger or a weaker form. The stronger form is stable but untenably extreme. The weaker form is less extreme but untenably unstable.

The stronger version of the reply appeals to:

"Strong Libertarianism": Absent consent, force may be used on Violet only to protect others from Violet's force.

This would rule out State Imposition, since the deterrents the state imposes on Violet will very often serve goods other than protection from Violet's force, such as protection from others' force or the "protection" from ignorance that education provides. The problem is that Strong Libertarianism also rules out Natural Imposition. Imposing deterrents on Flintstone for violations of natural prohibitions on force cannot be justified, in general, by others' interest in being free from Flintstone's force. Suppose that, following his violation, Flintstone is reformed, or incapacitated, so that there is no prospect of him using force in the future (Otsuka 2003, chap. 3). In that case, imposing a deterrent on Flintstone does nothing to serve the interest of his victim, Vic, in being free from Flintstone's force. It may well serve Vic's interests in being free from the force of another person, Dieter, since it reinforces Dieter's belief that anyone who uses force on Vic will pay. And, as Locke ([1689] 1960, sec. 8) assumed, this was much of the point of punishment: "as may make him repent of doing it, and thereby deter him, and by his Example others." But, according to Strong Libertarianism, Vic's interest in being free from Dieter's force cannot justify imposing a deterrent on Flintstone.[13]

To be sure, those committed to Strong Libertarianism can deny Natural Imposition. And they can still allow that nonconsensual force may be used in defense—which, again, includes some forms of "after the fact" restitution (Rothbard 1982, chaps. 12–13). Again, my argument is directed only against those who accept Natural Imposition. All the same, there are serious, perhaps intolerable, costs of rejecting it, which it isn't clear that advocates of Strong Libertarianism have squarely faced. If we reject Natural Imposition, then morality leaves Vic defenseless in cases like those just discussed.[14]

The weaker version of the libertarian reply appeals to:

"Weak Libertarianism": Absent consent, force may be used on Violet only to protect others not only from Violet's force but moreover from anyone's force.

Weak Libertarianism is compatible with Natural Imposition. Likewise, Weak Libertarianism is fully compatible with the minimal state, which imposes deterrents for violations of directives to contribute to efforts to protect rights: for example, to supply service or taxes to support policing and defense. So, Weak Libertarianism would support the Deontological Complaint only against a more expansive state. This would support the view, embraced by Nozick, that the minimal state represents a limit of legitimacy.

In any event, Weak Libertarianism is far less stable than Strong Libertarianism, extreme though the latter may be. Strong Libertarianism builds on a distinction that, vague and contested though it is, is accepted, in some form, by most nonconsequentialists: a distinction between what Violet does to others, regarding which morality makes relatively strong demands on Violet—either in terms of what morality requires Violet to do or in terms of what morality allows to be done to Violet—and what merely happens to others (albeit perhaps because Violet lets it happen), regarding which morality makes weaker claims on Violet. Then Strong Libertarianism carries this to an extreme: that morality makes no demands on Violet (at least in the sense that morality allows nothing to be done to Violet) with regard to what merely happens to others. Strong Libertarianism doesn't claim it isn't bad or doesn't matter when some ill befalls someone without Violet's doing while it is bad and does matter when some ill befalls someone from Violet's doing. "Yes," Strong Libertarianism agrees, "it's worse if your son dies of cholera as a child when Violet could have prevented it than if Violet forcibly detains him as an adult, for an indecisive fifteen minutes, before releasing him. But that isn't the point. The point is that Violet is responsible for what Violet does (again, in the sense that morality may make demands on Violet regarding what Violet does) in a way in which Violet is not responsible for what merely happens."

But once we deny Strong Libertarianism—once we grant that people's interest in protection from others' force, which are not Violet's doings, can justify uses of force against Violet—how else can we defend Weak Libertarianism? How else can we deny that their interest in protection from ills other than force, which are also not Violet's doings, can justify uses of force against Violet? If we can use force against Violet to protect ourselves from the violence of other people, then why can't we use force against Violet to protect ourselves from the ravages of wild animals? Why then can't we use force against Violet to protect ourselves from the ravages of microbes? And so on. Here the answer can't be that Violet is responsible only for what Violet does. Here it indeed begins to look like, in order to defend Weak Libertarianism, we do need to assert that it somehow isn't bad or doesn't matter when some ill befalls someone without anyone's doing but is bad and does matter when some ill befalls someone by someone's doing. And that idea is indefensible.

In sum, one can insulate Violet from state deterrents by insisting on limits to what she is responsible for—what morality puts her on the hook for. But that leads to Strong Libertarianism, which seems too restrictive. However, one cannot insulate Violet from state deterrents on the grounds that such deterrents protect others not from force but rather from natural mishap, unless we are prepared to say that suffering from sentient violence is somehow worse than suffering from mindless disease. And so, we cannot support the otherwise more attractive halfway house of Weak Libertarianism.

In conclusion, if we accept Natural Imposition, then we must accept State Imposition as well. This means that those who press the complaint against the state, so long as they accept Natural Imposition, cannot consistently hold that the state, by using force to impose deterrents for violations of its directives, violates the deontological Force Constraint, so long as the state does not satisfy a legitimating condition or a limit on legitimacy. This suggests what the Myth of the Omittites, in which the complaint against the state seemed to apply even against a state that used no force, suggested in another way: namely, that the complaint against the state is not that it uses force in imposing deterrents for violations of its directives. The target of the complaint must be some other relation of rule that the state involves. But what other relation of rule?

The next chapter considers and rejects the proposal that the relevant relation of rule has to do with the state's threats. But since this chapter has been driving, in a relentlessly negative way, deeper and deeper into the moral-philosophical weeds, let us raise our heads and take stock of where we are and where we are ultimately headed. In Part I, we are reviewing a first instance of the negative observation: that there are commonplace claims that cannot be explained by interests in improvement or rights against invasion. This first instance concerns the idea that there is some complaint against the state that is answered only by a limit on legitimacy or legitimating condition. What then is this complaint? In this chapter, we have considered the suggestion that the complaint is that the state uses force. So long as the state is using force to promote the public interest, it does not violate a claim to improvement. So, the thought would have to be that the state's use of force violates rights against invasion. But applying the Subtraction Test, in the guise of our Myth of the Omittites, we found that a similar complaint seems to apply against a state that didn't use force. And applying the Spare-Justification Test, we found that the state's use of force was permissible even without a limit on legitimacy or legitimating condition.

There is a deeper lesson here. It is natural to assume that your complaint against the state must arise from some specific, discrete thing the state does to you, such as that the state uses force on you. In other words, the complaint is about something one individual could do to another individual were their paths to cross, in a one-off encounter, in a state of nature. This assumption, I suspect, explains why the complaint against the state is so often motivated by first presenting some vignette about one individual doing such and such to another individual in a state of nature and then saying, in effect, "Wakey, wakey, sheeple! The state is doing precisely that to you!" (see, e.g., Narveson 2010, 262).

So long as we assume that the complaint against the state must have this character, however, we will be at a loss to identify a complaint against the state. In this chapter, we saw how this was so where the state's discrete treatment of you was the use of force. And we will see this lesson repeated in the next two chapters, where the discrete treatment is threatening you or using your external property. We come up empty handed because the complaint against the state is not against some specific, discrete treatment, of a kind that might be suffered, in an imagined primeval forest, at the hands of another private person.

Instead the complaint has to do with the state's hierarchical structure: with the distribution of power and authority the state represents and with the relations among people that involves. In other words, it is not incidental to the complaint against the state that the state is a state. The basic problem is that the state wields vastly superior, final and inescapable, power and authority over you. And yet the state is, when the robes and badges are stripped away, other people. Why then aren't you subject to the superior power and authority of other people? Notice how this is so even in the forceless state of the Omittites. The Guardian of the Ladder may not use force, but he still wields vastly superior power and authority over others. Suppose we posit that we have claims against inferiority: against standing in relations of inferiority to others. And suppose that such relations are constituted by asymmetric power and authority. Then we have a complaint against the state: that, in being subject to the state, we are subjected to the superior power and authority of those people whose decisions the state's decisions are. This is just an instance of our positive conjecture: that commonplace claims not explained by interests in improvement or rights against invasion are instead explained by claims against inferiority.

As I promised in the introduction, a reader who wants to get the general thrust of the argument can now skip to Part II, for the positive conjecture, and then to the book's conclusion. But those of you readers with an interest in the question of justifying or legitimating the state or in the morality of threats, or who are possessed of angelic patience, return now with me to the thicket.

3

Is the Claim against the State's Threats?

In the previous chapter, we considered and rejected the possibility that the complaint against the state, the complaint that lies behind calls to justify or legitimate the state, is a complaint against its imposition of deterrents: either that it is distributively unfair (the Distributive Complaint) or that, because it uses force, it violates the Force Constraint (the Deontological Complaint). In this chapter, we consider the possibility that the complaint against the state is instead a complaint against the state's threatening to impose deterrents, whether or not the state actually imposes them. This is a natural next thought. By "coercion," after all, many have in mind a species of threat.

3.1 The Myth of Our Trusting Future

We begin with the Subtraction Test. As in Section 2.5 with our Myth of the Omittites, we remove the candidate relation of rule and see whether this removes the intuitive complaint against the state. In this case, the candidate relation of rule is the state's threatening to impose deterrents on those subject to it.

Consider the "Myth of Our Trusting Future." Imagine that tomorrow common knowledge of dispositions to comply with the state's orders were to emerge spontaneously. And imagine that the state were to cease backing up its directives with threats. It continues to regulate our behavior. Its commands, even without the backstop of jails and gallows, continue to serve as decisively salient coordination points or tap dispositions to reflexive obedience. The state continues to shape our natural and social environment more or less as it currently does: through what are, and what are seen as, commands (as opposed to advice about what people have reason to do anyway).

It's just that, holding everything else fixed, there aren't any threats lurking in the background (Sangiovanni 2007).

Would the alleged complaint against the state disappear? Would the Harm Principle, say, or the requirement of public justification then no longer apply (Wall 2005; Bird 2014; Quong 2014, 271–273)? Would the state then be free to prohibit self-regarding choices or pursue policies based on a sectarian doctrine? One doubts that proponents of such limits of legitimacy and legitimating conditions would answer yes.

3.2 Conditioning and Announcing

This brings us to our second test, the Spare-Justification Test. Can the complaint against the state's threats be answered only by a legitimating condition or limit of legitimacy? Or can it be answered with sparer resources, which those who press the complaint against the state anyway accept?

We first need to clarify what the complaint against the state's threats might be. The way to get a handle on this, one might think, is to ask the general question of when and why anyone has a complaint against anyone's threats. However, I believe we carve the subject more closely at the moral joints if we ask a similarly general but somewhat different question: When and why does someone wrong someone else by, as I put it, "conditioning" or "announcing" a response to their choice? That is, why might Hablo wrong Audito by conditioning a response to choice, by making it the case that Hablo will Stick if Audito does not Obey and will Carrot if Audito does Obey? And why might Hablo wrong Audito by announcing a response to choice, communicating to Audito that Hablo has conditioned a response in the sense just defined?

"Conditioning and announcing a response to choice" is both broader and narrower than "threatening" in common usage. Some threats neither condition nor announce a response to choice. Hablo, a predestinarian, can threaten Audito with hellfire regardless of any choice Audito might make. And some announcings or conditionings of responses to choice do not threaten. Hablo may offer to Carrot if Audito Obeys. Or Hablo may warn Audito that Hablo will Stick if Audito does not Obey. For our purposes, distinctions among threat and offer, threat and warning, and so on, which preoccupy classic discussions such as Nozick (1999), are worth drawing only insofar as such distinctions matter for whether someone has been wronged or has a complaint. That remains to be seen.

3.3 Two Contrasts between Force and Threat

From the outset, it is worth highlighting two general differences between a complaint against the state's imposition of deterrents, which we considered in the previous chapter, and a complaint against the state's threats, which we are considering now. First, a complaint against the state's threats cannot be answered, as the complaint against the state's imposition of deterrents was answered, by appealing to opportunity to avoid, along the lines of the Avoidance Principle. For even if we have adequate opportunity to avoid the imposition of deterrents, by complying with the state's directives, we have no opportunity to avoid threats of their imposition. We are born to such threats.

Second, it is hard even to formulate, let alone defend, an analogue to the Force Constraint: a deontological constraint on threats. One might be tempted to say that just as force is wrong because it crosses a deontological barrier against invading another's body, so too threats are wrong because they cross a deontological barrier against invading another's choice. But while it is relatively clear what counts as invading another's body, it is less clear what counts as invading someone's choice. We know, more or less, what it is for someone to touch your body without your consent. But what is it, as it were, for someone to "touch your choice" without your consent? Presumably it isn't just to change your choices. Whatever I do changes your choices in some way. If I turn off my phone, then calling me (and getting through) is no longer an option. Nor can impermissibly "touching your choice" be identified, more specifically, with conditioning and announcing a response to your choices. I don't, in general, violate your rights by proposing a mutually beneficial exchange, for example. To be sure, political philosophers routinely speak of "interference in choice." But the routine should not lead us to assume that we know what they mean—or even that they know what they mean.

To anticipate, one might sum up the previous chapter on force and this chapter on threat as follows. When we press political philosophers' talk of "interference in choice," it collapses into one of two things. Either it means force—that is, acting on the chooser's body—or else it means making the chooser's choice situation unfairly worse—that is, worse in a way that isn't justified by what it gives to others. Therefore, political philosophers' talk of "interference in choice" faces a dilemma. On the one hand, if we interpret "interference in choice" to mean simply force, then it is far too narrow to cover many of the forceless episodes that will nevertheless be thought to involve interference in choice. On the other hand, if we interpret "interference in choice" to mean making the chooser's choice situation unfairly worse, then it is insufficiently deontological. It's no bulwark whatsoever against serving the public interest: against doing whatever improves choice situations in a fair way. So it licenses no objection to our ideal state, which serves the public interest, making everyone's choice situation as good as it can, compatibly with fairness to others.

This is not to deny that the fact that the state threatens those subject to it points to a genuine complaint against the state. It is to observe, instead, that it is difficult to say what it is and that an answer eludes us, so long as we look for it in a complaint one individual might have against another, were they to stumble on one another on the primordial heath. But, as I said, these remarks anticipate what is to come. We are getting ahead of ourselves.

3.4 From the Inheritance Principle to the Risk and Fear Principles

So, when and why does Hablo wrong Audito by conditioning or announcing a response to Audito's choice? Many are drawn to a simple answer, the:

> "Inheritance Principle": Hablo's conditioning or announcing a response to Audito's choice wrongs him when and because the response itself—that is, either Sticking when Audito does not Obey or Carroting when Audito Obeys—would wrong him (at least suggested by Haksar 1976; Murphy 1980, 22; Berman 1998, 2002, 2011; Scanlon 2008, 76; Shaw 2012, 168; White 2017).

Thus, McGer's conditioning and announcing to McGee, "Your money or your life," wrongs McGee at least because it would wrong McGee to take McGee's life if he does not surrender the money—that is, to Stick if he does not Obey.

Note that McGer's conditioning and announcing may also wrong McGee, according to the Inheritance Principle, because it would wrong McGee to take his money even while letting McGee live if McGee does surrender it (i.e., even while Carroting if McGee does Obey). McGee's consent to transfer the money under such a threat may not be valid because of a "value-of-compliance effect," of a kind described in Section 3.5 and then again in Section 19.3. So, McGer's taking the money may be theft. Other paradigmatically wrongful threats, such as threats used to commit sexual assault, have this same structure. Hablo's Carroting involves doing something to Audito that wrongs him unless he validly consents, and yet the conditioning and announcing itself invalidates his consent. Let us bracket, however, the possibility that the response that wrongs McGee is Carroting without McGee's valid consent, and suppose that the only response that wrongs McGee is Sticking—that is, killing McGee. If you like, imagine that McGer demands not that McGee give him money but instead that McGee twiddle his thumbs for a count of three.

Now, if the Inheritance Principle were the whole story, we would be home free. For we concluded in the previous chapter that the state does not wrong people by following through on its threats. So, for all that the Inheritance Principle tells us, the state does not wrong people by threatening to follow through. However, there are counterexamples to the Inheritance Principle. First, some announcements of wrongings don't wrong. If, in "Akratic Warning," King Fuse the Short can't control himself, and His Majesty, Fuse, will wrongfully thrash Jester if Jester does not put a cork in it, and His Majesty wishes to keep Jester safe, His Majesty does not wrong Jester by warning him of this (Julius 2013, 362, with names and stations added; compare G. Cohen's [2008, 40] "schizoid kidnapper"). Second, even some conditionings of wrongings don't wrong. In "Wrongful Retaliation," Capitalia, left with no other recourse, may permissibly condition—so long as it also announces!—nuclear retaliation in response to a first strike by Communia (and vice versa). However, to follow through on this threat would be, if not the gravest wrong ever, the clear runner-up (Berman 2011).

At any rate, even before we encountered these counterexamples, the Inheritance Principle should have called out to us for explanation. Why should a threat to wrong someone itself wrong him? One thought is that McGer's conditioning to wrong McGee can itself wrong McGee by making it more likely that McGer wrongs McGee. However, this thought supports not the Inheritance Principle but instead the:

> "Risk Principle": If Hablo would wrong Audito by Sticking, then Hablo, for that reason, wrongs Audito by making it sufficiently likely that Hablo Sticks, which Hablo may do by conditioning to Stick.

Wrongful Retaliation is no counterexample to the Risk Principle. If there is a good chance that Communia will attack no matter what, then it may well be wrong to condition retaliation, precisely because Capitalia makes it likely that it will do something wrong.

The Risk Principle says nothing about why announcing to wrong McGee might wrong McGee. Scanlon (2008, 76) suggests that McGer wrongs McGee by making McGee fear that McGer will wrong him. Perhaps the underlying principle is the:

> "Fear Principle": Hablo wrongs Audito by causing, without sufficient reason, Audito to fear something.

Since, as a rule, Hablo does not have sufficient reason to wrong Audito, Hablo usually does not have sufficient reason to cause Audito to fear that Hablo will wrong Audito. Akratic Warning and Wrongful Retaliation represent exceptions, in which there is sufficient reason to cause such fear: to help Jester avoid a thrashing that Fuse can't control and to prevent a nuclear conflagration.

In any event, if the Risk and Fear Principles were the whole story, then we would again be home free. For the Risk Principle, like the Inheritance Principle, applies only when the threatened Stick is wrong. The Fear Principle applies only when there isn't sufficient reason for the fear the threat may cause. And there is sufficient reason for whatever fear the state's threats cause. However, it seems doubtful that the Risk and Fear Principles are the whole story. Consider a case in which both McGer and McGee know full well that McGee will Obey and that McGer, being the professional he is, won't shoot (Anderson 2011). Then neither the Risk Principle nor the Fear Principle explains why McGer's threat wrongs McGee. For McGer's conditioning and announcing, "Your money or your life," neither makes it more likely that McGer takes McGee's life nor causes McGee to fear that McGer will.

3.5 The Choice Principle

So how else does McGer wrong McGee? Perhaps simply by making McGee's choice situation worse—worse, that is, than McGer owes McGee to make it. In other words, we have the:

> "Choice Principle": Hablo's conditioning or announcing a response to Audito's choice wrongs Audito when and because it leaves Audito's choice situation worse than Audito has a claim on Hablo to provide.

The Choice Principle is just a special case of a tautology: namely, that Hablo wrongs Audito when and because, in whatever way, he leaves Audito's choice situation worse than Audito has a claim on Hablo to provide. The Choice Principle represents, I think, the best sense to be made of talk of "interference in choice." To interfere in Audito's choice, in a way against which Audito might have a complaint, is to make Audito's choice situation worse than Hablo owes it to Audito to make it.

It is sometimes suggested that threats make Audito's choice situation worse simply insofar as they reduce Audito's "options" or "liberty." Indeed, this is sometimes meant in a baldly quantitative way, such that Audito is literally left with a lower count of options (Feinberg 1984, 207; Gaus 2011, 499). But this is too crude. There are many different ways in which choice situations can be better or worse and many different ways in which conditionings and announcings, in particular, can make them better or worse. Let us focus on five such effects (although I suspect there are still others): cost (or benefit), influence, capacity, value of compliance (or noncompliance), and compliance of others.

The "cost effect" is that Hablo's Sticking is added to Audito's not Obeying. If Hablo's Sticking is bad for Audito, this tends to make Audito's choice situation worse, other things equal. When Hablo's Carroting is good for Audito, then we can speak of a corresponding benefit effect that makes Audito's choice situation better, other things equal.

The cost effect of attaching Sticking to Audito's not Obeying depends on the significance of the option it is attached to, the relative loss of foregoing it given Audito's alternatives. Suppose Audito is making a move to turn down the Ethel Merman, which is giving him a splitting headache. Now Hablo comes along and threatens Audito with a noogie unless Audito turns the Merman down. Now, a noogie's a noogie. But, still, Hablo's threatening Audito with a noogie unless Audito turns the Merman down, as he is desperately moving to do anyway, has a less pronounced cost effect than his threatening Audito with a noogie unless he keeps it blaring. In the latter case, Audito avoids the cost only at the price of a forgone good: respite from the Merman. Not all forgone goods count alike, however. In a spirit similar to the Wrongful Benefit Principle from Section 2.7, we might hold that Audito's having to forgo the goods of dis-Obedience does less to amplify the cost effect when Audito has a duty to Obey. Audito can't claim as a hardship that in order to avoid the costly Stick, he must forgo what he would have gained only by failing in his duty. This helps explain why the threat in Wrongful Retaliation, but not in McGer's mugging of McGee, is permissible. It would be wrong for Communia to launch a first strike. Given that, and given this analogue to the Wrongful Benefit Principle, Communia has a fairly weak complaint that the consequences attached to a first strike make the benefits of a first strike prohibitively costly to obtain. By contrast, it would not be wrong for McGee to keep his own wallet. So, McGee has a very strong complaint against a choice situation that makes keeping it prohibitively costly.

The "influence effect" is that of making Audito more likely to Obey. If Obeying would be better for Audito (for reasons other than the avoidance of the Stick), the influence effect tends to improve Audito's choice situation, other things equal. (Of course, other things may not be equal; an adverse cost effect or adverse value-of-compliance effect, for example, may outweigh this beneficial influence effect.) Such is the brief, at least, for paternalistic threats (which we will consider in Chapter 19) meant to steer Audito from bad self-regarding choices. On the other hand, if Obeying would be worse for Audito, the influence effect tends to worsen Audito's choice situation. Tempting someone to make a deal that is bad for them, even when this does not involve deception, can worsen their choice situation in this way.

The "capacity effect" is a worsening or improvement of Audito's capacity to evaluate and select among the options he has. Informing Audito of what his options are tends to improve his capacity. By contrast, misinforming Audito of what his options are tends to worsen it. This is one reason why bluffing announcements can worsen a choice situation even without conditioning. Similarly, bringing to Audito's attention an option that will distract or confuse him, or flooding him with options so as to exhaust or paralyze him, also worsens his capacity.

"Value-of-compliance effects" are subtler and more varied. These effects involve a change in the value or normative character of Audito's Obedience itself. First, Hablo's conditioning or announcing may change the permissibility of Audito's Obeying. For example, it may be permissible for Audito to break a promise if coerced at gunpoint to do so. Second, even when it does not make it permissible for Audito to Obey, it may make him less blameworthy for Obeying. Third, it may keep Audito's Obeying from having its usual normative effect. When Audito says yes under threat, it may no longer count as a binding promise, or valid consent, or transfer of property. This is why McGer's taking the money that McGee surrenders amounts to theft. Fourth, it may give Audito reason to feel regret or remorse for his choice when he would not have otherwise. As Tadros (2016, chap. 12) observes, the famous choice put to William Styron's Sophie, to decide which of her children to save, made her a monstruous parent or at least left her to feel that she was. Finally, Hablo's announcement or conditioning may change the sort of relations to Hablo that Audito's Obedience would constitute. The very fact that Audito would be complying with a threat may make Obeying humiliating and servile (Scanlon 2008, 78).

Conditioning and announcing has "compliance-of-others effects" on Audito's choice situation insofar as it gets others to act in ways that worsen or improve Audito's choice situation. The state's threats, in particular, have important effects via the compliance of others. The fact that Audito is threatened may assure others so that they cooperate with Audito. Or the fact that they are subject to the same threat may induce them to act in ways that benefit Audito or protect him from harm.

In sum, these various factors—the cost, influence, capacity, value-of-compliance, and compliance-of-others effects—conspire to make Audito's choice situation better or worse. To know whether, in a given case, Audito has a claim on Hablo to a better choice situation, and so to apply the Choice Principle, we need to balance the burdens on Audito of a worse choice situation, on the one hand, against the burdens Hablo (and others) would have to bear for Hablo to make Audito's choice situation better, on the other.

If, in balancing these burdens, one considers only the burdens to Audito of a worse choice situation and neglects the burdens Hablo (and others) must bear to make Audito's choice situation better, one is liable to underestimate the explanatory power of the Choice Principle. Consider "Spit Bus," a case of Stephen White's. When I take this bus seat, I remove your option to sit there. Evidently, you are not entitled from me to a choice situation in which that option remains. However, it seems that I wrong you if, while not removing the option, I threaten to spit on you if you sit there (Julius 2013, 362; White 2017, 217). But this choice situation seems better, or at least no worse, for you. When I sit there, I remove your option to sit there, spat upon or unspat upon. When I threaten, I remove only the option to sit there unspat upon. So, it seems, the Choice Principle can't explain why this threat is wrong.

But this is to consider only your side of the balance sheet, neglecting my side. You are not entitled to my not worsening your choice situation when I have good reason for worsening it. I have good reason to sit—reason as good as you have. So, I may sit and so worsen your choice situation. But you are entitled to my not worsening your choice situation, even to a lesser degree, when this is gratuitous. I have no good reason for threatening. It only keeps you from taking a seat that would otherwise go to waste. So, I may not threaten and so worsen your choice situation even to that lesser degree.

Is there any general rule telling us how to strike the balance between Audito's claim to a better choice situation and the burdens Hablo (and others) must bear to provide it? I doubt it. To be sure, the fact that Audito is entitled from Hablo to Hablo's not Sticking when Audito does not Obey (or to Hablo's not Carroting when Audito does Obey) may be a strong indicator that Audito is entitled from Hablo to a better choice situation than one in which Hablo announces or conditions to Stick if Audito does not Obey (and to Carrot otherwise). In other words, the fact that Hablo would wrong Audito by following through is a strong indicator that Hablo wrongs Audito by threatening to follow through. Indeed, I suspect this is why many are drawn to the Inheritance Principle. Deep down, they are drawn to the Choice Principle, and they assume the Inheritance Principle is what the Choice Principle entails.

However, in some circumstances, Audito is entitled to Hablo's not Sticking, without being entitled to a choice situation in which Hablo does not condition or announce that Hablo will Stick. The counterexamples to the Inheritance Principle illustrate how these entitlements can come apart. First, holding fixed conditioning, announcing tends to have a beneficial capacity effect. If a cost has been attached to Audito's not Obeying, Audito is better off knowing about it. This is what His Majesty Fuse's akratic warning enables Jester to do. Holding fixed His Majesty's uncontrollable temper, the warning makes Jester's choice situation as good as His Majesty can make it. While Jester is entitled to His Majesty's not thrashing him, he is not perversely entitled to a choice situation in which His Majesty refuses to warn him.

Second, conditioning (provided it is announced) can have benefits that Sticking does not have. Capitalia's following through is pointless, and so it has no reason to follow through. By contrast, Capitalia's threatening deters a first strike, and so it has good reason to threaten. So, while Communia is entitled to Capitalia's not nihilistically following through, it isn't entitled, once Capitalia's reasons are taken into account, to a choice situation in which it is free to launch a first strike with impunity.

So, again, I doubt there is a general rule telling us how to strike the balance between Audito's interests in a better choice situation and the burdens Hablo (and others) must bear to provide it: a general rule telling us when Hablo owes Audito a better choice situation. Fortunately, we don't need such a rule to say whether the state's threats wrong us in the way the Choice Principle describes. They do not, if the state is ideally directive: if no alternative system of directives and enforcement would better meet our claims to improvement. In that case, its threats leave the choice situation of each of us as good as the state has it within its power to leave it, compatibly with fairness to others. How could any of us be entitled to a better choice situation from the state?

3.6 Coercion, Strictly Speaking

At this point, one might say that there is a distinctive complaint against coercion, strictly speaking, that isn't captured by the Fear, Risk, or Choice Principles. And the state's threats are coercion, strictly speaking. So, this is the complaint against the state. It is because the state coerces, in this strict sense, that it must satisfy some legitimating condition or limit of legitimacy. This appeal to coercion is a specific expression of a general impulse. This is to think that it must be possible to identify a special way of "interfering in choice" that is wrong in itself (at least absent special conditions), in something like the way that, according to the Force Constraint, physical invasion of someone's body is wrong in itself (at least absent adequate opportunity to avoid). What, then, is this special way of interfering in choice? Again, it is fairly clear what it is for someone to touch your body without your consent. But what is it for someone to "touch your choice" without your consent? Not just to affect your choice. We do that all the time. Nor is it just to condition and announce a response to your choice. A coffee merchant doesn't wrong you by offering to give you a latte in return for payment. So, what else can this special way of interfering in choice be? Coercion, strictly speaking, presents itself as the answer.

What, then, is coercion, strictly speaking? I consider, as representative, the conception suggested by Hayek (1960) and Raz (1986). On this conception, coercion, strictly speaking, is steering that compels (see also Yankah 2008). Hablo "steers" Audito, let us say, when Hablo intentionally gets Audito to do something or intentionally brings about a certain position or location of Audito's body. Hablo "compels" Audito when Hablo does one of the following two things. First, Hablo affects Audito's choice situation in such a way that Audito has "no other choice" but to Obey. Audito's having no other choice is reflected in especially pronounced value-of-compliance effects. For instance, Audito is justified or excused for Obeying, or Audito's Obedience is not "independent," in a sense to be explored more later. Second, Hablo compels Audito insofar as Hablo physically forces Audito's body into a position or location, so that there is not even an action to justify or excuse or to be independent.

The question then is what distinctive complaint Audito might have against coercion, so understood—that is, against compelling steering. In other words, what complaint might Audito have against compelling steering that is not already accounted for by the Risk, Fear, and Choice Principles? Granted, compelling steering has, by definition, especially pronounced value-of-compliance effects. But the Choice Principle already takes such effects into account.

Raz at times provides an answer to the question of what the complaint against compelling steering might be. He suggests that compelling steering distinctively expresses disrespect for autonomy (1986, 378, 416), unless a legitimating condition of "trust" is met (1986, 157, 419; 2001). But why should the ideal state's compelling steerings express disrespect for autonomy? The value of autonomy, for Raz, derives from the value of a worthwhile life that one selects and independently values. Insofar as the state's compelling steerings improve Audito's choice situation, they position Audito to live such a life. So why should they express disrespect for Audito's autonomy if they clearly aim to secure what gives Audito's autonomy its value (Quong 2011, 58)? A further puzzle is that Raz does not think that compellingly steering Audito to get him to fulfill his duties to support the autonomy of others, even absent a relationship of trust, expresses disrespect for his autonomy (1986, 157, 419; 2001). What does express disrespect for Audito's autonomy is compellingly steering him (absent trust) for the sake of Audito's autonomy. But why does only coercion for the sake of Audito's autonomy, but not coercion for the sake of others' autonomy, express disrespect for Audito's autonomy? One might have expected precisely the opposite. In any event, if coercion somehow distinctively wrongs, one doubts this can be explained in terms of what coercion expresses. For presumably coercion is supposed to wrong in a way that a blunt declaration of disrespect, for autonomy or whatever else, does not.

Setting aside what Audito's distinctive complaint against compelling steering might be, is there any positive evidence that Audito has a distinctive complaint against compelling steering? Such evidence would be provided by a clear case in which, holding fixed effects on the choice situation already accounted for by the Choice Principle, a noncompelling steering became impermissible by becoming compelling. It's not clear what such a case would be.

However, let us suppose, for the sake of argument, that Audito does have some distinctive complaint against compelling steerings. Could this be Audito's complaint against the state's threats? One difficulty is that the state's threats are not, as a rule, compelling steerings. Many people (not unreasonably) defy even threats of serious penalties such as long-term imprisonment (perhaps because they see the chances of being caught as sufficiently low as to be worth the risk). After all, if the state's threats were compelling steerings, wouldn't prisons be empty? The simple fact is that, although these threats are paradigms of "state coercion," they actually don't compel many of those whom they threaten and so don't count as coercion, strictly speaking.

Moreover, suppose that we find a given state threat that does compel. We can then perform the Subtraction Test on it. We can, in thought, gradually moderate the threatened bad consequence. Instead of imprisonment, there is some lesser loss of privilege; instead of a high fine, there is a lower one. Eventually, we will have moderated the threatened bad so that, while supplying some deterrent, the threat no longer compels—so that the threat does leave those it threatens with "another choice." Would moderating penalties in this way suffice to assuage the worry about state coercion? Would political philosophers who insist on the Harm Principle, or the requirement of public justification, think these no longer applied?

"Granted," one might reply, "some specific state threats don't themselves coerce. Nevertheless, all the state's threats are still backed by coercion. That—backing by coercion—is what the complaint is about." What does it mean to say that the state's threats are "backed by coercion"? My best guess is that it means that if Audito resists the state's following through on its noncoercive threat, then the state will coerce Audito (Yankah 2008). For example, if Audito refuses to pay the moderate, noncompelling penalty, the state will lay hands on him. If Audito, by contrast, complies with the noncoercive threat, then Audito will at no point have been actually coerced. However, even though Audito will not have been actually coerced, he will have been subject to a threat that was backed by coercion.

Suppose that the state's threats are backed by coercion in this sense. Why should Audito have a complaint about this? Even if we grant that Audito has a complaint against actually being coerced, it's not clear why it should follow that Audito has a complaint against, as it were, being merely counterfactually coerced: against its being the case that Audito would have been actually coerced had things gone otherwise. It is not generally true that if one would have had a complaint against suffering something had one suffered it, one does have a complaint about that counterfactual's being true. In any event, the state's threats are not always even backed by coercion in this sense. That is, it is not always the case that if Audito resists the state's following through on its noncoercive threat, then the state will coerce Audito. The state may be able to follow through on the noncoercive threat in a way that Audito is unable to resist in the first place. The state might simply withhold a benefit over which it has complete control.

To be sure, there is something to the idea that even the state's noncoercive threats are backed by coercion and that this itself points to a valid complaint against the state. It's just that we haven't been able yet to put our finger on what this something is.

3.7 Exploitative Offers

So far, I have argued that the Choice, Fear, and Risk Principles offer the most plausible explanations of when and why threats are wrong. Should we conclude, then, that the Choice, Fear, and Risk Principles, taken together, are the whole story? Is it the case that, for every threat that is wrong, either the Choice Principle, or the Fear Principle, or the Risk Principle explains why it is wrong? Or are there cases they don't capture?

The answer matters for our search for the complaint against the state. If the Choice, Fear, and Risk Principles, taken together, are the whole story, then the complaint against the state cannot be a complaint against its threats. For, as we have seen, neither the Choice Principle, nor the Fear Principle, nor the Risk Principle implies that the ideal state's threats are wrong. If there is some case of a wrongful threat that they don't capture, however, then some other principle besides the Choice, Fear, and Risk Principles must be invoked to explain why at least that wrongful threat is wrong. And perhaps that other principle, unlike the Choice, Fear, or Risk Principles, implies that the state's threats are also wrong. In that case, the complaint against the state might be a complaint against the state's threats after all.

In fact, I believe there are some cases of threats, "exploitative offers," that the Choice, Fear, and Risk Principles don't explain. Consider "Car Wash." Legitimate business reasons, such as declining sales or tardiness, make it the case that Boss would not wrong Employee by firing her. And presumably Boss does not wrong Employee by not firing her. Unless more is said, whether or not Employee has washed Boss's car has no bearing on this. That is, Boss would not wrong Employee by firing her in circumstances in which (in a more usual case) she has not washed his car. Nor would Boss wrong Employee by not firing her in circumstances in which (in a less usual case) she has washed his car (who knows why). All the same, Boss would seem to wrong Employee by conditioning and announcing, "Unless you wash my car, you're fired."

The Risk Principle isn't engaged by Boss's conditioning and announcing, since, for all that has been said, neither of Boss's responses would wrong Employee. Nor is the Fear Principle engaged, for similar reasons. Nor, finally, does the Choice Principle apply. Employee is not entitled from Boss to a choice situation in which Boss does not fire Employee, period. And the offer would seem to give Employee a better, or at least no worse, choice situation.

Now Employee has the option of keeping the job if she wants. Granted, the offer has an adverse value-of-compliance effect. Before the offer, Employee could volunteer to wash Boss's car as a free gift, which was in no way servile obedience. After the offer, washing Boss's car can no longer be a gift, and it does look like servile obedience. So, in one way, this makes Employee's choice situation worse. But this effect seems negligible. At most, Employee now can't give Boss a free gift she never had any intention or reason to give. Hence, the Choice Principle does not explain the case either; for all it says, the offer is permissible.

One might reply: "For as long as Boss is conditioning to not fire Employee if she does wash the car, he owes her the still better choice situation of not firing her even if she does not wash the car. As in Spit Bus, what he gains by refusing her that better choice situation is simply too little when compared to what she loses." A welcome suggestion, if it could be made to work. But, to a first approximation, Boss gains a washed car and Employee loses the labor of washing a car. Is this too little? After all, if I am willing to pay for a car wash from a commercial provider, I don't owe her the even better choice situation of being willing to pay the same amount for nothing in return.

In this chapter, we have been considering the possibility that the complaint against the state is not against its following through on threats but instead against its making the threats themselves. We now leave the discussion partly, but not entirely, resolved. In the meantime, let us sum up what we have found to this point. Insofar as the Risk, Fear, and Choice Principles together explain why threats wrong someone when they do, the ideal state's threats do not wrong anyone, since the state's threats do not violate the Risk, Fear, or Choice Principles. However, exploitative offers like Car Wash suggest that some threats—or, more generally, some announcings or conditionings—can wrong in a way that is not explained by the Risk, Fear, or Choice Principles. So, until we say what this way is, we haven't ruled out the possibility that the state's threats may wrong in this way. But, bracketing this possibility for now, let's move on to consider other possibilities for what the complaint against the state might be. Might we still account for it without appealing, as our positive conjecture conjectures, to claims against inferiority?

4

Last Attempts

We have been searching for the complaint, as opaque as it is familiar, against the state. We thought the target of the complaint might be the state's enforcement of its directives, either in the form of imposing deterrents for violations of its directives or in the form of threatening such imposition. But neither fit the bill. In this chapter, we consider two final candidates for the target of the complaint: the state's obligating us to obey and the state's invading our external property.

4.1 Is the Claim against Being Obligated to Obey the State?

I have not yet said much about "political obligation": a moral duty to comply with state directives, as such. We can include under the heading of "political obligation" the alleged duty to obey the law, as well as political de jure authority, understood as the state's power to create political obligations by issuing directives. We might also include under this heading the state's oft-discussed moral monopoly or exclusive right: namely, that where there is a state, it is morally impermissible for private agents to enforce natural prohibitions. This can be seen as a special case of political obligation: namely, to comply with the state's ban on private enforcement.

Recall that our ideal state issues directives to contribute to the public interest by meeting claims to improvement. As we saw, such directives go beyond the prohibition of the Force Constraint. And because of the Directive/Duty Gap, such directives will also go beyond any natural Duty to Improve. Thus, if there are political obligations to comply with the ideal state's directives, we are morally constrained to a greater extent than we would be if we faced those directives with only natural duties, even on an expansive view of what those natural duties are. Put another way, if there are no political obligations, then sometimes disobeying the state's directives violates no moral duty whatsoever, not even a Duty to Improve.

Might the complaint against the state, then, be somehow a complaint against political obligations? One can speak, intelligibly enough, of an objection to being bound by political obligations. Presumably, this objection doesn't take the form of first granting that there are political obligations and then railing against Moral Reality for having put us in chains. Instead, the objection comes earlier, as a reason why Moral Reality doesn't, in fact, so obligate us. In general, the thought would be, agents who would be bound by any putative moral requirement have objections, of a kind, to being so bound. In Scanlon's (1998) terms, they have "reasons to reject" principles that would require them to act in the relevant way. Unless those objections are outweighed by sufficiently important values that the requirement serves, there simply is no such moral requirement. Since the objections to being bound by political obligations are not answered by sufficiently important values, the thought concludes, there are no political obligations.

In evaluating whether this sort of objection to political obligations is our sought-after complaint against the state, we again apply our two tests. First, there is the Subtraction Test. Does removing the target of the complaint remove the complaint? Second, there is the Spare-Justification Test. Can the complaint against the target be answered, at least by the lights of those who insist there is a complaint, even without the legitimating conditions and limits on legitimacy that they invoke?

Let's begin, in reverse order, with the Spare-Justification Test. Even those who press an objection of this kind to political obligations are likely to accept that there are some natural duties. Presumably, there is an objection to natural duties, as there is to any putative moral requirement. So, they accept that this objection to natural duties is overcome. Why, then, isn't the objection to political obligations also overcome? What is the relevant difference between natural duties and political obligations?

Is the difference, first, that political obligations ask more of those they bind than natural duties and so give them more to object to? But political obligations are not, as a rule, more burdensome. For instance, political obligations to refrain from private enforcement are requirements simply to let the state take a distasteful chore off one's hands. Or is the difference, second, that political obligations are imposed on us by another person or will whereas natural duties are not? But this is an illusion. The basic principle that we are morally required to comply when a state issues a directive to us, if there is such a principle, is not itself imposed by any state. Rather, the state determines how it applies, as a result of making certain choices: namely, choices to issue certain directives. The same is true of natural duties. The basic principle that you may not step on my foot is not imposed by me. Rather, I determine how it applies, as a result of making certain choices. If I move my foot from here to there, then you may no longer step there (van der Vossen 2015).[1]

Perhaps, then, the difference is, third, not that it's somehow more objectionable to be bound by political obligations than by natural duties; it's not that there's more to be said against being bound by political obligations. Instead, the difference is simply that there is less to be said in favor of being bound by political obligations. There are just no sufficiently important values in the pro column. After all, what's to be said in favor of complying with political obligations? Given the Duty/Directive Gap, one can often serve the public interest at least as well without complying with political obligations. So, even if complying with political obligations is no more burdensome than not complying, what is the positive point of complying with political obligations?

Perhaps, if one has promised to comply, then that could give compliance a positive point. The value of fidelity to promises would be an important value in the pro column. If that's the only reason in favor of compliance, however, then something like consent is, after all, a kind of legitimating condition. For the free act of will involved in making a promise would then be a necessary condition for political obligation. Interestingly, on this view, this free act of will legitimates the state not by waiving an objection but instead by creating a positive reason. The act of will makes for a promise, and it is the value of fidelity to promises that gives one positive reason to comply with political obligations when compliance would otherwise be pointless.

Let us grant, for the sake of argument, that this is so: that we can't answer the objection to being bound by political obligations without appealing to a legitimating condition like consent. Then, as far as the Spare-Justification Test is concerned, we still have a live candidate for the complaint against the state. However, we still need to consider the Subtraction Test: Does removing the candidate target remove the complaint? Imagine that we didn't have political obligations. (Or, if you don't believe we have political obligations, just remind yourself of what you already believe.) This means that disobeying the state's directives will sometimes violate no moral duty whatsoever. Otherwise, however, imagine that the state relates to us in the same way. It still issues and enforces its directives. Does the fact that we don't have political obligations to comply with these directives, which the state nonetheless issues and enforces, silence the complaint? It would seem not.

The residual complaint, some might say, is that the state, in issuing its directives, asserts, falsely, that we have political obligations. But can the complaint be merely that the state asserts untruths? In any event, imagine that the state does not even assert that we have political obligations. (Is any imagination required? Do states actually assert that we are morally required to obey them?)[2] For example, although the state freely admits that it holds no moral monopoly on enforcing the Force Constraint, it nonetheless announces that it stands ready to imprison anyone else who tries to enforce it. Does the state's conceding that we aren't obligated to comply with these directives, which it nonetheless issues and enforces, quell the felt complaint? Presumably not.

It may seem obvious what the target of the residual complaint is. The state is enforcing our compliance with its directives. The state's concession that we are free from any moral bonds of political obligation to comply with its directives does nothing to answer this complaint about what the state still does to us in enforcing those directives. Indeed, if we accept Force Requires Duty, which says we can be enforced to do only what we have duties to do, then the fact that we have no political obligations only intensifies the complaint about what the state still does to us. The state is wronging us by enforcing directives with which we have no duty to comply. But then we are back to enforcement as the target of the complaint. And we have already discussed that.

4.2 Is the Claim against the State's Expropriation?

One last try. Perhaps the complaint against the state is against the state's use of our external property, not simply in compensation or deterrent fines but also in taxation.[3] To be clear, we have discussed complaints against two other forms of state treatment that might be described as "the use of our property." First, we discussed complaints against the state's use of force in imposing deterrents, which is the state's use of our bodies, which might be said to be our property. Second, we discussed complaints against the state's inducing us, by threat, to contribute to the public interest. The state might induce us to build a well or stand sentry. This might be described as the use of our labor, which might also be said to be our property. Whether or not such descriptions are accurate or illuminating, we have already discussed what they purport to describe.

The complaint we have not yet discussed is a complaint against the state's use of our property in the most natural, literal interpretation of the phrase: its use of some object, not itself part of our bodies, that nonetheless belongs to us. It might be argued that just as there is the deontological Force Constraint on the use of our bodies, so too is there a deontological constraint on the use of our external property. And it might be argued that taxation violates this deontological constraint. Taxation does something morally akin to invading and removing parts of our bodies or draining the blood from our very veins.

Once again, we apply our two tests. The Subtraction Test, in this case, consists in imagining that the state does not use our external property. We already performed this test, implicitly, when we told ourselves the Myth of the Omittites. We did not assume that the Guardian of the Ladder taxed his subjects. The complaint against his empire would remain, I take it, even if his empire was self-financed.

On to the Spare-Justification Test, which asks whether those who hold that there is a complaint against the state can consistently hold that state taxation violates a deontological constraint, akin to an invasion of the body, even in the absence of a legitimating condition or limit on legitimacy. In order to hold this, it seems, they would need to accept:

> "Natural Property": There are rights in property other than those assigned by a system that reliably achieves the public interest: that is, a system that meets claims to improvement.

For taxation by an ideally directive state is itself part of a system that reliably meets claims to improvement. If one denies Natural Property, if one holds that people have property rights only in what such a system assigns them, then taxation defines, rather than violates, their property rights. So, again, one can hold that state taxation violates a deontological constraint only if one accepts Natural Property.

Yet some who hold that there is a complaint against the state reject Natural Property. An example is Nagel, who voices the complaint against the state (1991) while rejecting Natural Property (Nagel and Murphy 2004). So their complaint against the state can't be that taxation violates property rights. Moreover, even if one accepts Natural Property, the Avoidance Principle may still license taxation. With a carbon tax, for example, there might be adequate opportunity to avoid taxation, just as there is adequate opportunity to avoid the force used in deterrents.

Suppose, however, that one holds both Natural Property and that there is not adequate opportunity to avoid taxation. Then, I grant, one could hold that there is a complaint against taxation. But it bears emphasizing how strange the resulting position would be. For it has already been granted that there is no complaint against the state's use of our labor: its directing us, under threat, to act in certain ways. The resulting position would be that there is a complaint only against the state's use of the material fruits of our labor. And yet one might have thought that the complaint against the state's use of our labor had far greater power than the complaint against the state's use of its products. Nozick (1974, 169–171), for example, implicitly acknowledges this when he argues that taxation is objectionable because it is "on a par with forced labor." He tries to get our blood pressure up by making (seemingly innocent) taxation look like (manifestly noxious) impressment, not by making impressment look like taxation.

II

The Positive Conjecture

Claims against Inferiority

In the previous part, I made the case for one instance of the negative observation: that the felt claim against the state, which calls for its justification or legitimation, resists explanation by appeal to interests in improvement or rights against invasion. In this part, I present the materials for my positive conjecture: that this and other commonplace claims are explained, instead, by what I call claims against inferiority. Toward the end of this part, I explain how the claim against the state can be understood as a claim against inferiority. In Parts III, V, and VI, I consider a number of other commonplace claims, arguing, as the negative observation has it, that they are not explained by interests in improvement or rights against invasion and then proposing, as the positive conjecture would have it, that they are explained instead by claims against inferiority.

5

Relations of Inferiority

A "claim against inferiority" is, roughly, a claim against standing in a "relation of inferiority" to another person: against being subordinated to another or set beneath them in a social hierarchy. Relations of inferiority are the natural-historical legacy of pecking order in other social animals, albeit irrevocably transformed by symbol and self-consciousness. This heritage may account for the primitive depth and inarticulateness of our consciousness of relations of inferiority.

My discussion of claims against inferiority takes inspiration from two strains of thought. The first is the revival and development of the republican (or neo-Roman) tradition—by Pettit (1997, 2012, 2014), Skinner (1998, 2002, 2008), and Lovett (2010), among many others—and of Kant's political philosophy—by Ripstein (2009), Stilz (2009), Pallikkathayil (2010, 2017), and Forst (2013). These theorists emphasize complaints that look very much like complaints against inferiority: complaints against domination or dependence, against having a master, or against being vulnerable to an arbitrary, unilateral, or private will. Moreover, these complaints resist explanation as improvement or invasion complaints. For they are not complaints against any (independently intelligible) foregone improvement or actual invasion. Indeed, they are complaints not against how one is actually treated or provisioned at all but instead against the mere fact that one is exposed to the possibility of certain kinds of treatment at the hands of another will. The philosopher's fictions of the benevolent despot, the kindly slave master, the husband who keeps his wife in a gilded cage, the aristocrat given to noblesse oblige, the colonial administrator who selflessly bears the "White man's burden," and so on are meant to elicit such complaints.

The second strain of thought from which I take inspiration is what has come to be known as "relational egalitarianism," represented, most notably, by the work of Anderson (1999) and Scheffler (2003) (see also Miller 1997; Norman 1997; Wolff 1998, 2015, 2019; Scheffler 2005, 2015; Anderson 2010a, 2010b). These philosophers have suggested that unless we attend to "relational equality," we risk an incomplete view of what is required for an acceptable distribution of income and wealth. Among other things, they observe that an otherwise fair and efficient distribution of income and wealth—and so one that might not give anyone, in my terms, improvement complaints—might still be a highly unequal distribution (compare G. Cohen 2009, 34). And this highly unequal distribution might lead to objectionably inegalitarian relations between people, in which some are dependent on others or in which there are hierarchies of status. In many societies, for example, inequality arose through debt peonage, which itself was the natural result of fair contracts and the distribution of option luck. Even though the inequality might not be unfair or inefficient, people might have a complaint about finding themselves in, and compelled to support, such a society. And this complaint seems more than a mere preference for a certain public culture, such as a preference that the prevailing mores governing interaction among strangers were more open and less reserved. This complaint against relational inequality looks like what I describe as a complaint against inferiority. It is not an improvement or invasion complaint. Again, we are imagining a distribution that is fair and efficient and does not violate anyone's natural rights.

If the paths are so worn, why trod them again? What does this book add? One might be put in mind of a criticism commonly, if possibly erroneously, attributed to Samuel Johnson, "The work is both good and original. That which is good is not original, and that which is original is not good." First, as I noted in the introduction, claims against inferiority animate a broader range of political commitments—namely, our various commonplace claims—than has been appreciated. For the most part, for instance, relational egalitarianism has focused only on the implications for the distribution of material goods.[1] Second, I try to give a clearer and more specific analysis of what relations of inferiority are. Third, relatedly, I try to distinguish claims against inferiority from other moral ideas, with which they are at times confused.[2] Finally, also relatedly, I present claims against inferiority as part of a pluralist view. By contrast, writers in both the republican and relational egalitarian camps have at times proposed nondomination or relational equality as a kind of master value that could shoulder the whole weight of a political philosophy. But this seems to me a mistake. Interests in improvement, rights against invasion, and claims against inferiority are simply distinct and irreducible concerns. This excessive ambition, I suspect, is partly responsible for the unclarity and confusion just noted.

5.1 Three Abstract Conditions, Two Paradigms

What, then, are relations of inferiority? To start, we can give at least three necessary conditions. Abstract though they are, they do considerable work, even without further specification. First, relations of inferiority involve genuine relations. These relations need not be face-to-face encounters. But they must involve either interactions of some kind, perhaps across borders, or comembership in a common society. So, on the one hand, there are no relations of inferiority between people who live in altogether different times and places. You, reader, stand in no relation of inferiority to the ancient Egyptian pharaoh Ramses II. On the other hand, it is not in itself sufficient for a relation of inferiority simply that some have more or are better off. The mere fact that some contemporary in your society (let alone someone living in an altogether different time and place) discreetly enjoys, in the privacy of their own home, some labor-saving convenience that you don't enjoy does not put you in a relation of inferiority to them.[3] (This is not to deny that you can have improvement complaints against the long-dead Ramses or provoked by your more convenienced contemporary. Perhaps Ramses, or whoever better convenienced your contemporary, could have improved your situation without unfairness to others but failed to do so.)

Second, relations of inferiority involve an unequal ranking. There is one party who can be identified as higher in the hierarchy, the other as lower. One is above, the other below. Third, relations of inferiority are relations between individual, natural persons. They are not relations between an individual, natural person and an artificial person, collective, or force of nature. The second point, that relations of inferiority involve rankings as superior or inferior, partly explains the third point, that they are not relations between individual natural persons and entities of an entirely different moral category, such as a force of nature, a collective, or an artificial person. What would it even mean for you to have equal, inferior, or superior status with a hurricane? Of course, we can make sense of a difference in power between you and a hurricane. A hurricane can have effects that you can't. The question is whether the difference in power constitutes something further that is of concern—something we want to describe as, say, subordination—or whether it is just a difference in power.

Similarly, what would it mean to say that you have equal, inferior, or superior status with a collective or artificial agent, such as Indonesia, the Roman Catholic Church, or Procter and Gamble? Again, we can say, and indeed I have said, that a collective, such as the state, can have greater power over you. But is there a question of the state itself having inferior, superior, or equal status in relation to you? It seems to me a kind of category mistake.[4]

Presumably, claims to equal status are symmetrical. If I have a claim of equal status with you, then you have a claim of equal status with me. So, if you have a claim of equal status with the state, then the state has a claim of equal status with you. But does the state have such a claim? Does the state have an objection on its own behalf should it have less power than you? Granted, in the case of some collectives, such as nations, it may be possible to speak of their having equal or subordinate status with one another. Moreover, members of those collectives might have vicarious claims that their group not be subordinated to another group. We consider this possibility in Chapter 10. But do all collectives have claims to equal status with each other, as all individuals do? Does the City of Albany have a claim to be the equal of California or the United States? Is there some standing objection Albany has on its own behalf that it has to take orders from Sacramento? Or, coming at it from another angle, if I am the equal of the City of Albany, the State of California, and the United States, and if equality is transitive, would the city, state, and nation then be equals? And if it doesn't make sense to have equal status with a collective, what sense does it make to be ranked as superior or inferior to a collective—as opposed to neither equally nor unequally ranked with respect to a collective?[5]

So, we have some abstract necessary conditions of relations of inferiority. Here is another point of entry. We can identify relations of inferiority by their two most extreme forms. On the one hand, there is "bondage," epitomized by the relation between slave and master. Here the republican epithets of "domination" and "dependence" apply most readily and with the least qualification. On the other hand, there are cases of "caste," epitomized by the relation of Dalits to Brahmins in India or Black people to White people under Jim Crow. Caste consists in the stratification of classes across a society. While bondage and caste often travel together, they can come apart. There might be an isolated relation of bondage between two individuals, without the inferior in that relation belonging to some caste that is recognized as lower in the broader society. If a Gothic slave slips the fetters and speaks Latin without an accent, perhaps he can blend in.

Now—and I can't emphasize this enough—I am not claiming that all instances of relations of inferiority are, or are morally equivalent to, instances of bondage or caste. Rather, I am saying that bondage and caste are extreme forms—aggravated cases of the pathology—that might instruct us about milder cases. They are cases in which the constituents of relations of inferiority are particularly intense or pronounced and where the factors that elsewhere "temper" such relations, as I put it, are sparse or absent.

5.2 Power, Authority, and Regard

What do relations of inferiority consist in? Put another way, what are these admittedly extreme examples, bondage and caste, extreme examples of? I suggest that Loman's standing in a relation of inferiority to Hyman consists in one or several of the following five things.

First, Loman's standing in a relation of inferiority to Hyman can consist, to a first approximation, in Hyman's enjoying an untempered "asymmetry of power over Loman": that Hyman has greater power over Loman than Loman has over Hyman. Hyman has more power over Loman to the extent, first, Hyman has the capacity to make decisions to affect Loman more significantly and, second, Hyman faces lower cost or difficulty in making these decisions. This power need not be to interfere in Loman's choice or invade Loman's person or property. Nor need the power be to bring Loman to have certain attitudes or to perform certain actions. The power might be of another kind, such as to withhold goods from Loman or shape Loman's environment. The power need not be a capacity to overcome resistance. Hyman's power to withhold goods from Loman, for example, may be so absolute that there is nothing Loman might do that would count as resistance.[6]

Second, Loman's standing in a relation of inferiority to Hyman can consist, to a first approximation, in an untempered "asymmetry of de facto authority" over Loman: that Hyman has greater de facto authority over Loman than Loman has over Hyman. Hyman has more de facto authority over Loman, first, insofar as Hyman can command (to put it with deliberate vagueness) a more significant range of actions from Loman; second, insofar as Hyman faces lower cost or difficulty in making these commands; and third, insofar as Loman is more likely to obey. By "commands," I mean, at a minimum, that Hyman's directives are not presented as advice, which merely informs Loman of reasons that would have obtained even in the absence of the communication. By "obey," I mean that Loman performs the commanded action at least partly because it was commanded (or at least while being so disposed that, in the absence of other motivating reasons to perform the commanded action, Loman would perform it at least partly because it was commanded). However, the authority is "de facto" in the sense that the commands need not create, claim to create, or be believed to create reasons, let alone moral reasons, for compliance. People may be acting out of habit, to avoid punishment, to preempt a contretemps, or because the command has solved a coordination problem. For brevity, I drop the qualifier "de facto," taking it to be implied.

All authority over Loman is power over Loman.[7] However, it is worth distinguishing authority over from other forms of power over, since asymmetries in authority over may be distinctively objectionable in a way in which asymmetries in other forms of power over Loman are not. Not all power over Loman is authority over Loman, as can be illustrated with the following points. First, Hyman might "lord his power over" Loman, but for the benefit of an audience other than Loman himself and so where Hyman commands nothing of Loman. To anticipate the case of Silent Car Wash of Section 12.3, Boss might say to his pal: "I'm all set to fire that loser. But—check it out, Biff—if she volunteers to wash my car, then I won't." Or think of "that exultation of the mind" that Hobbes called "glorying": the "joy arising from the imagination of a man's own power" ([1651] 1994, chap. 6), which largely meant greater power than another (chap. 10). Second, even where Loman is Hyman's intended audience, Hyman might toy with Loman precisely by not giving Loman any commands: "Maybe I will, maybe I won't, and there's nothing that you can do about it." Finally, Hyman might simply bully, hector, harass, or, as the chickens do, peck Loman, without giving Loman any orders. One might reply that in such cases Hyman is somehow ordering Loman to avoid him. But Hyman may not intend, by his bullying, to get Loman to behave in any particular way, let alone to avoid him. After all, if Loman avoids him, then Loman deprives him of the pleasures of bullying.

Third, Loman's standing in a relation of inferiority to Hyman can consist in Hyman's enjoying an untempered "asymmetry of power in comparison with" Loman: in Hyman's having greater power over others, in some group to which Hyman and Loman both belong, than Loman has over those same others. Note that what matters is Hyman's greater power over others than Loman has, not simply Hyman's greater power over things than Loman has. My neighbor with his larger-capacity washing machine has greater power than I have, at least to wash larger loads in one go. But my neighbor does not have greater power over me or greater power than I over others, unless he somehow uses his surplus capacity as leverage.

Fourth, Loman's standing in a relation of inferiority to Hyman can consist in Hyman's enjoying an untempered "asymmetry of authority in comparison with" Loman: in Hyman's having greater authority over others, in some group to which Hyman and Loman both belong, than Loman has over those same others.

Finally, Loman's standing in a relation of inferiority to Hyman can consist in an untempered "unmerited disparity of regard": that Hyman enjoys, whereas Loman does not, certain kinds of favorable responses from others, in some group to which they both belong, such as, among other things, respect, courtesy, and a willingness to serve interests.

I have said that a relation of inferiority can consist, "to a first approximation," in an asymmetry of power over or asymmetry of authority over. More precisely, it can consist in (i) Hyman's exercised greater power (or authority) over Loman, (ii) Hyman's "endorsement" of Hyman's (perhaps unexercised) greater power (or authority) over Loman or what Loman believes (perhaps mistakenly) is Hyman's greater power (or authority) over Loman, or (iii) Loman's "submission" to what Loman believes (perhaps mistakenly) is Hyman's greater power (or authority) over Loman. Hyman "endorses" an asymmetry of power (or authority) over Loman insofar as Hyman (a) welcomes it, (b) deliberately exploits it (such as by accepting placating gifts), (c) desires that Loman submit to it, or (d) desires that others take it as a basis for regarding Hyman more highly than Loman. Note that what is endorsed in such cases is not the power (or authority) itself but the asymmetry of power (or authority): the fact that Hyman can do things to (or command things of)

Loman that Loman can't do to (or command of) Hyman. By contrast, I might endorse my power to heal you without also endorsing your powerlessness to heal me. Loman "submits to" Hyman's real or believed greater power (or authority) over him insofar as Loman's belief that Hyman has greater power (or authority) over him leads Loman to (a) experience fear, anxiety, or concern about adverse uses of that asymmetric power (or authority); (b) feel grateful or indebted to Hyman for benign use (or nonuse) of that asymmetric power (or authority); or (c) act in ways that, sincerely or insincerely, express or display such emotions.

Why the need for all these qualifications? Let us focus on power for simplicity; the same considerations carry over to authority. Suppose my neighbor, Grande, who is physically stronger than I am, could, in principle, push me around. So, he has greater power over me than I have over him.[8] However, as we both implicitly know, Grande will never exercise his greater power over me, however I may act. Indeed, this implicitly known, never-to-be-exercised greater strength scarcely registers with either us, let alone rises to the level of an "issue" between us. Grande doesn't endorse it, and I don't submit to it. We just go about our business as if it didn't exist. It seems doubtful that anyone, at least prior to a great deal of philosophical priming, would view me as thereby subordinated to him. This sort of asymmetry of power seems too inert to define our social relations. The point is not that this asymmetry of power is tempered by other factors. The point is deeper: that it just isn't an asymmetry that needs tempering to begin with. For brevity, however, I will avoid repeating these qualifications and speak simply of asymmetries of power and authority over.[9]

The specification of these five constituents of relations of inferiority explains and gives content to the first abstract feature listed in the previous section: namely, that relations of inferiority presuppose genuine relations between people. To the extent that Hyman and Loman do not interact, Hyman cannot have greater power or authority over Loman. And where Hyman and Loman do not come under the same appraising eye, Hyman cannot enjoy greater authority over others or higher regard than Loman. For that requires that there is a common judge, Miro, of Hyman and Loman who responds more readily to Hyman's commands or regards Hyman more highly.[10]

This indicates some structural differences among constituents of relations of inferiority. On the one hand, we might divide the constituents in terms of their association with the paradigms of bondage and caste. What bondage carries to extremity is Hyman's having greater power and authority over Loman, whereas what caste carries to extremity, by contrast, is Hyman's enjoying greater power, authority, or regard in comparison with Loman. On the other hand, we might divide the constituents in terms of their dependence on the responses of a third party, Miro, to Hyman and Loman. In order for Hyman to have greater authority over others than Loman, there must be some Miro who complies more readily with Hyman's directives than with Loman's. And in order for Hyman to enjoy higher regard than Loman, there must be some Miro who regards Hyman more favorably than Loman. By contrast, Hyman can have greater power or authority over Loman, or greater power over others than Loman, without the responses of any Miro.

With five different constituents of relations of inferiority, which in turn can be grouped in different ways, with what right can we still view relations of inferiority as a unified category? Or, pragmatically setting aside questions of right, with what expectation of illumination do we view relations of inferiority as a unified category? For all these differences among constituents of relations of inferiority, they still share the abstract features identified in the previous section: they presuppose genuine relations, they are rankings as superior and inferior, and they are between natural individuals. And, most importantly, they are targets of complaints on behalf of those set in the inferior position.

5.3 Is Objectionable Hierarchy Just Disparity of Regard?

Still, some may argue that the fivefold list of constituents could be much shorter and unified. "It is only disparities of regard, not asymmetries of power or authority, that are, strictly speaking, constitutive of relations of inferiority," they may say.[11] "After all, Hyman might have and exercise greater power or authority over Loman without anyone viewing or treating Loman as inferior to Hyman. This might be because, in some imagined social context, greater power or authority does not attract higher regard. Or, even if greater power or authority, when known, does attract higher regard, no one may know that Hyman has greater power or authority over Loman. (Here we would have to imagine a case in which, while Hyman may command and Loman may obey, neither Hyman nor Loman, let alone anyone else, realizes it is Hyman's commands that Loman is obeying.) In such cases, there would be no objectionable hierarchy of Hyman over Loman."

Granting that there could be such cases, why should we agree with the conclusion that they would not be cases of objectionable hierarchy? Let us return to our paradigms as starting points and try to analyze what they involve. In the paradigm of bondage, the mere fact of the master's greater exercised power and authority seems to suffice, as a matter of ordinary English usage, for the enslaved person to be "subordinated" to the master, whether or not this is further attended by a disparity of regard.[12] Similarly, Orwell's "picture of the future," as of "a boot stamping on a human face—forever" ([1949] 2017, 256), seems a paradigm of subordination, even though the picture itself depicts nothing of regard but just a boot, a face, and infinite time left on the clock.

Perhaps a proponent of this reduction of objectionable hierarchy to disparities of regard might try to defend it in this way. (1) When is there no objectionable hierarchy among a group of people? Just when those people relate to one another as equals, as opposed to superiors or inferiors. (2) However, relating to someone as an equal, superior, or inferior entails having states of mind that bring them under the relevant description of equal, inferior, or superior. (3) Regard does bring people under a description as equal, inferior, or superior. (4) However, mere asymmetries of power and authority, even when exercised, need not bring people under a description as equal, inferior, or superior. (5) Therefore, asymmetries of power and authority themselves, when not attended by a disparity of regard, do not make for objectionable hierarchy.

As I argue in Chapter 22, I do not think, against (1), that the negative absence of objectionable hierarchy must be identified with the positive presence of an activity of "relating to others as equals." For one thing, objectionable hierarchy might be avoided by avoiding social relations altogether. For another, even where there are social relations, the absence of objectionable hierarchy might be better described as not being related to others as inferiors or superiors or not standing to others as inferiors or superiors, which, unlike the more active phrase "relating to others as," does not imply or connote bringing others under some description.

In any event, against (4), why shouldn't at least Hyman's knowingly wielding greater power and authority over Loman count as bringing Loman under the description of Hyman's inferior? If this is granted, then the argument would have to turn on the more exotic possibility that Hyman wields greater power or authority over Loman without anyone's knowing about it. In such a case, no one might bring Hyman or Loman under the description of superior or inferior. Even so, would this mean no objectionable hierarchy between them obtains? One imagines that if Loman were to discover the truth—that all this time he has been pushed or bossed around by Hyman—it might come as a nasty surprise. But what bad has Loman discovered if not that of objectionable hierarchy?

Finally, premise (2)—roughly, that there is no objectionable hierarchy but that thinking makes it so—has implausible implications. If it is a necessary condition of relating to someone as, say, an inferior that one brings them under that description, then egalitarian good intentions are self-fulfilling. If one believes that one is relating to someone as an equal, then one cannot, in fact, be relating to them as an inferior.

5.4 The Primary Tempering Factors

I have so far defined relations of inferiority as consisting in asymmetries of power and authority and in disparities of regard. And I have suggested that those who find themselves in the inferior position, at least, have claims against being in it. But surely this is too broad as it stands. Not every asymmetry of power and authority, and not every disparity of regard, gives rise to an objection. Such asymmetries and disparities are everywhere, in clubs, schools, mass transport, and houses of worship. Flight attendants and college professors, for example, tell passengers and students what to do. We greet these asymmetries and disparities more or less with equanimity. What's more, we don't always view such asymmetries or disparities as bitter compromises, concessions to necessity, or the tragic price paid for efficiency. Indeed, such asymmetries or disparities—between mentor and mentee, priest and parishioner, and so on—may be constitutive of social forms that we find valuable in themselves. So how can it be said that asymmetries of power and unmerited disparities of regard are objectionable or regrettable? As Berlin (1956, 313) observes, "Even the most convinced social egalitarian does not normally object to the authority wielded by, let us say, the conductor of an orchestra. Yet there is no obvious reason why he should not."[13]

We greet these asymmetries and disparities with equanimity, I suggest, because of certain "tempering factors" that we tend to take for granted, noticing them only by their absence. These tempering factors bound, contextualize, or transform these asymmetries or disparities so that they count less, or not at all, as objectionable relations of inferiority. What constitute objectionable relations of inferiority, therefore, are not asymmetries of power and authority and disparities of unmerited regard but rather such asymmetries and disparities when untempered. The idea, to be clear, is not that these tempering factors somehow outweigh or compensate for the bad of inferiority. The idea is instead that when these tempering factors are present, the asymmetries and disparities are not a bad, or less of a bad, to begin with. If we like, we might still describe those asymmetries and disparities as hierarchies, but as unobjectionable ones.

In this section, I lay out what I call the "primary tempering factors," which will be supplemented later by the (equally imaginatively titled) "secondary tempering factors." Before listing these, some general comments. First, we can identify certain tempering factors by noting that when they are present, the asymmetries and disparities are further from the paradigms of caste and bondage. Second, we can identify other tempering factors by noting that when they are present, the superior power or authority is less that of another natural individual, with whom one has a claim to equality. Third, we can identify still other tempering factors by noting that when they are present, it is publicly acknowledged that the person subject to asymmetric power and authority has a pro tanto objection to being so subject. Finally, even when the factors temper disparities and asymmetries in a scalar way by making disparities further from the paradigms of caste and bondage or by making the superior power or authority less that of another natural individual, the tempering factors, as they accumulate, can have a dichotomous effect. A threshold may be crossed beyond which the tempering factors make the asymmetry or disparity no longer such as to ground a claim against inferiority at all.

A first tempering factor, "Episodic Character," is that the asymmetries or disparities arise only in chance, one-off encounters, instead of being entrenched in an established, ongoing social structure. For example, in an upbeat mood, Benny might offer supererogatory help to a stranger, Indy, such as giving Indy a lift, without any plan to do the same for another stranger,

Altra. Benny performs a "random act of kindness."[14] This may be an unmerited disparity of regard, but it is tempered by the fact that there are no established, ongoing relationships among Benny, Indy, and Altra constituted by these fleeting interactions. It is compatible with this, however, that there are other established, ongoing relationships among the trio. It is just that if there are other relationships, they are constituted by something other than these fleeting interactions. (For instance, Benny, Indy, and Altra might stand in the established, ongoing relationship of cocitizen, which is constituted by the interactions of each of them with the same state.) Note that this tempering factor is not necessarily sufficient in itself. If the asymmetry or disparity is particularly pronounced, such as if Hyman happens, for the moment, to hold Loman's life in his hands, then the asymmetry's being one-off may not suffice to temper its objectionable character. (Recall that Hyman has greater power over Loman insofar as Hyman has the capacity to make decisions to affect Loman more significantly.)

A second tempering factor, "Context Limitation," is that the asymmetries or disparities are limited to certain contexts, including certain times, places, and social roles. Teachers might only be able to tell students what to do in class and only for a given semester or course of schooling. Flight attendants might be able to tell passengers what to do only for that interval between when they board and deboard the plane.

A third tempering factor, "Content Limitation," is that the asymmetric power or authority is limited in content: that is, in what can be done or commanded. Teachers and flight attendants might simply be ignored if they were to command students to perform tasks that had no bearing on their own or their fellow students' education or were to command passengers to do things that have no bearing on a safe and decorous flight. Another important form of Content Limitation is that the power and authority do not set ends for people to pursue. Rather than setting ends for people to pursue, the power and authority regulate only the means people take to their own ends. For example, sound traffic regulations don't command where motorists are to travel, let alone if they are to travel at all. Instead, they command certain means of travel, which facilitate the pursuit of each motorist's independent ends by coordinating their pursuit of those ends with the like pursuits of other motorists. This example also illustrates another kind of Content Limitation: that activities are regulated only in a coarse-grained way, leaving much to agents' discretion. Traffic regulations don't command motorists to take the quickest or cheapest route to their destination, for example.

To some extent, the first three primary tempering factors—Episodic Character, Context Limitation, and Content Limitation—reduce, in a more or less quantitative way, Hyman's power and authority over others. But they also temper asymmetries in power and authority in ways that seem more qualitative than quantitative. Consider, for example, the significance of the fact that Hyman commands only means (such as rules of the road), rather than ends (such as destinations), or that the commands concern only one easily compartmentalized aspect of others' lives (such as occasional air travel).

A fourth tempering factor, "Escapability," is that the asymmetries or disparities may be escapable, at will, with little cost or difficulty.[15] To take an extreme case, if one can exit a slave contract at will, then it is not clear in what sense one really is enslaved. Another way of putting this is to say that what matters for relations of inferiority is not so much inequality in exercised power or authority and actual regard but instead inequality of opportunity for power, authority, and regard, where equality of opportunity is understood not as equal ex ante chances to end up on the winning end of the asymmetry or disparity but instead as retained freedom to exit the relations in which the asymmetry or disparity arises. The point is not that, while being on the losing end of asymmetries or disparities is always a burden, one forfeits one's complaint when the burden is self-imposed—that one has no one to blame but oneself.[16] It is rather that the freer one is to exit what would otherwise be an objectionable relation of inferiority, the less it seems an objectionable relation of inferiority to begin with. Importantly, what matters is freedom to exit an otherwise objectionable relation of inferiority of a given kind. It is not enough that one is free to exit a relation of that kind to one individual if, upon exiting that relation to that individual, one is constrained to enter into a relation of the same kind with another individual. We must keep in mind Marx's ([1849] 1978) insight that the proletarian's freedom from any given capitalist is compatible with her subjection to (to put it somewhat misleadingly) the capitalist class.

A fifth tempering factor, "Downward Equalization," has two parts. First, the asymmetries or disparities are not "final"; they are themselves regulated by higher-order decisions, such as a court of appeal or a decision further up the chain of command. Second, these higher-order decisions are not themselves marked by the same asymmetry or disparity. What managers can ask of workers, for example, might itself be regulated by bargains struck at the start of each year. In brief, inequality at a lower level in a decision-making hierarchy is tempered by equality at a higher level. It tempers whatever hierarchy there is that it is regulated from a standpoint of equality.

The last tempering factor, "Egalitarian Relationship," is that the people in the relationship marked by the asymmetry or disparity might also stand as equals (such as enjoying equal consideration) in some other recognized relationship. Once the plane lands, passenger and flight attendant are simply private citizens looking for ground transportation.

This helps explain why the extreme cases of caste and bondage are extreme: namely, that these primary tempering factors are absent. Bondage, for its part, involves virtually unlimited power and authority over another. Castes, for their part, are woven into the fabric of social relations; they are not cabined to any one time, place, or context; they cannot be exited; and they often preclude any other recognized relationship within which one is the equal of all the others in one's society.

5.5 The Structure of Claims against Inferiority

We turn now from relations of inferiority to claims against such relations. Those who find themselves in the inferior position in untempered relations of inferiority, I suggest, have complaints against being so positioned. True, those in the superior position may also have a complaint about their position. However, I believe this derives from the complaint of those in the inferior position. The superiors have a complaint about themselves having to stand in relations to which those in the inferior position have a complaint.

Strictly speaking, claims against relations of inferiority are not claims against the relations of inferiority themselves but instead claims addressed to certain agents to perform or refrain from certain actions (or to conditionally intend to perform or refrain from certain actions) that involve relations of inferiority. First, Loman has a claim on Benny not to directly contribute to Loman's standing as an inferior, in the sense that (i) Benny is not to exercise or endorse untempered greater power or authority over Indy, (ii) Benny is not to exercise or endorse untempered greater power or authority than Indy over others, and (iii) Benny is not to give Loman untempered lesser regard than Benny gives Hyman, where this is not merited. Claims of this kind have a deontological or agent-relative character. Benny is not himself to directly contribute to Loman's standing as an inferior, whether or not this reduces the overall incidence of cases in which someone stands to someone else as an inferior.

Second, even if Benny does not himself directly contribute to Indy's standing as an inferior, Indy may still have a claim on Benny that Benny work, where he can, to temper relations of inferiority that Indy stands in with others or bring it about that Indy avoids those relations. Claims of this second kind have a consequentialist or agent-neutral character. Benny is to contribute to reducing the overall incidence of cases in which someone relates to someone else in the objectionable way.

Complaints of the agent-relative kind are more likely than complaints of the agent-neutral kind to be held by a particular person, rather than by every member of some group to which that person belongs. Insofar as I do nothing to combat sexism, perhaps all women equally have that complaint against me. But no woman seems to have that complaint to a greater degree than any other. By contrast, if I myself undervalue the contributions of a certain female colleague because she is female, then that is a complaint that she, in particular, has against me. However, even complaints of the agent-neutral kind can be held by someone in particular. If I don't intervene in or actually acquiesce in another colleague's overlooking her contribution, then the overlooked colleague may have a complaint against me because I could have intervened in her case or refrained from acquiescing.[17] In any event, even when agent-neutral complaints are held equally by every member of a group, such as all women, they are still, as it were, "claimant relative." Even if every woman has the same complaint, it is a complaint that men don't similarly have.

6

Disparities of Regard

I begin with some general remarks about the genus of disparities in regard before turning to its three species: disparities of esteem for particular qualities and achievements, disparities of consideration for persons, and purely expressive disparities.

6.1 Regard in General

First, recall that a disparity of regard between Hyman and Loman is always relative to some judge, Miro, who regards Hyman more favorably than Loman. Moreover, how far Miro's regarding Hyman more highly than Loman contributes to Loman's inferiority to Hyman depends on who or what Miro is. In general, higher regard from a person or body that wields greater power or authority, or from a person who themselves enjoys higher regard, counts for more than higher regard from a person or body that wields lesser power or authority or from a person who themselves enjoys lesser regard. To be the favorite of a superior is itself a kind of superiority.

Second, disparities in regard are to be distinguished from agent-relative partiality. Simply believing that a special relationship to one's friend or child gives one agent-relative reason to serve their interests, which one does not similarly have to serve the interests of strangers, does not make for a disparity of regard. To see one person and not another as a friend, for example, is not to regard the latter as though they belonged to a lower stratum. She's just not a friend, and she has other people, but not you, as friends. In social hierarchies marked by disparities of regard, by contrast, people regard members of the higher stratum more highly than members of the lower stratum, regardless of any further relationship to them. Indeed, members of the lower stratum regard members of the higher stratum more favorably than they regard fellow members of the lower stratum, including themselves.

Third, some disparities in regard are merited, whereas others are unmerited. In the case of a merited disparity of regard, Miro regards Hyman more highly than Loman in some respect because, first, Miro accurately judges that they differ in some respect and, second, it is constitutive of Miro's properly understanding and appreciating certain independent values that, on the basis of Miro's judgment that they differ in that respect, Miro should regard Hyman more highly than Loman in that respect. It is constitutive of understanding and properly appreciating musicality, for example, that one appraises a more musical person more highly, as musical, than a less musical person. It is only unmerited disparities of regard, not merited disparities, that make for objectionable relations of inferiority. This is one of several reasons why, against Berlin (1956, 326), equality need not require "the minimization of all differences between men, the obliteration of the maximum number of distinctions, the greatest degree of assimilation and uniformity to a single pattern." No doubt a merited disparity can be said to constitute a social hierarchy of a kind, and people may care intensely about their relative position within this hierarchy of merit. But it does not make for relations of inferiority against which anyone has a complaint.

Finally, often when there is an unmerited disparity of regard between Hyman and Loman, Hyman attracts higher regard because Miro believes Hyman to have (or have to a greater degree) and Loman to lack (or have to a lesser degree) a certain "basing trait," such as having no close ancestor with dark skin, tracing a noble lineage, being blessed with divine favor, or simply belonging to the conquering side. In such cases, Miro gives Hyman higher regard than Loman because Miro judges that Hyman has the basing trait whereas Loman lacks it. However, Miro need not believe the basing trait justifies the higher regard in any further sense. More generally, an unmerited disparity of regard need not be based on a belief that there is a noninstrumental reason, or even a reason, for the disparity. For example, Lackey might be conspicuously solicitous of Patron's interests out of pure self-interest, simply to curry favor. Accordingly—and this is a point that bears emphasis—it is not necessary for an unmerited disparity of regard that it be believed that the social inferiors are unworthy of the greater regard the social superiors receive. So, in particular, it is not necessary that it be believed that because the social inferiors lack some relevant basing trait, they are not fully human, have lesser basic or fundamental moral status, or have interests and claims of lesser weight (compare Manne 2018, chap. 5; contrast Hellman 2008, 38; Viehoff 2019, 19). Miro can regard Hyman more highly than Loman from motivations that do not depend on any such belief.[1] Miro may be responding from unthinking habit. Miro may be temporizing or responding strategically (such as by catering to the interests of Hyman because of his greater purchasing power) whether out of self-interest or for more altruistic reasons. In order to ease the work of organizing who does what or who tells what to whom, Miro may be relying on salient coordination points (such as that others are likely to defer to the White man in the group, whether or not he is otherwise the best person to lead it; Ridgeway 2019) or importing distinctions or emulating models with which Miro is familiar elsewhere (Tilly 1998). Or, last but not least, people can simply take pleasure in belonging to the in-group or in triumphing over those whom they have defeated, as they themselves acknowledge, only by the whims of fortune, without any illusion that their superiority has some deeper justification. To overlook this is to underestimate the human genius for social distinctions.

It might be suggested that what may appear to be objections to unmerited disparities of regard are really objections to something else. On a first reductive proposal, the apparent objections to unmerited disparities of regard themselves are really objections to something that unmerited disparities of regard express, such as that the inferiors are less worthy of higher regard. Yet why should disparities of regard express this if they need not be based on a belief that the inferiors are less worthy of higher regard? It might be replied that disparities express this because they would be unjustified unless inferiors were less worthy of higher regard (Viehoff 2019, 19). To begin with, it is not true, as a general principle, that an action or attitude that would be unjustified unless something is the case expresses that it is the case. If I say to my fellow audience member, "Nice weather we're having," I don't express that the performance hasn't yet begun, even though my utterance is unjustified, because disruptive, if the performance has begun. But let us set this aside. To say that the disparity of regard would be unjustified unless something is the case is to presuppose that there is already some objection to the disparity of regard that would not be answered unless that were the case: that is, that there is already an objection to the disparity of regard that is independent of what it might express. Thus, the reductive explanation presupposes what it aims to reduce.

A second reductive proposal is that what appears to be an objection to a comparative unmerited disparity of regard between Hyman and Loman is simply an objection to a noncomparative withholding of merited regard for Loman. Loman's objection is not to being regarded less highly than Hyman in comparative terms but instead to being regarded less highly than Loman merits in absolute terms. A number of replies are in order here. First, what sort of regard Loman merits, in absolute terms, may be underdetermined. There may be a range of responses that count as regarding Loman adequately, in absolute terms, given Loman's merits. Suppose that Loman is so regarded. Still, it seems that Loman may have an objection if Hyman is more highly regarded despite having no greater merit. Second, suppose, as a baseline, that Loman and Hyman are not adequately regarded given their equal merits. Suppose that Hyman, but not Loman, is then adequately regarded. If the objections were only to noncomparative withholding of merited regard, then this would only remove an objection. But instead it seems to add an objection that wasn't there before: namely, Loman's objection that while Hyman is adequately regarded, Loman is not. Finally, suppose that Loman is not adequately regarded, in absolute terms, given his merits. Does Loman have an objection, of any moral weight, about this? Where the inadequate regard takes the form of consideration for persons, Loman may well have an objection of a moral character. But where the inadequate regard takes the form of esteem for particular qualities and achievements, one might wonder. Suppose, for the sake of argument, that we grant that there is some identifiable threshold of esteem that every composer of a given caliber merits at a minimum. Suppose that every composer of that caliber is equally esteemed but at some degree below that threshold (whatever that might mean). Do those composers have a moral complaint about this deficit in esteem? That's what I wonder. By contrast, the complaint takes on more of a moral character, or so it seems to me, when some, but not others, of those composers are esteemed more highly. This is all the more so when the disparity in esteem tracks a basing trait such as race or gender.

6.2 Esteem for Particular Qualities and Achievements

I distinguish three broad kinds of disparity of regard: disparities in "esteem for particular qualities and achievements," disparities in "consideration of persons," and "purely expressive" disparities. This section considers disparities in esteem for particular qualities and achievements. Esteem for a person's particular qualities and achievements consists in positive appraisal of or expression of positive appraisal of certain (actually or merely supposed) independently valuable qualities they possess, such as grace or beauty, or (actually or merely supposed) independently valuable achievements they have attained, such as acquired skills or contributions to industry or medicine, letters or science, art or sport.

Note, first, that such esteem need not have any further practical upshot. It need not incline the appraiser to do anything beyond simply favorably appraising the qualities and achievements and expressing that appraisal (Runciman 1967, 225). In particular, it need not incline the appraiser to the responses I describe in the following section as consideration. And note, second, that such esteem can be focused on the quality or achievement itself. It need not spread to the person as a whole. We can appraise a sprinter highly along the dimension of speed, for example, without this bleeding into our responses toward him as a whole.

Esteem for particular qualities and achievements is, in general, the sort of thing a person can merit. Where a disparity in esteem is merited, it need not make for a relation of inferiority, about which the person who enjoys less esteem has a complaint. This is, of course, not to deny that such merited disparities in esteem might be regrettable in other ways. To be sure, to lack a quality or achievement, especially one that one has sought, can give one reason to be disappointed or count oneself a failure. At very least, one lacks reason to feel satisfied or count oneself a success. And to be without that quality or achievement just is not to merit, noncomparatively, esteem for it. It is another question whether one has distinct reason to feel bad, in a further way, about either the comparative fact that others have, whereas one lacks, the quality or achievement or the further comparative fact that they enjoy, whereas one does not, merited esteem from others for having it. In a suitably philosophical frame of mind, one might be puzzled about what such distinct, comparative reasons could be. One might look on Oscar ceremonies and Olympic podia, as it were, with bemusement. It is clear why one should care that one lacks the quality or achievement. But why, one might wonder in this philosophical mood, should one care whether others have it or whether they are recognized for it? There is no denying, of course, the psychological fact that such comparisons do make people feel bad. They are a source of anguish for strivers everywhere (for the author big-time). Perhaps while these comparisons don't give people reason to feel bad in a further way, they nevertheless draw their attention to what we have granted they already have reason to feel bad about: namely, the lack of the quality or achievement itself. In any event, there is reason to reduce this psychic harm by broadening the range of qualities and achievements for which people can gain merited esteem (Fishkin 2014, chap. 3) and by reducing the salience, at least to those who merit less esteem, of the disparities, perhaps by what Rawls (1999, 470) called "non-comparing groups" (Fourie 2015; Scanlon 2018, 32–36). However, to say that there is reason to take such steps to mitigate the suffering that might be caused by believing one merits less esteem, or even to say that those who so suffer might have a complaint when those steps are not taken, is not to say that those who merit less esteem have a complaint about meriting less esteem itself or enjoying only so much esteem as they merit itself.

Be this as it may, there can also be unmerited disparities in esteem for qualities and achievements, and these can be partly constitutive of relations of inferiority. Often these unmerited disparities in esteem track a basing trait, such as gender. Part of what makes a culture sexist, for example, is that it systematically overlooks or discounts the intellectual or leadership contributions of women in comparison with men (which does further harm, for example, by suggesting that women can gain esteem only for other qualities or achievements, such as physical attractiveness or nurturing others).[2]

"But," one might protest, "is this not absurdly overgeneralized? Surely there need not be a relation of inferiority whenever there is a mistake, even an honest one, in comparative appraisal of qualities or achievements!" Agreed, but here, as elsewhere, it is crucial to remember the tempering factors, such as Episodic Character.[3] Granted, accidental, isolated unmerited disparities of esteem, which are not woven into the fabric of ongoing social relations, will not make for objectionable relations of inferiority. However, the systematic discounting of the intellectual or leadership contributions of women, for example, is not tempered in this way. It is systematic and so, I suggest, grounds a complaint.

6.3 Consideration for Persons

The second species of regard is what we might call "consideration for persons." I begin by listing some subspecies of consideration for persons. Then

I identify some characteristics of the species of consideration for persons and distinguish it from esteem.

A first subspecies of consideration for a person is treating them with courtesy. Treating some with greater courtesy than others will therefore amount to a disparity in consideration. In some cases, Miro may not only treat Loman comparatively with less courtesy than Hyman but also noncomparatively with insufficient courtesy. In the latter case, Loman might have an independent, noncomparative objection to Miro's treatment, quite apart from an objection to the relation of inferiority constituted by the comparative disparity in courtesy.[4] However, not every disparity in courtesy need involve Loman's receiving insufficient courtesy. Miro might show Hyman, as it were, supererogatory courtesy.[5] Indeed, there may be no fact of the matter whether such and such amounts to sufficient courtesy in absolute terms. The only question to ask may be whether it is the same courtesy that others receive in these parts.

A second subspecies of consideration for a person is concern for their interests, which include not only interests in improvement but also the interests that underlie rights against invasion. Again, where there is a disparity of concern for interests, Miro may display not only comparatively less concern for Loman's interests than for Hyman's but also insufficient noncomparative concern for Loman's interests. In such cases, where the insufficient concern may take the form of unjustified violence or an unfair distribution of resources, the noncomparative wrong of this insufficient concern will, entirely appropriately, loom much larger. But not every disparity in concern for interests need involve Loman's receiving insufficient concern. Miro might show Hyman, as it were, supererogatory concern (as in the case of the Half-Warm Society discussed in Section 13.1).

A third subspecies of consideration for persons is recognizing them as moral agents, who can owe things to others; as moral patients, who can be owed things by others; and as members of the moral community, who have standing to blame others for wrongs done others. Here a disparity in consideration would consist in Miro holding, in the absence of any independently justifying difference between their situations, that Hyman would be wronged by a wider range of actions than Loman would be; that, although Hyman can wrong others, Loman would wrong others by a wider range of actions than Hyman would; and that Hyman has standing to blame others for a wider range of wrongdoing than Loman has (Wallace 2010; Lippert-

Rasmussen 2018, chap. 4). In the case of such disparities, it is likely that Miro will be simply mistaken about what someone owes, is owed, or has standing to blame others for. In that case, someone may have a noncomparative objection. For example, suppose that in holding that Loman would wrong Vic by an action that Hyman would not, Miro is mistaken in holding that Hyman would not wrong Vic by that action but nevertheless is correct in holding that Loman would wrong Vic by that action. Then Vic has a noncomparative objection: namely, that Miro fails to recognize what Vic is owed by Hyman. However, it seems that Loman also has a comparative objection about the fact that Miro regards Hyman as not bound by the same moral requirements as Loman.

Fourth, there can be a similar disparity of consideration involving social norms or expectations of behavior, which may not be, or may be thought of as, moral requirements. By a "social expectation that *X* do *Y*," I mean, roughly, either that others are disposed to sanction *X* for failing to do *Y*, if only by ridicule, shunning, or disapproval, or that others (and perhaps *X* too) view *X*'s failing to do *Y* as in some sense inappropriate or out of order around here—at very least the sort of thing that, whether or not in some deeper sense inappropriate, risks a social encounter out of joint.[6] Here a disparity of consideration would consist in having a more restrictive set of social expectations on Loman's behavior than on Hyman's, as in Runciman's (1967, 228) example where "civilians never speak to soldiers until spoken to." There is a difficulty here, however. In many cases, the social expectations on the intuitively more highly regarded can be more, or at least no less, restrictive than the social expectations on the intuitively less highly regarded. The social expectations of the two castes are just different. In such cases, I suggest, insofar as the difference in social expectations constitutes a disparity of regard, it is as a purely expressive disparity, which we consider in the next section.

A fifth subspecies of consideration for a person is trusting them by default. Trusting people by default might be thought of as the reverse of what Moreau (2020) calls "censure." Her example of censure is assuming that any Muslim must sympathize with terrorism or extremism. That is, I would say, a disparity of consideration: namely, the withholding of default trust extended to others. If trusting people by default also includes listening to them and taking them at their word, then one way of looking at Fricker's (2007) path-breaking work on "epistemic injustice" is as an exploration of disparities of consideration, often along lines of gender, constituted by disparities in listening to people and taking them at their word.

A sixth subspecies of consideration for a person is simply noticing and attending to them. It is not for nothing that, in social scientific studies, one of the main indices of social rank is simply "visual attention received" (Cheng and Tracy 2014, 7, 13; Ridgeway 2019, 9–10). Consider Moreau's (2020) insightful discussion of "structural accommodation"—architecture, literal and social, that presupposes that the needs, interests, and abilities of a privileged group are normal, such as the ability to climb stairs to access spaces otherwise open to the public. To be sure, those unable to climb stairs presumably have an improvement complaint about this. Their situation could be improved without unfairness to others. However, they have a further complaint about the fact that this simply fails to see them or take their needs into account while seeing and taking into account the needs of the privileged group. I would say (although Moreau herself argues against this interpretation) that this counts as a disparity of consideration, where the consideration in question consists in seeing someone and taking their needs into account. Something similar might be said of Moreau's (2020) example of how representations of, as it were, "the man in the street" overlook people from certain groups—such as, to wit, people who aren't men. (Compare also Young 1990, chap. 6.)

A final subspecies of consideration for a person that we will consider here is attending to their particular attributes and so treating them as an individual.[7] Notice that treating people as instances of stereotypes, rather than as individuals, is possible even when the stereotypes are otherwise favorable (see Berlin [1958] 1997, 227; Eidelson 2013, 2015; Beeghly 2018). Eidelson (2013) gives the example of assuming that a female Asian American musician who has a technically imperfect audition must just be having a bad day. For his part, Eidelson suggests that the intuitive objection so naturally described as "failing to treat someone as an individual" is a general objection to failing to respect someone's autonomy by neglecting evidence of past choices or assuming an incapacity for future choices. Now, perhaps there is such a general objection, which would apply when someone assumes that someone who is unusually tall, presumably not by choice, plays basketball (Eidelson 2013, 208). At the very least, your taking offense when someone "makes assumptions" about you is intelligible in a way in which your taking offense when, say, someone who knows of your good deeds admires them is less intelligible. But, as Eidelson acknowledges (2013, 208), the objection seems significantly clearer and more forceful when the assumption is based on a view about a minority or disfavored protected class, such as being an Asian American female. But why should this be if, as Eidelson proposes, the objection is a general objection to someone making assumptions about you? Moreover, there seem to be similar objections to your "failing to treat someone as an individual" even if you draw inferences from that person's acknowledged choices: for example, that a man who has chosen to wear a yarmulke will be combative or a woman who has chosen to wear a headscarf will be retiring. Conversely, it seems that you can fail to treat someone as an individual by neglecting evidence of some unchosen trait they have, such as refusing to believe the mounting evidence that someone of African descent is congenitally beat deaf and so will never "have rhythm."

This suggests to me that failing to treat someone as an individual matters, when it does, because it contributes to a disparity of consideration, where the relevant form of consideration is precisely attending to people's particular traits, whether chosen or unchosen. The disparity of consideration, in other words, consists in one's attending to the individual traits of some people but not of others. This is, I suspect, part of what is meant by saying that Whiteness is "invisible" or "weightless" in a way Blackness is not. If you are White, others "see through" the pane of Whiteness to your particular qualities. If you are Black, that is all others see. Their sight never reaches your particular qualities, since the reflection on the dim pane of stereotype is too fictitiously vivid (Fanon 1952, chap. 5; Yancy 2018, 35, 57).[8]

Why should this matter, especially if the individual traits that are overlooked in your case, but attended to in the case of others, are defects? Among other things, it matters because people whose particular traits are not attended to are thereby disbarred from forms of association, such as love and friendship, that require attention to particular traits. In other words, to view people as merely instances of a stereotype, even a favorable stereotype, is to keep them always at a distance. It also matters because it keeps others from recognizing one's particular qualities and achievements. If it is assumed one has these desirable traits by default, then one's traits are never seen, only, as it were, veridically hallucinated. It is a disparity of consideration, I submit, when members of the majority or favored protected class treat one another as individuals, attending to their particular qualities, while treating members of the minority or disfavored protected class as merely instances of a stereotype, even if it is the stereotype of a "model minority."

Having given a list, which may not be exhaustive, of the subspecies of consideration for persons, I now say something more general about the species of consideration for persons and how it differs from esteem for particular qualities and achievements. First, consideration of persons is typically directed toward some practical response to the person, whereas esteem can be mere detached appraisal, of the sort an uninvolved spectator might make, such as that Genghis Khan was an able archer. Second, consideration for persons, unlike esteem for particular qualities or achievements, is not focused on specific, distinguishing traits but instead extends to the person as a whole. Even when higher consideration for Hyman tracks a basing trait, the consideration focuses not on the trait itself but spreads to Hyman as a person. Because Herr Geldsack has the trait of high net worth, for example, one is particularly courteous to him and solicitous of his interests.

Third, at least in egalitarian cultures, equal consideration for persons is extended by default, without prior appraisal of any distinguishing traits. Finally, and relatedly, consideration, unlike esteem, is rarely something a person merits because of anything distinctive about them. Insofar as a person "merits" consideration, it is, for the most part, simply in virtue of being a person. Accordingly, most *disparities* in consideration of persons will be *unmerited*. However, there may be some exceptions. Perhaps there are withdrawals of at least certain forms of consideration from a person that are merited by what one subsequently learns about their character or conduct. For example, it may no longer be fitting to hear Flake out because he has shown himself to be untrustworthy, or it may be fitting to withdraw goodwill from Mustache because he has seriously wronged others.

With esteem and consideration distinguished, we can note that lesser consideration of Loman is compatible with higher esteem for Loman's qualities and achievements.[9] Buyers in a slave market can discern skills or beauty in their prospective "purchases." We can also note the possibility that the basing trait that underlies an objectionable, unmerited disparity of consideration for persons may be a quality or achievement that grounds an unobjectionable, merited disparity in esteem for that quality or achievement. Grace and beauty might, in some society, take the place of race or lineage.

What is unmerited, and so objectionable, in such a case is a disparity of consideration for the person based on those qualities and achievements, where that consideration consists in responses of the kind that we have been describing, which differ from the mere expression of esteem for those qualities and achievements.

To allow that merited disparities in regard are not objectionable, therefore, is not to endorse, say, grafting the pattern of consideration characteristic of an aristocratic order onto "meritocratic" competitions: that is, simply replacing lineage with qualifications or careers as the basing trait. This is because there is no reason to think that qualifications or careers merit such responses. Qualifications, to the extent that they are admirable, merit admiration. But admiration is not, for example, acting to advance someone's interests. And your being better qualified, as we will see in Section 17.1, means simply that others will benefit more from your getting the job, which in turn answers the objections that other job seekers may have for their not getting the job. But this is not a response to merit; it's purely instrumental.

Of course, some might say, not without justice, that we do currently view qualifications and careers in the way in which aristocratic orders viewed lineage (Arneson 1999, 93–94). But it isn't clear to me as a conceptual matter that qualifications and careers, however scarce and desirable, must be freighted with such further significance. The fact that someone spends his days doing something I would prefer to spend my days doing need not mean he has a higher rank, any more than that he enjoys, in the privacy of his own home, some labor-saving convenience that I don't. This is not to deny that the distinction may be psychologically difficult to sustain (Williams 2005, 113–114). Nor is it to deny that the distribution of such goods—desirable work or conveniences—is of concern. It is of concern, and there are claims to improvement that such goods be distributed fairly. The point is just that the concern is not rooted in a claim against inferiority.

6.4 Purely Expressive Disparities

The third and final kind of disparity in regard, in addition to disparities of esteem and disparities of consideration, are purely expressive disparities. Consider the social expectation that Black people sit only in the back of the bus, whereas White people sit only in the front. This seems to be an objectionable disparity of regard, in which, one wants to say, White people are more highly regarded than Black people. Yet there is no disparity of esteem for particular qualities or achievements. Nor is there a disparity in consideration, at least not in any of the forms we have distinguished. For example, it is not clear that seating someone in the back, as opposed to the front, in itself involves giving less weight to their interests. Sitting in the back of the bus might not be, in general, less desirable than sitting in the front. Some might prefer to sit in the back. Nor, if White people are expected to sit only in the front, are the social expectations of Black people more restrictive than the social expectations of White people. What is objectionable, one wants to say, is what the difference in expectations expresses.

I take it that an act, *A*, expresses a content, *C*, only insofar as some people in the relevant culture either intend to communicate *C* by *A* or interpret others as doing so (Ekins 2012). If *A* does not bespeak or invite such intentions or interpretations, then it simply does not express *C*. Whether *A* expresses *C* will, of course, depend on convention, context, history, and more general cognitive limits of intention and interpretation.

The key question, then, is what content is expressed by the difference in social expectations for White people and Black people. We've already seen reason to doubt the answer that what, in general, is expressed is that Black people are less worthy of something, let alone that Black people are less worthy because Black people are less than fully human. The answer, I think, is instead that what is expressed (possibly insincerely or as mere lip service) is an endorsement of independent relations of inferiority. Those independent relations of inferiority might be constituted by a disparity of regard of another kind or by an asymmetry of power or authority. Whether or not it is expressed that anyone is less worthy, in other words, the social fact of the inferiority of some to others is embraced or ratified.

These expressions depend "recursively," in two ways, on independently existing relations of inferiority. First, to repeat, the content expressed is an endorsement of some independent relation of inferiority of Loman to Hyman. Again, it is endorsement of that social fact, whether or not that endorsement is grounded in some further judgment that, for example, Loman lacks full moral status. Second, the vehicle of expression may be some difference in response to Hyman and Loman that, apart from independently existing relations of inferiority, would not express an endorsement of relations of inferiority. Whether it counts as lesser regard to be required to sit in the back of the bus, as opposed to the front, is impossible to say without knowing whether it is the superiors or inferiors (as determined by other contexts) who are required to sit in the back (Hellman 2008, 27). Holding other things fixed, if Black people had been forbidden from sitting in the back of the bus, "going to the back of the bus" would have had the opposite valence.

7

Reductive Gambits

Must we posit claims against inferiority? Few would deny that there are complaints, to put it mildly, against the extreme cases of bondage or caste. But some may contend that those complaints are not against relations of inferiority as such but instead against something else. In this chapter I consider some contentions along these lines to the effect that there is something in the conceptual vicinity of claims against inferiority but that I misinterpret what it is.

7.1 Expression

A first alternative interpretation of the complaints that are intuitively provoked by cases such as bondage or caste suggests that these complaints are, in fact, not against relations of inferiority themselves but instead against what those relations express or symbolize. What, then, do relations of inferiority express or symbolize? Relations of inferiority themselves? To be sure, if relations of inferiority are objectionable, then expressions of those relations (e.g., statues of colonial oppressors, Confederate flags) may be objectionable. But this just presupposes that relations of inferiority are objectionable. Something similar can be said of the suggestion that the objection is not to relations of inferiority themselves but instead to the vices of superiority (for example, haughtiness) and inferiority (for example, obsequiousness) to which they give rise (Rawls 2001a, 131). To count these as vices seems to presuppose that relations of inferiority are a bad thing.

Do relations of inferiority instead express a lack of concern for interests in improvement or rights against invasion? It would seem not. After all, relations of inferiority can obtain where there are no unmet claims to improvement and no violated rights against invasion.

Do relations of inferiority instead express judgments that some lack the basis, such as humanity or rationality, for basic moral status, so that, among other things, their interests count for less? As we have seen, unmerited disparities of regard need not be based on such judgments. Unmerited disparities of regard might simply be based instead on the brute fact that fortune smiled on us at the decisive moment, your city fell to our arms, and we took you captive. Such judgments might be affirmative, or else silent, on the question of whether the inferiors have equal basic moral status. Or unmerited disparities of regard might be avowedly arbitrary, without any grounds. And asymmetries of power or authority over need not involve any judgments. They may simply be a matter of brute force. So, it seems, relations of inferiority need not express such judgments. And yet relations of inferiority seem objectionable even when they do not express such judgments.

Do relations of inferiority instead express that some have superior virtue, wisdom, or judgment? For similar reasons, relations of inferiority need not express that. And, in any event, expressing that is not, in general, objectionable. Some people do have superior judgment, and giving merited esteem to this superior judgment, in a way that takes care not to cause gratuitous offense, is not objectionable.

7.2 Psychic Cost

The next alternative interpretation of the complaints that are intuitively provoked by cases of bondage or caste is that these complaints are, in fact, not against relations of inferiority themselves but instead against the psychic cost that, if recognized, they impose. The psychic cost might be unpleasant feelings. Or it might be a loss of confidence, which in turn limits one's opportunities to lead a fulfilling life. This is part of Rawls's account of the parties' reasoning in the original position. They are to care about the "social bases of self-respect" because without the social bases of self-respect, those whom the parties represent will not be motivated to pursue their conceptions of the good.[1]

To be sure, recognizing that one stands in these relations of inferiority can take such a toll on one's psychology. But saying that relations of inferiority matter only because they have such psychic costs seems like saying that the insincerity of one's (seeming) friend matters only because one will be sad if one finds out about it. In both cases, there are, to be sure, psychic costs. But they are occasioned by the recognition of some underlying bad: relations to others that one had reason to want to be otherwise. That is, if Loman's recognition that Loman stands in certain relations of inferiority has these psychic costs, then it is presumably because Loman independently views the relation of inferiority itself as something bad. But if people independently view relations of inferiority as bads, then why not take their value judgments seriously in their own terms? Why should we second-guess them (especially when, as it seems, they are us)? I suspect political theorists find it appealing to invoke only the effects of a value judgment that relations of inferiority are objectionable because this allows them to avoid committing themselves to the value judgment itself. But there is something unstable in the attempt to avoid an allegedly controversial value judgment by assuming that, as a matter of psychological fact, everyone makes it.

Moreover, this underlying objection explains why we take the psychic costs to matter in the way we do. After all, we don't feel obligated to forestall or mitigate every psychic cost a person might experience. By and large, people are left to their own devices to cope with life's disappointments. But we view differently the costs associated with Loman's perceiving himself to stand to others as an inferior. It is because we think Loman has a complaint against others about the relations of inferiority that occasion the feeling that we think that Loman has a complaint against others about being made to feel it.

In any event, the relations of inferiority seem objectionable even when purified of the psychic costs. Suppose Loman so thoroughly internalizes the lesser regard he receives that he ceases to be pained by it. Would this solve the problem? And, human frailty being what it is, the superiors are usually buoyed by the greater regard.[2] Is this an unambiguous good? Or suppose people are largely unaware of the fact that there are untempered, unmerited disparities of regard among them. If some are dismayed to discover these disparities, are they dismayed only about the psychic costs that will be borne henceforth? One imagines they will be dismayed in part about how things have been. And that dismay cannot be about the psychic costs that have been borne until now because no psychic costs have been borne until now.

7.3 Recognition

The next alternative interpretation of the complaints that are intuitively provoked by cases such as bondage or caste is friendlier to the idea that these are complaints against relations of inferiority themselves. It's just that we don't go deep enough. In fact, claims against inferiority represent merely a special case of a more general claim to have our social roles acknowledged and affirmed by others (Miller 1997, 231–232). To illustrate, imagine Hierarcadia—a "chivalric paradise," as Joseph Raz and his seminar once put it to me—in which people are attached to their social roles, even though these roles constitutively depend on relations of inferiority. Their attachment to them does not stem from false consciousness (contrast Miller 1997, 234) or ignorance of the alternatives. As even we can see, their social roles provide them with meaning, orientation, and the possibility of a fulfilling life. Moreover, relations among members of the society, while hierarchical, are nonetheless what we might call "role respectful": everyone relates to everyone else in a way that acknowledges and affirms the value each person takes his own role to have. The value that those on the lower rungs take their stations to have is a value that is manifestly affirmed in how those higher up relate to them. The servant who finds his own worth in being his liege's loyal and dependent retainer is acknowledged and affirmed as such in his liege's relations with him.

Ought the Hierarcadians to avoid relations of inferiority, presumably by refashioning their social order? It is hard to be confident that they ought. What then explains why they lack the reasons to avoid relations of inferiority that we have? The explanation, it may seem, is the suggestion under review. The claim against relations of inferiority is only a special case of a more basic claim: to wit, a claim on others to acknowledge and affirm the value one takes one's own social role to have. In our society, everyone values his or her role as an equal. In Hierarcadia, by contrast, everyone values his or her role in the hierarchy. This is why relations of inferiority are bads in our social context but not in Hierarcadia.

This explanation might be right. If it were right, it would not change all that much in our treatment of relations of inferiority, apart from an ever-present qualification that relations of inferiority are bads only in a social context like ours. And it would smack less of cultural imperialism.

However, I do wonder whether we can accept this explanation. We may be stuck with the cultural imperialism. For this explanation, it seems, fails to account for a crucial asymmetry. Suppose doubts set in about the value of social roles in Hierarcadia and those lower down claim to be treated as equals. Their claims would have a weight that the claims of their superiors to continue to be treated as superiors would lack. Yet if at root everyone's claims were the same—that others acknowledge and affirm the value one takes one's own social role to have—then everyone's claims would be on a par. So, I find myself drawn to another explanation. While relations of inferiority are still bads in Hierarcadia, and while they provide the Hierarcadians with reasons to avoid them, these reasons are outweighed or excluded by the Hierarcadians' attachments to their social order.

Here we might view relations of inferiority in a way similar to how some view (putative) disabilities, such as deafness. Just as, on this view (to which I don't mean to subscribe), deafness is a bad wherever it occurs, so too we might say that relations of inferiority are bads wherever they occur. However, just as there are distinctive goods that are possible only within deaf communities (for example, certain personal relationships, modes of expression, senses of humor), so too there are distinctive goods possible only within an unequal order like Hierarcadia (for example, certain social roles and role-respectful relations). Should Hierarcadia become egalitarian, a bad would be eliminated, but genuine goods would also be lost. Attachments to such distinctive goods, formed by life within such communities, may provide members not only with overriding reasons against seeking to ameliorate the bads on which the goods constitutively depend but also with exclusionary reasons against even ambivalence: against seeing such bads as bads at all (Wallace 2013). Their attachments give them compelling reasons, if not to believe a falsehood, then at least not to give thought to a truth: that disability and relations of inferiority are, in themselves, something to be regretted.

In this chapter, I considered objections of the following form: that while there is a complaint in the conceptual vicinity of a complaint against inferiority, I have mischaracterized what it is. According to these objections, it is not a complaint against standing in a relation of inferiority as such but instead against some expression or symbol, against some psychic cost, or against a failure to receive what counts, in this time and place, as due recognition. I have resisted these contentions. In Part IV, I consider other contentions of this form, which submit that what I describe as a complaint against inferiority is better understood as a complaint against what republicans call "domination" or a claim to what relational egalitarians call an "egalitarian relationship."

8

The State and the Secondary Tempering Factors

So far in this part, I have sought to explain what claims against inferiority are and have considered attempts to reduce them to claims of a different kind. In this chapter, I suggest, as a first instance of our positive conjecture, that the claim against the state, which we sought for in vain in Part I, is a claim against inferiority. I then introduce the secondary tempering factors, which address this claim against inferiority and provide the explanatory materials for the subsequent instances of the positive conjecture.

8.1 A Claim against the Hierarchy of the State

What, then, do claims against inferiority imply for the state? Part of what they imply is clear enough. People have claims on the state not to cause, and even to prevent or undo, untempered asymmetries in power and authority and untempered, unmerited disparities in regard, constituted by how individuals subject to the state relate to one another. The state should support marital and employment protections. The state should combat caste distinctions. And so on. However, there are not only (to use Pettit's 2012 term) "horizontal" relations of inferiority between one individual subject to the state and another individual subject to the state to consider but also "vertical" relations of inferiority between one individual and the state itself—or rather between those individuals who are subject to what the state decides and those individuals whose decisions the state's decisions are.

And here dark clouds gather. After all, the state wields vastly greater power and authority over the individuals who are subject to it. At the same time, the state just is, like *l'enfer* of Sartre, other people. So, it would seem, those other people wield vastly greater power and authority over the rest of us.

Why, then, isn't subjection to the state's decisions a kind of subordination to those individual, natural persons whose decisions the state's decisions are? Why don't we have complaints against standing in relations of inferiority to those individual, natural persons?[1]

This would not be a problem if our relations to the state were tempered, in the way relations to a teacher might be. But, on the contrary, the tempering factors seem to be conspicuously absent in our relations to the state. First, the state is an established social structure, and our relations to it are ongoing. Second, the state has extensive reach. As far as the law is concerned, the classroom extends all the way to the border, and class is always in session. Third, there are few limits on what the state can do to us or command us to do. Fourth, it's costly and difficult to avoid relations to the state within whose jurisdiction one presently resides or to whose jurisdiction one presently belongs and all but impossible to escape the jurisdiction of some state. Recall that Escapability requires not only freedom to exit an asymmetry or disparity with respect to certain individuals; it also requires that at least some exit options do not involve a relation of the same kind with other individuals. Fifth, the state's decisions are typically final: that is, they sit at the apex of the hierarchy, above which there is no further appeal (short of the "appeal to heaven"). The state's decisions are generally treated as overriding or nullifying any other decision. Therefore, there can be no recourse to a decision higher up the chain of command, with a different character.

Finally, one relation within which you might stand as an equal with others, whatever other asymmetries or disparities might mark your relations with them, is equality of citizenship: that you stand as an equal with them insofar as you and they interact with the state. If equality of citizenship with others is not available because, say, they, but not you, decide what the state does, then it is not clear what other relation of equality with them will be available. Granted, you may stand to some other individuals as equals in a local club or parish. But it is unlikely that, for every other individual in your society, there is some socially recognized relationship within which you stand as equals. This is especially likely to be the case in a society with cultural, religious, regional, and professional diversity.

What I now suggest is that the complaint against the state that we sought in vain all through Part I is precisely this complaint. The state wields vastly greater power and authority over us, who are subject to it. And, where the state is concerned, the tempering factors are conspicuously absent. Yet, the state just is, when the robes and badges are stripped away, other people. So, unless more is said, we have a complaint against standing in relations of inferiority to those natural persons whose decisions the state's decisions are.

This understanding of the complaint against the state finally explains why the complaint is still felt to apply in our Myths of the Omittites and Our Trusting Future. Even though those mythical states use no force or threat against anyone, they still wield vastly superior, final, and inescapable power and authority over people. At the same time, this understanding of the complaint would explain why the complaint against the state is nevertheless so often expressed in terms of "coercion." What the word "coercion" gestures toward, I suggest, is the final character of the state's power and authority: that the state is the highest link in the chain. And it is natural enough that the word "coercion" should so gesture since the power to coerce, strictly speaking—that is, to compellingly steer—is usually necessary for holding final power and authority: power and authority that regulate and control the exercise of other powers and authorities. In the ordinary run of human affairs, setting aside the Myth of Our Trusting Future, some can enjoy final power and authority over others only if they can, when push comes to shove, compellingly steer them. In other words, "coercion," in such contexts, functions as a metonym.

This, in turn, explains why the complaint against the state is so often described as a complaint against decisions being backed by coercion, even when it is granted that the state doesn't actually coerce. At the end of Section 3.6, we found that puzzling. If at root the complaint is about coercion, why should it apply when the state is not actually coercing? We can now solve the puzzle. The complaint that finds expression as a complaint against backing by coercion is not, at root, a complaint against coercion itself. It is instead a complaint about something that usually requires "backing by coercion," understood as the capacity to compellingly steer. That something is wielding final and inescapable power and authority over others.

To sum up, in Part I, we sought in vain for the complaint against the state. I first proposed the complaint was against the state's use of force. Then I proposed it was against the state's issuing threats. Then I proposed it was the state's disposing of property. The mistake, in each case, was to assume that the complaint against the state had to be a complaint against some specific, discrete treatment, of a kind that, in some isolated episode, might be suffered at the hands of another private person but that, in this instance, was suffered at the hands of the state. What we have learned is that the complaint instead concerns the state's hierarchical structure: the untempered asymmetries of power and authority that the state involves and what this implies for relations among the people who decide what the state does, on the one hand, and the people who are subject to those decisions, on the other hand. It is not incidental to the complaint against the state, therefore, that the state is a state. The complaint could not be brought against an agent that did not have the features of a state.

8.2 Secondary Tempering Factors

So that's the question: If the state just is *les autres*, if it wields vastly superior power and authority over each of us, and if our relations to the state are not tempered by the factors listed in Section 5.4, then how can they not be relations of inferiority?[2] The answer, I suggest, lies in certain "vertical secondary tempering factors"—or "vertical factors," for short—which, to a first approximation, make our subjection to the superior power and authority of the state less our subjection to the superior power and authority of other individuals and so less relations of inferiority to them. These factors are "secondary" in that they are called for to address relations of inferiority that are not tempered by independently obtaining primary tempering factors.

These vertical factors, about which more will be said later, are:

- "Impersonal Justification": that asymmetries of power and authority are offices justified by impersonal reasons.
- "Least Discretion": that officials occupying those offices exercise no more discretion than serves those impersonal reasons.
- "Equal Application": that exercises of superior power and authority apply as much to those who wield it as to those who are merely subject to it.
- "Equal Influence": that those subject to what would otherwise be superior power and authority have equal opportunity to influence it.
- "Downward Accountability": that those with superior power and authority are accountable for their use of power and authority to those subject to it.

- "Upward Unaccountability": that those subject to superior authority are not accountable to those who wield it.[3]

In addition to the concern that we stand in relations of inferiority to other individuals as agents of the state, there is also the concern that we stand in relations of inferiority to other individuals as patients of the state. This concern is addressed by two further "horizontal secondary tempering factors":

- "Equal Consideration": that the state shows equal consideration to its citizens.
- "Equal Citizenship": partly in virtue of Equal Influence or Equal Consideration, those subject to the state stand in at least one relationship of equality to one another, namely that of equal citizenship, whatever other asymmetries and disparities there may be.[4]

In virtue of having claims against inferiority, individuals have claims to these secondary tempering factors, in the absence of which they would stand in untempered relations of inferiority. Many of the commonplace complaints left unexplained by interests in improvement and rights against invasion express, in effect, unmet claims to these secondary tempering factors.

Observe that the vertical factors differ from many of the legitimating conditions or limits of legitimacy traditionally said to be necessary for the state's justification or legitimacy, as discussed in Section 2.1. In order to satisfy the vertical factors, the state doesn't need to restrict its efforts to protecting people from invasion of their person or property but could promote other goods as well. Nor need the state secure consent or reasonable acceptability.

We can also explain more clearly and directly why the vertical factors count as answers to the complaint against the state than why these traditional legitimating conditions or limits of legitimacy count as answers to the complaint against the state. If the complaint against the state is supposed to be that the state uses force, for example, how does it answer that complaint that the use of force has a justification that does not rest on sectarian premises or that it is not meant to prevent or deter self-regarding choices? How does that—that the force has a nonsectarian justification or is used only to prevent or deter other-regarding choices—make it any less a use of force? And if it does not, then how does it address the complaint against the state, which, allegedly, was precisely that the state uses force? By contrast, the vertical factors, as we will see, address the complaint against the state directly. If the complaint is that, in being subjected to the state, we are subordinated to the superior power and authority of other individuals, then the vertical factors aim to make it the case that, in being subjected to the state, we are not, or at least less, subordinated to the superior power and authority of other individuals.

8.3 Inferiority or Heteronomy: Self-Sovereignty as a Case Study

I have just said that on our interpretation of the complaint against the state, there is a clear and direct explanation of why the secondary tempering factors count as answers to the complaint against the state. On other interpretations of the complaint against the state, by contrast, it is less clear why the familiar legitimating conditions or limits of legitimacy count as answers to the complaint against the state. This leads us to a more general point, which is a hinge of this book. To preface the point, note that, for all I have said, the complaint against the state might be not to inferiority—which we understand for the present purposes just as being subject to the alien power and authority of a superior individual—but instead to what we might call heteronomy—being subject to alien power or authority, period—whether natural or artificial, individual or collective, or superior, inferior, equal, or none of the above. The Myth of the Omittites, for example, does not distinguish between these possibilities. Yet they have crucially different implications. This is because, in brief, while all inferiority is heteronomy, not all heteronomy is inferiority. This means, first, that heteronomy is harder to avoid simply because it is more widespread. And it means, second, that there are fewer ways to address heteronomy than inferiority. If the problem is heteronomy, being subject to alien power and authority, then the only solution is to make the power and authority no longer alien. Whereas, if the problem is inferiority, subjection to the power and authority of a superior, then there is another solution: to make the power and authority, even if alien, no longer that of a superior. In sum, if the problem is inferiority, rather than heteronomy, then there is less to put us at odds with our social world, and there are more routes to reconciling us to it.

Elsewhere in this book, I have occasion to illustrate specific instances of this general point. It will recur when I distinguish inferiority from domination (Chapter 23), which is a kind of heteronomy. It will also recur when I distinguish noninferiority from the ideal of self-rule, which underlies much of democratic theory (Part V), including a strain of thought in Rousseau (Conclusion). The absence of such self-rule is another kind of heteronomy. For the present, it may be useful to illustrate the point by speculating about a possible value I call "self-sovereignty" (and return to in Section 20.3).

The speculation is that there is an objection to being subject to alien, de facto authority as such: an objection to being addressed by (or perhaps merely exposed to) the commands of an alien will—whether natural or artificial, individual or collective, or superior, inferior, equal, or none of the above—whose commands are generally obeyed. Now, it seems implausibly broad to suggest there is a complaint against being addressed by commands from anyone, such as those of a universally ignored sidewalk crank who urges "Repent!" on each passerby.[5] If there is a potentially viable suggestion in the neighborhood, it is rather that there is an objection to being addressed by the commands of a de facto authority whose directives are broadly treated as commands. This would contrast with an objection to the analogous constituent of inferiority, that of being subject not to any de facto authority but rather to the superior de facto authority of another natural individual.[6]

The idea of an objection against mere commands, where this does not constitute any inferior standing, may seem like moral shadowboxing, and perhaps it is. Suppose, however, that what is to be avoided is a kind of objectionable social standing (as G. Cohen [2011, 191–192] speculates). Then perhaps one could argue that there is an objection to being addressed by those commands of a de facto authority: commands that, in virtue of being routinely obeyed, have social reality as commands. For whatever else one's social standing may depend on, it would seem to depend on how one is addressed, where that in turn depends not simply on what is said to one but also on the broader, recognized significance, in one's society, of what is said. Such, at least, would be the picture. Put negatively, being addressed by the commands of a de facto authority is objectionable heteronomy. Put positively, one enjoys a certain kind of social standing insofar as de facto authorities do not command one. One is sovereign over oneself, one might say. No other earthly authority—natural or artificial, individual or collective, or superior, inferior, equal, or none of the above—tells one what to do or bosses one around. While this self-sovereignty would consist in the absence of a certain kind of objectionable social standing, this objectionable social standing would again be different from the objectionable social standing of inferiority to others.

But now consider, if there is this speculative objection to subjection to alien de facto authority in general, how we might answer it. To begin with, subjection to alien de facto authority is much more widespread than subjection to the de facto authority of a superior. In a world in which each individual's rights are respected, each individual has de facto authority over what others do to their person. When I can command you not to infringe my rights, you are thereby subject to my alien de facto authority. If you have an objection to being subject to alien authority, then you have at least a pro tanto objection to this. By contrast, you are not subject to the authority of a superior. You have authority over your person, just as I have authority over mine. Each of us is queen of her own castle.

Second, there is more than one way to temper or correct subjection to the necessarily alien authority of a superior. Either we can make the authority no longer alien or we can make it no longer the authority of a superior. The vertical factors of Impersonal Justification, Least Discretion, Equal Application, Downward Accountability, Upward Unaccountability, and Equal Influence aim to do the latter. Likewise, some of the primary tempering factors, such as Egalitarian Relationship, address the specifically inferiorizing character of subjection to authority. Part of what makes the authority of teachers and flight attendants less objectionable, I have suggested, is that, so long as Equal Citizenship obtains, that authority is embedded in a relation of citizenship, in which one stands as an equal to others. By contrast, if the objection is to subjection to alien authority as such, then we seem to have only the former way to address it: namely, to make the authority no longer alien. But how else are we to do this if not by making the commands of the authority somehow commands that you give yourself? And how are we to do that compatibly with, say, your living under a state?

It might be replied that, even if you do not give the commands to yourself, nevertheless, so long as the commands have the right content, you do only what you have most reason to do in complying with the commands. Now, it is not clear how this addresses the alleged problem: namely, subjection to the commands of an alien authority. You are still subject to the commands of an alien authority. It is just that, as it happens, you already have your own reasons to do what the authority commands. But, setting this aside, what sort of state would issue commands of the right content? If we deny that even the ideal state issues commands of the right content, then one wonders what other commands could have the right content. How could the content of the ideal state's commands be improved? If, alternatively, we accept that the ideal state issues commands of the right content, then the ideal state would, in itself, suffice to avoid heteronomy. But then we lose sight, once again, of the complaint against the state, for that complaint was supposed to apply even to the ideal state.

In any event, the ideal state does not command you to do whatever it is that you have most reason to do. It might be argued that insofar as the commands of the ideal state command you only to fulfill your duty to serve the public interest, the ideal state commands you to do only what you have most reason to do. However, as we saw in Section 2.6, while the commands of the ideal state will serve the public interest, they will not necessarily command you to fulfill your own duty to serve the public interest.

Alternatively, it might be said that the state's commands are one's own commands when one somehow identifies with the state. Presumably, identifying with the state is a matter of having (or being disposed to have) certain attitudes toward the state. But if all that is needed to avoid heteronomy, understood as not being subject to an alien authority, is that we in fact identify with the state, then the escape from heteronomy seems too cheaply won. The ugliest of regimes can free us from heteronomy so long as we in fact identify with them. Or suppose the state meets whatever other conditions one can imagine but still one refuses to identify with it. Does one then have a complaint about one's resulting heteronomy? Perhaps it might be replied that the state's commands are one's own so long as one has reason to identify with it. But then when does one have reason to identify with the state? When the state secures, as the ideal state does, the public interest? But then, once again, we lose sight of the complaint against state, which was supposed to apply even to the ideal state.

No doubt one could try to pursue further this line of thought: namely, that the complaint against the state is a complaint against subjection to alien authority as such and that this complaint can be addressed by making the state's authority somehow one's own authority. Although I am not optimistic that there is forward progress to be made, I will not press that criticism. The thing to remind ourselves of, and to emphasize, is the crucial contrast. If the complaint is against subjection to alien authority as such, then there is only way to address it: namely, to make the authority one's own. By contrast, if the complaint is against subjection to the authority of a superior, then there is, in addition, another way to address it: namely, to make the authority not that of a superior. There are simply more possibilities for reconciling ourselves to our social world.

8.4 Impersonal Justification and Least Discretion

Let us now examine the vertical factors in greater detail. The first vertical factor, Impersonal Justification, is that the relevant asymmetry of power and authority of Offe over Indy constitutes an impersonally justified office. To say that the asymmetry constitutes an "office" is, for our purposes, just to say that it consists in Offe's capacity to make, by certain processes, certain decisions that have certain implications for Indy. And to say that an office is "impersonally justified" is to say that its existence and operation—that is, Offe's making decisions of that kind, by processes of that kind—serves impersonal reasons, against the relevant background, at least as well as any alternative and better than any alternative not marked by a similar asymmetry.

By "impersonal reasons," I mean either "globally impersonal" or "locally impersonal" reasons. Let us focus first on globally impersonal reasons. These are reasons that simply are not personal: not grounded in the agent's interests, projects, or relationships as such. What is being ruled out is that it could justify my otherwise untempered asymmetric power or authority over you that the asymmetry would serve my interests, projects, or relationships, as opposed merely to someone's interests, projects, or relationships. The pronoun "my," as it were, can add no weight to the justification. What is crucial is that the reasons that justify my otherwise untempered asymmetric power or authority over you are no more my reasons than they are yours.

To be sure, personal reasons are universalizable. If I have reason to promote my own projects specially, then everyone has similar reason to promote their own projects specially. But, even so, the reason I have to promote my project, because it is mine, is different from the reason I have to promote someone's project, simply because it is someone's. The latter sort of reason does not recommend my favoring my project over other people's projects. For my project is no more and no less someone's project than is someone else's project.[7]

To be sure, my personal reasons, where the pronoun "my" does add weight, are genuine reasons. More than that, they are reasons that can justify my acting in ways to which someone would otherwise have a complaint. For example, you might have no complaint about my passing up some opportunity to help your child because my child needs my attention instead. What Impersonal Justification requires is that personal reasons of this kind have no bearing on whether my otherwise untempered asymmetric power or authority over you is justified. It can't justify my otherwise untempered asymmetric power or authority over you that it would mean that my child gets attention, as opposed merely to some child getting attention. If my otherwise untempered asymmetric power or authority over you is justified, the case must be made in terms of impersonal reasons.

Note that Impersonal Justification is significantly stronger than the requirement, which goes without saying, that the justification of asymmetric power and authority be compatible with the truth that everyone's interests are equally important. This goes without saying because there is no justification of anything that is incompatible with the truth that everyone's interests are equally important. Even justifications based on personal reasons are, in general, compatible with the truth that everyone's interests are equally important. When I help my child instead of yours, on the grounds that it is my child, I don't somehow presuppose that my child's interests are more important than your child's. If I did, then I would think you have the same reason to help my child instead of yours.

This ban on personal reasons is not a ban on all agent-relative reasons. First, there may be agent-relative restrictions, such as the Force Constraint, that make reference not to the agent's interests, projects, or relationships but instead merely to the structure of the choice the agent faces, such as that the agent may not use force (at least absent adequate opportunity to avoid force) even to bring about a greater good. Note that such agent-relative restrictions apply not only to natural individuals but also to artificial or corporate agents, which don't have personal reasons because they don't have interests, projects, or relationships.

Second, there may be personal reasons that are nonetheless shared by everyone who is at one or the other end of the relevant asymmetry. These are locally impersonal reasons with respect to the group involved in that asymmetry. Suppose you and I share personal reasons to aid our compatriots, as opposed merely to aiding people. These reasons are personal insofar as they are not shared by our noncompatriots. However, these reasons are locally impersonal with respect to us insofar as they are no more mine than yours and no more yours than mine. These reasons would be impersonal, one might say, if there were no noncompatriots. If an asymmetry between just us compatriots serves locally impersonal reasons with respect to us, then this can satisfy Impersonal Justification with respect to that asymmetry. By contrast, if an asymmetry involving not only us but also noncompatriots served the same reasons, which are more ours than theirs, then this would not satisfy Impersonal Justification with respect to that asymmetry.

Finally, there can be impersonal reasons to follow policies of prioritizing one's own projects or relationships. Perhaps military esprit de corps is better overall when members of a given unit look after their own first. Compare the sort of impersonal justification that Williams (1982) famously believed would, on the lips of a spouse, involve "one thought too many."

Among globally impersonal reasons are presumably reasons to promote the public interest: to improve the situation of everyone, as far as is possible compatible with fairness to others.[8] We can also include, as globally impersonal reasons, those of the kind given by claims against inferiority and rights against invasion. This does not exclude the possibility of other globally impersonal reasons, such as reasons to protect the environment or promote the arts.[9] And there can be an even wider range of locally impersonal reasons, such as reasons to work for the greater glory of a shared faith.

The second, and closely related, vertical tempering factor, Least Discretion, is that the official should exercise only so much discretion in decisions about how to use the office as serves the impersonal reasons that justify it. If the official could serve the impersonal reasons no less well without such and such discretion, then the official should not exercise it. Note that Least Discretion presupposes that there are impersonal reasons that justify the office (or at least that would justify it if the official were to use it appropriately), in the service of which whatever discretion is permitted is permitted. Impersonal Justification and Least Discretion imply several subsidiary principles that are discussed in later chapters: the Duty to Execute, the Duty to Exclude, and Equal Treatment by Officials.

So far, our discussion has been stipulative. What might explain the stipulation? Why do Impersonal Justification and Least Discretion temper asymmetries of power and authority? To begin with, they jointly effect a separation of the office from the natural individual who occupies it. This distinction between office and occupant, as has long been noted, is particularly pronounced in the modern Western conception of the state (Van Klaveren 1957; Huntington 1968; Weber 2019). As Ripstein (2009, 192) puts it, "An official is permitted only to act for the purposes defined by [a] mandate. The concept of an official role thus introduces a distinction between the mandate created by the office and the private purposes of the officeholder."[10] Consequently, the superior power and authority of the office are less that of the natural person who occupies it. Thus, you are not at all or less subject to him, the person occupying the office, and rather only or more subject to the office alone. To be sure, you are no less subjected to the asymmetric power and authority of the office itself. However, whatever the office is, it is not another natural person. It is not the sort of entity to which relations of inferiority (or superiority or equality) are possible.

Why doesn't the office count as another natural person? Insofar as Impersonal Justification is satisfied, the existence and operation of the office in the first place serves reasons, as opposed to the arbitrary whims of the occupant or particularized considerations such as that she is Dolly Parton (as opposed the globally impersonal reason that she is someone and the locally impersonal reason that she is a national treasure). Moreover, the office serves only impersonal reasons, which are no more the reasons of the occupant of the office than they are the reasons of those subject to the office. And insofar as Least Discretion is satisfied, the official's decision-making is limited to the service of those impersonal reasons. The office, as Ripstein puts it, "exhausts" the occupant.

8.5 Equal Application

The vertical factor of Equal Application obtains when exercises of asymmetric power and authority apply as much to those who wield it as to those who are simply subject to it. The commander addresses the same command to herself as she addresses to others and is just as inclined to follow it. The wielder of power exercises power in a way that affects himself as much as it affects others. In general, the decision maker is someone to whom their own decision applies.

Contrast the paradigm of bondage. There, Equal Application is glaringly absent. Masters do not order themselves to do what they order slaves to do. In this case, there are two differences between Hyman and Loman. Hyman makes decisions, whereas Loman does not, and Loman takes those decisions, whereas Hyman does not. When Equal Application holds, by contrast, the latter difference is absent. The relationship is, to that extent, removed from the paradigm of bondage.

To say that Equal Application is a tempering factor is not to say that exercises of asymmetric power and authority are necessarily objectionable if Equal Application does not obtain: if the decisions do not apply to the decision maker themselves. There may be other tempering factors. In particular, even when Equal Application is violated, Impersonal Justification may still be respected. There may be an impersonal justification why the decision does not apply to the decision makers themselves. For example, being a boss, monitoring and directing the activity of the enterprise, may be a full-time job. It may be inefficient or impossible for the boss to comply with the commands they give others.

8.6 Downward Accountability and Upward Unaccountability

A further pair of factors that temper relations of power and authority concern accountability.[11] By "accountability," in this context, I mean not something constituted by moral facts, such as that one person is entitled to resent another for what they do, but instead something constituted by social facts, which depend on actual attitudes and dispositions.

The first of these two tempering factors is the absence of Upward Accountability: while Hyman has superior authority over Loman, it is not the case that Loman is accountable to Hyman for obedience to Hyman's commands. That "Loman is accountable to Hyman for obedience to Hyman's commands" might mean one of several things. First, it might mean that Loman may be punished, at Hyman's discretion, for disobeying Hyman's commands. Second, it might mean that Loman is subject to Hyman's expressions of resentment for disobeying or to others' expressions of indignation on Hyman's behalf. (These expressions, however, might be insincere in that the expresser may not believe that a moral demand has, in fact, been flouted.) Finally, it might mean that Loman is expected to justify to Hyman any failure to obey or any discretion exercised in obedience. These expectations may be backed, in turn, by punishment or resentment and indignation. Or they may be social expectations, in the sense introduced in Section 6.3, where Loman's refusal to justify is met with, for example, surprise and confusion.

The second of these two tempering factors is the presence of Downward Accountability. While Hyman has superior power and authority over Loman, Hyman is accountable to Loman for Hyman's use of it. That "Hyman is accountable to Loman for Hyman's use of superior power and authority" might mean any of the following things. First, it might mean that Hyman is subject to being punished, at the discretion of Loman, for uses that wrong Loman. Or it might mean, second, that Hyman is subject to Loman's expressions of resentment for uses that wrong Loman or to others' indignation on Loman's behalf. Such expressions are not discouraged, for example, by social expectations. (Of course, Loman is, in any case, morally entitled to express resentment for Hyman's uses of power and authority that wrong him, as he is morally entitled to express resentment for any action by anyone that wrongs him.) Or it might mean, third, that Hyman is subject to Loman's expressions of, if not resentment, then a kind of displeasure akin to resentment, at Hyman's poor use of superior power and authority, even when it does not wrong Loman. Or it might mean, fourth, that Hyman is subject to being removed from his position of superior power and authority, at the discretion of Loman, for Hyman's use of that power and authority. Or it might mean, finally, that Hyman is expected to provide explanations to Loman, for Hyman's use of his superior power and authority, that reveal both the process by which the decision was made and why, perhaps in part by being made by that process, the decision was justified.[12] Since these forms of Downward Accountability all increase the costs Hyman faces in exercising power and authority over Loman, they reduce Hyman's power and authority. However, they have a further tempering significance not shared by other kinds of costs Hyman might face in exercising power and authority.

Contrast the paradigm of bondage. Upward Accountability is glaringly present. Slaves are accountable to masters for obedience. Downward Accountability is glaringly absent. Slaves can in no way hold masters to account for how masters wield their power and authority over slaves. So, simply put, the absence of Upward Accountability and the presence of Downward Accountability shift asymmetries of power and authority further from the paradigm of bondage.

Moreover, we can make sense of why this is. Where Upward Accountability to the natural person, Hyman, is absent, Loman's obedience is not understood as something Hyman is owed, something Hyman himself has a claim to. Hyman's superior authority over Loman is less Hyman's personal possession. Where Upward Accountability to an office that Hyman occupies is absent, Loman is even less subject to the superior authority of Hyman than Loman would otherwise be in virtue of the office alone. For a clear example of how one might not be upwardly accountable to someone who nonetheless wields superior authority, suppose that Stentor, because his voice alone carries far enough, is the only person capable of solving a particular coordination problem. Once Stentor commands "Drive on the right!" disobeying his command may now wrong other drivers, but it does not wrong Stentor, in particular. If we further suppose that Stentor's community is one that expresses resentment and indignation just when they are called for, then Upward Unaccountability will be absent, despite Stentor's superior authority.

Where Downward Accountability is present, Loman has a kind of reciprocal power and authority, albeit different in kind, over Hyman. The relationship is, in that way, more symmetrical. Furthermore, where Downward Accountability is present, it is publicly acknowledged that the person subject to asymmetric power and authority has a pro tanto objection to being so subject.[13]

These tempering factors can obtain in the case of state officials. State officials may be Downwardly Accountable to those subject to their superior power and authority. And those subject to their superior power and authority may not be Upwardly Accountable to those who wield that superior power and authority. It may be understood that obedience to the commands of state officials is not owed to them, even in their official capacities, but instead to other citizens.

8.7 Equal Influence

I will be brief here about the vertical factor of Equal Influence because Parts V and VI are devoted to it. Equal Influence is satisfied insofar as any individual who is subject to superior untempered power and authority has as much opportunity as any other individual for informed, autonomous influence over decisions regarding how that power and authority are exercised. The rationale is straightforward. If I have as much opportunity for informed, autonomous influence over a decision how to exercise power and authority as anyone else has, then there's no one to whom I can point and say that because that individual had greater influence, I, in being subjected to that decision, am subordinated to that individual. I may have far less influence than has the collective as a whole. But that collective is not another natural person, with whom a question of equality arises. Indeed, Equal Influence does not so much change the character of the asymmetry of power and authority as replace asymmetry with symmetry entirely.

It may seem like the tempering effect of Equal Influence can be realized only insofar as offices are abolished. For offices give decision-making powers to some and not to others. But this is to overlook the primary tempering factor of Downward Equalization: that equality at a higher level in the decision-making hierarchy tempers inequality at a lower level. So long as Equal Influence is enjoyed over decisions higher up in the decision-making hierarchy, this tempers the asymmetries of power and authority constituted by offices lower down. I return to this point in Section 27.4.

One might object that no matter what institutions we imagine, presumably some individuals will have greater power than others. There will be military officers, say, who could, if they had a mind to do so, ignore civilian control. However, so long as these military officers are disposed to respect democratic, civilian control precisely because they respect Equal Influence, then Equal Influence, as I understand it, is achieved. Equal Influence can rest on the disposition of people to wield whatever greater power and authority they have only in ways that respect Equal Influence. This is a difference from republican views, which I discuss in Chapter 23.

8.8 Ruling and Being Ruled in Turn

Aristotle recognized a problem similar to ours: How is the rule of some over others compatible with the equality of all? To be sure, whereas we assume that all human beings have claims against inferiority, Aristotle held that some human beings are naturally inferior to others and so social institutions that reflect this, including slavery, are not unjust. However, Aristotle at least entertained the possibility that some, if not all, human beings both are natural equals to one another and not inferior to any other human beings (which perhaps is what he meant by calling them "free"). So, he faced the question of how it can be just for one such natural equal to rule over another, which appears to occur whenever one natural equal holds a special office to which another natural equal is subject. The solution, which Aristotle seems to treat not only as obvious but also without any serious competitors, is rotation in office. Everyone who is ruled at one time takes a turn at ruling at another time so that, over time, the distribution of ruling and being ruled is equal (e.g., *Politics* I.12 1259b4–6, II.2 1261a38–1261b2; 2017, 18, 23). This suggests that rotation might represent a further secondary tempering factor.

There is the obvious practical difficulty that this rotation is unavailable when the ratio of the citizenry to offices is too high. However, there is also the more fundamental question of whether, how, and how far rotation tempers subjection to asymmetric power and authority. Granted, rotation provides temporary relief from such subjection and equally distributes this temporary relief. For in those moments when one wields the superior power and authority, one is not subjected to it. And, granted, to endorse someone's taking a turn in rotation is to deny that they have some permanent trait, such as being a natural slave, that makes it more appropriate for them to be subjected to asymmetric power and authority than it is for anyone else among whom the office rotates to be subjected to it. But does it provide relief in those moments when one is subjected to asymmetric power and authority? By analogy, is the wrong of discrimination somehow mitigated, at the time when one is discriminated against, by the fact that in a year's time, a different group, and not yours, will be discriminated against? Granted, one can look forward to relief from discrimination, and one can rest assured that the basing trait is not permanent. But does that go to the heart of the problem?

Perhaps, for Aristotle, rotation was not a solution to the problem of inferiority, as we are understanding it. It was a solution instead to a problem of fairly distributing opportunities for political activity (see Section 26.2), in a context in which claims to opportunities for political activity were particularly urgent. We imagine Aristotle holding the following. First, to exercise the virtues, including political virtue, just is happiness. Second, holding office is necessary for the exercise of political virtue. Third, natural equals have an equal capacity for the exercise of political virtue. So, for someone to be a natural equal, but to be deprived of office, is for them to be deprived of the opportunity for happiness that they might otherwise have enjoyed. Rotation is the fairest way of distributing a scarce, positive good: namely, the opportunity for exercising political virtue. Indeed, it seems a fair solution to the problem that not all can engage in a valuable activity at the same time that they should each have a turn to engage in it. This seems a better solution than distributing a nonrotating office by lottery. Lottery suggests itself only when the good is indivisible, but in this case, the good is divisible. Each can exercise political virtue, at least for a time, by taking turns.

While we acknowledge there is an interest in political activity, which gives people claims to a fair distribution of opportunities for political activity, we see the interest as not being as urgent as Aristotle understands it. This is because we recognize the possibility of a valuable life without political activity (Constant [1819] 1988). This, along with the fact that we recognize opportunities for political activity without holding special office, makes the case for rotation less compelling. There may be other ways of fairly distributing opportunities for political activity. In any event, the main point for the present is that a concern for the fair distribution of opportunities for political activity is a different concern from a concern to avoid inferiority. Rotation might address the former problem without addressing the latter problem.

8.9 Equal Consideration and Equal Citizenship

In Sections 8.4–8.7, I discussed secondary tempering factors that address concerns about "vertical" relations to the state: about standing, insofar as one is subject to the decisions of the state, in relations of inferiority to the agents of the state, who decide what the state does. In this section, I discuss secondary tempering factors that respond to concerns about "horizontal" relations involving the state: about standing, insofar as one is subject to the decisions of the state, in relations of inferiority to other patients of the state, who are likewise subject to the state's decisions. These horizontal factors are Equal Consideration and Equal Citizenship.

The best way to introduce Equal Consideration may be to anticipate the discussion of discrimination in Chapter 13. There we will see that discrimination represents one way a disparity of consideration can be untempered. Where there is discrimination, a basing trait serves as a focal point for a coordinated pattern of greater or lesser consideration (or, more broadly, regard) for those who have or lack the trait, from many different persons and institutions, across society. It is this coordination, made possible by the basing trait, that makes the disparity of consideration untempered: ongoing, pervasive, and inescapable. It makes the disparity unlike a fleeting episode of lesser consideration from a lone individual, such as a driver who performs a random act of kindness by picking up another hitchhiker but, deciding that is enough for the day, not you.

With discrimination in mind as one example of an untempered disparity of consideration, what should be said about another kind of disparity of consideration: a disparity constituted by the responses of the state itself, even when it is not connected to any pattern of discrimination, so understood? If it is objectionable for the rest of society, coordinating on a basing trait, to, say, count your interests for less in the provision of public services, might it also be objectionable, for a similar reason, for the state, without the cooperation of the rest of society and independent of any basing trait, to count your interests for less in the provision of public services?

One might answer no. "After all, it isn't objectionable for the isolated, randomly kind driver to show you lesser consideration, again so long as they treat you adequately and so long as this isn't connected to any independently existing pattern of discrimination—that is, so long as there isn't any coordination on a basing trait. So, likewise, it isn't objectionable for the state to show you lesser consideration, so long as it treats you adequately and so long as this isn't connected to any independently existing pattern of discrimination."

However, the reason why the isolated individual's lesser consideration of you was unobjectionable, I said, was that tempering factors were present. The lesser consideration was not ongoing, pervasive, or inescapable. It was both regulated by higher-order structures with a different character and occurred against the background of other structures within which you enjoyed equal standing with the person who enjoyed greater consideration from that isolated individual. By contrast, relations to the state are ongoing, pervasive, and inescapable and not regulated by higher-order structures. And if, in your relations with the state, you do not enjoy equal standing with other individuals, there may be no other structures in which you do enjoy equal standing with them. In other words, because the tempering factors are absent, the state seems to play something more like the role of "the rest of society" in a case of discrimination and less like the role of a single stranger who performs random acts of kindness. Moreover, the state's consideration is special in a further way: it is the consideration of a body that wields superior power and authority. A disparity in the state's consideration, therefore, does more to constitute those it favors as superior than would a disparity in any individual's consideration.

This suggests the state is under a more stringent requirement to show equal consideration for those subject to it than private persons, such as the randomly kind driver, are under to display equal consideration for one another. As far as their duties with respect to disparities of consideration are concerned, private persons are required, perhaps, only to refrain from contributing to patterns of discrimination. The state, by contrast, is required to show equal consideration even absent any pattern of discrimination or any coordination on basing traits. This more stringent requirement is the horizontal factor of Equal Consideration. This view assumes that the state, understood as the agency that wields final power and authority, has a certain unity, even over time, even when distributed into a multitude of offices. And insofar as the state's consideration takes an expressive form, it also assumes that what the state does can have expressive significance. Both assumptions are open to question, granted. But they seem to me plausible.

Now let us turn to Equal Citizenship. Suppose the state satisfies Equal Influence and Equal Consideration. And suppose, moreover, that those subject to the state have not only equal influence over it but also sufficient positive influence over it and that the state shows them not only equal consideration but also sufficient positive consideration. Then those subject to the state enjoy a kind of socially recognized equal status with one another in virtue of the relations of each of them to the state. In virtue of Equal Influence, one is an equal "active" citizen. One has the same say as any other citizen has in what the state does. In virtue of Equal Consideration, one is an equal "passive" citizen. One enjoys the same consideration from the state as any other citizen does. This means that, as a kind of happy by-product, the state satisfies the last of the primary tempering factors listed: namely, Egalitarian Relationship. Whatever other asymmetries or disparities there may be between members of society, they stand as equals to one another in at least one other recognized relationship: namely, the relationship of Equal Citizenship, which is constituted by their relations with the state. Moreover, because the state wields final power and authority, which regulates all other relations, citizenship is, in one sense of "fundamental," one's most fundamental standing with respect to others in society (Miller 1997, 234).

Note that Equal Citizenship provides further support for Equal Influence and Equal Consideration. This is because Equal Influence and Equal Consideration are constituents of Equal Citizenship. Where there is reason for the thing constituted, there is reason for the things that constitute it. Also note that Equal Citizenship requires not only Equal Influence in or Equal Consideration by the state but also sufficiently positive influence or consideration. If the state plays little role in people's lives, for example, it might trivially satisfy Equal Consideration. However, it would not go very far in satisfying Equal Citizenship, since the relationship of equal citizenship that it established would be relatively thin; it would not amount to much.

This argument for Equal Citizenship may remind the reader of Rawls's second argument for the priority of the equal basic liberties. The arguments share the main premise that it is important to secure for everyone a kind of equal status: that, whatever other hierarchies there may be in society, there be at least one socially recognized relationship in which members of society stand as equals to one another (see also J. Cohen 1997).[14] The difference between the arguments lies in what this socially recognized relationship is taken to be. Rawls suggests it is realized by a basic structure that secures the equal basic liberties and, moreover, gives that equality priority over the distribution of other goods. By contrast, I have been suggesting that the relevant equal status of Equal Citizenship is constituted by Equal Influence and Equal Consideration (where there is sufficiently positive influence or consideration). It is equality in the relations, active and passive, that each of us bears to the state.

Rawls's focus on the equal distribution of liberty as the guarantor of equal status is puzzling in several ways. First, it is at best misleading to characterize the equality in question as concerning the holdings of any kind of good, let alone concerning the holdings of liberty. Instead, it concerns how the state relates to its citizens, and the same holdings of goods can be the end result of different relations to the state. To anticipate the discussion of Chapter 16, it is hard to explain why some inequalities in "holdings" of liberty, such as those that result from home security systems purchased on the open market, are unobjectionable, unless one attends to the arm's-length role the state plays in bringing about those inequalities.

Second, even if we grant that equal status requires equality in the holdings of goods of some kind, why should the goods be all and only the liberties? Why not money, or less than all the liberties, or some of the liberties and some money? A natural reply is that it is easier to tell whether there is equality of liberty than whether there is equality of other goods. But this isn't obvious, as Shiffrin (2004b) observes. On the one hand, with appropriate reporting requirements, we could monitor equality in income and wealth. On the other hand, monitoring equality in some of the basic liberties can be quite difficult. Another reply is that Rawls independently establishes that only liberty should be distributed equally. So liberty is the only candidate for the guarantor for equal status. However, much of the argument for the equal distribution of liberty seems to depend on the idea that it is a guarantor of equal status. Moreover, as we will see in Section 16.2, it is difficult to say how liberty even differs from money—let alone differs in such a way as to make different principles of justice appropriate to each.

Having enumerated these secondary tempering factors, I leave open the possibility that, even in the case of the state (or state-like arrangements in which the tempering factors are absent), not all these factors are required. Among other things, I leave open the possibility that the distinctively democratic tempering factor of Equal Influence is not required. To be sure, I devote a great deal of space to Equal Influence in Parts V and VI. But that should not be read as ignoring the possibility that the other secondary tempering factors might be enough.

9

The State and the Firm

Although I have introduced the secondary tempering factors as addressing a complaint against the state, this is in two ways too narrow. First, claims to the secondary tempering factors may be made of arrangements that, on the one hand, aren't counted as "states," either by ordinary usage or by the specialized usage of lawyers or social scientists, but that, on the other hand, are still, for our purposes, "state-like" in the sense that they, like the state, are not tempered by the primary factors. Thus, claims to the secondary tempering factors may be just as pressing against, on the one hand, international bodies with power and authority over states or, on the other hand, clan elders or warlords in "pre-state" or "failed-state" societies. And claims to the secondary tempering factors may be just as pressing against agents who occupy "privatized" offices within a society governed by a state, such as that of a warden in a for-profit prison or a private detective in a company town. Even if, by other criteria, these offices do not count as part of the state, nevertheless they are not tempered, which is what matters for our purposes. The for-profit warden might as well be the warden in a state-run prison, and the private detective might as well be a police officer. Second, claims to at least some of the secondary tempering factors may also be made of arrangements where some of the primary tempering factors are present: arrangements that not only are not counted by ordinary or specialized usage as part of the "state" but also are not fully state-like in the sense that matters for our purposes: namely, that none of the primary tempering factors are present. The most important of these arrangements is, arguably, the workplace or firm.

9.1 Reviving the Parallel-Case Argument

There are familiar "parallel-case arguments" of the form: because the firm is relevantly like the state, the firm must meet some condition required of the state (Walzer 1983; Dahl 1985; J. Cohen 1989). The thought, it would seem, is that workers in the firm have the sort of complaint against the firm that those who are subject to the state have against the state. However, if the complaint against the state is against its enforcement of its directives, as is so often thought (Section 2.2), then it is not clear there would be a parallel complaint against the firm. For, as many parallel-case arguments concede, the firm does not enforce its directives (Tawney 1912, 34–35; Dahl 1985, 113; Anderson 2017, 38).[1] As I have argued, however, it is a mistake to think the complaint against the state is to its enforcement. The complaint is instead against the hierarchical structure of the state itself: that those who control the state wield asymmetric power and authority over those who are subject to it. Even if the state, for contingent reasons, must enforce in order to wield asymmetric power and authority, the complaint against the state is not against those acts of enforcement themselves but instead against the ongoing relations of asymmetric power and authority that those acts sustain. If this is the complaint against the state, then it puts parallel-case arguments on a new foundation. For the firm, like the state, is open to the same objection. The firm, like the state, wields ongoing asymmetric power and authority over those subject to it.

Observing bosses in the wild, we find that they have ongoing discretion to do some or all of the following with respect to their workers:

1. to hire, fire, promote, demote, and reassign workers;
2. to determine workers' compensation;
3. to issue directives at least about how, when, and where workers are to work, including, importantly, setting ends for workers to pursue;
4. to control working conditions, such as time, location, noise, temperature, and safety;
5. to monitor and review performance, including as a reference for other employment;
6. and to encroach on workers' privacy (e.g., reading emails, requiring drug tests) or workers' sphere of control over their own person and effects (e.g., hairstyle), when workers are working, using the employer's property, or otherwise representing the employer.

This means, first and perhaps most significantly, that bosses have de facto authority over workers. They boss workers. Indeed, the workplace is one of the few settings in modern society, outside of relations with the state itself, in which some adults give other adults, for most of their waking hours, orders that they are expected to obey (Herzog 2018, chap. 4). Second, bosses have superior, ongoing power over workers. This superior power may be the source of superior authority, as when the boss's power to fire or otherwise discipline workers induces workers to obey the boss's commands. However, the boss can have superior power that does not support authority: power that is not deployed in order to get workers to do anything. Examples are depriving workers of safe or sanitary working conditions, snooping on their email, or firing them out of personal animosity.

Contrast one-off, quid pro quo market exchange of goods or services for which there is a sufficiently complete contract. Here there are no ongoing relations of asymmetric power and authority. While there may be asymmetries of power, they tend to be episodic, rather than ongoing (Walzer 1983, 291–292; González-Ricoy and Queralt, 2021). On one market day, one seller can bargain up the price of a commodity, whereas on another day, a buyer can haggle it down. And there aren't ongoing relations of asymmetric authority—or of authority at all. Neither market participant submits to future direction by the other.

This is an instance of a broader point: that in the wide genus of human interaction, one-off, quid pro quo market exchange is a special and perhaps somewhat artificial species. Part of the function of such exchange is to extinguish further normative (or pseudonormative) relations among the participants. Buyer and seller can go their separate ways without further normative entanglements. Consider Lewinsohn's (2020) insight that one-off, quid pro quo market exchange (as opposed to, say, gift exchange) functions to preempt future obligations of gratitude. Similarly, I am suggesting, one-off, quid pro quo market exchange functions to preempt the future submission of one participant to the superior authority or ongoing superior power of the another. Seen in this light, the problem with the exchange of labor for a wage is not, as Julius (2013) argues, the strategic, quid pro quo character of the contractual exchange. The problem is that, because the quid the worker is contracted to supply is submission to authority, it becomes a relation of subordination.[2] In sum, insofar as workers are subjected to the superior power and authority of their bosses, they are at risk of standing in an objectionable relation of inferiority to them, just as those subject to the state are at risk of standing in an objectionable relation of inferiority to those whose decisions the state's decisions are.

9.2 The Firm and the Primary Tempering Factors

How far this parallel-case argument succeeds, however, depends on whether the tempering factors that are absent in the state are likewise absent in the firm. Like the state, the firm is an established, ongoing social structure. Indeed, as we have seen, this is part of how employment, with its characteristic submission to authority, differs from one-off, quid pro quo market exchange. So the tempering factor of Episodic Character seems absent in the firm as in the state.

Whether Context and Content Limitation are absent in the firm seems largely to depend on the economic and legal structure. Granted, "at will" employment undermines Context and Content Limitation in most jurisdictions in the United States. But there can be labor laws that ensure Context Limitation. Managers might be able to tell workers what to do only on the shop floor, when they are on the clock. Likewise, with sensible labor protections, there might be Content Limitation. Managers might be able to tell workers to perform only work-related tasks. They might be able to fire them only with cause. They might not be able to use their power and authority in the workplace as a lever to extract personal favors or support for their political or religious aims. They might not be able to monitor nonwork-related communications.

Whether the firm is escapable also largely depends on the broader economic and legal structure. With a generous social safety net, opportunities for worker retraining, support in searching for new employment, and the state as an employer of last resort, the asymmetries of subjection to a particular employer may be escapable, at will, with low cost or difficulty. However, there are two general reasons to doubt that such freedom of exit will be entirely sufficient. First, there is again the Marxist point that one does not enjoy freedom of exit of the relevant kind if, upon exiting subjection to one employer, one is constrained to enter into a relation of the same kind with another employer. If all firms are alike, then although one can escape subjection to this boss, one cannot escape subjection to some boss. Second, there is reason to expect that exit will carry some cost or difficulty. For example, the worker may lose their investment in firm-specific human capital when they move to a new firm. And, as the theory of efficiency wages predicts, employers may pay higher wages than whatever fallback the welfare state provides. That is, employers may find that the incentives to productivity this potential loss in wages provides workers with more than compensates for the higher wage bill itself.

Against a backdrop of democratic political institutions, however, Downward Equalization will be present in the case of the firm. The asymmetries or disparities will not be final: that is, they will themselves be regulated by a higher court of appeal or a decision further up the chain of command that is not itself marked by that asymmetry or disparity. The firm itself will be regulated by a legal order that workers have equal opportunity to influence. The hierarchy of the firm will itself be controlled from a standpoint of equality (compare McMahon 2009, 12). Finally, against a backdrop of Equal Citizenship, Egalitarian Relationship will also be present in the case of the firm. The persons in the relationship marked by the asymmetry or disparity stand as equals in some other recognized relationship. Once the whistle blows, the manager is just another citizen.

In sum, some of the primary tempering factors wholly absent in the case of the state are more present in the case of the firm. Boss and worker do stand in another recognized relationship of equality—citizenship. The state is a higher court of appeal than the firm. Various measures could make exit less difficult or costly. Other measures could limit the time, place, context, and content of the asymmetries of power and authority. The greater presence of these primary tempering factors in the firm than in the state suggests that the case for secondary tempering factors is weaker in the firm than in the state. This casts parallel-case arguments into some doubt.

One possible conclusion is that some, but not all, of the secondary tempering factors that are called for in the case of the state are called for in the case of the firm.[3] In particular, one might suggest that since bosses are relevantly like state officials (Tawney [1912] 1972; McMahon 2009), bosses must at least meet the conditions of Impersonal Justification and Least Discretion that apply to state officials. As we will see, "abusive" or "arbitrary" treatment by bosses, which intuitively wrongs their employees, can be explained as violations of Impersonal Justification and Least Discretion. Indeed, this is how we will analyze the case of Car Wash. However, one might deny that the secondary tempering factor of Equal Influence is called for. This would fit the conventional moral wisdom in capitalist systems, which is friendlier to prohibiting "abusive" or "arbitrary" treatment of employees than to requiring workplace democracy.

9.3 Impersonal Justification and Least Discretion in the Firm

Grant that the firm calls for at least the vertical factors of Impersonal Justification and Least Discretion. Then, in order to apply Impersonal Justification and Least Discretion to the firm, we need some understanding of how the structure of offices in which the firm consists serves impersonal reasons, against the background of other social institutions, at least as well as any alternative and better than any alternative not marked by a similar asymmetry.

The answer, I assume, lies in the economic theory of the firm, pioneered by Coase (1937) and developed by later economists such as Williamson (1973, 2010). The basic idea is that the high costs of market transactions make it inefficient to organize certain processes of production by market transactions among autonomous buyers and sellers of the relevant factors of production, including labor. Organizing those processes instead under the hierarchical direction of a boss—which is what, for Coase at least, defines the firm—lowers those transaction costs. The resulting improvements in efficiency stand to benefit everyone.

Why might hierarchy offer lower costs than the market? For one thing, as Coase observes, even under conditions of certainty, there are the costs to negotiating complete labor contracts. Under uncertainty, there is the difficulty that such contracts cannot foresee all the contingencies that might require, in the interests of efficiency, a change in what the worker does. The problem is solved, Coase suggests, by an incomplete contract to submit to the direction of a boss. "For this series of contracts is substituted one. . . . The contract is one whereby the factor, for a certain remuneration . . . agrees to obey the directions of an entrepreneur *within certain limits*. . . . The details of what the supplier is expected to do is not stated in the contract, but is decided later by the purchaser. When the direction of resources (within the limits of the contract) becomes dependent on the buyer in this way, that relationship which I term a 'firm' may be obtained" (Coase 1937, 391–392). In other words, the boss is, in effect, the creature of incomplete contracts: an office established to specify the contractual terms left unspecified for the purpose of efficient production. Williamson's later developments emphasized the further effects of incomplete contracts when there is asset specificity, in which suppliers of factors of production make investments in assets, including human capital, that "cannot be redeployed to alternative uses and users without loss of productive value" (2010, 680). The selective investment in specific assets, in turn, transforms a situation with a large number of buyers, and so competitive bidding, into a situation with only a small number of buyers, and so something like monopsony power. This in turn creates openings for costly, opportunistic renegotiation of contracts. And the prospect of such changes disincentivizes investment in specific assets in the first place. A boss is thus needed to coordinate and resolve such intrafirm disputes. For other theorists, the principal role of the boss is to monitor workers' productivity and compensate them or dismiss them, accordingly. For Alchian and Demsetz (1972), the need for such monitoring becomes particularly acute with inseparable, "team" production, which makes individual contributions harder to identify.[4] This encourages shirking, which lowers productivity. (Note that this might be a problem from the point of the view of the workers themselves. They may be caught in a low-effort, low-productivity, and so low-wage equilibrium when they would each prefer a higher-effort, higher-wage equilibrium.) Alchian and Demsetz's solution, roughly, is a single boss who contracts with and monitors each of the workers independently and so is able to renegotiate the contract with each worker independently, in light of that worker's monitored performance.[5] Bowles and Gintis (1993, 79) also emphasize the cost or difficulty of external enforcement of labor contracts by courts (which might be a problem even if the contracts themselves were complete). In place of the discipline of external enforcement of contracts, there is submission to the discretionary discipline of a boss, who can change compensation or fire.

If the office of the boss is justified in some or all of these ways, then it makes sense that the boss would have some or all of the discretionary capacities we attributed to bosses earlier: to direct workers, fire them for cause, and so forth. And, to a first approximation, the relevant impersonal reasons would be those that favor efficient production by the firm itself. However, this does not mean the office of boss should be geared exclusively toward efficient production by the firm. For that might not serve, as it were, efficient production overall: the public interest, understood as fairly meeting the claims to improvement of all. It might result in workers bearing unfair costs for a given increase in the firm's productivity. It may not be fair to ask a canner to risk life and limb simply to get slightly cheaper fish to market. Moreover, blinkered pursuit of the firm's productivity might come at the expense of impersonal reasons arising from claims against inferiority, as when discriminating against workers might be efficient from the perspective of the firm. Hence, the office of boss may be impersonally justified only if the pursuit of the firm's productivity is constrained by certain protections for workers.

9.4 A Case for Workplace Democracy?

Earlier, I suggested that, since more of the primary tempering factors are present in the case of the firm than the state, the argument for the secondary tempering factors is less compelling in the case of the firm than in the state. Perhaps the conclusion to draw, I proposed, was that the secondary tempering factor associated with democracy, Equal Influence, is not required in the case of the firm, whereas the secondary tempering factors concerning office, namely Impersonal Justification and Least Discretion, do apply in the case of the firm. I then asked, in order to apply Impersonal Justification and Least Discretion to the firm, what impersonal reasons the firm serves. I have, however, overlooked three further considerations that tend in the opposite direction: considerations, that, other things equal, make the argument for Equal Influence stronger in the case of the firm than the state.

First, there is the fact that, in certain ways, the asymmetries of authority in the workplace are less Content Limited than the asymmetries of authority in the state (Anderson 2017, 63). First, the boss's orders impose ends on the worker in which the worker typically has no investment; they don't simply regulate how the worker pursues their own independent ends. Second, as Taylorism famously codified, the boss's orders are often exceedingly fine grained. They significantly constrain how, when, and where those ends are to be achieved, leaving little to the worker's discretion. By contrast, much of a liberal state's orders—its laws—don't assign ends to citizens. Nor do they much constrain how, when, and where those ends are to be achieved. Rather, its laws are meant to facilitate the pursuit of citizens' own ends, in a fair way, with the main constraints deriving from the need to fairly provide like opportunity to others. Consider, for instance, the orders a dispatcher gives to drivers, which give them specific destinations, routes, and arrival times. Contrast that with the state's traffic regulations, which simply set up a framework that allows citizen motorists to drive safely and efficiently, in a way that is fair to all, to whatever destinations, by whatever routes, and at whatever times those citizens have chosen for themselves (Anderson 2017, 67). The law of contracts likewise leaves largely open what the content of those contracts are. The laws of incorporation leave largely open what the corporations are incorporated to do. The tax code leaves largely open how one goes about acquiring the funds that are to be sent to the treasury. Building codes (or at least sensible ones) leave largely open what structures are built and for which purposes.

Second, the secondary tempering factor of Equal Application seems more likely to obtain in the case of the state than in the case of the firm. Equal Application, recall, obtains just when exercises of asymmetric power and authority apply as much to those who wield them as to those who are simply subject to them. The highest officials in the state, such as legislators and chief executives, are themselves typically subject to the laws and executive orders they make. By contrast, bosses are not typically subject to their own orders. Issuing and monitoring compliance with workplace orders is a full-time job, with no time left over to fulfill the orders one has issued.

Finally, the secondary tempering factor of Upward Unaccountability seems more likely to obtain in the state than in the firm. Upward Unaccountability obtains, recall, when, even though Hyman has superior authority over Loman, Loman is not accountable to Hyman for obeying Hyman's commands. In general (apart from, say, findings of contempt of court or Congress), obedience to the commands of state officials are understood to be owed not to them even in their official capacities, but instead to other citizens. However, it is less clear that this is true in the case of bosses: that, say, working the night shift is understood as owed to fellow workers, let alone citizens as a whole.

So, where does this leave us? Is what is required of the state—both the tempering factors concerning offices, Impersonal Justification and Least Discretion, and the tempering factor concerning democracy, Equal Influence—also required of the firm? Are the parallel-case arguments to these conclusions sound? It is hard to say. In some ways, the case for these tempering factors seems stronger with respect to the state than the firm. In other ways, however, the case for these tempering factors seems stronger with respect to the firm than the state. I cannot claim to have proposed a resolution of pretheoretical controversy over workplace governance. But I have proposed a theory of the deeper sources of the controversy.

10

Collective Inferiority

In describing complaints against inferiority, I have been describing complaints of individuals against relations of inferiority to other individuals. However, there may be a different, but related, phenomenon. This is a complaint of individuals that a group to which they belong is subordinated to another group. Such vicarious, collective subordination would be possible even where otherwise there are no relations of inferiority among individuals.

This objection to vicarious, collective subordination might explain objections to persistent minorities, which are consistently outvoted. After all, as I return to in Section 29.5, each member of a persistent minority enjoys equal influence with each member of the majority. There is no subordination of any member of the minority, as an individual, to any member of the majority. However, the persistent majority as a group enjoys superior influence, indeed decisiveness, over the persistent minority as a group. So the objection of each member of the minority may be that, although, in the first instance, she is not individually subordinated to any other individual, a group to which she belongs is subordinated to another group. For that reason, she, and every other member of her group, is vicariously subordinated to each member of the other group.

This objection to vicarious, collective subordination might also explain objections to colonial annexation. Suppose the United States were to have annexed Iraq as the fifty-first state. Assuming that every member of the first fifty states stood as an equal with every other, it would seem that every member of the now fifty-one states stands as an equal with every other. The objection of each annexed individual may again be that, although that individual is not, in the first instance, individually subordinated to any other individual, a group to which that individual belongs is subordinated to another group and so that individual is subordinated to each member of the other group. Note that, conversely, relations of inferiority among individuals are possible even where there is no vicarious, collective subordination. Anti-colonial movements, for example, might see their people as liberated once the colonizing power has been thrown off. But not all anti-colonial movements are democratic (Berlin [1958] 1997, 228–229).

One challenge for this idea that there is an objection to vicarious, collective subordination is to say what the relevant groups are. Why should any given member of the minority be counted as a member of the minority, rather than as a member of the electorate as a whole or, indeed, of any number of other intermediate groups, such as the majority plus that individual? In the cases I have discussed, however, a division of groups suggests itself. The divide between persistent majority and persistent minority may track a divide between salient ethnic, racial, or religious groups between which there has been a history of oppression, hostility, or mere separation, even if presently there is no substantively unfair treatment. It is certainly intuitive that such distinctions might plausibly make the majority and minority—the first fifty versus Iraq, polarized White voters versus Black voters, metropole versus colony—relevant groups.

III

Further Instances

In Part I, I described the materials of the negative observation: interests in improvement and rights against invasion. I introduced one instance of a commonplace claim, the claim against the state. And I argued for the negative observation with respect to that commonplace claim. That is, I argued that the claim against the state cannot be explained by interests in improvement or rights against invasion. In Part II, I introduced the materials of the positive conjecture: relations of inferiority and claims against standing in such relations. And I advanced the positive conjecture with respect to the first commonplace claim: that the claim against the state is a claim against inferiority. Now, in Part III, I follow the same routine with a number of other commonplace claims. I introduce a commonplace claim. I make the negative observation: that that commonplace claim can't be accounted for by interests in improvement or rights against invasion. And then I propose the positive conjecture: that the claim can instead be understood as a claim against inferiority.

11

Claims against Corruption

The Negative Observation

In this chapter, we begin by considering a new commonplace claim, a claim against corruption. In its broadest use, "corruption" means regress from a pure, healthy, or virtuous state. Our interest, however, will be in a narrower use, where the paradigms of "corruption" are bribery, nepotism, cronyism, self-dealing, and embezzlement. We might say that such "official corruption" consists in using an office or role within an institution for the purpose of benefitting oneself or people close to oneself when one shouldn't. We may need to adjust this definition later, but it gives us a place to start. It is commonly thought that such official corruption wrongs "the public." That is, everyone related in some relevant way to the office has a complaint against such official corruption. The questions for this chapter are: When and why does official corruption wrong the public?[1]

To be sure, some official corruption wrongs people in "office-independent" ways. That is, we can explain the wrong without appealing to the fact that an office was used. Whatever else embezzlement is, for example, it is theft. It would still be theft even if weren't an inside job. Likewise, dangling a pardon before a coconspirator to get them not to cooperate with the prosecution is obstruction of justice. It would still be obstruction of justice if a private citizen offered a cash quid for a similar quo. However, not all official corruption wrongs the public in such an office-independent way. And even when corruption does wrong the public in some office-independent way, it seems wrong in some further office-dependent way. So much is suggested by the slogans that official corruption is wrong because it "subverts the public to the private" or "breaches the public trust" (Lowenstein 1985, 806; Philp, 2002). But how are we to understand these slogans? When and why does official corruption wrong "the public"? Those are our questions.

11.1 The Duty to Execute

The obvious explanation, it might seem, is that official corruption wrongs the public because it leads to worse official decisions: worse exercises of office. This proposed explanation, more fully spelled out, would be:

1. There is a "Duty to Execute." A holder of an office, Grafton, because she holds that office, owes it to those subject to the office to make good official decisions.
2. Corrupt decisions are bad decisions.
3. Therefore, corrupt decisions violate the Duty to Execute. Grafton's corruption wrongs the public, understood as those who are subject to her office, by failing in the Duty to Execute that she owes them.

The proposed explanation, as it stands, leaves something unexplained. Even a noncorrupt official, Ness, can make a bad decision as an honest mistake. However, it seems to wrong the public in a further way for Grafton to make a bad decision because Grafton is on the take (Philp 2002). A more plausible view would revise (1) and (2) slightly:

1* There is a Duty to Execute. An officeholder, Grafton, because she holds that office, owes it to those subject to the office to take due care to make good official decisions.
2* Corrupt decisions fail to take due care.

Unlike Ness's honest mistake, it might be said, Grafton's corruption violates that duty of due care. When Raz describes "abuse of power," he seems to have something like this in mind. Grafton's act is done "with indifference as to whether it will serve the purposes which alone can justify use of that power" or with the "belief that it will not serve them" (Raz 1977, 220; see also 2019, 7).

So far, so good. But now let us ask: Why do officeholders owe it to those subject to the office to take due care to make good official decisions? It seems so obvious that there is a Duty to Execute that it sounds almost silly to ask why. But once posed, the question is surprisingly hard to answer. One's first thought may be to appeal to the idea that everyone has a Duty to Improve: to serve the public interest. The Duty to Execute is just a special case. When a sometime civilian finds herself, as it were, behind the wheel of an office, the way for her to fulfill her Duty to Improve is to make official decisions that serve the public interest. On this view, the only difference between officials and civilians is that officials, but not civilians, happen to be (now going nautical) at the tiller: to have special access, which civilians don't have, to a lever, namely the office, to promote the public interest. To help this reductive argument along—that the Duty to Execute is a special case of the Duty to Improve—let us assume, for the time being, that good official decisions just are decisions that serve the public interest.

A first difficulty with this reductive argument is the "prerogative problem." The official's Duty to Execute is more exacting than the civilian's Duty to Improve. As a civilian, even if I have some opportunity to serve the public interest, I might not have a duty to take it. This might be because the reason I have to serve the public interest is outweighed by my personal reasons: such as my own interests, relationships, or projects or those of people close to me. If promoting the public interest, by doing Great rather than Good, would mean some sacrifice of my own interests (say, a loss of income) or the interests of those close to me (say, my nephew's foundering on the job market because I can't spend the time to help him polish his resume), then, at least within certain bounds, I don't have a duty to do Great. Or, at very least, it would be controversially rigoristic to say that I have a duty to do Great. By contrast, it doesn't seem even controversially rigoristic, it seems rather like common sense, that such personal reasons carry no (or far less) weight against an official's Duty to Execute. Suppose Grafton is offered a bribe to make an official decision for Good over Great, to exercise the office in that way. If Grafton instead decides for Great over Good, then Grafton thereby sacrifices some income: namely, the bribe. But surely that doesn't release Grafton from the Duty to Execute. Likewise, if Grafton were to forgo nepotism, then Grafton would have to sacrifice the interests of her nephew.[2] In both cases, however, the same things seem to be at stake on either side of the scales: the public interest, on the one hand, and personal reasons, on the other.[3]

A second difficulty with the reductive argument—that the Duty to Execute is a special case of the Duty to Improve—is the "modesty problem." We have been assuming that good official decisions are just decisions that serve the public interest. But this is questionable. It seems intuitively permissible for an official to make a decision that fails to take due care to serve the public interest. Does a customs official, Offe, act impermissibly when he decides to let this particular shipment pass because the proper duties have been paid, without first checking whether that promotes the public interest overall? Good official decisions are not, or at least not exclusively, decisions that directly promote the public interest. They are instead, or at least also, decisions that issue from certain decision-making processes that partly define the office, such as to let all and only those shipments pass on which duties have been paid. Perhaps Offe would even violate the Duty to Execute in pursuing the public interest directly, in contravention of the decision-making processes that define the office. But, at very least, Offe does not violate the Duty to Execute in not pursuing the public interest directly, so long as Offe follows the decision-making processes that define the office.

In response to both the prerogative and modesty problems, one might argue that the official, unlike the civilian, has a special duty because the official, unlike the civilian, leads others to expect—say, by seeking or accepting the office—that she will make, or take due care to make, good decisions.[4] This reply offers a fairly literal interpretation of the slogan that corruption "breaches the public trust." The Duty to Execute is more or less a promissory duty. In general, when one promises to *X*, personal reasons that otherwise would have made it permissible not to *X* no longer do so. Likewise, in this special case, where the promised *X* is to take due care to make good official decisions, personal reasons that otherwise would have made it permissible to fail to take due care no longer make it permissible. The problem is that this makes the official's Duty to Execute hostage to Grafton's giving an actual promise, or Grafton's inviting actual expectations, or whatever else it is that gives rise to a promissory duty. But what if Grafton makes it clear that she will neglect her office? And what if the public is resigned to this (as publics in corrupt systems often become)? All the same, Grafton comes to occupy the office. One wants to say that, even though there has been no promise, and even though no actual expectations have been created, others are still entitled to expect that Grafton will take due care to make good decisions.

One might reply that even if none of the other usual conditions of promissory obligations are satisfied, the very fact that Grafton enters into the office or refuses to relinquish it triggers a sui generis promissory obligation to execute it well. But this feels more like a restatement of what we want to explain than an explanation of it. To be clear, I am not denying that there is a Duty to Execute. Surely there is. I am just observing that we haven't yet explained it.

11.2 Must Corruption Disserve the Public Interest?

In addition to the prerogative and modesty problems, there is a further problem with the strategy under review: that of explaining the wrong of corruption as a violation of the Duty to Execute and the Duty to Execute, in turn, as a special case of the Duty to Improve. Let us again assume, for the sake of argument, what we just questioned: namely, that good official decisions are just decisions that serve the public interest. The "permissiveness problem" is that there are intuitively corrupt actions that don't violate the Duty to Execute because they are not official decisions that serve the public interest worse.

There are three kinds of cases. First, some official corruption uses an office without exercising it: that is, without making an official decision. For example, it seems corrupt for Grafton to "leverage" her office for gifts that Grafton would not otherwise receive, even though the gifts aren't conditioned on any official decision at all, let alone an official decision that disserves the public interest. Suppose, to take an example suggested to me by Paul Weithman, Grafton is a head of state who convinces a resort owner to give her a free stay, in return for the resort owner's publicizing Grafton's visit, as a way of attracting business. Grafton's decision about where to go on vacation is itself not an official decision or an exercise of the office. So the Duty to Execute doesn't apply. But Grafton is still using the office: leveraging it for a gift.[5]

Second, even when corruption does exercise the office, so that the Duty to Execute does apply, the official decisions that are induced by bribes, say, may predictably serve the public interest better than the alternatives. It's a serious, if contested, thesis that corruption can, under certain conditions, be economically efficient (Leff 1964; Nye 1967; Friedrich 1972; Huntington 1968; Huang 2018). The rough idea is that corruption, by allocating resources to those most willing to pay, puts them to their most productive use. Suppose that Grafton, convinced by the relevant social science (which we can moreover suppose is correct), unilaterally adopts a policy of auctioning decisions to the highest bribe. Grafton is not violating the Duty to Execute. Grafton is fulfilling it. Still, one feels ambivalent about applauding Grafton as a pioneering reformer who is just taking the initiative.

Finally, even when corruption does exercise the office, so that the Duty to Execute applies, it can be the case that, even after having taken due care to identify a decision that serves the public interest, Grafton finds herself with an underdetermined decision. Grafton has several options open to her, and, at least as far as Grafton is in a position to judge, each of them would serve the public interest equally well or in incommensurable ways such that neither option can be said to serve the public interest worse. Thus, whatever decision Grafton makes, Grafton will not violate the Duty to Execute. Still, it seems wrong for Grafton to resolve the underdetermination for a bribe or in order to favor her nephew. Call this the "Argument from Underdetermination."

While I am myself making this Argument from Underdetermination, I caution that it needs to be handled with care. Sometimes what looks like underdetermination is not, in fact. First, consider cases in which Grafton is allocating a scarce, indivisible good (such as a construction contract or a subsidized housing unit) and there are two parties with tied cases to receive it, Kleene and Greaser. In that case, it is intuitive that the allocation should be by what was referred to in Section 1.4 as a "highest fair chance lottery." Flipping a coin gives each of Kleene and Greaser the best chance of receiving the good compatible with fairness to the other. If Grafton is bribed to give the good outright to Greaser, therefore, Grafton wrongs Kleene simply by giving Kleene less than a 0.5 chance, which is worse than Kleene is entitled to. In this case, a Duty to Execute does seem to explain why Kleene is wronged. That is, upon closer inspection, we see that the decision is not underdetermined after all. The determined decision is to distribute by lottery. Kleene's complaint against Grafton for giving the good to Greaser for a bribe is simply an improvement complaint: that Kleene was thereby deprived of a better chance at the good, a better chance that Kleene could have been given without unfairness to Greaser. Notice that this improvement complaint does not depend on the fact that Grafton was bribed. What matters is simply that Grafton failed to conduct a fair lottery, not why Grafton failed. However, presumably there are other official decisions that don't concern (at least not directly) the allocation of a scarce, indivisible good among equally compelling claimants and that can be genuinely underdetermined. The complaint against Grafton's making such a decision for a bribe cannot be simply the improvement complaint that it deprived someone of a better chance in a lottery for a scarce, indivisible good.

A second caveat about the Argument from Underdetermination: as I discuss in greater detail in Section 14.1, it can violate a norm of equal treatment to make a decision in Greaser's favor in one case but then not to do the same in Kleene's relevantly similar case. This is so even though, because each decision taken in isolation is underdetermined, either decision taken in isolation would be unobjectionable. Kleene's complaint against Grafton's making a favorable decision for Greaser, but not for Kleene, because of a bribe might then simply be that Grafton's treatment of them was unequal. This equal treatment complaint does not depend on the fact that the unequal treatment resulted from a bribe. What matters is that Grafton treated them unequally, not why Grafton did so. Again, however, this does not cover all the relevant cases. Not all underdetermined official decisions treat different people differently. The underdetermined decision might concern only Kleene's case, with no Greaser on the scene.

A final caveat about the Argument from Underdetermination concerns the cumulative effects of making underdetermined decisions on certain grounds. Granted, Grafton's breaking a tie for a bribe may not do any harm; it's a tie, after all. But if all the relevant officials were to break ties for bribes, then perhaps it would do harm. That overall pattern would not be "tied" with the alternative. Even if this is so, however, it would not explain why Grafton wrongs the public when she breaks the tie for a bribe, so long as she has taken due care that other officials won't do the same so that the cumulative harm will not occur. Perhaps Grafton wrongs the other officials by not constraining herself as they constrain themselves. But the other officials aren't the (whole) public. They aren't (all) the people wronged by the official corruption.

11.3 Unjust Enrichment

So, even assuming a Duty to Execute, we have not yet explained how, in at least some cases, official corruption wrongs the public. Consider now a different possible explanation, which we might call "Unjust Enrichment." Suppose that Grafton rents out the township's snowplow and pockets the proceeds. Grafton steals from the public, it might be said. This is because the public has property rights in the snowplow. And those property rights include rights to any proceeds from the use of the snowplow. Yet Grafton is keeping those proceeds, which belong to the public, for herself. Likewise, it might be said, the public has property rights in Grafton's office itself, just as the public might have property rights in equipment, patents, or broadcast frequencies. In brief:

"Office as Property": Offices are the public's property.

Therefore, the public has property rights in any proceeds from the use of the office. By keeping a bribe, which Grafton acquired by using the office, Grafton is stealing from the public. The "public is subverted by the private," on this view, insofar as the public's property is made private "property" (Strauss 1995, 148).

Two initial worries about this proposed explanation, Unjust Enrichment, can be addressed fairly easily. First, one might worry that it implies officials must work for free. After all, Grafton's salary is something she gains only by using the office. The natural reply is that the public has consented to Grafton's keeping these proceeds: her official salary. The complaint is about Grafton's keeping proceeds the public hasn't consented to. Second, one might worry that Unjust Enrichment cannot distinguish between corruption and honest mistake. After all, unjust enrichment is a matter of mere possession, not intent. Suppose that, despite Station Chief's efforts to disabuse her, Ambassador Doofus continues to labor under the misconception that the local potentate would be so offended by Doofus's refusal of personal gifts as to mar diplomatic relations. As a result, Doofus has accumulated a snuffbox collection that really belongs to the Smithsonian, as though she unwittingly inherited stolen art. The natural reply is that Doofus's honest mistake differs from corruption because Doofus at least takes due care to avoid unjust enrichment, whereas Grafton does it deliberately.

In addition to dispatching these initial worries, Unjust Enrichment offers nice explanations of two things that have so far puzzled us. First, Unjust Enrichment explains our ambivalence about commending Grafton for forward-looking institutional reform when she starts taking bribes, after having been independently convinced by the social scientific research that says this will allocate resources more efficiently. Even if this allocates resources more efficiently, we can now say, the resulting social surplus is not Grafton's to keep. The money should be going into the treasury. Second, Unjust Enrichment explains why not only exercises of office but also other uses of office can be corrupt. Even if Grafton leverages the office for gifts that aren't conditioned on Grafton's official decisions, she still claims for herself the proceeds of an office that belongs to others.

So far, so good. But Unjust Enrichment seems incomplete. Nepotism doesn't enrich Grafton, although it advantages her nephew. Nor is Grafton enriched by bribes with no cash value, such as honors, sexual or administrative favors, or, as the Emoluments Clause of the US Constitution lists, "Office, or Title." These are forms of official corruption that wrong the public, it would seem. But they do not involve, in any straightforward sense, the accumulation of property that should be, but is not, shared with members of the public.

11.4 The Duty to Exclude

We are thus left, it seems, with forms of official corruption that wrong the public but without failing to take due care either (i) to serve the public interest or (ii) to avoid unjust enrichment. For example, Grafton might take a bribe to decide an underdetermined decision in a particular way where the bribe in question is not property that somehow ought to be shared with others or deposited in some public treasury. For those who read Section 3.7, note that Boss's exploitative offer to Employee in Car Wash had this structure. To all appearances, it looks like such official corruption is wrong because of the purposes for which Grafton uses the office (Ryan 2013; Teachout 2014). Grafton wouldn't wrong the public by making either underdetermined decision on the merits. Grafton only wrongs the public by making one of those underdetermined decisions for a bribe. The issue, it looks like, is the reason for which the official acts. In other words, it looks like corruption violates the "Duty to Exclude": a duty that officials have, because they hold offices, to avoid using those offices for certain "improper" reasons.

The exclusion of a reason can be accomplished in several ways. Things can be engineered so that the reason simply never obtains, as when an official recuses himself from cases that would present a conflict of interest. Or the official can be kept ignorant of such reasons as do obtain by screens, blind trusts, redactions, sequestrations, or conferences in chamber. Or, as a last line of defense, the decider may give those reasons that the official does know of no weight as reasons in his decision, as Raz's (1990b) "exclusionary reasons" require.[6] It is hardly a new thought that in various contexts, for various reasons, a decider may be expected to exclude reasons that would discriminate against race or gender or reasons that some authority, such as the law, has instructed them to disregard. What the Duty to Exclude requires, more specifically, is that officials in general exclude improper reasons.

In order to articulate and defend the Duty to Exclude, however, we need to answer two questions. First, which reasons are improper? That is, which reasons does the Duty to Exclude exclude? Surely, one might think, self-interest is one such reason. But it can't be right, without further qualification, that making an official decision out of self-interest suffices for corruption. Consider, for illustration, how Teachout's (2014, 283–285) proposal to use the criminal law to prevent corruption risks backfiring if corruption, as Teachout at times suggests, consists in acting from self-interest. If politicians act from fear of criminal punishment, they are already acting from self-interest. Far from preventing corruption, therefore, the criminal law dangles an almost irresistible temptation to it. Anti-corruption statutes become a kind of entrapment.

Second, once we have identified the improper reasons, which must be excluded, why does Grafton wrong the public by acting for those reasons? Why is the Duty to Exclude owed to the public? Granted, when Grafton acts for a base reason, that might be a reason to think less of her. But it isn't clear that improper reasons are always base—at least in a sense that antedates the judgment that they are corrupt. After all, isn't wanting your nephew to find a job just being a good auntie? And, in any event, acting from a base reason isn't, in general, grounds for someone else to complain—to claim they have been wronged. While I care that "Representative Barbara Lee speaks for me," why should I care, so long as she does speak for me, what hidden springs set her tongue in motion? After all, it hardly stokes resentment to learn, from Adam Smith, that it's not from the benevolence of butcher, brewer, or baker that we expect our dinner. In sum, if corruption scandals merely revealed base reasons, why should they inflame?

One might be tempted to return to Office as Property to explain why Grafton owes the Duty to Exclude to the public. Perhaps, in general, if we own something, we can permit others to use it only for certain purposes. If they then use it for other purposes, they have wronged us. Why not say that we, the public, permit the official to use what we own, namely the office, only for certain purposes?

I doubt this will work. To begin with, we need to scrutinize Office as Property—the idea that the public owns the office—more closely than we have so far. There is a danger that saying that we own the office just restates what we want to explain: that the official owes it to us, the public, not to use it for certain purposes. To explain why the official owes it to the public, the office needs to be the public's property in some more substantive sense.

The idea would be, I suppose, that, in general, when one contributes to the establishment and upkeep of something, one acquires property rights in it. Since we, the public, have contributed to the establishment and upkeep of the office, we have acquired property rights in the office. To be sure, this relies not only on a controversial theory of natural property but also on a speculative extension of it to the case of offices. But let us grant all that. Three further difficulties remain. The first difficulty is that, on this view, only people who have contributed to the establishment and upkeep of the relevant office can be wronged by the corrupt use of it. Only they count as the public. But then noncontributors—such as asylum seekers, children, the infirm, the indigent, new hires, freshmen, or occupied peoples—would have no objection when an official, to whose decisions they are (in some other sense) subject, was influenced by bribes.

A second difficulty is determining what is supposed to count as the public's consent to the use of its property. Things are clear enough if I tell you that you may use my property only for certain purposes. But when and how did the public tell Grafton for which purposes she could use the office? Is it the law that represents the public's telling Grafton for which purposes she may use the office? In that case, corruption would consist only in violating the law (as, indeed, some have argued: Leff 1964; Nye 1967; Friedrich 1972; Gardiner 1993). Yet one might have thought corruption would be wrong even if there were no law against it. (Indeed, one might have thought that was why there are laws against it.) Moreover, if one examines actual laws against corruption, one finds they quite often pass the buck to extralegal, moral standards to decide which purposes count as corrupt.

Finally, why should the public care, in the first place, to put such restrictions on the purposes for which its property is used? Absent further explanation, it is as though I were to say: "You may borrow my turntable, and you may play records on it. (Moreover, of course, you may enjoy the music that comes from it. It goes without saying that I have no property rights in your enjoyment!) But you may not play records on my turntable in order to enjoy the music that comes from it." I guess, having said this, I could resent you for playing the record in order to enjoy the music. But it is bizarre why I should have put this condition on your use of it in the first place. By contrast, it doesn't seem bizarre, it seems taken for granted, that we would care about offices being used for bribes or nepotism. But then why do we care? What's at stake?

12

Claims against Corruption

The Positive Conjecture

In the last chapter, we saw that in order to make sense of the commonplace claim against corruption, we face two explanatory tasks: to articulate and explain the Duty to Execute and the Duty to Exclude. In the last chapter, I also argued for the negative observation with respect to the commonplace claim against corruption. Neither the Duty to Execute nor the Duty to Exclude is explained by the public interest, which is to say that neither is explained by interests in improvement. As the permissiveness problem shows, violating the Duty to Exclude need not come at any cost at all to the public interest. As the prerogative problem shows, even if we understand the Duty to Execute as a duty to make decisions that promote the public interest, violating the Duty to Execute need not come at any cost to the public interest beyond what the Duty to Improve, to which civilians are subject, already permits for the sake of personal reasons. And as the modesty problem shows, if we understand the Duty to Execute as a duty to follow certain decision-making procedures that define the office, then satisfying the Duty to Execute, on a particular occasion, may come at a cost to the public interest. I turn now to the positive conjecture with respect to the claim against corruption: that the Duties to Execute and Exclude can be explained by claims against inferiority.

12.1 Impersonal Justification Explains the Duty to Execute

Recall the vertical tempering factor of Impersonal Justification. Where there are otherwise untempered asymmetries of power and authority, they must be impersonally justified offices. An office is impersonally justified if and only if, against the relevant background, impersonal reasons are served, in general and over the long run, at least as well as any alternative, and better than any alternative without the asymmetries, when, first, there is that office and, second, the occupants of that office, in exercising it, follow, in general and over the long run, the decision-making processes that partly define the office. This means that Impersonal Justification with respect to a given office is realized just when, first, its occupant follows generic decision-making processes, applying their individual judgment and powers of perception only in the ways that those processes allow, and, second, the generic decision-making processes themselves serve impersonal reasons, not (except indirectly or coincidentally) personal reasons (let alone things that aren't reasons at all, such as bare whims or desires). Together, these two elements of Impersonal Justification—that those wielding superior power and authority follow a generic process and that the process itself serves only impersonal reasons—effect a distinction between the superior power and authority of the office and the natural person who occupies it. By effecting that distinction, they lessen the degree to which exposure to the otherwise untempered power and authority of the office is subordination to the natural person who occupies it. Underlying the whole structure is a claim against being so subordinated: a claim against inferiority.

Suppose, then, that you find yourself the occupant of an office that otherwise satisfies Impersonal Justification. How are you to make official decisions? You have a duty to realize Impersonal Justification with respect to your office by following the generic decision-making processes that define it. This duty would seem to be the Duty to Execute that we sought. First, it is a duty, unlike the Duty to Improve, that only officials, not civilians, have. Second, solving the modesty problem, it is a duty, unlike the Duty to Improve, that you fulfill just when you follow the decision-making processes that define your office. And, finally, solving the prerogative problem, it is a duty such that your personal reasons are weightless in determining what it requires you to do (except in "indirect" cases, in which giving them weight itself has an impersonal justification), since the processes are justified in a way that is insensitive to your personal reasons.

Now, two objections. First, one might ask why you don't do your part to realize Impersonal Justification overall by seeing to it that other officials follow the decision-making processes that define their offices. This would suggest that one is required, in an analogue to the "paradox of rights," to depart from the decision-making process in one's own case in order to see to it that several others don't depart from the decision-making process in their case. However, I argued in Section 5.5 that claims against inferiority call on one to refrain from entering into relations in which one is superior and to give this priority over working to avoid relations of inferiority among others. By failing to follow the decision-making process yourself, you are entering into relations to those subject to the office as their superior, insofar as you are failing to maintain what tempers the asymmetric power and authority you exercise over them.

Second, one might ask why the duty just described is not, like the Duty to Improve, limited by a prerogative to serve your personal reasons. Granted, the duty of officials just described is not, as it were, "internally" sensitive to personal reasons, insofar as what it directs you to do is to follow an impersonally justified decision-making process. But, likewise, the Duty to Improve is not "internally" sensitive to personal reasons, insofar as it directs you to promote the public interest. Granted, the Duty to Improve is "externally" sensitive to personal reasons, insofar as you do not have a duty to do what it directs you to do (that is, to promote the public interest) when it would come at too great an expense of your personal reasons, such as helping your nephew find a job. But why isn't the duty that we have described similarly externally sensitive to personal reasons, so that you would not have a duty to do what it directs you to do (that is, to follow the decision-making processes) when it would come at too great an expense of your personal reasons, such as helping your nephew find a job? The answer, I suggest, is that in departing from the decision-making process, you are doing something more like active harming; you are placing yourself in a position of superiority to those subject to your office. By contrast, in not promoting the public interest, you are doing something more like failing to aid. And it is a familiar thought that personal reasons can make permissible failures to aid in a way in which they do not make permissible active harms.

Note that the Duty to Execute, so understood, rests on an indirect, two-level structure of justification, of the sort exemplified by rule utilitarianism. The Duty to Execute is, roughly, a duty to follow a generic decision-making process such that if it were followed in general and over the long run, impersonal reasons would be served. Why then isn't the Duty to Execute vulnerable to the familiar objection to indirect, two-level theories? If the thing that ultimately matters is serving impersonal reasons, then why isn't your duty simply to serve those impersonal reasons directly, which might require, on some particular occasion, that you depart from the decision-making process that, if followed in general and over the long run, would serve impersonal reasons? The reply is that the impersonal reasons are not the only thing that ultimately matters. It also ultimately matters that you maintain the distinction between office and occupant. And that is a distinct value that is served by each particular instance of following the generic decision-making process.

12.2 Least Discretion Explains the Duty to Exclude

If I have articulated and explained the Duty to Execute, I have not yet articulated and explained the Duty to Exclude. Whatever the decision-making processes are that serve impersonal reasons, they will presumably leave some decisions underdetermined. Put another way, a process such that, for some case, one follows the process in that case whichever decision one makes might be a process that serves impersonal reasons at least as well as any alternative. Why then is it wrong to make the decision on the basis of "improper" reasons? Similarly, when one uses an office for improper reasons but does not exercise the office, one does not depart from the decision-making process that defines the office.

Where the vertical factor of Impersonal Justification explained the Duty to Execute, the vertical factor of Least Discretion explains the Duty to Exclude: the duty to exclude what we described, with deliberate vagueness, as improper reasons. Least Discretion is, like Impersonal Justification, a vertical factor, meant to address otherwise untempered asymmetries of power and authority. So as to keep the exposure to the office from being subordination to its occupant, Least Discretion requires that the office holder, Offe, exercise only so much discretion—that is, deliberative or motivated decision-making—in decisions about how to use the relevant office that Offe presently occupies as serves the impersonal reasons that justify that office.[1] If Offe could serve the impersonal reasons that justify the office just as well without this discretion, then Offe should not exercise this discretion.

In violating the Duty to Exclude, in deciding from an improper reason, however, our corrupt official, Grafton, is exercising just such discretion, violating Least Discretion. At least this is so if we understand an improper reason as a reason such that Grafton could serve the impersonal reasons that justify the office just as well without being sensitive to it, even if sensitivity to improper reasons, in any given case, might not mean Grafton served the impersonal reasons any worse. Insofar as Grafton does not exclude improper reasons, insofar as Grafton is sensitive to them, Grafton violates Least Discretion. Grafton exercises excess discretion—discretion beyond what Grafton needs—in order to serve the impersonal reasons that justify the office.

The paradigm cases of corruption, such as bribery or nepotism, consist in failing to exclude reasons of personal gain or the gain of one's nephews. These reasons are improper. Grafton doesn't need to be sensitive to them to serve the impersonal reasons that justify the office. Corruption thus "subverts the public to the private" by turning exposure to the asymmetric power of an impersonally justified office into subjection to the private person who occupies it. All those who are subject to the decisions of the office, therefore, have a complaint.

Why say, more restrictively, that a reason is improper if Grafton could execute the office just as well without being sensitive to it? Why not say, more permissively, that a reason is improper only if Grafton would execute the office worse if she were sensitive to it? For one thing, the more restrictive prohibition is more in keeping with the spirit of Least Discretion. And the more restrictive prohibition implies, as we sought, that Grafton's taking bribes to resolve underdetermined decisions still counts as a violation of the Duty to Exclude. For that is sensitivity to a reason—namely, the bribe—that does not serve the impersonal reasons that justify the office (even if it does not disserve those reasons either).

In underdetermined cases, Offe needs to make some decision. How should Offe decide, compatibly with the Duty to Exclude? A lottery among the options is the natural alternative to exercising discretion (that is, deliberative or motivated decision-making) among the options. The Duty to Exclude thus offers a second justification for using lotteries to distribute scarce, indivisible goods among equally compelling claimants, Dee and Dum. This justification is not, as in a highest fair chance lottery, to give Dee the highest chance of the good, compatibly with fairness to Dum. It is instead that a lottery gives Offe a way of deciding who will receive the good without being sensitive to an improper reason, such as that Offe happens to like the cut of Dee's jib.[2]

What of cases in which Grafton uses the office for, say, a bribe, but without exercising the office? The decision to use the office for that reason is itself an instance of discretionary (that is, deliberative or motivated) use of the office that is not required for the office to serve impersonal reasons. For Grafton, any further uses of the office, beyond those uses that are required for the office to serve impersonal reasons, should be off the table.

To say what the Duty to Execute or the Duty to Exclude requires in any given case, we need to know which decision-making processes enable the office, given the relevant background, to serve impersonal reasons. This is because the Duty to Execute says to follow those processes in exercising the office, and the Duty to Exclude says to exclude, in the use of the office, reasons not specified by such processes (reasons sensitivity to which does not serve impersonal reasons). What are these processes? To begin with, processes will better serve the impersonal reasons insofar as they are "accurate": insofar as they identify the particular decision that, in the circumstances, would best serve the impersonal reasons. If officials were omniscient, then a perfectly accurate decision-making process could be described in this way: "Identify the decision that, in the circumstances, best serves the impersonal reasons." But given human limitations, a more accurate process might involve deciding only on more concrete, proximate considerations: for example, to decide that this shipment should pass customs on the basis of a judgment that duties on its full value have been paid.

Moreover, accuracy isn't the only virtue. There is also the cost, speed, transparency, and predictability of the process; the incentives created when others expect the process in the future; and the relationships the process would foster or rupture. These factors may also argue for deciding on more concrete, proximate considerations. It may also be important, for democratic values or for pragmatic responses to disagreement, that the office can be occupied by people with a range of opinions on matters of policy, legal interpretation, and so forth. This argues against, for example, processes that are defined exclusively in the terms of a specific, contentious economic policy or jurisprudence. This implies that by deciding on the grounds that the decision best serves the public interest, most low-level officials would violate the Duty to Exclude. For many offices, that a decision would serve the public interest is itself an improper reason. A process in which low-level officials stepped back and tried to take in the big picture would serve the big picture worse.

A fortiori, the improper reasons need not consist in some benefit to oneself or those close to one. So, there can be violations of the Duty to Exclude that do not meet our initial definition of "official corruption," which specified acting for the benefit of oneself or those close to one. Nor need improper reasons be base. They might otherwise be morally praiseworthy, such as avuncular affection, a sense of gratitude (Teachout 2014; Lessig 2015, 91–99), devotion to a charitable cause, or loyalty to a foreign prince. Nor need there be a quid pro quo: an explicit, prearranged agreement that a specific official act will be performed in return for a specific personal favor.[3]

In all of this, there is the difficulty of specifying the "relevant background." What sort of concessions, if any, do we make to the "crooked timber" of humanity: to received habits or expectations, to temptation or ignorance, and so on? That is, to what extent do we "take men as they are"? And what sort of concessions, if any, do we make to imperfections elsewhere in the institutional structure? I note these difficulties without proposing to resolve them. I do observe, though, that our ambivalence about which reasons are improper may stem from our ambivalence about how concessive to imperfection we should be in specifying the relevant background. Consider (without necessarily accepting as accurate) Fukuyama's (2011, x–xiii) description of present-day Papua New Guinea. Each local *wantok* expects that its "Big Man," once elected to the national parliament, will simply try to siphon off as much public spending for it as he can. Pork-barrel politics is all there is. If we feel ambivalent about criticizing Big Men as corrupt, perhaps this is because, barring a profound change in the relevant culture, excluding such reasons would serve the relevant impersonal reasons worse. It would extinguish the traditional relationship of Big Man to his *wantok,* with no other source of social trust to replace it. Even in other societies, similar concessions may argue against otherwise desirable processes. Refusing to give or receive small favors, for example, might cause offense or weaken esprit de corps.

No doubt, all of this makes it murky and controversial where to draw the line between proper and improper reasons in any particular case. Nevertheless, we can explain the relative clarity and consensus in condemning paradigmatic cases of corruption, such as bribery and nepotism. The explanation is that even if we don't confidently agree on which reasons are proper, we may still confidently agree that benefits to oneself or one's relatives are not among them. Whether decisions to lease public land should be sensitive to environmental or business concerns, for example, all can confidently agree that they need not be sensitive to whether the lessee is the official's nephew. Whether legislators should be trustees or delegates, all can confidently agree that floor votes should not be sold for cash payments.[4]

Setting aside where to draw the line between proper and improper reasons, there is another problem. The Duty to Exclude might seem to police officials' motivations. It's not just that this is rigoristic. It also leads to paradox. If the Duty to Exclude says that officials can't be motivated by self-interest, why doesn't an official violate the Duty to Exclude by refusing a bribe from self-interested fear of penalties for bribery? As asked in Section 11.4, why aren't anti-corruption laws entrapment?

We need to distinguish. On the one hand, there is excluding certain considerations as reasons in one's decision-making. The Duty to Exclude does police this. On the other hand, there are the second-order reasons why one excludes those considerations: one's motivations for excluding them. The Duty to Exclude does not police this. It calls only for exclusion, not for exclusion from certain motives in particular. Different officials might exclude the same considerations, giving them no weight in decision-making, from a variety of different motives, such as fear of penalty, disaffected routine, or a desire to impress. If this seems puzzling, recall that one can exclude reasons externally by keeping oneself in ignorance of them (e.g., by screens, redactions) or by publicly committing to abiding by the result of a lottery. Excluding reasons of which one is aware internally, by sheer willpower, as it were, is just maintaining the last line of defense when these other methods are unavailing. Clearly, one can decide to exclude reasons externally from a variety of motives. Likewise, it seems, one can decide to exclude reasons internally from a variety of motives.

If, then, an official refuses the bribe, then their decision-making isn't sensitive to the bribe. This is so even if the reason they made their decision-making insensitive to the bribe is entirely self-interested, such as to avoid a penalty.[5] We might think less of them that they needed special incentives to exclude the bribe. But so long as they did exclude it, we have no complaint against them. The separation of office and occupant was thereby maintained.

12.3 Exploitative Offers as Violations of the Duty to Exclude

With the Duty to Exclude in hand, we can finally explain Employee's complaint about Boss's exploitative offer in Car Wash: namely, the offer to keep

Employee on if Employee washes Boss's car. Recall from end of Chapter 3 that this was the fly in the ointment in our effort to explain, in general, when and why Hablo's conditioning and announcing of a response to Audito's choice wrongs Audito. In most cases, we observed, the explanation was given by the Choice Principle: namely, that Hablo left Audito's choice situation worse than Audito was entitled to from Hablo. But Car Wash was a stubborn exception. For Boss's offer leaves Employee with, if anything, a better choice situation than Employee is entitled to from Boss: namely, Boss's firing Employee flat out.

With the Duty to Exclude, we have a fresh lead. As I argued in Chapter 9, Boss's superior power and authority over Employee, despite the presence of some tempering factors, makes the boss a kind of public official, subject to Impersonal Justification and Least Discretion and so to the Duty to Exclude. Observe, next, that firing Employee is an exercise of office and that conditioning or announcing firing Employee, whether or not it is an exercise of office, is certainly a use of office. Finally, observe that whether or not Employee washes Boss's car is not, in the main run of cases, a reason that serves the impersonal values that justify the asymmetry. The hierarchical structure of the firm, to be sure, serves some impersonal values. That social structure allows for efficient production, where transaction costs among autonomous producers would be prohibitive. But doing personal services for Boss plays no role in that justification.

Thus, firing Employee for not washing Boss's car violates the Duty to Exclude and so Least Discretion. So too does Boss's either conditioning or announcing it. It can be tempting to think that what is wrong about Car Wash has to do with Boss's attempt to get Employee to do his bidding (what we have called "steering") or Boss's interference in Employee's deliberation (Shaw 2012). But these are red herrings. Consider a variant of Car Wash where Boss only conditions, without announcing. In "Silent Car Wash," Boss, to impress his buddy, says: "I'm all set to fire that loser. But—check it out, Biff—if she volunteers to wash my car, then I won't." Boss still wrongs Employee, but now Boss does nothing to influence Employee's choice or affect her deliberations.[6] The source of the problem is simply what Boss is doing with his office.

Does this cover all wrongfully exploitative offers? In "Melodrama," Mater cannot pay for treatment that will save her child's life, and Mustache offers to pay for the treatment in return for sexual favors (Feinberg 1986)—or, dialing back the villainy, a kiss or some obsequious display. If Mustache has a duty of rescue to pay for the treatment, then the Choice Principle might explain straightaway why the offer is wrong. She is entitled to a choice situation in which Mustache will pay for the treatment whatever she decides to do and Mustache would wrong her by not paying for it. But, if the treatment is costly enough, then Mustache's paying for the treatment seems supererogatory. In that case, the offer would seem to improve her choice situation beyond what she is entitled to from Mustache. So the Choice Principle seems not to explain the case.

Melodrama differs from Car Wash in at least two ways. First, the asymmetry of power and authority is not established and ongoing. Still, while there is no established, ongoing relationship, that fact may not temper the relevant asymmetry. Mater is nonetheless in desperate need of what Mustache is able to provide—so desperate that, if not for the excessive cost to Mustache, he would have a duty of rescue to provide it. One might have thought that the argument for a social safety net is in part that it would prevent this sort of asymmetry from arising. The argument is not only that people should get aid when they need it but also that they shouldn't be made dependent in this way on others (Satz 2010). But this brings us to a second difference between the cases. While the asymmetry between Boss and Employee, we are supposing, serves impersonal reasons, the asymmetry between Mater and Mustache does not. Mater should not be dependent on Mustache in this way to begin with. So Least Discretion has nothing to apply to. What would it be for Mustache to use the asymmetry for proper reasons, which serve the impersonal reasons that justify that asymmetry? There are no impersonal reasons that justify that asymmetry.

Why then is Mustache's offer objectionable? One possibility is that Mustache thereby endorses the asymmetry of power over Mater, which is, as suggested in Section 5.2, part of what makes asymmetries of power objectionable in the first place. As Mustache should acknowledge, Mater should not be dependent on Mustache in this way. Now it's one thing if Mustache acts as he would if he were duty bound to provide the aid, accepting no more than compensation, a fair return, or a free gift after the fact. And it's one thing if he just opts not to help, as he would if he decided he has his own life to live. But it's quite another if he conveys that he embraces Mater's dependence on him by demanding favors or making a production of the fact that whether the child lives is up to him to decide, say, by ostentatiously flipping a coin.

12.4 Corruption without Inequality?

Official corruption, I have suggested, violates either the Duty to Execute or the Duty to Exclude and so, in turn, violates Impersonal Justification or Least Discretion. Impersonal Justification and Least Discretion are vertical tempering factors that address otherwise untempered asymmetries of power and authority between officials and those subject to them. To violate Impersonal Justification or Least Discretion is to remove the tempering factor: to let the asymmetry take an objectionably "personal" form. So, this complaint against official corruption, I am claiming, is, at root, a complaint against inferiority. One might question this, however. Is the complaint against official corruption necessarily a complaint against inferiority? To begin with, complaints against official corruption might be voiced by those, such as Confucians, otherwise at peace with hierarchy (as Teachout [2014, 282] notes). Surely theirs is a coherent position!

I wonder. First, it is not clear that these inegalitarian objections are to official corruption as we understand it—the violation of the Duty to Execute and the Duty to Exclude—as opposed to poor government more generally. Second, these objections might not be quite as inegalitarian as it might at first seem. They might instead express the position that, while hierarchy does need some tempering factors, Impersonal Justification and Least Discretion are sufficient tempering factors. Further tempering factors, such as Equal Influence, are not necessary. In other words, these inegalitarians aren't at peace with hierarchy tout court. They agree it is a problem needing some solution. They are at peace with hierarchy only insofar as officials abide by the Duties to Execute and Exclude. If that is their position, then nothing I have said so far implies that it is incoherent. Indeed, in some moods of democratic pessimism, I wonder whether their position might not be correct. In any case, the disagreement, if there is any, would not be about whether hierarchy poses a problem. Nor would it be about whether Impersonal Justification and Least Discretion are part of the solution to the problem. The disagreement would only be about whether they are the whole of the solution.[7]

There is another worry about the idea that the complaint against official corruption is a complaint against inferiority. Can't someone be wronged by Grafton's official corruption—broadly defined as Grafton's use of an institutional role for personal gain (see the start of Chapter 11)—even though Grafton's office does not involve an asymmetry of power or authority over that person? However, this too is not, in itself, a challenge to anything I have said. It would be a challenge only if there was a good argument that the wrong in the cases I discussed earlier, which did involve asymmetry, had to be the same kind of wrong as in these cases, which don't involve asymmetry. But when we consider particular cases, it's not clear that they do involve the same kind of wrong.

Consider a proposed counterexample, from Sophia Moreau, of official corruption without asymmetry. A lawyer in a civil case, Saul, fails to disclose documents to the opposing lawyer, Dooright, for personal gain. Whether Saul wrongs anyone else, surely Saul wrongs Dooright, who has a professional interest in winning cases. Yet Saul does not wield asymmetric power and authority over Dooright. However, I think we can explain, in other terms, how Saul wrongs Dooright. In a word, Saul cheats. The value of competitions (or their outcomes) typically depends on competitors, referees, and judges observing certain constraints on the means taken to bring it about that a given competitor wins (or achieves what but for the cheating would have counted as winning). Breaching such constraints—that is, cheating—wrongs those who have an interest in the relevant value. Note that breaching such constraints, unlike violating the Duty to Exclude, does not depend on the reasons for which Saul acts. Saul wrongs Dooright in the same way if he fails to disclose documents from carelessness or misunderstanding of the law.

13

Claims against Discrimination

We have now considered two commonplace claims: against the state and against corruption. In this chapter, we consider a commonplace claim against discrimination: against, roughly, adverse treatment on the basis of, or disparate outcomes that track, membership in "protected classes," such as gender, race, sexual orientation, or religion. In the first section, I make the case for the negative observation, arguing that complaints against discrimination cannot be fully explained as improvement complaints. In the second section, I propose the positive conjecture: that complaints against discrimination are often complaints against inferiority.

13.1 Claims against Discrimination: The Negative Observation

Can complaints against discrimination be explained as improvement complaints? To be sure, discrimination often does give rise to improvement complaints (Moreau 2010; Arneson 2013a; Lippert-Rasmussen 2014). Employment discrimination, for example, deprives someone of a chance for a job in a way that isn't required for fairness to others' chances. Still, even when discrimination does give rise to improvement complaints, there seems to be a "discrimination complaint" that goes beyond this. It's one thing to be denied a job because an employer is absentminded and happens to space out at the precise moment in the late afternoon when, as chance has it, they reach your application in the stack. It's another thing to be denied a job because you are transgender and the employer consciously or subconsciously views this as a minus.

Moreover, there can be discrimination complaints where there are no improvement complaints. Consider a set of admittedly stylized contrasts. Imagine, first, the Cold Society, in which every private person treats every other private person well enough that no one has any improvement complaint but does nothing more for anyone. Now contrast it with the Warm Society, in which everyone takes every opportunity to do more for everyone. Supererogation is the norm. Your neighbors help you move in, hold doors when you are struggling with groceries, drive your kids to school when you've slept through your alarm, and so on. Some in the Cold Society might well prefer that their society were more like the Warm Society. But none of them, even someone prepared to innovate, has a complaint (or much of one, at any rate) against anyone else. But now imagine the Half-Warm Society. Everyone now treats right-handed people in the ways everyone treats everyone in the Warm Society while treating left-handed people in the ways everyone treats everyone in the Cold Society.[1] It seems the left-handed in the Half-Warm Society have a discrimination complaint, even though they have no improvement complaint—or no more improvement complaint than anyone has in the Cold Society.

What is this distinctive discrimination complaint? Alexander (1992, 159, with second thoughts in 2016) suggests that the distinctive wrong of discrimination is that "a person is judged incorrectly to be of lesser moral worth and is treated accordingly." I don't doubt it is wrong to treat people as having less moral worth than they in fact have. But I doubt this can explain all the relevant discrimination complaints (compare Arneson 2013a; Lippert-Rasmussen 2014). First, discrimination complaints, as Alexander's own formulation implicitly acknowledges, seem to be comparative. They aren't complaints that one might have to a consistent amoralist, who underestimated everyone's moral worth.

Second, discrimination complaints apply only when the treatment tracks membership in a protected class, not when it is motivated by, say, personal animosity. It is a further question what a protected class is: how one should generalize from the paradigms of race or gender. Is it a class that one is not responsible for being a member of? Is it a class defined by some visible or salient trait? Is it a class that has been mistreated in the past? This last answer risks a kind of regress if the mistreatment in question is itself supposed to consist in discrimination. For then a group is discriminated against in the present only if that group was discriminated against in the past. But then how could discrimination of that group ever begin? To be sure, there may be a way to avoid this regress if we suppose the past mistreatment can be identified in terms other than discrimination, such as a failure to meet claims of improvement or a violation of rights against invasion. But no mistreatment of that kind is presupposed in the Half-Warm Society. Again, left-handed people are treated as everyone is treated in the Cold Society, where there is no mistreatment.

The final problem with Alexander's account is that there can be a discrimination complaint about differential treatment that does not involve any underestimation of moral worth. As I have described the Half-Warm Society, no one judges left-handed people to be of lesser moral worth any more than anyone in the Cold Society judges anyone to be of lesser moral worth. People in the Half-Warm Society simply withhold supererogatory treatment from left-handed people on the grounds that they are left-handed. They don't overthink it.

13.2 Claims against Discrimination: The Positive Conjecture

In the last section, we saw, as another instance of our negative observation, that ordinary complaints against discrimination are not always or entirely improvement complaints. Even when discrimination gives rise to an improvement complaint, as it often does, there is still a further complaint that goes beyond that. Absentmindedness is one thing, transphobia another. And we can imagine discrimination, as in our hyperstylized Half-Warm Society, that gives rise to no improvement complaints at all. In this section, we turn to the positive conjecture. The residual discrimination complaint is a complaint against inferiority. More specifically, it is a complaint about a disparity of regard, which is neither merited nor tempered in that it is ongoing, inescapable, pervasive, and not cabined to any one time, place, or context.

Discrimination is a certain kind of untempered, unmerited disparity of regard. What distinguishes discrimination from other such disparities in regard is that the disparity "tracks" a basing trait across various social settings and institutions. Put another way, the basing trait serves as a focal point, which allows people and institutions across society to coordinate in giving greater regard to some than to others, depending on whether they have or lack the trait.[2] This coordination makes the disparity untempered: ongoing, pervasive, and inescapable. It is one thing if a lone stranger, here and there, does a good turn for someone else but not for you. It is something else if everyone does this.

Earlier I asked what counts as a "protected class" such that treating people differently based on their membership in that class gives rise to a discrimination complaint. How should we generalize from the cases of race and gender? I now suggest that a "protected class" is simply any group defined by a basing trait around which an untempered, unmerited disparity of regard has gathered (or threatens to gather). What matters is simply that the basing trait serves as a focal point of coordination, which in turn makes the disparity untempered. That's all that's required of the basing trait to make discrimination possible.

The relevant basing trait, therefore, needn't be visible or salient, so long as it can be tracked in some other way. Nor need the basing trait be one for which the bearer is not responsible: a trait they cannot choose or were born with. This is as it should be. It does not make discrimination against race and gender acceptable that people can, in some cases, successfully "pass" or change their birth gender (Boxill 1992, 12–17). Nor, as we saw in Section 6.3, is it obvious that it would be acceptable to graft the pattern of consideration characteristic of an aristocratic order onto meritocratic competitions, simply replacing lineages with test scores as the basing trait, even if people are responsible for success in those competitions.

Protected classes are sometimes defined as classes that have been subject to discrimination in the not-too-distant past. I worried that this risked a regress. In order to be discriminated against now, the class would have to have been discriminated against in the past, and in order to have been discriminated against in the past, the class would have to have been discriminated against in the further past, and so on. How could discrimination ever start? The present suggestion avoids this regress since it does not define protected classes as those that have been subject to discrimination in the past. All that matters is that their basing trait is a focal point for a disparity of regard now. That said, there is something right in the suggestion that protected classes are classes that have been subject to discrimination in the not-too-distant past. This is because of the second sort of "recursion" as discussed in Section 6.4: namely, that a response that would not express an endorsement of a relation of inferiority may express such an endorsement because of a history of relations of inferiority. A response to a basing trait that would not otherwise count as lesser regard can come to have that meaning within a not-to-distant past of lesser regard for people with that trait. In this way, what would not otherwise be discrimination may become discrimination because of existing discrimination. Consider an example, discussed by Hellman (2008), of a principal segregating Black and White students for a school photo, which might have been an innocuous aesthetic choice, like clustering taller people in the center, if not for the history of segregation by race.

I can now explain our misgivings at the end of the previous section about Alexander's suggestion that the distinctive wrong of discrimination is rooted in judging a person to be of lesser moral worth. I observed, first, that as Alexander's own formulation reveals, the discrimination complaint seems to be a comparative objection to a judgment of lesser moral worth than others have. It's not the objection one might have to a consistent amoralist, who underestimated everyone's moral worth. I have now explained why this is. In the case of the consistent amoralist, there is no disparity of regard. Second, we worried that there seems to be a further objection when the underestimation of moral worth is based on one's being a member of a protected class, such as race or gender, as opposed, say, to being a judgment motivated by some personal jealousy, enmity, or dislike. In the latter cases, but not the former, the tempering factors are absent. Personal animosity is typically localized in time, place, and context, limited in its effects, and escapable. There is not coordination, facilitated by the basing trait's role as a focal point, on a disparity of regard. Finally, we worried that there can be a discrimination complaint about differential treatment that does not involve any underestimation of moral worth, as in the Half-Warm Society. This is because, as we saw, there can be a disparity of regard without any underestimation of moral worth.

This account of discrimination might explain why people have complaints about discriminatory patterns of responses in society. But, one might ask, does it explain why the victim of some specific discriminatory response has a special complaint about that specific response and not just a complaint about the broader pattern or others' support of it? It does. Their complaint is that, on this occasion, a specific person related to them as an inferior, in the sense explained in Section 5.5. Granted, in the absence of the broader social pattern, the same treatment would not have counted as responding to them as an inferior, and so they would not have had that complaint about it. But this is compatible with their complaint still being against that specific response toward them, not only about the social pattern. Something can be a condition of a complaint without being the only thing (or without even being one of the things) it is a complaint against.

Indeed, what is ordinarily meant by "discriminating against you," I suggest, is giving you lesser regard as part of a system of differential regard that tracks a basing trait. However, the complaint that someone has discriminated against you is only one kind of discrimination complaint that you may have. You may also have a discrimination complaint against, as it were, bystanders, who don't themselves discriminate but fail to take measures to combat discrimination by others or otherwise support or acquiesce in the system.

What does it mean to say that the disparity of regard "tracks" a basing trait? The most straightforward way is that the "judges" whether the judges are people or institutions—categorize the judged people as having the basing trait and show differential regard on the grounds of that categorization. This would correspond to one understanding of direct discrimination. Note, however, that this judged categorization might be unconscious or implicit.

However, there are at least two other ways of tracking a basing trait. First, paradoxically, the lesser regard may partly consist in the judges being insensitive, rather than sensitive, to the basing trait or to people who have it. Consider the phenomenon of structural accommodation described in Section 6.3, where design choices overlook the needs of people with disabilities. Similarly, noticing only the other hotel guests but not the hotel staff is itself a disparity of regard, even though, insofar as one does not notice the staff at all, one does not judge them to have any traits.

Second, although the judges' regard is not sensitive to their categorization (if any) of the judged as having the basing trait, their regard might be sensitive to a factor that is correlated with that basing trait. This corresponds to one understanding of indirect discrimination. Imagine that women are paid less than men for the same work only because men, perhaps due to overconfidence, are more likely to press for higher pay in negotiations. Insofar as pay is a way of valuing contributions, and insofar as valuing contributions is a form of regard, employers show lesser regard for women in a way that tracks that they are women. At least given the broader disparity of regard between men and women, this supports the conclusion that employers discriminate against women. In principle, there might be a system of discrimination that was entirely indirect in this way. In that case, it might be a discovery to all involved that the disparity of regard even existed. However, in practice, systems of discrimination are usually anchored by direct discrimination. Indirect discrimination only sustains or amplifies it. For example, educational institutions deny members of the disfavored group access on the explicit grounds of some basing trait, and promotions are then conditioned on tests, which are impossible to pass without the relevant education.

While this account covers many forms of indirect or implicit discrimination, it admittedly does not cover, so to speak, egalitarian discrimination. Suppose that a culture believes in a gendered division of labor, although (somehow) this is in no way linked to asymmetries in power or authority or disparities of regard (Lippert-Rasmussen 2014, 41). Or suppose that two equal groups just do supererogatory things for their own members, without any suggestion of a hierarchy, just as members of different families do. If there really is no connection whatsoever to hierarchy, then, I submit, the problem, if there is one, is different. In the gendered labor case, for example, the problem is just that everyone is pointlessly limited by their gender in the opportunities they can pursue.

This account may also seem to overlook cases of wrongful discrimination against members of a group that do not involve any broader pattern of discrimination against that group. Consider Hellman's (2008, 41) example of a "state law forbidding people with freckles from voting," Eidelson's (2015, 30) example of "a firm [giving] preference in hiring to blond-haired applicants . . . even if hair color bears little significance in social life writ large," or Moreau's (2020, 141–142) real-life example of "heterosexual couples in the U.K. who claim that they are wrongfully discriminated against if they are not, like same-sex couples, allowed the option of entering into a civil partnership." While I agree that there may be a complaint in such cases, and indeed a complaint against inferiority, it is different in kind from complaints about discrimination on the basis of sex or race. Notice that it is essential to these cases, where there is no systematic coordination on a disfavored basing trait, that it is the state or some official (e.g., the firm's human resources officer) directly distributing some benefit or privilege unequally. If it were merely a private person distributing a benefit unequally, then it would be less clear that it was wrongful. If you choose to pick up only hitchhikers with freckles, or Freemasons, or whatever, that's your affair. This suggests that the complaint in such cases is about a violation of a norm of equal treatment that applies to the state or, at any rate, to officials. That there is such a norm is our next commonplace claim.

14

Claims to Equal Treatment

Suppose that the state provides a benefit, *B*, for one citizen, Tweedle Dee, that it does not provide for another citizen, Tweedle Dum. The benefit might be some positive good or service, such as roads, schools, or disaster relief. Or it might be exemption from some rule, duty, or penalty. Suppose, further, that there is no "justifying difference" between Dee and Dum, no positive reason for this difference in treatment. When the state does this, Dum is often thought to have a complaint of unequal treatment by the state, which is expressed in comparative terms: that the state is favoring Dee over Dum or that since the state gave *B* to Dee, it should also give *B* to Dum. Call the principle thereby violated "Equal Treatment by the State." The issue is one of, as is sometimes said, comparative justice or treating likes alike.

A similar complaint can be leveled against certain nonstate officers, such as teachers, administrators, employers, or even custodians of children, when they provide a benefit, *B*, to one student, administratee, employee, or child in their custody, Dee, but not to another, Dum, when there is no justifying difference between them. When this occurs, Dum is often thought to have a complaint of unequal treatment by an official—or "favoritism"—which is expressed in similarly comparative terms. Call the principle thereby violated "Equal Treatment by Officials."

Unequal treatment complaints are not much discussed in the philosophical literature, with some notable exceptions being Greenawalt (1983), Gosepath (2015), and Scanlon (2018, chap. 2). Perhaps this is in part because the principle to "treat like cases alike" seems straightforward (Berlin [1956] 1997, 302; Hart 1992, 160), uncontroversial, or empty (Westen 1982). However, unequal treatment complaints seem at least as common in actual political discourse as complaints that states or officials are simply not doing enough for people in absolute terms. Equal treatment complaints, moreover, are often especially rhetorically potent. This may be, in part, because they are often easier to establish. One only needs to show that one group isn't getting the same as another group, whatever "the same" happens to be. One doesn't need to show that it is the right amount in some absolute sense. That people have a claim to equal treatment by the state or by officials seems to merit the appellation of a "commonplace claim."

14.1 Claims to Equal Treatment: The Negative Observation

Once again, our question is: Can we explain these apparently comparative, equal treatment complaints as noncomparative, improvement complaints? If not, then we have another instance of our negative observation. One might suggest, to the contrary, that equal treatment complaints are really noncomparative, improvement complaints in disguise. Dum's complaint is really just that the state or official could have given *B* to Dum. That the state in fact gave *B* to Dee is immaterial.[1] But I doubt this, for several reasons. First, suppose that the state or official provides *B* to neither Dee nor Dum but that each has a claim to *B*, with the result that each has an improvement complaint. If those improvement complaints were all that were at issue, then the state's or official's now giving *B* to Dee but not to Dum would only subtract a complaint. But, intuitively, it seems to add one (Greenawalt 1983, 1173).

Second, suppose *B* cannot be given to Dum. A case of this so common as to be overlooked is the application of the same rule to different people at different times. Here the benefit, *B*, is exemption from the rule. The state or official, applying the rule, required something of Dum in the past but now faces the question of whether to require it similarly of Dee. Dum has no improvement complaint about what the state now does for Dee, since that has no bearing on what the state could have done for Dum. Still, Dum might seem to have an equal treatment complaint about exempting Dee. When, in the office of teacher or administrator, I'm asked for an extension, waiver, exception, or so on that I've denied before, I hear myself saying, "What would I tell the other people I've already said no to?"

Finally, consider cases in which neither Dee nor Dum would have an improvement complaint if they did not receive *B*. Giving *B* to anyone is either supererogatory or discretionary. Still, if the state or official gives *B* to Dee,

Dum may have an equal treatment complaint that the state does not give *B* to Dum too (Scanlon 2018, 17).

One might wonder whether anything can be supererogatory for the state. The state isn't a person who can say: "I've done enough for others; I have my own life to lead." Of course, the state may rein in current expenditures to save for a rainy day, but this is for the benefit of people when the rain comes, not for raisons d'état. However, first, when the benefit, *B*, is the extra time or effort of an official beyond what can otherwise be fairly asked of them, we can speak of supererogation. If the official volunteers that extra effort for Dee, then Dum has a complaint if the official doesn't similarly do so for Dum. Second, even if the state is not a person with its own life to lead, still the state's giving *B* to Dee or Dum may be supererogatory with respect to what the state must do for Dee or Dum. In that case, presumably, giving *B* to Dee or Dum unfairly burdens some third party, Tercero, by, for example, reducing services, raising taxes, or increasing risk. If the state nonetheless gives *B* to Dee, then the state now has a reason to give *B* to Dum too. This might unfairly burden Tercero. In that case, meeting Dum's equal treatment complaint by "leveling up," by giving *B* to Dum too, would conflict with Tercero's improvement complaint not to be burdened unfairly. However, giving *B* to Dum too might not unfairly burden Tercero. There may be slack or waste in the system that already unfairly burdens Tercero. Using some of that slack to give *B* to Dum too, assuming it would not go to Tercero anyway, would not add to Tercero's burdens. Moreover, the state's or official's decision might be not supererogatory but instead discretionary. That is, the state's or official's decision whether to provide people with benefit *B* or instead a different benefit *B'* is tied or incommensurable. In that case, no would-be recipient of *B* such as Dum has an improvement complaint if *B'* is provided instead. But if *B* is provided to Dee, then Dum does have an equal treatment complaint if *B* isn't provided to Dum, absent a justifying difference.

So far, then, it seems that equal treatment complaints resist reduction as improvement complaints. However, equal treatment complaints need some escape clause. For example, Dum may have no equal treatment complaint if Dee needs medical care that Dum does not or Dum's parents already provide Dum with school lunch. And once we clarify what the escape clause is, one might argue, equal treatment complaints will reduce to improvement complaints.

Scanlon suggests the following escape clause. Dum has a complaint only if the state's or the official's giving *B* to Dee but not Dum "would be unjustified if the interests of all those affected were given appropriate weight" (2018, 19, or "sufficient" and the "same" weight, 21). But this clause allows too much to escape. Suppose that the state or official, giving Dee's interests appropriate weight, correctly determines that giving *B* to Dee is optional: giving *B* to Dee is not unjustified but also not giving *B* to Dee is not unjustified. Knowing that Dum is in exactly the same situation as Dee, the state or official, in giving *B* to Dee but not to Dum, does something that would not be unjustified if the interests of all were equally given their appropriate weight.

What I think Scanlon should say instead is that Dum has an equal treatment complaint just when the state or official gives *B* to Dee but not to Dum, unless some difference between Dee and Dum justifies not giving *B* to Dum. In other words, equal treatment is the default, unless there is a "justifying difference" between them. It is sometimes said that treating likes alike also requires treating different cases differently (Hart 1992, 159). But this doesn't follow. There is no default to treat different cases differently, pending some showing of a "justifying similarity." A justifying difference will have to be an impersonally justified difference. It cannot be a justifying difference, for example, that Dee is my nephew. By contrast, it could be a justifying difference that Dee needs medical care that Dum does not or that Dum's parents already provide Dum with school lunch. More generally, a justifying difference for giving *B* to Dee rather than to Dum will often be that giving *B* to Dee rather than to Dum will more fairly satisfy improvement interests (including, perhaps, the improvement interests of third parties, such as those who benefit from a job's being given to Dee rather than to Dum).

But if we say that, in general, a justifying difference for giving *B* to Dee but not to Dum just is that this will more fairly serve improvement interests, does it follow that equal treatment complaints collapse into improvement complaints? It does not follow. First, equal treatment complaints can arise in cases without any such justifying difference in, say, need or ability to pay. Dum might need the medical care just as much or leave for school just as bereft of lunch. Second, the appeal to justifying differences is a defense of the unequal provision of *B* to Dee but not to Dum. When there is equal provision of *B* to Dee and Dum, no defense is called for. So, while there need not be an equal treatment complaint about means-tested benefits—since Dee's having more limited means is a justifying difference—there also need not be an equal treatment complaint about non-means-tested benefits that are equally provided—since no justifying difference needs to be adduced in the first place. Finally, when the state or official cannot give *B* to Dum (say, because it enforced the rule in Dum's case) but can give *B* to Dee (say, by exempting Dee from the rule), it would better satisfy improvement claims to give *B* to Dee. It would be an inequality-increasing weak Pareto improvement. But it is not obvious that this fact counts as a justifying difference.

Equal Treatment suggests a third argument for lotteries, besides giving highest fair chances (Section 1.4) or excluding improper reasons (Section 12.2). If an official actually gives Dee some chance of *B*, then Equal Treatment requires that the official give Dum the same chance of B, unless there is some justifying difference between them. Note that such "equal chance lotteries" do not require the official to maximize the chances of either Dee or Dum. Equal chance lotteries require only that each have equal chances. So, an equal chance lottery might be to flip a fair coin twice and award *B* to Dee if the outcome is both heads, to Dum if the outcome is both tails, and to neither if the outcome is mixed.

If improvement complaints don't explain equal treatment complaints, then what does? It isn't clear.[2] And making the matter more challenging is that equal treatment complaints pattern in distinctive ways.[3] First, Dum has a complaint of unequal treatment by a state, *S*, only if Dum is a citizen, or at least a resident, of *S*. If Dum is a nonresident alien, then Dum may have a humanitarian complaint about foreign aid being too low but not the sort of comparative complaint residents have that they don't have access to the same benefits as other residents (Scanlon 2018). Similarly, Dum has a complaint of unequal treatment by an official only when Dee and Dum stand in the same relevant relationship to that official.

Second, Dum does not have a complaint against a private person, Benny, who gives *B* to Dee but not Dum, unless either this differential treatment contributes to a pattern of discrimination or Benny stands in some special relationship, of the same kind, to Dee and Dum (such as that Benny is the parent of Dee and Dum).[4] In general, if you do something supererogatory for one person, such as pick up one hitchhiker, you don't have to do it for everyone, even if there is no justifying difference. Such random acts of kindness are permitted.

Third, equal treatment complaints differ from discrimination complaints. On the one hand, discrimination complaints arise not only against the state or officials but also against private strangers, as happens in the Half-Warm Society (Section 13.1). On the other hand, Dum can have an equal treatment complaint even if the state's or the official's differential treatment has nothing to do with Dee and Dum belonging to different protected classes. The state or official might favor Dee for other reasons.

Fourth, equal treatment complaints apply to what the state or the official directly provides. If you pave your private driveway up to the public thoroughfare, but I do not pave mine, I do not have any equal treatment complaint about this, even though the state permitted, in Rawls's terms, a basic structure that let it come to pass that your private driveway but not mine was paved. Finally, equal treatment complaints are typically triggered by inequalities in specific benefits—per-pupil spending across districts or exemption from certain rules—without a detailed accounting of overall net receipts. There may be other kinds of localization or compartmentalization, such as differentiation by age cohort. If kids these days get better schooling, their elders may not have a complaint. If a rule is repealed, those who were bound by the rule in the past may not have a complaint.

One might wonder, though, why we are making such hard work of this. Equal treatment is easy to explain. It just follows from the general moral principle of simple fairness, of treating like cases alike, of following rules (Berlin [1956] 1997, 305), of not making arbitrary distinctions. This response, however, overlooks two difficulties. First, a general moral principle of simple fairness, or treating like cases alike, or not making arbitrary distinctions, would explain too much. There isn't a requirement to treat like cases alike in general. Again, the requirement applies only to states and officials, only with respect to people who stand in the same relationship to them, only with respect to direct provision, and only with respect to certain goods. In our ordinary dealings with people, by contrast, we aren't required to treat like cases alike. We don't wrong people by performing random acts of kindness. Second, this response doesn't explain why we should care about simple fairness, or treating like alike, or not making arbitrary distinctions. What is at stake? Why not regard it as a foolish consistency, Emerson's "hobgoblin of little minds"? Why isn't it "rule worship" to adhere to the rule applied to Dum when violating it in the case of Dee does no harm to the purposes the rule is supposed to serve?

14.2 Claims to Equal Treatment by the State: The Positive Conjecture

In the last section, I registered the negative observation with respect to the commonplace claims to Equal Treatment by the State and by Officials. These norms cannot be explained by interests in improvement. We now turn, as usual, to the positive conjecture. I propose an explanation of Equal Treatment by the State in this section and an explanation of Equal Treatment by Officials in the next. Each is explained by a claim against inferiority, but in a different way.

Recall the horizontal tempering factor of Equal Consideration of Section 8.9. There is a more stringent requirement on the state to show equal consideration for those subject to it than there is on private persons, such as randomly kind drivers, to display equal consideration for one another. For the most part, the only requirement on private persons, not acting in any official capacity, with respect to disparities of consideration is simply to refrain from contributing to patterns of discrimination, which coordinate a disparity of consideration on basing traits. The state, by contrast, is required to show equal consideration even absent any pattern of discrimination, any coordination on basing traits. Recall also that Equal Consideration gains further support from Equal Citizenship. Insofar as the state shows equal consideration for those subject to it, it constitutes them as equal citizens and so provides them with at least one relationship in which they stand to one another as equals, whatever other hierarchy there may be in society. From Equal Consideration, Equal Treatment by the State follows as a special case. In general, to give a benefit *B* to Dee but not to Dum, absent a justifying difference between them, is to show greater consideration for Dee than for Dum. So, insofar as the state is required to show equal consideration for Dee and Dum, it is required to refrain from giving *B* to Dee but not to Dum, absent a justifying difference.

Moreover, this explains why Equal Treatment by the State patterns in the way it does. It is because Equal Treatment by the State is a special case of Equal Consideration that it applies to what the state directly provides. An agent's providing something directly is that agent's treatment and expression in a way an agent's merely countenancing something to be provided, via the intervention of other agencies, is not. What one says oneself is a more significant expression of one's state of mind, for example, than what one suffers others to say. Thus, when the state unequally provides something that it directly provides, this is a more significant expression of the state's unequal consideration than when something, via the actions of the state and intervening agencies, is unequally provided. This, in turn, assumes a distinction between what the state directly does and what it indirectly allows to happen. In the latter case, what happens is more the result of independent initiative by other agents, who, even if regulated by the state in what they do, are not implementing its directives or carrying out its express charges. This means that, for present purposes, the state may be something less than Rawls's basic structure, insofar as the basic structure includes some of those regulated but not directed or charged agents, such as participants in a market economy.

One might worry that this makes it too easy for the state to slip the fetters of Equal Treatment by the State. All it needs to do is "privatize" (Patten 2014, sec. 4.4). However, first, much that goes by the name of "privatization" would not be "indirect" in the relevant sense. The state's contracting with nonstate employees to do what state employees would be in their place directed to do, for example, makes little difference. Those "private contractors" are still carrying out the state's express charges. Second, there are reasons against replacing direct provision even with genuinely indirect provision. One is simply that people might be worse served by indirect provision. Another reason against indirect provision is that it would undermine Equal Citizenship. Granted, the state might fully satisfy Equal Treatment by providing equally little to everyone. After all, the Aztec Empire trivially satisfied Equal Treatment with respect to you and me by giving neither of us anything. But if the state provides equally sufficiently much to everyone, then it provides them with Equal Citizenship. That is something the Aztec Empire, despite its flawlessly equal treatment, does not provide us with.

My proposal, that Equal Treatment by the State is a special case of Equal Consideration, also explains why Dum has no equal treatment complaint when Dum is a nonresident alien of the state in question. In that case, Dum's relations to that state are not ongoing, pervasive, and inescapable, and that state does not play the same final, regulating role over Dum's society. This proposal also explains why Dum can have an equal treatment complaint even if the unequal treatment does not stem from Dee's and Dum's belonging to different protected classes and so is not, in that sense, discriminatory. The root objection is to an untempered disparity of consideration. Again, the disparity in this case is untempered not, as in the case of discrimination, because of coordination across many agents on some disfavored basing trait but instead because it is the state whose consideration is at issue. This proposal further explains why equal treatment complaints typically apply to specific benefits. Giving people the same benefits is typically, given the cognitive limits of interpretation, a less ambiguous expression of equal consideration than compensating lesser provision of a certain good with greater provision of another.

Finally, this proposal suggests that what counts as a "justifying difference" will similarly depend, in part, on the contingencies of what expresses what. Perhaps the fact that the state cannot give *B* to Dum (because, say, the rule was already applied in Dum's case) but can now give *B* to Dee might be enough for the unequal provision not to express unequal consideration. But, then again, it might be less ambiguous, and more of a positive statement of equal consideration, simply not to give *B* to Dee under the circumstances.

One might object: "You grant that what counts as equal consideration depends, in part, on 'what expresses what.' What if prevailing interpretations were such that the state cannot express unequal consideration by how it henceforth acts so long as it henceforth acts in whatever way brings it about, directly or indirectly, that interests in improvement are best satisfied overall, treating any mistakes it might have made in the past as water under the bridge? In that case, once the state determined how best to satisfy improvement claims going forward, Equal Consideration would impose no further constraint on its deliberations." In reply, it's not clear that, given the general cognitive limits of interpretation, what expresses what is so malleable. And in any event, even if we grant that Equal Consideration imposed no independent constraint, it would still be a further reason to satisfy improvement claims (at least within a given society).

14.3 Claims to Equal Treatment by Officials: The Positive Conjecture

In the previous section, I explained why the state, in particular, is under the requirement of Equal Treatment by the State. The positive conjecture appealed to the horizontal factors of Equal Consideration and Equal Citizenship. However, that explanation appealed to special characteristics of the state. It is less clear that this explanation applies to many nonstate offices, such as teachers, administrators, employers, and custodians of children. Yet they too are under requirements of equal treatment. So, what accounts for Equal Treatment by Officials? Why is it the case that when an official, Offe, provides a benefit, *B,* for one person subject to the office, Dee, that Offe does not provide for another person subject to the office, Dum, when there is no justifying difference between Dee and Dum, Dum has a complaint? Again, the answer will appeal to claims against inferiority, but in a different way.

The answer might seem obvious: a violation of Equal Treatment by Officials is a violation of the Duty to Exclude. To be sure, Offe might decide to benefit Dee, or not to benefit Dum, for a reason that does not serve the impersonal reasons that justify the office. Perhaps Dee is Offe's nephew, or perhaps Dum refused to pay Offe a bribe. In that case, in violating Equal Treatment, Offe would be violating the Duty to Exclude. But consider the following possibility. If Offe were to follow decision-making process *A,* which conforms to the Duty to Exclude, Offe might decide to grant Dee an exemption. However, if Offe were to follow a different (or perhaps even the same) decision-making process, *B,* which also conforms to the Duty to Exclude, Offe might decide to deny Dee an exemption. In other words, Dee's case might be underdetermined, such that Offe could reach either decision without violating the Duty to Exclude. Now imagine that Dee's case is, in fact, like this. Then Offe might grant the exemption to Dee but not to Dum, while conforming all the while to the Duty to Exclude. So not all violations of Equal Treatment by Officials are violations of the Duty to Exclude. We need some other explanation of Equal Treatment by Officials.

Even if, by violating Equal Treatment by Officials, Offe does not violate the Duty to Exclude, Offe still violates the broader principle of Least Discretion from which the Duty to Exclude derives. Offe, exercising discretion, has granted an exemption to Dee. Holding that fixed, why shouldn't Offe simply apply to Dum whatever judgment was reached in Dee's case? Why should Offe have the further discretion to deny Dum an exemption, assuming there is no justifying difference between Dee and Dum? This seems like unjustified, excess discretion, which does not serve impersonal reasons. So Offe's unequal treatment violates Least Discretion. To be sure, we're not denying that a decision-making process that leaves Offe with discretion may serve impersonal reasons. The point of offices is largely to reap the benefits of Offe's exercise of judgment about particular cases. But once it is settled that, exercising that judgment, Offe has reached a certain decision in Dee's case, nothing is lost if Offe henceforth applies the same judgment to every case that in all relevant respects, as Offe acknowledges, is the same as Dee's. (Moreover, it seems that some things are gained. Offe doesn't have to rethink the case. And Dum now knows what the decision in his case will be.)

In sum, Equal Treatment by Officials is, like the Duty to Exclude, a special case of Least Discretion. Equal treatment curbs what would otherwise be the excess discretion of officials. At first glance, Equal Treatment by Officials, like Equal Treatment by the State, might appear to be concerned with maintaining horizontal equality among the various people subject to the office. But this appearance is misleading. Insofar as Equal Treatment by Officials is explained by Least Discretion, it is concerned, instead, with avoiding a vertical relation of superiority of the natural person who occupies the office over anyone subject to it.

Consider now three objections to this proposed explanation of Equal Treatment by Officials. First, Least Discretion implies something broader than Equal Treatment by Officials. By the same logic, Least Discretion should rule out inconsistent treatment of a single person, over time, by an official. For that too is "excess" discretion. Is this not an overgeneralization? No, on reflection, it seems to me the right result. There is a recognizable complaint against an official who grants you an exception one day but not the next while acknowledging that there is no relevant difference between the cases, other than, apparently, how they feel from one moment to the next. This brings out the point just made that insofar as Equal Treatment by Officials stems from Least Discretion, it is not really concerned with maintaining horizontal equality among the various people subject to the office. It is concerned, instead, with a kind of limitation of official discretion, which is itself, in turn, called for in order to avoid a vertical relation of superiority of the natural person who occupies the office over anyone subject to it.[5] By contrast, Equal Treatment by the State, which is based on the horizontal factors of Equal Consideration and Equal Citizenship, is concerned with equality among people subject to the state.

Second objection: What if Offe simply made a mistake in, say, denying Dum an exemption in the past? In that case, in granting Dee the exemption, Offe is simply saving Dee from Offe's past mistake. This sort of discretion is not unjustified. It corrects an error. So, Dum has no complaint, at least on the grounds of Least Discretion, in this case. But, intuitively, it may be thought, Dum does have a complaint. Perhaps, however, the complaint is simply the noncomparative complaint that Offe made the mistake in Dum's case—a complaint Dum would have even if Dee hadn't appeared on the scene.

Final objection: Suppose Offe denies Dum the exemption but grants it to Dee, even though there is no justifying difference. Our proposal suggests that not only Dum but also, oddly, Dee has a complaint against Offe: namely, that Offe violated Least Discretion by not applying the same judgment to them both. Indeed, this objection is a more general objection to Least Discretion, even when Least Discretion appears under the guise of the Duty to Exclude, rather than Equal Treatment by Officials, and even when what is at stake is the noncomparative treatment of one person, rather than the comparative treatment of two. If Grafton uses her office to benefit someone subject to the office on a mere whim, then that too is a violation of Least Discretion. I grant that it may sound odd. But I suspect the oddity is just the general oddity of one's complaining about an action that benefits one. In many cases, the oddity has to do with the "affirmation dynamic" illuminated by Wallace (2013): that is, that there is a tension in regretting the necessary conditions of something that we affirm. How can we complain of, and so regret, the act while affirming the benefit it brought us? But, as Wallace (2013) observes, that tension doesn't change the fact that the act gives us grounds for complaint. So, I would maintain, as Least Discretion implies, that even when someone subject to the office is benefitted by a violation of Least Discretion, such as a favor granted on a whim, they have a complaint about it, even if there is some oddity or tension in their complaining of it. Consider "a case reported a number of years ago when a judge told a defendant convicted of a reasonably serious crime that he would ordinarily send him to prison, but would not because it was the judge's birthday" (Bingham 2010, 53). The defendant, at least if they had a healthy self-respect, might have felt mixed emotions.

15

Claims to the Rule of Law

We are now in a position to see how the secondary tempering factors we have discussed so far help explain another commonplace claim: the claim to the rule of law. These secondary tempering factors, taken together, support many, although not all, of the elements of the complex ideal of the rule of law. Among the main elements are:

1. "Constraint": Officials follow the law or are constrained by the law in making new law (Bingham 2010, chap. 4).
2. "Equality": Officials treat like cases alike. No one is above the law. The law treats equally those subject to it, and each has equal access to the courts (Bingham 2010, chap. 5).
3. "Noncorruption": Officials are not corrupt (Raz 1977; Bingham 2010, chap. 6).
4. "Impersonality": Rule is, in some sense, "by law, not by men" (Hayek 1960; Tamanaha 2004, 122–126).
5. "Guidance": The law purports to guide those subject to it (Hayek 1944; Fuller 1969; Raz 1977; Hart 1992, 207; Bingham 2010, chap. 3).

Other features of the rule of law, such as that the law must be prospective, stable, clear, knowable, and general (or at least regulated by law that is such), seem to be consequences of these elements. Guidance and Noncorruption, in most circumstances, require these features. And Equality implies a certain stability and generality.

The secondary tempering factors support many of the main elements of the rule of law. Least Discretion straightforwardly supports Constraint. Equal Influence also supports Constraint. For Equal Influence, as we will see, requires that, when laws have been made in a way that grants all equal opportunity for informed, autonomous influence, officials execute or respect those laws. If they do not, then they deprive others of that equal opportunity. (This reason to obey specifically democratic law is simply the answer to what we call, in Chapter 24, the "Question of Authority," as applied to officials.) Least Discretion, via Equal Treatment by Officials, also supports Equality, insofar as it requires that officials treat like cases alike.[1] Equal Consideration, via Equal Treatment by the State, supports Equality. Insofar as the state directly provides a system of legal enforcement and redress to some, it should provide it to all. Equal Application supports Equality, insofar as those who make the law are themselves subject to it.

Reflecting on the law, one might be tempted anew to reduce the principle of treating like cases alike to something else. One might argue, "Isn't the principle of treating like cases alike just a by-product of the correct application of a rule (Hart 1992, 161; Westen 1982)? Granted, existing rules may underdetermine the decision in some particular case. But when an official makes a decision in that case, they are promulgating a new rule. Thus, the apparent pressure to treat all like cases in the future alike is simply the pressure to follow the newly promulgated rule." First, while it is natural to view many judicial decisions in a common-law system as promulgating new rules, it isn't a natural interpretation of many other official decisions, even judicial ones, such as sentencing. And yet the apparent pressure to treat all like cases in the future alike applies to these other decisions. Second, in any event, it needs to be explained why there would be an objection if the official decision did not promulgate a new rule. Is the objection that if the decision did not promulgate a new rule, the system would be passing up an opportunity to reap the benefits of Guidance: the benefits of a predictable framework for future actions? But this wouldn't make sense of Dee's complaint when Dee was denied a benefit that Dum later received. It isn't as though Dee's expectation of the benefit was somehow disappointed by Dum's getting it later. Moreover, one can imagine cases in which the failure to treat like cases alike would not have any cost in predictability because, for example, the decisions will not be publicized in any event or because the moods that lead the official to treat like cases differently are themselves predictable. (Thus, petitioners were warned not to cry in front of Tolstoy's Karenin because it set him off.) Finally, how is the duty to make rule-bound decisions itself to be explained, if not by appeal to materials such as Least Discretion and Equal Consideration?

Least Discretion, via the Duty to Exclude, supports Noncorruption: that officials are not corrupt. Impersonal Justification and Least Discretion support Impersonality.[2] Insofar as the superior power and authority of the office are used only in the service of impersonal reasons, one is subject not to the natural person who occupies it but instead to the office itself, which, whatever it is, is not another natural person. Moreover, Equal Influence supports Impersonality in another way. When Equal Influence is realized, the law is no more the will of one natural person than of any other natural person.

16

Claims to Equal Liberty

We have now considered a number of commonplace claims: against the state, corruption, discrimination, unequal treatment, and departures from the rule of law. In this chapter and the next, we consider two further commonplace claims: to equal liberty and equal opportunity. Students of Rawls will recognize here Rawls's first two principles—or, perhaps one should say, Rawls's first one and a half principles—of justice. And, indeed, it is illuminating to frame the discussion of equal liberty and equality of opportunity as a meditation on a puzzle about Rawls's theory of justice.

16.1 The Puzzle of Rawls's Egalitarianism

The puzzlement starts with noticing that the parties in Rawls's "original position" exclusively press interests in improvement. That is, they seek a larger share of "social primary goods," understood as means to advance one's "life plan" or "conception of the good," for those they represent. In other words, the aims of the parties—to get the largest share of primary goods for those they represent—are, at the most basic level, noncomparative. They want the most for those they represent, period. They do not care what others enjoy, at least so long as this does not affect what those they represent themselves enjoy. This last clause is an important qualification. In some cases, what a given person enjoys in absolute terms is affected by what others enjoy in comparative terms. For example, the mere fact that Altra has a greater share of primary goods than Indy may affect Indy's share itself because it puts Indy at a disadvantage in competition for other goods or because it has adverse effects on Indy's psychology, which makes Indy less able to pursue Indy's conception of the good. Nevertheless, the main point stands. At the most basic level, what the parties care about is the absolute share of those they represent. What others get in comparative terms matters only insofar as it affects that absolute share.

Why should this fact, that Rawls's principles answer simply to interests in improvement, be puzzling? Because Rawls's principles have more structure—and more comparative, egalitarian structure—than one would expect if they simply answered to interests in improvement. First, different principles regulate different goods. In the crudest terms, the different goods are: liberties, (chances for) jobs, and money. To be sure, there are other primary goods, notably the "social bases of self-respect." However, these other primary goods are supposed to be properly distributed just when the other primary goods are properly distributed.[1]

Second, the principles governing liberty and jobs require strict equality. It is only the principle governing money, the difference principle, that sanctions inequality, and then only insofar as it benefits the worst off.[2] I know, I know: the fine print actually allows inequality in liberty and jobs, so long as it benefits those with less (Rawls 1999, 266). According to the fine print, the real structure of the theory is, first, the difference principle for liberty, then the difference principle for jobs, then the difference principle for money. But I think the fine print is at odds with the rest of the document. The first principle is certainly advertised as a principle of equality ("equal right to . . . equal basic liberties"). And the second argument for the priority of the equal basic liberties works only if they are indeed equal (477: "And this distribution being equal . . .").

Finally, liberty takes lexical priority over jobs, which take lexical priority over money. This bit of structure—the priority of the basic liberties—has attracted a great deal of criticism, with which I am sympathetic (van Parijs 2003, 225).[3] But my main focus is on the other bits of structure: the regulation of the distribution of different primary goods by different principles and the egalitarian character of those principles.

The puzzle, in brief, is: Why equality, and why equality in just these goods? Why not instead a single principle: improve the overall situation of each as far as possible, except where this would deprive another of an improvement, in which case trade off between them fairly? Or, coming at it from the other direction: If equality is the right way to distribute some goods, such as liberty, then why isn't equality also the right way to distribute other goods, such as wealth? I have been framing the issue as a problem within Rawls's system: How can his selectively comparative, egalitarian principles be derived from the noncomparative motivations of the parties in the original position? But our interest in the issue is not exclusively exegetical. We can put the point in the terms of our negative observation. Rawls's principles, or at least the aspects of his principles that are the focus of this and the following chapter, reflect commonplace claims. The principles of equal basic liberty and fair equality of opportunity seem like liberal commonsense. The question is: Can these commonplace claims, which appear to have a comparative structure, be explained by noncomparative interests in improvement?

16.2 Equal Basic Liberty: The Negative Observation

Making this meditation on Rawls more concrete, consider two specific puzzles about liberty. Since political liberties are discussed at greater length in Parts V and VI, I assume it is nonpolitical liberties that are at issue. The first puzzle is why the parties should treat liberty and money differently. Rawls suggests that liberties matter as means to certain activities. But money is also a means to many of the same activities. Consider freedom of movement. I take it that you enjoy freedom of movement, understood as what Rawls calls a "basic liberty," insofar as the state, first, does not issue and enforce commands that you not travel and, second, prevents others from obstructing your travel. Granted, you can't travel if you lack freedom of movement. But you also can't travel if you lack bus fare. So not only freedom of movement but also money are a means to activities that require getting from point *A* to point *B*.

One might reply that liberty is a special kind of means: a means that consists in being able to predict that others will not coercively prevent one from that activity. (As I argued at length in Chapters 2 and 3, I don't think we know what we mean by "coercively" here, but set that aside.) If one lacks freedom of movement, then others will coercively prevent one from traveling. By contrast, if one lacks money, one just can't pay for travel. One problem with this reply is that it's obscure why protection from coercion—which is what liberty is supposed to provide—should be governed by one principle whereas protection from, say, disease—which is likewise a means to certain activities—should be governed by another principle. Insofar as the parties in the original position simply want to pursue the relevant activities, it is not clear why they should care whether what prevents them from pursuing those activities is coercion or disease. Whether the impediment to pursuing those activities is sentient or nonsentient, it's an impediment either way.

Another problem with this reply is that, on closer inspection, it does nothing to distinguish freedom of movement from bus fare (Hale 1923; G. Cohen 1995, 56; 2011, chap. 8; Sterba 2010). Without freedom of movement, one will be stopped by domestic passport control, which will call on the police for enforcement. Without bus fare, one will be stopped by the driver, who will call on the police for enforcement. If being stopped by domestic passport control counts as coercive interference, then so too does being stopped by the police. So, lacking money is being unable to predict that others won't coercively interfere with you as you pursue certain activities. So, setting aside why anyone should care about the distinction between liberty and money, it's elusive what the distinction, in suitably general terms, even is.

Now on to the second puzzle. To my knowledge, Rawls never addresses—and, in any event, justice hardly seems to require—the full range of restrictions that would be required to secure equal basic liberty. Suppose that some people buy home security systems on the open market. This means they are better protected from "interference" than others, but (let us suppose) no one is worse protected in absolute terms. The basic structure is predictably resulting in inequality in liberty (and, moreover, inequality that does not work to the advantage, even if not to the disadvantage either, of those with less liberty). As far as I understand the distinction, this is inequality not in what Rawls calls the "worth" or "value" of liberty but instead in liberty itself—freedom from interference.

To repeat, these are not just puzzles about Rawls, since Rawls is, by and large, reflecting widely shared judgments: commonplace claims. We would find unequal legal prohibitions on movement intolerable, even though we are more or less reconciled to inequality in bus fare and home security upgrades. Interests in improvement don't explain why.

16.3 Equal Basic Liberty: The Positive Conjecture

What might solve these puzzles—these features of the equal basic liberties not accounted for by interests in improvement? As always, I reach for the positive conjecture: that claims to the equal basic liberties are rooted in claims against inferiority. In particular, claims to equal basic liberties are explained by the horizontal factor of Equal Consideration. Equal Treatment by the State is a special case of Equal Consideration, and the equal basic liberties are a special case of Equal Treatment by the State. The truth in Rawls's doctrine of the equality of the basic liberties is just Equal Treatment by the State as applied to the state's directly issuing and enforcing prohibitions on what its citizens do and protecting citizens from interference by others. If the state directly issues and enforces prohibitions for some citizens, then it should do the same for the other citizens. Otherwise those other citizens would enjoy the benefit of freedom from those prohibitions without a justifying difference. And if the state directly protects some citizens from interference, then it should directly protect other citizens, on pain of withholding from the latter the benefit of protection.

What is the difference between freedom of movement and bus fare even supposed to be, setting aside the question of why the difference should matter? When the state denies freedom of movement, it directly issues and enforces a prohibition. There is little or no intervention by other independent agencies. By contrast, when the state allows or facilitates an economic structure that ends up leaving one unable to find a private transportation service willing to transport one for what one is able to pay, the state's role is less direct. One's inability to travel is due to a greater extent to the intervention of independent agencies.

To be sure, this is a difference in degree rather than in kind. Insofar as it is in the state's power to regulate those other agencies, the difference is in how directly one is treated by the state: how far one's treatment is mediated by the decisions of other agencies. And degree of directness may be hard to measure; in some cases, there may be no answer as to whether one sort of provision is more or less direct than another. But it is still a difference. This difference matters if, as I have suggested, Equal Treatment by the State applies more stringently to what the state more directly provides. This may mean that one has an equal treatment complaint about inequality in freedom of movement that one lacks about inequality in bus fare.

This view, of course, differs in several ways from Rawls's doctrine of equal basic liberty. First, the focus is not on individuals having equal amounts of some privileged good. The focus is rather on the state's providing equal amounts. If some threshold of basic security has been provided equally, there is no violation if some have additional security because they have purchased it on the open market. Second, the comparative complaint doesn't attach to some privileged kind of good, such as liberty. It is rather that there is special pressure on the state to provide whichever goods it directly provides equally. It isn't violated when the state simply upholds an otherwise justified economic system with the predictable but indirect result that some, but not others, can induce a private provider of transportation services to provide them. If, by contrast, in a command economy, the state distributed bus vouchers only to party members and not to others, then that would be like the state's granting freedom of movement only to party members. In that case, there wouldn't be a significant moral difference between a bus voucher and an internal passport, as seems intuitive.

If we understand the equality of the basic liberties to be a special case of Equal Treatment by the State—namely, where the state directly provides protection from interference—then we can explain why it isn't violated when the state, while providing equal police protection to all, in addition upholds an otherwise justified economic system with the predictable but indirect result that some, but not others, have home security systems.

This proposal is thus relieved of the need to draw a clear, general distinction between liberty and money. And this proposal does not imply that protection from sentience is somehow more important than protection from disease. The state's directly providing sewers to only some would be objectionable in the same way as its providing police protection to only some.

Finally, there is no insistence on the priority of distributing one kind of good over any other. Again, the idea is simply that the unequal provision of goods directly provided by the state, but not the mere unequal holding of goods that are not directly provided by the state, gives rise to a comparative equal treatment complaint.

One might object that this gives the state carte blanche to stand aside as some are assaulted, defrauded, and so on by others. After all, the state plays only an "indirect" role in those violations of liberty! But this objection is multiply mistaken. First, people would have an improvement complaint if the state did not give them sufficient protection from assault, fraud, and suchlike: that is, if the state could have given them greater protection without unfairness to others. Second, it would violate Equal Consideration for the state to provide better protection from assault to some people than to others. Finally, Equal Citizenship might independently require not only equal but also sufficient protection.[4]

17

Claims to Equality of Opportunity

After the equal basic liberties, Rawls urges equality of fair opportunity, requiring, roughly, equal chances for jobs. Opportunities for positions are to be distributed equally, and this equal distribution is to take priority over the distribution of the remaining goods, such as income and wealth, by the difference principle. As with the equal basic liberties, this Rawlsian principle resonates. It too has some title to being considered a liberal democratic commonplace. In the first section, we consider the formal component of equality of opportunity. In the second section, we consider the substantive component. The arguments of these two sections go rather against the grain of the rest of the book. For we find that much, although not all, of formal equality of opportunity can be explained by interests in improvement. There is a bit of a negative observation to register, and a bit of work for the positive conjecture, but not much. Furthermore, I suggest that all of substantive equality of opportunity can be explained by interests in improvement. This is a point worth making, however, since, as we will discuss, substantive equality of opportunity can at first seem to be largely comparative.

17.1 Formal Equality of Opportunity

The formal component of equality of opportunity says something like the following:

> "Equal Qualifications": For any given position, *P*, if Barred has no worse qualifications than Beckoned for *P*, then Barred has a complaint if Barred has worse chances than Beckoned of being selected for *P*, if both apply.

Principles of this kind are usually formulated as requiring only that equal qualifications receive equal chances. But that formulation seems too narrow. It recognizes no complaint of Barred's against Beckoned's enjoying much better chances than Barred, even though Beckoned's qualifications are much worse. This is why I favor the formulation that no worse qualifications receive no worse chances (compare G. Cohen 2008, 367).

Our question in this section is: Can Barred's complaint in Equal Qualifications be understood as an improvement complaint: that some individual or institutional agent, by improving Barred's chances for *P*, could have improved Barred's situation without unfairness to Beckoned or others? If not, then this would be an instance of our negative observation.

I begin by distinguishing several kinds of improvement complaints relevant to the allocation of positions. Along one axis, we can distinguish between improvement complaints from those who would be served by work—"beneficiaries"—and from those who aspire to do the work—"workers." Along another axis, we can distinguish improvement complaints about which positions are made available, about how they are filled, and—although I won't discuss this until the next section—about how people are trained for them.

Thus, to begin with, beneficiaries may have an improvement complaint if, by making different positions available, their situation could be improved without unfairness to others. If we make the position of baker available, for example, consumers will have baked goods to eat. Call these "beneficiary-position complaints." Workers may also have an improvement complaint if, by making different positions available, their opportunities could be improved without unfairness to others. If we make the position of baker available, some workers will have the opportunity to spend their days as bakers. Call these "worker-position complaints."[1]

Of course, beneficiary- and worker-position complaints may conflict. "Inefficient" positions may improve the situation of workers but worsen the situation of beneficiaries. Such "inefficiency" does not support a beneficiary-position complaint, however, if this is a fair trade-off. Nor does it count as a genuine inefficiency, with the scare quotes removed. The relevant sense of efficiency is simply promotion of the public interest, and the "inefficient" positions do promote the public interest. Note that making positions available might consist not only in creating baking jobs but also in changing the structure of baking jobs so that certain workers can do them: for example, providing equipment to help lift heavy bags of flour or offering flexible scheduling to allow bakers to care for elderly parents. Again, this may make the positions less "efficient," but it may be a fair trade-off and so, in the sense that matters, a gain in efficiency.

Now consider complaints about how positions are filled. A beneficiary may have an improvement complaint if, by filling the positions in a different way, their situation could be improved without unfairness to others. Call this a "beneficiary-selection complaint." A worker may have an improvement complaint if, by filling the positions in a different way, they could have had a better chance for the position, without unfairness to others. Call this a "worker-selection complaint."

One worker's having a better chance might be unfair to others in two ways. First, there may be competition, by which I mean that improving one worker's chances of obtaining the position reduces another worker's chances of obtaining the position. In this sense, lotteries are competitive, even though they don't involve rivalrous exertion. Note that not all cases of filling positions are competitive. For instance, there may be at least as many positions as applicants, in which case your obtaining one position does not prevent me from obtaining one of the open positions that remain. I assume that Equal Qualifications applies even when there is no competition.[2]

Second, one worker's having a better chance might serve beneficiaries worse, in which case beneficiaries have selection complaints. This is the main reason, I think, why a worker's being qualified for a position is morally relevant. If Arbeit is more qualified for a position than Boulot, then giving Arbeit the position costs beneficiaries less. It's beneficiaries, not Arbeit, who have a complaint if, despite Arbeit's better qualifications, he has no better a chance at the position than Boulot.[3] And beneficiaries might not have a complaint; the importance to Boulot of a chance at the job may mean that the loss of "efficiency" that beneficiaries bear is not unfair (and so not, in the relevant sense, a loss of efficiency). Imagine, for example, that the "inefficiency" comes only from the cost of accommodating Boulot's occasionally disruptive need to care for an elderly parent.

For another illustration of the ways in which one worker's having a better chance for a job may or may not be unfair to others, suppose selection processes *X* and *Y* have a zero false-positive rate—they never overestimate qualifications—and fill all the positions. However, *X* has a lower false-negative rate—unlike *Y*, it does not overlook qualified *F* workers—and settles ties by lottery. Then *F* workers may complain that their chances for the job could be improved by *X*. Selection process *X* would not be unfair to beneficiaries, since *X*, with the same zero false-positive rate as *Y*, serves beneficiaries' interests just as well. Granted, in raising the chances of *F* workers (from zero), *X* lowers the chances of non-*F* workers (from something above zero). By construction, the case is competitive. But far from being unfair to non-*F* workers, this trade-off—raising some from zero while lowering others from above zero—seems positively required by fairness.

Insofar as qualifications play this justificatory role, they are nothing more than traits such that beneficiaries' situations are fairly improved by a system where people with those traits are given the position. To say that Barred is more qualified than Beckoned for a position is to say that Barred's and Beckoned's traits are such that beneficiaries' situations would be fairly improved by giving people with Barred's, rather than Beckoned's, traits that position. This should be read so as to accommodate the following point about comparative advantage, raised by Daniels (1978, 210). In the ordinary usage, Barred is "more qualified" than Beckoned for position 1 when, holding other things equal, including how well other positions are filled, giving Barred position 1 would better serve beneficiaries. Suppose now that Barred is more qualified than Beckoned, in this sense, for both position 1 and position 2. Compatibly with that, however, it might be the case that beneficiaries would benefit more from having Barred in 1, given that this will mean that Beckoned is in 2, than they would from having Barred in 2, given that this will mean that Beckoned is in 1. (This is just an application of David Ricardo's famous doctrine.) In that case, Barred does not have a selection complaint about having worse chances than Beckoned for position 2, even though, in an ordinary sense, Barred is "better at the job." The morally relevant sense of more qualified should not hold other things equal. In that sense, Barred is more qualified than Beckoned for position 2 only if giving Barred rather than Beckoned position 2 would better serve beneficiaries, given the effects of that decision on how well other positions are staffed.

As this point about comparative advantage indicates, qualifications, so understood, don't answer to any independent notion of merit. Nor are they limited to what we might ordinarily think of as on-the-job skills (Daniels

1978; Scanlon 2018, 48). They include, among other things, that the worker would serve as a role model, helping to combat the impression that members of an underrepresented group would be unsuccessful (or simply unhappy) in it or to "foster social trust and cooperation among [deeply divided] groups" (Arneson 2013c, 319). Granted, it's not clear whether this is how Rawls understood "qualifications." But it is hard to see how else he could have understood them in a way that is consistent with the rest of his outlook.

The phrase "to be qualified" is significantly ambiguous. On a narrow reading, to be qualified is to have traits such that beneficiaries' situations are improved when people with those traits have those positions, abstracting from the process of selecting those people. For example, someone who would have passed a certification exam, even though they in fact neglected to take it, is just as qualified, in this narrow sense, as someone who is in fact certified. On a broad reading, to be qualified is to have traits such that beneficiaries' situations are improved when there is a process of selecting people with those traits for those positions. A certification may well be a qualification in this broad sense since it efficiently assures others that the certified person is qualified in the narrow sense. Insofar as qualifications are simply factors that affect the complaints of beneficiaries in the way described, I believe they should be understood in the broad sense. Suppose that while *X* is a better qualification than *Y* in the narrow sense, *X* is impossible to detect whereas *Y* is not (or *X* is prohibitively costly to detect or attempts to detect *X* are intolerably more prone to error). Then beneficiaries would have a complaint about selection processes that sought to ascertain *X* instead of selection processes that sought to ascertain *Y*.

Have we overlooked a further complaint that workers might have? Scanlon (2018) suggests it would be wrong to use proxies rather than more direct evidence of narrow qualifications, even if there was no worker-selection complaint, because it made no difference to applicants' chances of the job, and no beneficiary-selection complaint, because proxies were more efficient. This is so, he writes, because "people have further reason to want to be taken seriously as candidates for these positions, and considered on their (institutionally determined) merits" (51).[4] I doubt, though, that one has a significant interest in simply having one's narrow qualifications attentively reviewed, for its own sake, much less an interest that gives one a claim on others to bear the cost of satisfying it. It becomes all the more questionable when we remind ourselves of what narrow qualifications amount to in this context. Perhaps there's some plausibility in the suggestion that one has an interest in having one's narrow qualifications attentively reviewed (if not in the suggestion that this interest gives one much of a claim on others) when the qualifications in question are traits that one has independent reason to take pride in. But one's "(institutionally determined) merits" needn't be that. I may "merit" a place in nursing school simply because I plan to move to St. Louis after I graduate, because my partner has work there, and since a new hospital will be opening, there's expected to be relatively high demand for nurses in St. Louis. A valid reason, to be sure, but it's not clear that it's a fact about myself that I have a claim that people take notice of.

Let's now return to our main question. In this section so far, I have described various improvement complaints, from workers and beneficiaries, about positions and selection, concerning the distribution of jobs. Do these improvement complaints fully account for the sort of complaint described in Equal Qualifications: Barred's complaint of having worse chances for a job when Barred has no worse qualifications? Here I make three observations. First, Equal Qualifications conflicts with these improvement complaints—that is, avoiding the complaint described by Equal Qualifications gives rise to these improvement complaints—only on the narrow reading of "qualifications" but not, as far as I can tell, on the broad reading. To illustrate, suppose we can create a kind of beneficial and desirable position, for which *X* workers and *Y* workers would be equally narrowly qualified. However, the only selection process available to us would fail to pick up on the qualifications of the *Y*s. Creating and filling the position would violate Equal Qualifications on the narrow reading, since *X* workers would have better chances than *Y* workers, despite being no more qualified, in the narrow sense, than *Y* workers. However, if we don't create and fill the position, beneficiaries and *X* workers would have position complaints. So, there is a conflict between Equal Qualifications and these improvement claims. On the broad reading, by contrast, *Y* workers are simply not as qualified as *X* workers. So, the fact that their chances are lower than those of *X* workers does not violate Equal Qualifications. So, on the broad reading, which I believe is the correct reading, Equal Qualifications does not conflict with the improvement claims I have described.

The second observation is that, even when Equal Qualifications is satisfied, workers can still have improvement complaints. Equal Qualifications is satisfied when every worker has the same improvement complaint: where no one occupies the position that should be created or everyone's qualifications for a given job are neglected. So, Equal Qualifications needs at least to be supplemented by the improvement complaints I have described in order to have a complete theory of justice in employment.

The final observation is that, when Equal Qualifications is violated, this often indicates that Barred has an improvement complaint. Suppose that Barred is no less qualified but only Beckoned is considered. Barred can complain that Barred's chances could have been improved by also being considered, without unfairness to Beckoned or, since Barred is no less qualified, to beneficiaries. This complaint does not rest on any comparison, let alone any inequality. If there was no Beckoned and the position was simply left unfilled, Barred would have exactly the same complaint: that considering Barred would improve Barred's situation without unfairness to anyone else.

These three observations suggest a kind of reduction, or error theory, of Equal Qualifications. Violations of Equal Qualifications matter only as indicators that Barred has an improvement complaint. Noncomparative improvement complaints tell the whole story, and we could simply drop the comparative-seeming principle of Equal Qualifications. This is almost right, but not quite. Consider a case in which an employer, at a scale larger than a family business, hires no one, even though hiring someone wouldn't harm business, even though Barred and Beckoned are equally qualified (in either sense), and even though Barred and Beckoned would each find the job rewarding. In this case, perhaps each has an improvement complaint. But now contrast this with a case in which the employer refuses to consider Barred's application and hires Beckoned. If improvement complaints were the only thing at issue, then what the employer does in the second case should be less objectionable. But, if anything, it seems more objectionable. At any rate, Barred has a complaint about this, which has a comparative character. It arises only because, while Barred wasn't given a chance for the job, Beckoned was given a chance. So, it seems we need Equal Qualifications as an independent principle. If it isn't explained by improvement complaints, what is it explained by? If the negative observation is, to this extent, vindicated, can we expect some help from the positive conjecture?

I believe we can. As we saw in Section 8.4, Least Discretion is a vertical factor that keeps otherwise untempered asymmetries of power and authority from amounting to an objectionable relation of inferiority to those who wield the power and authority. And as we saw in Section 14.3, from the vertical factor of Least Discretion follows Equal Treatment by Officials. And Equal Treatment by Officials, in turn, explains the residuum of Equal Qualifications: why Barred has a comparative complaint when the employer refuses to consider Barred's application and hires Beckoned. Equal Qualifications is thus just a special case of Equal Treatment by Officials, where the official act in question is considering Beckoned and Barred for the job. Barred has an equal treatment complaint against an employer who gives Beckoned a greater chance of a job, when there is no justifying difference between them. One justifying difference might be that Beckoned has better qualifications. But, when the antecedent of Equal Qualifications is satisfied, Beckoned does not have better qualifications.

This explanation assumes that employers count as officials to whom Least Discretion applies. While employers may not be officers of the state, they still occupy positions of superior power and authority that are insufficiently tempered. True, some tempering factors may be present. Workers may be able find work elsewhere, and there may be labor protections. Nevertheless, as we observed in Chapter 9, workplaces involve particularly pronounced asymmetries of power and authority. Most notably, they represent rare settings in modern society, outside of the formal state itself, in which some adults give other adults, for most of their waking hours, orders that they are expected to obey (Anderson 2017; Herzog 2018, chap. 4). So it should not be surprising that at least some of the vertical factors, in particular Least Discretion, are called for in relations between employers and employees.

17.2 Substantive Equality of Opportunity

We turn now from the formal side of equality of opportunity to its substantive side. Substantively, equality of fair opportunity seems to imply something like:

> "Equal Potential": For any kind of opportunity to acquire a qualification (where the opportunity might be, e.g., a certain educational setting), if

> at a given time Barred has no worse potential than Beckoned, then Barred has a complaint if at that time Barred has a worse opportunity of that kind than Beckoned has.

As in the previous section, our question is whether improvement complaints explain Equal Potential. As we will find, bucking the trend of the arguments elsewhere in the book, improvement complaints do explain what is plausible in Equal Potential. Although at first there appears to be a negative observation in the offing, that appearance will be revealed to be misleading.

Some comments on Equal Potential. First, someone has more "potential," let us say, to the extent that they are more likely to acquire the qualification if they are given the opportunity. Second, I set aside opportunities to actualize oneself in ways other than the acquisition of qualifications, such as learning to play a musical instrument for purely amateur purposes, speak the native language of one's in-laws, or appreciate poetry in one's spare time, whether or not any of these accomplishments improve one's chances for formal employment. I make two comments, however. First, with respect to such opportunities, having greater potential may be even less important. A lower level of actualized musical skill may be just as rewarding for the less talented learner than a higher level for the more talented learner. (Or so I tell myself.) Second, such opportunities are less likely to be competitive. Your learning to play the piano usually doesn't prevent me from learning to play.

Finally, equality of fair opportunity is typically formulated in terms of potential at birth. But suppose Barred had greater potential than Middling at birth, but because Barred was not offered some educational opportunity, Barred now has the same potential as Middling. It isn't clear why Barred should now have a greater claim than Middling on educational opportunities going forward. Barred may have a complaint that Barred was not given certain opportunities in the past, but it isn't clear why that should give Barred priority over Middling now, except perhaps under the separate heading of reparative justice.

We can distinguish two kinds of improvement complaints relevant to Equal Potential. A worker has an improvement complaint if her opportunity to acquire qualifications could have been improved without unfairness to anyone else. Call this a "worker-development complaint." Beneficiaries have improvement complaints if, by changing the scheme of opportunities, beneficiaries' situations would be improved, without unfairness to anyone else. On the one hand, beneficiaries benefit from superior qualifications. On the other hand, beneficiaries may have to bear the costs of changing the scheme of opportunities. Call such complaints "beneficiary-development complaints."

Now consider two observations. The first is that many such improvement complaints don't show up as violations of Equal Potential. Suppose Barred has less potential than Beckoned relative to the current educational setting (e.g., where there are no accommodations for dyslexia) but Barred would have at least as much potential in a restructured educational setting. While Equal Potential is satisfied in the current educational setting, Barred may well have a development complaint, which argues for a different educational setting altogether. (This is similar to cases from the last section, in which a worker who is currently less qualified, because they can't lift the sacks of flour, might be just as qualified if positions were restructured.) So, Equal Potential needs at least to be supplemented by development complaints.

The second observation is that violations of Equal Potential often indicate that Barred has a development complaint. Suppose Beckoned has better opportunity than Barred and we could redistribute some of that opportunity from Beckoned to Barred. If Beckoned had more potential, then beneficiaries might have a development complaint if Barred rather than Beckoned had that opportunity, since it is more likely to lead to better qualifications. And if Beckoned had more potential, then the opportunity might be worth more to Beckoned than to Barred, since it has higher odds of resulting in a qualification. But since Equal Potential applies only if Barred has no worse potential than Beckoned, neither consideration argues against redistributing some of Beckoned's opportunity to Barred. So, Barred may have a development complaint: an improvement complaint that Barred's opportunity could be improved, without unfairness to anyone else.

These two observations suggest a possible reduction or error theory: namely, that violations of Equal Potential matter only as indicators that Barred has a development complaint. I think this reduction is, in fact, correct. While so far I have been highlighting what improvement complaints can't explain, here we find something that improvement complaints can explain. This takes some work to see, however, since this reduction faces a challenge. The challenge is that there seem to be violations of Equal Potential where, intuitively, the person in Barred's position has a complaint but where, it seems, that person has no improvement complaint.

Suppose that White and Blue have, as children, equal potential. White's parents give White additional education in high school. Blue's parents do not, either because they could not or because they chose not to. Crucially, assume that prior to White's parents giving White additional education, neither Blue nor White had any improvement complaint, against either the school system or their own parents, that their education could have been improved without unfairness to others. Everyone was already doing enough for them; White's parents just volunteered to do more. Because White was given this additional education and Blue was not, White has more potential for a college education.[5] As a result of that enhanced potential, White receives a college education, whereas Blue does not, and so White becomes more qualified for a desirable job. And as a result of those better qualifications, White gets the job, whereas Blue does not.

Blue seems to have a complaint that, because White got additional education, White, but not Blue, got the college place and later the job. And this complaint, unlike an improvement complaint, seems to have a comparative character. It's only because White's parents do something for White that Blue has a complaint. How can we explain it without Equal Potential? As this same case illustrates, satisfying Equal Potential might seem to come at the cost of improvement complaints. By hypothesis, others have already provided Blue with whatever opportunities it was not unfair to ask of them to provide (e.g., by paying taxes or being deprived of other services). Isn't it unfair for them now to be required to provide more for Blue to bring Blue up to the level of White (Arneson 2013c, 318)?

Something else is puzzling about this case. The intuition that Blue has a complaint seems oddly fixated on employment. Contrast a case in which the Hausers don't give Junior additional education but save the money and give Junior the down payment for a house. Later in life, Hauser has no better job than Renter, but Hauser owns, whereas Renter has to rent. Might Renter have a complaint like Blue's: that the broader social structure permits parents' desires to do things for their children to translate into significant advantages for them? I suspect most people who think that Blue has a complaint would deny that Renter does. The difference between Renter and Hauser, they think, unlike the difference between Blue and White, involves no problematic violation of equality of opportunity. But why should it be less concerning if Hauser's parents just give him the financial advantage directly, without laundering it, as the Whites do, through a diploma? Why the fixation on employment?

Is the answer that, while no one can deserve a house, someone can deserve a job? But we are setting aside desert—let alone the idea that jobs and educational opportunities are rewards for desert. Is it that not getting a job has unique importance, say, because a job is a unique opportunity for self-realization (Shiffrin 2004b, 1666–1667)? But Hauser's house pride can also be a kind of self-realization.

Is it that Blue and White, and Hauser and Renter, live in a "meritocratic" society, in the pejorative sense, in which the disparity of consideration characteristic of an aristocratic order has been grafted onto meritocratic competitions? In such a society, which bears perhaps an uncomfortable likeness to our own (Arneson 1999, 93–94), qualifications or careers supplant lineage as the basing trait. Qualifications and careers attract regard that exceeds, in quality or extent, what they intrinsically merit, such as admiration for skill or a job well done. By contrast, no similar pattern of regard has coalesced around owning, rather than renting, a domicile. So that is why the inequality of White and Blue presents a problem that the inequality of Hauser and Renter does not. But this is not the difference we are looking for. First, Hauser and Renter needn't live in such a society; to suppose that they do is to write more into the example than is already there. And, second, if the problem is a disparity of regard of a kind that could not be merited by competitive success, then it is not clear how tinkering with the competitions, by making them satisfy Equal Potential, could be a solution.

Instead, I suspect the difference in our reactions to White versus Blue and Hauser versus Renter has to do with competition as I earlier defined it. Hauser's getting the house doesn't prevent Renter from getting it. Renter wouldn't have gotten it anyway (Shiffrin 2004b, 1670–1671). To test this suggestion, suppose White was not competing with Blue. There are two unfilled spots for anyone who meets the threshold of qualification. White's additional education pushes him over the threshold, whereas Blue remains below it. This seems less objectionable. If the crux is competition, then jobs are not somehow different in kind from other forms of advantage. There isn't, in that sense, a meritocratic bias. If housing were competitive, Renter would have a complaint like Blue's. Imagine there's a land rush and the Hausers outfit Junior with a party of advance scouts and the fastest team of horses money can buy. In this competitive context, a complaint about a violation of equality of opportunity gains intuitive traction.

Why, then, should competition matter? Because, if a competition isn't fair, then the outcome is less likely to track genuine desert or merit? Again, we set desert and merit aside. Instead, I suggest, competition between Blue and White matters simply because it means that White's additional education reduces Blue's absolute opportunity. White's chances of getting the college spot increase from 0.5, which, given competition, means that—and this is what really matters—Blue's chances decrease from 0.5.[6] Blue has a noncomparative, improvement complaint after all. Blue's chances could have been improved by keeping Blue from dropping below 0.5, and this would not have been unfair to White. Fairness does not require lowering Blue's chances below 0.5 so as to raise White's chances above 0.5. So, we don't need to appeal to Equal Potential after all. Blue just has a straightforward improvement complaint. In effect, Blue was denied a highest fair chance lottery, in the sense defined in Section 1.4.

Or, rather, Blue may have an improvement complaint. By hypothesis, people other than White benefit from White's additional education. In effect, White's parents are making voluntary contributions to augment the stock of human capital. Once we take this into account, whether Blue still has an improvement complaint—that his opportunity could have been improved without unfairness to others—depends on whether it is unfair to trade off the reduction in Blue's opportunity for these benefits to others. It may be unfair in some cases but not in others.

Suppose the case is one in which it is unfair, so Blue does have a complaint. To answer it, must we prevent White's parents from giving White the additional education, which is invasive, or require others to give Blue the additional education, which is expensive? Maybe, but maybe there's a third alternative: to make the college admissions process insensitive to White's greater potential.

Isn't this to sacrifice "efficiency"? No, because "efficiency" is served just insofar as the public interest is served: insofar as people's situations are improved in a way that makes trade-offs among people fairly. And the insensitive process, in this case, improves people's situations in a way that makes trade-offs among people fairly. Granted, the process (if Blue should be admitted) reduces the benefits others would receive from White's greater qualifications. But the insensitive process improves Blue's situation. And we are imagining a case in which it is fair to improve Blue's situation, even when this reduces others' benefits.

To recap: The case of Blue and White is a paradigm violation of Equal Potential. At first, it seemed that Blue does not have an improvement complaint, which suggested that Equal Potential is an independent constraint. On closer inspection, however, Blue does have an improvement complaint when but only when two conditions are met: (i) Blue and White are in competition and (ii) it is unfair to trade off the reduction in Blue's chances (brought about by White's additional education) for the benefits to others (also brought about by White's additional education).

Does Blue have a complaint when (i) and (ii) do not hold? I don't think so. In the noncompetitive case, Blue may have, as it were, a cosmic complaint about being unlucky in not having wealthier or more generous parents. But that's like Renter's cosmic complaint about not having wealthier or more generous parents or like the cosmic complaint of someone who finds themselves in a society where their talents happen to be in either high supply or low demand.

So, in sum, improvement complaints do appear to explain what needs to be explained about the substantive principle of Equal Potential. Again, however, improvement complaints don't seem to explain all that needs to be explained about the formal principle of Equal Qualifications. The formal principle requires supplementation by Equal Treatment by Officials, which is to say by claims against inferiority.

18

Claims against Poverty, Relative and Absolute

This book has said little about "economic" or "material" justice—or "distributive justice," in the narrow sense. One reason for this is that economic justice has been the focus of earlier work by relational egalitarians. I have been exploring what other ideas might be accounted for by materials like those to which relational egalitarians appeal. Another reason for this is that I am skeptical that there is a philosophically distinct or interesting topic of economic or material distributive justice. To be sure, there is an interesting topic of how to improve the choice situations that people face. But improving their choice situations involves not only economic measures to affect their income and wealth but also noneconomic measures to expand their liberties. I am broadly sympathetic to Marxist doubts that we can distinguish these economic and noneconomic contributions to choice situations. Granted, I did try to argue back part of the distinction between liberty and money in Section 16.3, in terms of a distinction between what the state directly provides and what it indirectly provides. But this was work of partial reclamation from a baseline of more fundamental puzzlement about what morally significant distinction there could be.

If we suppress our fastidiousness, however, we can ask whether complaints about relative or absolute poverty are always improvement complaints. If not, then we would have another instance of the negative observation. And if we then had to appeal to claims against inferiority, then we would have another instance of our positive conjecture. To be sure, as I noted in Chapter 5, complaints about poverty can indeed be improvement complaints, which can even arise in the absence of any relations of inferiority. I might have an improvement complaint that someone else enjoys, in the privacy of their own home, some labor-saving convenience that I don't have, even though this does not amount to any hierarchy between us. Likewise, I might have a complaint that earlier generations did not invest enough for my generation.

Notice, however, that there can be poverty, even relative poverty, in the sense of simply having less than others, even where there are no improvement complaints. First, the poverty might arise from choice situations about which no one had an improvement complaint. In many societies, the origin of much relative poverty was debt resulting from poor option luck: in particular, voluntary contracts followed by poor harvests. It might not be unfair to let such relative poverty stand; indeed, it might be unfair to mitigate it. Second, inequality-increasing weak Pareto improvements for the more affluent might not come at the absolute expense of the relatively poor at all, and so not unfairly at their expense. In that case, the poor could have no improvement complaint about the improvement for the more affluent.

Even where poverty gives rise to no improvement complaints, it may still give rise to complaints against inferiority. First, relative poverty might be the more or less proximate result of something against which someone has an inferiority complaint. Relative poverty might be the result of discrimination on the basis of another trait. Or it might be the result of a violation of Equal Treatment. Second, relative poverty may lead to dependence on the relatively rich: specifically, dependence on them for, not to put too fine a point on it, money. So, it may lead to untempered asymmetries of power over the relatively poor (Thomas 2017). One imagines that relative poverty is more likely to have this effect when it is combined with absolute poverty. For it is absolute poverty that makes the need for money urgent. Third, being relatively poor can itself mean having less authority than the relatively rich. This is all but guaranteed where money is accepted in exchange for services. Finally, if poverty is a basing trait, then relative poverty can result in a disparity of consideration, either by individuals or the state. If one is shabbily dressed, private citizens and public officers may not give one the time of day. Again, relative poverty is more likely to have this effect when it is combined with absolute poverty, which places one below some threshold of consideration.

As I have described things so far, poverty is just one cause, among others, of asymmetric power and authority and just one basing trait, among others, that can attract a disparity of regard. However, poverty differs in an important way from other causes of asymmetry and other basing traits. In those other cases, the remedy is exclusively to prevent those causes from resulting in asymmetric power and authority or to prevent the basing trait from attracting disparate regard. It is not to change the causes or traits themselves. Women should not have to become men, for example, to have their work valued at the same rate. In the case of poverty, however, there is a stronger case for remedying the problem by changing the causes or traits themselves: that is, for simply lifting people out of poverty. If people without housing are being overlooked for public services because they have no mailing address, for example, then one remedy is to make those public services less dependent on a fixed residence: to prevent the trait of being without housing from attracting lesser regard. But another remedy is just to change the trait: to provide them with housing.

The answer to the question of how fairly to distribute (even cooperatively produced) goods when there will be no (further) interaction among people is governed solely by interests in improvement. By contrast, the answer to the question of how, all things considered, to distribute goods when there will be ongoing interaction among people needs also to respond to claims against inferiority. If, as I have been arguing, there can be complaints against inferiority about poverty even when there are no improvement complaints about poverty, then the correct answer to the latter question—how, all things considered, to distribute goods when there will be ongoing interaction among people—may differ from the correct answer to the former question—how fairly to distribute goods when there will not be ongoing interaction among people.

19

Claims against Illiberal Interventions

The Negative Observation

What underlies the demand for a liberal society—or at least a liberal government? What accounts for, as I put it, the commonplace claim against "illiberal interventions"? The liberals I have in mind believe a person, Prudie, has a complaint against a state that "intervenes" in Prudie's "protected" choices.[1] Prudie should not face a fine or jail time, for example, for choosing a particular religion or pastime. This is so even when such interventions improve the choice situations of Prudie and others by making them less likely to make choices that are worthless or bad bargains.[2] This prohibition on illiberal interventions is sometimes itself viewed as a limit of legitimacy: a constraint on what the state does that the state must respect in order to avoid the complaint against state. This is one way of viewing Mill's ([1859] 2015) Harm Principle: that the state may not intervene in choices except to prevent harm to others.

Imagine your adult child was to join the Order. The Order is such that you think your child is making a bad choice, throwing their life away. If there were any hope of success, you ought to make every effort to dissuade them. All the same, if you are a liberal, committed to religious freedom, you would oppose the state's prohibition of the Order.

Why is this? Why prohibit illiberal interventions? Of course, one might have pragmatic misgivings about illiberal interventions. Even if it is possible to intervene to good effect in theory, it might be said, states will intervene to bad effect in practice. The state's instruments may be too blunt. If long-term imprisonment is the only cure, it may be worse than the disease (Raz 1986, 418). Or the state may know less than the chooser. This is often the case with "matching" choices, such as choices about a career or mate in which the suitability for Prudie depends on her specific tastes, talents, temperament, endorsements, and values. However, many seem to think that even if the state overcame these limitations, Prudie would still have a complaint against its intervention in her protected choices. Perhaps they overgeneralize. But in this chapter and the next, I want to explore what sense might be made of the thought. If Prudie would still have a complaint, what might this complaint be?

In this chapter, I present the case for the negative observation: that the claim against illiberal interventions cannot be explained by interests in improvement or rights against invasion. Since I will rely on the arguments of Chapters 2 and 3, the reader is advised to read those chapters before this one. In the following chapter, I present the positive conjecture: that the claim against illiberal interventions is a claim against a certain kind of disparity of consideration. Put in a more general way, if there is sense to be made of the liberal idea, it has less to do with personal liberty—whether understood as being provisioned to pursue one's choices or as insulation from invasion and more to do with interpersonal equality—with one's standing with respect to others.

19.1 Illiberal Interventions

Before pursuing this question, one might ask, reasonably enough, for more guidance on what it means for the state to intervene in protected choices. Which choices are protected? Which interventions matter? While I doubt any pat answers can be given, I assume we have at least some material with which to start: more or less confident particular judgments that this or that intervention in this or that protected choice would be impermissibly illiberal. As we learn more about the values that ground these particular judgments, of course, our confidence in some of these particular judgments may wax while our confidence in others may wane. However, I doubt there is some clear, succinct intermediate formula that, by defining "protected" and "intervention," encapsulates these particular judgments and shows how they follow from the grounding values. To the question of how to define the terms "protected" and "intervention," the only general answer may be: as the balance of grounding values implies.

To see this, it is instructive to consider the shortcomings of the most natural candidate for such an intermediate formula: Mill's Harm Principle, perhaps interpreted or amended in some way (Hart 1963; Feinberg 1984;

Raz 1986; Leiter 2013).[3] As defined by the Harm Principle, protected choices are choices that don't (themselves, nonconsensually) harm others. And protected choices are protected from, roughly, threat, coercion, force, social sanction, enforcement, imprisonment, punishment, and criminalization—Mill's ([1859] 2015, 13) "compelling . . . visiting with evil"—but not from mere advice—"remonstrating . . . reasoning . . . persuading . . . entreating."

First, the Harm Principle doesn't draw a very clear line between prohibited "interventions" and other ways of affecting someone's choices. The literature often casually treats the items on the list of prohibited interventions—threat, coercion, force, imprisonment, punishment, and criminalization—as, on the one hand, interchangeable with one another and, on the other, clearly distinct from other ways of affecting choice. Yet the items on the list of prohibited interventions differ significantly, in morally relevant ways, from one another, and they can be hard to distinguish, in morally relevant ways, from items left off the list.

Second, it's notoriously unclear what counts as harm to others and so which choices are, because they don't harm others, protected. On the one hand, if one counts as harming others simply by helping make a bad choice available to them, then the Harm Principle does not protect very much.[4] On the other hand, if one counts as harming others only when one violates natural rights, then, except in the opinion of libertarians, the Harm Principle protects too much, prohibiting the state from intervening to ensure contributions to public services. In search of a middle ground, we might say that one harms others when one fails in a duty owed to others. However, as Chapter 2 argued, it's a mistake to think that intervening in someone's choice is permitted only when they would otherwise fail in a duty. At very least, we rejected Force Requires Duty.

A third problem with the lines the Harm Principle draws is that some interventions to prevent harm to self seem permissible. "End interventions," designed to steer people from bad choices of final, organizing ends, such as religion, career, or relationship, are indeed illiberal. But many otherwise liberal states engage in "means interventions," designed to steer people from bad choices of all-purpose materials for pursuing such ends, such as health, safety, or financial security. They impose sin taxes, for example, which at least profess to aim at reducing alcohol, tobacco, or sugar consumption (even if one worries that they are politically expedient but regressive ways to raise revenue). They regulate prescription medicine (Conly 2013, 18). They require that goods for commercial sale have built-in mechanisms, such as seat-belt buzzers, to deter imprudence. One might reply that such means interventions conform to the Harm Principle on the grounds that the choosers would otherwise harm others by exposing them, for example, to secondhand smoke or higher insurance premiums. But such arguments seem to me strained.

A final worry is that the Harm Principle, even on the broadest definition of harm to others, doesn't protect enough. Consider, again, advice: simply informing someone of reasons that independently obtain. According to the Harm Principle, advice is the one thing that, unlike, say, coercion, is supposed to be unproblematically permissible. But not even this is clear. Although it may be permissible for individuals to advise one another to avoid a particular religious choice, is it permissible for the state to do so?

19.2 Cost Effects

We turn now to ways in which a liberal might support the prohibition on interventions in protected choices. Again, we rely, for lack of something better, on our particular judgments, rather than any intermediate formula such as the Harm Principle, to guide us about what counts as an intervention and what counts as a protected choice. To begin with, it might be argued that illiberal interventions in Prudie's choice simply worsen Prudie's choice situation. Again, Prudie will be our recurring character, whose bad choice of the Order, or smoking, or what have you is the target of an illiberal intervention. Her complaint against illiberal interventions is simply an improvement complaint. The state could have improved her choice situation by not so intervening.

I believe this is more or less the approach that Rawls (1971, 1993) takes. He views the basic liberties as means to the pursuit of certain abstractly conceived activities, such as the pursuit of a determinate conception of the good. The reason why the parties in the original position seek to secure the basic liberties for those they represent is to better position them to live fulfilling lives or to develop and exercise their moral powers. However, Rawls may not even be trying to answer our question: Why not intervene to lead people to better choices? Since citizens are conceived to have an interest in a determinate conception of the good, whether or not that conception is worthwhile, no case can be put to parties in the original position for a more discriminating principle, which would secure the conditions for the pursuit of a worthwhile, but only a worthwhile, conception of the good. In Rawls's text, the argument for liberalism is largely off the page.

Returning to the usage of Section 3.6, we understand "steering" Prudie to be attempting to get Prudie to do something by means other than simply informing her, as advice does, of the reasons there are to do it independent of that very attempt. One way to steer Prudie away from a bad choice is to raise the cost of her making it and then inform her that the cost has been raised. Threats of forcible imprisonment certainly do this. But so do threats of other penalties or fines, as well as fees and taxes.[5]

Does raising the cost, and informing Prudie of this, make her choice situation worse? On the one hand, there is the cost imposed on Prudie if she makes the bad choice and the threat is carried out. Still, imposing this cost on Prudie might fairly improve the choice situation of others by upholding the credibility of the threat, which steers others in beneficial ways. Why then should it wrong Prudie to impose the cost? If we reply that it invades Prudie by breaching some deontological constraint like the Force Constraint, then our objection is no longer necessarily to the cost imposed but instead to the invasion that imposes it. We consider this in Section 19.4.

On the other hand, there is threatening Prudie with a cost if she makes a bad choice. Even if Prudie avoids the threatened cost, it might be said, the threat itself wrongs her. As I argued in Section 3.5, the usual way in which a threat would wrong Prudie is by violating the Choice Principle: by leaving her choice situation worse than she is entitled to from the threatener. Again, how good a choice situation she is entitled to from a given agent depends on balancing the burdens she bears in being deprived of a better choice situation against the burdens others would have to bear for the agent to provide her with a better choice situation. Now, threatening to attach a cost to an option, to be sure, tends to make Prudie's choice situation worse by making that option more costly. The question is why this negative cost effect on Prudie's choice situation isn't outweighed by the positive influence effect on Prudie's choice of making her more likely to choose what is better for her, which tends to improve her choice situation. Indeed, we might expect the cost effect to be small in this case. For, as I noted in Section 3.5, the cost effect tends to be smaller when the threat attaches a cost to a choice (such as leaving the Ethel Merman blaring) that is less valuable to the threatened person. In Prudie's case, the illiberal threat attaches a cost to a bad choice, which is not valuable to her.

In any event, the cost itself might not be severe: a night in jail (Kleiman 2009) or, if we imagine away technological limitations, a whine that persists until Prudie abandons the bad choice. Moreover, steerings needn't threaten costs at all. They might instead increase the benefit or lower the cost of Prudie's avoiding the bad choice. This is what offers and subsidies, in contrast to threats and taxes, are said to do. Or steerings might make the psychological feat, as it were, of the bad choice harder or less likely, by mind control, what Thaler and Sunstein (2008) call "choice architecture," or by simply issuing a command to someone reflexively disposed to comply. Or, finally, steerings might make successful execution of the bad choice harder or less likely even if one could otherwise psychologically choose it. This might be done by making it difficult or impossible to obtain the necessary means (what G. Dworkin [1972] calls "impure paternalism"). These means might be commodities or services whose sale or provision might be prohibited, even if their use was not. Or the means might be institutional or associational supports: the enforcement of a contract, the recognition of a marriage, or the mere presence of like-minded people. In sum, it looks like the positive influence effect of an illiberal steering might well outweigh its negative cost effect. If so, then why can't the illiberal steering improve Prudie's choice situation overall? And if it does, then why should it violate the Choice Principle?

19.3 Value-of-Compliance Effects

Even if an illiberal steering's influence effect outweighs its cost effect, however, it still might not improve Prudie's choice situation overall. This is because the illiberal steering might have negative, value-of-compliance effects. Precisely because her choice was influenced by intervention, Prudie's choice of the good option over the bad option may lack the value it would otherwise have. One might first propose that fear of a penalty or promise of a reward might corrupt one's motivations. Even if Prudie makes (what would otherwise have been) a good choice, she might do so for the wrong reasons. This deprives her choice of its value (R. Dworkin 2002, 217, 218, 269; Shiffrin 2004a; Moreau 2010, 2020, chap. 3).

However, not all interventions need to involve penalties or rewards that would displace more intrinsic motivations. Moreover, this suggestion fails to explain why liberals are specially exercised about steering: measures intended to get one to make certain choices. After all, the relative costs and benefits—penalties and rewards—of options are in constant flux even without steering. Suppose that the cost of an option increases via organic processes: it becomes too expensive on the open market or goes out of fashion. The effect on the option's relative cost, we might imagine, is precisely the same as would have been brought about by a tax or fine deliberately imposed to steer people away from the option. If contemplation of the increased cost imposed by the steering displaces intrinsic motivations, then so too does the increased cost resulting from organic processes. Yet, while the steering seems objectionably illiberal, few clamor to halt or reverse organic processes with the same effect, at least not so as to ensure that motives aren't corrupted by those organic processes.

Next one might propose that some options have value, or at least a certain kind of value, only if they are, as I put it, "selected" from an adequate range of acceptable alternatives. This is one component of Raz's (1986) definition of "autonomy." If threats attach sufficiently grave costs to alternatives, for example, then they may no longer count as acceptable. And if threats do this to a sufficient number of alternatives, then there may no longer be an adequate range. These threats will then have an adverse value-of-compliance effect. The chosen option will not count as selected. However, a more limited regime of threats might still leave enough acceptable options (Hurka 1993). Imagine that the state steers people away from a single option, such as the Order, while leaving lots of other options available. This might still seem objectionably illiberal. And this appeal to selection, like the earlier appeal to corrupted motivation, does not explain why steering should have a value-of-compliance effect that organic processes do not. Changes of fashion and market forces can narrow the range of options to precisely the same extent as steering. And yet organic processes aren't thought to compromise choice in the same way.

This leads us to a third suggestion. Steering has an effect that other changes in the cost and availability of options do not. In particular, Raz suggests that steering deprives Prudie's choice of "independence" by making Prudie the steerer's tool, making her do his will. This independence is another component of Raz's (1986) definition of "autonomy." To be sure, not all steering undermines independence. Meryl Streep's career as an actor is presumably independent, even though studios steer her to perform by offering her pay. So, what kind of steering undermines independence? Raz suggests that it is coercion, strictly speaking, that compromises independence: not only steering Prudie to do something but also steering her compellingly so that Prudie has "no other choice" and accordingly is justified or at least excused in complying (see Section 3.6). The terms of Streep's employment, attractive though they may be, don't compel her to perform. This is why her acting, even when induced by payment, still counts as independent. It's only when another compels Prudie, sees to it that Prudie has no other choice, that it seems most apt to say that Prudie has become their tool or that Prudie's will has become theirs.

Might one then argue that illiberal interventions wrong Prudie because they compellingly steer her, which deprives even her good choices of independence, which, in turn, worsens her choice situation? One problem is that few illiberal interventions, even when backed by threats of long-term imprisonment, are compelling. If the state's threats were compelling, as I noted in Section 3.6, prisons would be (closer to) empty.

Another problem is that even if illiberal interventions were compelling, it is implausible that they would deprive Prudie's good choices of independence. Set aside illiberal interventions for the moment and consider the ordinary liberal criminal law. Suppose, further, that the ordinary liberal criminal law is compelling. Thus, the ordinary liberal criminal law compellingly steers us away from the bad choice of a life of crime. Now, perhaps it's plausible to say that this makes us nonindependent, mere tools of the state, insofar as we make the general, negative choice of not a life of crime. But the ordinary liberal criminal law surely does not make us nonindependent, or mere tools of the state, insofar as we choose some specific, positive choice that is compatible with not leading a life of crime: insofar as we choose some particular noncriminal relationship, career, or faith. If the ordinary, liberal criminal law deprives those choices of independence, then it is not clear how any choices could be independent.

If, then, Prudie's specific good choices that are compatible with not leading a life of crime can be independent even though the ordinary liberal criminal law compellingly steers her away from a life of crime, why shouldn't Prudie's specific good choices, which are compatible with not pursuing some particular bad option, Bad, also be independent even though some illiberal intervention compellingly steers her away from Bad? Perhaps the fact that Prudie is compellingly steered from Bad means that Prudie cannot independently choose the negative option of not-Bad. But why can't Prudie independently choose one from among many of the specific, positive, good options that are compatible with not choosing Bad? By analogy, if compelling steering removes the option of badminton, then perhaps one cannot independently choose the general, negative option of not-badminton. Still, one might independently choose the specific, positive option of tennis or the specific, positive option of ping-pong (Miller 2010). This possibility is obscured by stylized cases with only two alternatives, Bad and Good. Since they present Good and Bad as the only alternatives, we equate the negative option of not-Bad with the positive option of Good. Since Prudie can't independently choose not-Bad, we conclude that she can't independently choose Good. But if there are many alternatives to Bad—Good 1, Good 2, Good 3, and so forth—then it no longer seems plausible that, if Prudie can't independently choose not-Bad, she can't independently choose, say, Good 2. So much for independence.

R. Dworkin suggests another way steering might undermine the value of compliance: that steering makes Prudie's good choice no longer Prudie's own achievement. The problem is not so much an evil (such as becoming the tool of another) as the absence of a good: namely, that the choice no longer counts as Prudie's achievement. The underlying thought is that Prudie faces a kind of problem or challenge, which is defined relative to a benchmark of how things stand prior to any steering. By analogy, imagine a competition to make a collage from found objects on a beach or a dinner from whatever happens to be in the cupboard. Contrast cases in which the objects were cast about by the tides or the ingredients left there by the natural ebb and flow of kitchen inventory with cases in which the same objects or ingredients were deliberately selected and placed in that order so as to suggest a certain arrangement or dish. In the former case, one's creation counts as one's achievement, one's own solution to the problem. In the latter case, it seems more the achievement of the intelligence selecting and placing the objects. One might not feel that one had been reduced to a mere instrument of another's will. But one might still take less pride in what one had thought was one's own achievement.

Again, we need to explain why the studio's paying Streep to act doesn't rob her of that achievement. For R. Dworkin, what matters is not whether the steerings compel (2002, 273; 2011, 212) but instead whether they are motivated by a judgment that a certain way of life is good or bad (2002, 282; 2011, 369). It is only such "end steerings" that rob Streep of her achievement. Presumably, a studio's efforts to get Streep to take the part are motivated by its bottom line or artistic ambitions, not by her quality of life. The rationale is that the challenge involves, in part, coming to one's own conclusions about what one values. If the state intervenes on the basis of a judgment that a certain way of life is good or bad for Prudie, then the state has done the work for Prudie, as it were, and it is not her own achievement.

Let us grant that illiberal interventions are end steerings. Still, it is implausible that an end-steered choice cannot count as Prudie's achievement. After all, there are all manner of private efforts to "end steer" people to appreciate the arts or adopt a particular religion. These efforts range from private support for the arts to private provision of houses of worship and religious texts. Surely these private efforts don't objectionably diminish one's achievement in appreciating the arts or finding religion. If they did, then it is hard to see how any choices could count as one's own achievement. So, the thought must be that while private end steerings don't compromise one's achievement, public end steerings do. But why should this be? In both cases, the contribution is coming from some other agency, apart from oneself. Isn't that what matters to whether it counts as one's own achievement? So, if private agents' end steerings don't objectionably compromise one's achievement, then it seems that the state's end steerings should not compromise one's achievement either.

19.4 Responsibility

So, let us grant that the influence effect of illiberal interventions can outweigh their cost and value-of-compliance effects. This means that illiberal interventions might improve Prudie's choice situation. Illiberal interventions fairly meet claims to improvement. Still, it might be said, illiberal interventions are impermissible because they violate Prudie's rights, provoking a complaint against invasion. In this vein, Feinberg (1986, 27) models "autonomy as sovereignty" as something like the right of an owner over her property or of a sovereign nation over its territory. Unfortunately, Feinberg's descriptions of what the right protects are as vague as they are rousing. "The life that a person threatens by his own rashness is after all *his* life; it *belongs* to him and to no one else. For this reason alone, he must be the one to decide—for better or worse—what is to be done with it" (59). But which actions violate his right "to decide what is to be done with his life"? Not all actions that somehow affect his life. Just about any action affects "his life" in some way.

Feinberg's analogies to property and territory, however, suggest a more definite, if literal-minded, answer. The right protects against physical invasion of one's bodily space. Indeed, liberalism aside, one might think we have a right against such force, whose core incident is expressed by the Force Constraint. The prohibition on illiberal interventions that use force would just be, on this view, a special case of the Force Constraint. For Kantians and libertarians, in particular, the impermissibility of illiberal interventions follows simply from the more general impermissibility of nonconsensual force. Kantians may speak here of equal external freedom (Pallikkathayil 2016); libertarians may speak of self-ownership. Self-ownership, as noted in Section 1.6, may involve more than simply the Force Constraint: it may imply that one is morally permitted to do whatever one likes with one's body; that one can permit, by consent, anything to be done to one's body (whether or not it achieves a greater good); or that one can transfer such rights over one's body to someone else.[6] But all we need here is the less controversial Force Constraint. Suppose, for the sake of argument, that illiberal interventions do use force. Would that mean illiberal interventions violate the Force Constraint?

In Section 2.7, I argued against the idea that state imposition must violate the Force Constraint. I suggested that if we accept Natural Imposition, then we should also accept State Imposition. If Flintstone's neighbors can use force on Flintstone to deter violations of natural rights, then so too may the state use force on Violet to deter violations of state directives. There is no morally relevant difference. So, let us consider a similar strategy of argument. If we accept Natural Imposition, should we not also accept the following (Conly 2013, 34–35)?

> "Illiberal Imposition": The Force Constraint is lifted, for the purposes of deterrence, when the target has violated the state's illiberal prohibition of a bad choice.

If we may use force on Flintstone for the purpose of deterring violations of natural rights, why may we not also use force on Prudie for the purpose of deterring bad choices like hers? What's the difference between Flintstone and Prudie?

As far as the Avoidance Principle is concerned, the two situations might seem similar. Like Flintstone, Prudie could have complied with the state's directive to refrain from the bad choice. Granted, some illiberal interventions would not give Prudie adequate opportunity to avoid the state's force. For instance, it would not, as far as the Avoidance Principle is concerned, lift the Force Constraint to implant devices in Prudie's body to deliver a shock when she contemplated the choice; to manipulate her brain, as a kind of puppetry, to get her to choose differently; or to confine her forcibly and preemptively (Quong 2011, 55). But we are mostly considering cases in which Prudie is given a chance to comply and told what is in store if she doesn't. Why isn't that choice situation as good as what Flintstone had?

Moreover, just as to provide Flintstone with an even better choice situation (e.g., to require his present consent) in order to impose a deterrent would burden others severely, so too to provide Prudie with an even better choice situation (e.g., to require her present consent) in order to impose a deterrent would burden others. Just as others rely on the deterrent in Flintstone's case to protect them from harm, so too they rely on the deterrent in Prudie's case to protect them from bad choices. If the state gives Prudie better opportunity to avoid force, by requiring her consent after violation, then it must give the same opportunity to everyone. But that means depriving them of the threat's protection. For if one can avoid the threatened force merely by refusing consent to its imposition, then the threat loses its power to influence. It no longer protects.

The liberal might here invoke Force Requires Duty: that it is permissible to impose a forcible deterrent only for the violation of a duty. Since Prudie had no duty to act otherwise, it is wrong to impose a deterrent on her. To this, one might reply that Prudie has a duty to refrain from bad choices. Perhaps she has a duty to herself (Arneson 2013b,d). Or perhaps she has a duty to Sage to spare him of one more bad example or potential partner in crime (Wall 2013a,b,c). But the liberal can reasonably counter, first, that even if there are duties to self, Force Requires Duty requires not just a duty, but a duty to others, and, second, that there is no duty to others to refrain from bad choices. After all, when making major life choices, we don't fret about whether we are fulfilling a duty to set a good example.

The problem for the liberal is instead that, as we saw, Force Requires Duty is unmotivated. In particular, recall from Section 2.7 the two error theories for Force Requires Duty. First, it is easy to confuse Force Requires Duty, which forbids using force when the target hasn't wronged others, with the almost tautological Condemnation Principle, which deems unfitting condemning the target for wronging others when the target hasn't, in fact, wronged others. If we grant, for the sake of argument, that unfitting implies impermissible and that punishment involves condemnation for wronging others, then the Condemnation Principle forbids the state from punishing choices that don't wrong others, as we are imagining that Prudie's choice does not (Husak 2005). But, again, the Condemnation Principle would not forbid the state from, as it were, subtracting from punishment the element of condemnation for wronging others. The state could still correctly declare that choice to be bad and impose other, nonexpressive aspects of the penalty (compare Tadros 2016, chap. 6). Yet that would be impermissibly illiberal. Second, it is easy to confuse Force Requires Duty with the Wrongful Benefit Principle: that if the target had a duty to *X*, her opportunity to avoid force by *X*-ing was adequate. However, the opportunity to avoid force by *X*-ing can be adequate even if the target had no duty to *X*. This is especially likely to be so in Prudie's case, where *X*-ing is just abstaining from a bad choice.

So far, then, Prudie's situation seems, in relevant respects, just like Flintstone's. Following through on the threat to Prudie seems permissible, just like following through on the threat to Flintstone. But here, I think, there is a way for the liberal to drive a wedge between the cases. This is to invoke the:

> "Responsibility Principle": The fact that force would protect others from their own choices carries no (or at least diminished) weight in lifting the Force Constraint.

Whereas the force used on Flintstone protects others from harms that do not arise from their own choices, the force used on Prudie protects others from harms that do arise from their own choices. That's the difference. Vic has no other way to avoid the harms except to limit Flintstone's control. By contrast, Sage—a representative person whose opportunities are improved by the illiberal threat to Prudie—clearly does have a way to avoid the harms other than to limit Prudie's control. Since the harms would come from Sage's own choices, he can avoid the harms by choosing appropriately. Why isn't that his responsibility? Why is it fair to limit Prudie's control when Sage, by choosing appropriately, could enjoy the same benefits?

To be sure, much will depend on whether it is fair to treat the harm to Sage as his responsibility. Was he in a position to know what he was getting into? Was his judgment impaired by disease or drink? It seems fairer that Prudie's control should be limited so as to protect Sage from his faultlessly ignorant or impaired, so-called lower *c* "choices" than from his well-informed, cool-headed, capital *C* Choices. Thus, the Responsibility Principle suggests a stable explanation of an idea that Arneson (1989, 2005) calls an "unacceptable halfway house": namely, the idea that "soft-paternalistic" force—which enforces directives that prohibit ignorant or impaired "choices" (e.g., "You may not engage in this activity until you have passed a quiz and a breathalyzer test")—may be permissible when "hard-paternalistic" force—which enforces directives that prohibit Choices—may not be. Soft-paternalistic force on Prudie is justified as a way of protecting Sage (as always via a credible deterrent) from harms that wouldn't, in the relevant sense, be due to his Choices. That is like protecting Vic from Flintstone. Hard-paternalistic force on Prudie, by contrast, would have to be justified as a way of protecting Sage from his own settled will. That isn't like protecting Vic from Flintstone. At that point, it's up to Sage, not Prudie, to protect himself. Therefore, the objection to hard-paternalistic force against Prudie—or, rather, to following through on forcible threats meant to deter Choices—is not that it is paternalistic. It is instead that it is unfair, at least to Prudie's interest in control over others' use of force against her. For Prudie's control is limited in order to provide protection that Sage could provide for himself. By contrast, soft-paternalistic force against Prudie—or, rather, following through on forcible threats meant to deter "choices"—provides protection that Sage cannot provide for himself, just as the force against Flintstone provides protection that Vic cannot provide for himself.

So, there are reasons to think that when illiberal interventions use force, they may violate the Force Constraint. However, do illiberal interventions need to use force? First, even if illiberal interventions impose costs, they might not use force to impose them. Consider the Omittite emperor's forceless imprisonment (Section 2.5) or automatically deducted fines. Second, as we saw in Section 19.2, illiberal interventions might not even impose costs. They might provide subsidies, structure choices, make means unavailable, or, finally, simply issue advice. So, applying the Subtraction Test, we find that if even if we remove the force from illiberal interventions, the complaint against their illiberality remains.

19.5 Public Justification

We have not yet considered a prevalent approach to explaining the prohibition on illiberal interventions, which is often associated with the phrases "public reason," "public justification," and "reasonable acceptability." It runs roughly as follows:

1. Prudie has a "right against what she cannot accept." That is, she has a right against being treated in certain problematic ways, which is lifted only if she could "reasonably accept" grounds that, if true, would justify that treatment.
2. Illiberal interventions treat Prudie in these problematic ways.
3. There is no justification of illiberal interventions that Prudie can reasonably accept.
4. So, illiberal interventions violate Prudie's right against what she cannot accept.[7]

A now vast literature proposes rights against (or at least prohibitions of) what a person cannot reasonably accept, with Rawls's (1993) "Liberal Principle of Legitimacy" being perhaps the best-known instance (see also Nagel 1991; Larmore 2008).

Two comments before we assess whether the argument is sound. First, "reasonably accept" can be understood in two ways. On a stronger reading of "reasonably accept," the grounds in question must be compatible with Prudie's actual, particular religious, moral, philosophical, or comprehensive commitments (J. Cohen 2009; Estlund 2008; Gaus 2011; Quong 2011, 168; Tadros 2016, chap. 8), unless these commitments are "unreasonable." On a weaker reading, the grounds in question may instead be relevantly "generic"—based on ideas from the "public political culture" or "common human reason"—even if they aren't compatible with Prudie's actual, particular commitments (Rawls 1993; Freeman 2007, 236–237).

Second, one might wonder why (1) takes the form it does. Why does respecting the right require only that Prudie could reasonably accept the grounds, even if Prudie does not actually accept the justification? Perhaps the idea is, on the one hand, that Prudie has a stronger complaint against the problematic treatment to the extent that Prudie is further from actual acceptance of its justification but, on the other hand, that this complaint has to be balanced against the burdens others would have to bear if the problematic treatment is forgone. Hence the fact that Prudie could reasonably accept the grounds may be close enough, in light of the burdens others would have to bear either to bring Prudie closer or to forgo what would be gained only by the problematic treatment of her. Second, it may be fair to ask others to do their part in bringing it about that Prudie is not subject to problematic treatment whose justification Prudie does not accept. But they can do their part either by refraining from the treatment or by helping Prudie accept it. If others have ensured that Prudie could reasonably accept the grounds, they have given adequate help. It's not their responsibility if Prudie refuses to actually accept the justification. This is especially so if Prudie's refusal is epistemically unreasonable (e.g., intellectually lazy) or morally unreasonable (e.g., unwilling to take others' interests into account).[8] If this reconstruction is correct, however, then the right against what Prudie cannot reasonably accept would seem to require not only that there be grounds that Prudie could reasonably accept but also that others give Prudie sufficient help to actually accept the justification, such as by trying to convince Prudie of it. It is worth noting that this further requirement, to make efforts to actually convince others, seems largely overlooked in the literature.

With these two comments out of the way, on to the central issue: Is the argument is sound? Of course, the argument also needs to show (3): that there is no justification of illiberal interventions that Prudie can reasonably accept. But some illiberal interventions might be justified on grounds, such as domestic peace, that are either generic or compatible with a wide range of particular views (Arneson 2014; however, see J. Cohen 2009, 238). And even illiberal interventions that can be justified on grounds that are compatible only with a narrow range of particular views might nevertheless take place in a society whose members agree on those particular views.[9]

But let us set that challenge aside. The deeper questions are: What is the problematic treatment? And why, as (1) claims, is reasonable acceptability required to solve the problem? After all, if the problematic treatment is force, then why isn't a sufficient solution, as the Avoidance Principle holds, that Prudie has adequate opportunity to avoid the force? Or if the problematic treatment is instead a kind of threat, then why isn't a sufficient solution, as the Choice Principle holds, that Prudie's choice situation is left no worse than she is entitled to? Why insist on reasonable acceptability as a further requirement?

It's hard to find explicit answers in the literature. One exception is Gaus (2011), who views the problematic treatment not as force or threat but instead as holding attitudes, such as resentment, toward Prudie that presuppose that she has, or had, a duty to act otherwise. Holding such attitudes toward Prudie is appropriate, he then suggests, only insofar as Prudie could reasonably accept that she has that duty. Why think this? Gaus suggests it offers the best explanation of why it is inappropriate to resent children or the mentally impaired for what would otherwise count as a violation of duty. It is inappropriate because they could not reasonably accept that they had that duty. In any event, this doesn't quite give us something of the form of (1), which we might restate as:

> One wrongs Prudie by treating her in a certain way, unless she could reasonably accept grounds that, if true, would justify one's treating her in that way.

Instead, it gives us:

> It is inappropriate to hold attitudes toward Prudie that presuppose that she has a duty, unless she could reasonably accept that she has that duty.[10]

Even if, for whatever reason, we grant (1)—that Prudie has such a right against problematic treatment that she cannot reasonably accept—why should (4) follow: that illiberal interventions on Prudie are prohibited? We still need to show (2): that illiberal interventions treat Prudie in the problematic ways. But, as we have seen, illiberal intervention need not involve force or threat. So, this argument would present no barrier to illiberal interventions in the Omittite Empire (Section 2.5) or Our Trusting Future (Section 3.1)—just as this argument presents no barrier to the sermons of private citizens. And, turning to Gaus's view—that the problematic treatment is presupposing that Prudie has a duty to do otherwise—illiberal interventions need not presuppose that Prudie has a duty. This is so even if the illiberal interventions use force, at least if we reject Force Requires Duty.[11]

19.6 Paternalism, Strictly Speaking

One last try. Perhaps the complaint about illiberal interventions is a complaint against "paternalism, strictly speaking": against others aiming to benefit Prudie by means other than advice when she in advance refused, or now refuses, to consent to being so benefitted. The argument would run as follows:

1. Prudie has a right against paternalism, strictly speaking.
2. The illiberal interventions against which Prudie has a complaint treat her paternalistically, strictly speaking.

However, against (2), not all illiberal interventions, even interventions that make Prudie less likely to choose badly, treat Prudie paternalistically, strictly speaking. First, if aiming to benefit Prudie is required to make the intervention paternalistic, then the same intervention might avoid the charge of paternalism simply by aiming not to benefit Prudie but instead to please God. But that would not make it any less objectionably illiberal. Second, not only Prudie but also her neighbor, Prudhomme, benefits from the state's intervention. And the state cannot benefit Prudhomme without benefitting Prudie. Either the state illiberally intervenes with everyone or with no one. So, in illiberally intervening with everyone in order to benefit Prudhomme, the state needn't treat Prudie paternalistically. And it needn't treat Prudhomme paternalistically if he consents to it (de Marneffe 2010, 81). Yet Prudhomme's consent should not make it permissible to subject Prudie to an illiberal intervention. Finally, assuming that mere advice is not paternalistic, a right against paternalism would not rule out the state's advice against the Order, which, again, seems objectionably illiberal.

Moreover, against (1), the right against paternalism is itself mysterious. Many suggest that the problem with paternalism has to do with what it expresses: for instance, that the target's judgment (or agency) with regard to his own good (or what lies within his "legitimate agency") is inferior (Shiffrin 2000; Quong 2011; Cornell 2015; Cholbi 2017). But it's not wrong to report that someone has inferior judgment about his own good (setting aside independent moral prohibitions on misleading, causing gratuitous pain, etc.). And a person may take as much pride in his judgment about his duties to others or impersonal values as in his judgment about his own good. Why then isn't it as objectionable for others to express that his judgment is inferior in those other domains?

20

Claims against Illiberal Interventions

The Positive Conjecture

In the last chapter, we sought to identify a complaint or complaints against illiberal interventions. We indeed found some such complaints, grounded in interests in improvement and rights against invasion. But we did not find complaints that, even jointly, would cover all the relevant instances in which there is, at least by the lights of liberals, an illiberal intervention that provokes a complaint. Count this as another instance of our negative observation. Now turning to the positive conjecture, I suggest that at least some of these remaining instances might be accounted for by a claim against inferiority. Certain illiberal interventions constitute a disparity of consideration by the state. They violate Equal Consideration and so, among other things, undermine Equal Citizenship. Moreover, the disparity has the characteristics of discrimination, insofar as it tracks the basing trait of a social identity associated with the choices that those interventions target. It threatens to be a disparity of consideration not only by the state but also by society at large.[1]

20.1 Condemnation of Choice as a Disparity of Consideration

Picture the intervention against the Order—and you needn't go to extremes. There aren't any house-to-house searches or forced confessions. Rather, when the practice of the Order is so blatant that peace officers can't pretend it escaped their notice, they will issue a citation, which will escalate, after repeated violation, from a warning to confiscation of ritual equipment, a small fine, or a night in jail. Nothing terribly ham handed or Orwellian. Yet how could this fail, in a social world anything like those we are acquainted with, to mark members of the Order as "beneath" others?

Why is this? It can't be said that the illiberal interventions amount to a disparity of consideration by the state because they are less concerned to advance the interests of members of the Order than those of others. They are intended to improve the choice situation of members of the Order precisely by dissuading them from the Order. Moreover, they might be, in principle, known to have precisely that aim—although, in that case, at least the members of the Order will think they are well-intentioned mistakes. Instead, the illiberal interventions contribute to a disparity of consideration. The interventions condemn the Order, if not as a practice that wrongs others, then as no way to live. And in a social world anything like ours, to condemn that choice is to rank those who are defined by the choice, whether or not they themselves make it, as inferior. In this context, there is no way to distinguish condemnation of the choice from subordination of the identity that choice is assigned. Compare the tension in declaring: "People are just objectively uglier when they have the physical characteristics associated with your race. But I don't mean that in a racist way." It's not just a matter of disentangling the trait from the identity in one's own thoughts or conveying to others that one has so disentangled them. It's also a matter of what the context even makes it possible to say (Eisgruber and Sager 2007; Hellman 2008). This may be compounded by the second sort of recursion mentioned in Section 6.4: namely, that where there is an existing disparity of regard, a response that otherwise would be neutral or even beneficial (such as a seat at the back of the bus) may take on a negative valence. The targeted choices may be associated with groups of a kind, such as religious groups, among which there is a not-too-distant history of disparities of consideration.

Illiberal interventions will be objectionable, on this account, insofar as they condemn, or will be seen as condemning, the relevant choice. Criminal punishments otherwise reserved for serious wrongs to others will surely be seen to condemn the choice. The same is true of public prohibitions, even if not backed by any penalty. And the same is true of mere advice when it comes from the state. Imagine state-funded television spots featuring the admonitions of celebrities. (The crusty-but-benign judge intones: "I'd advise you to steer clear of the Order. It's no way to live.") Nothing totalitarian, but the stigma seems clear.

However, whether further measures condemn, or will be seen as condemning, a certain choice is a contingent matter. As is the nature of expression, a great deal will depend on history and context. In particular, the fact that a line was drawn in the past may give crossing it a significance it would not otherwise have. The establishment of a Federal Church of America is not only constitutionally but also morally unthinkable. But comparable alarm about the Church of England, given what it has become, may seem provincial (like certain arguments for the necessity, in all times and places, of judicial review of primary legislation).

Does a concern for disparities of consideration then give us a reason to refrain from otherwise justified criminal penalties on the grounds that they condemn the choice to commit crime and so condemn the criminal (Wall and Klosko 2003, 20; Wall 2005, 299–300)? Or, setting aside criminal penalties, may the state simply criticize hate speech while permitting it? First, not all criminal penalties need to target an existing identity, as a career criminal, or assign a new identity, as a convict. In many cases, it would be better if they focused on particular violations of the law, imposing the regrettably necessary deterrent cost in a way that is more or less cabined from the rest of the target's social identity. Second, as we observed in Chapter 6, disparities in consideration are less objectionable when they are merited: when the difference in consideration is internal to the recognition of other values. Lesser consideration of a criminal—say, a withdrawal of default trust and goodwill—may be merited when they have wronged others. Lesser consideration of them may be the flip side of recognizing the claims of the others whom they have wronged. But the Order does not wrong anyone or deny anyone's equal standing. It is less clear that recognizing the flaws of the choice of members of the Order requires lesser consideration of the members themselves. Of course, other responses to bad religious choices may be merited, such as a disinclination to take life advice from someone who has made them. Finally, the state's penalizing crime or criticizing hate speech is done precisely to uphold Equal Citizenship, whereas steering people away from a bad religious choice is not.

If it is wrong for the state to advise people away from the Order, then why isn't it wrong for a nonstate actor to advise people similarly? First, individuals, as well as certain associations, cannot but form and express judgments about the worth of certain choices. This is simply part of their deciding how they themselves are to live or part of their associative purpose. The state, by contrast, does not need to make up, let alone express, its mind (Nagel 1991). Second, the advice of nonstate actors, since it does not affect Equal Consideration by the state, doesn't undermine Equal Citizenship. Finally, if the state does provide for Equal Citizenship, then this, in turn, provides a context in which nonstate actors can offer the same advice to individuals while recognizing their equal standing as individuals. One citizen can preface her advice to another with something like the line Hall puts on the lips of Voltaire ("I disapprove of what you say, but I will defend to the death your right to say it"): "While (i) you are, or would be, making a mistake in remaining within or joining the Order, (ii) I oppose any intervention in your doing so that threatens your standing as an equal citizen." The advice is thus focused explicitly on the value of the choice and not the social standing of the person. The state, by contrast, can't say this without a kind of pragmatic contradiction. For, in saying (i), the state does the very thing it commits itself to oppose in (ii).

Now, this account—which might be caricatured, with some justice, as "liberalism as identity politics"—has an obvious limitation. It protects only those choices that are associated with an identity that might attract a disparity of consideration. Religious affiliation—along with its negative image, the rejection of any religious affiliation in an overtly religious society—may be such a choice. But other choices are not associated with such an identity. Choices of means, such as health or finances, and of some ends, such as engagement with the arts, need not be associated with social identities. So, on this account, if end intervention is usually more objectionable than means intervention, it is because social identities usually coalesce around ends rather than means. These implications are not unwelcome, however. These interventions—concerning means, such as health or finances, and certain ends, such as engagement with the arts—don't seem objectionably illiberal, at least not in the way a ban on the Order would be.

This account of the prohibition on illiberal interventions contrasts with the account suggested by the right against what one cannot accept, as discussed in Section 19.5. The mere fact that some cannot reasonably accept certain state policies whereas others can reasonably accept those state policies is not enough for a disparity of consideration among them. This is because the presence or absence of such an abstract justificatory relationship might well lack the requisite social salience. For instance, the mere existence of state funding of the arts, based on premises that some cannot reasonably accept, would not tend to make them an underclass—nor would state policies implementing liberal justice, based on premises that some established academic philosophers, because they are committed on abstract philosophical grounds to utilitarianism, cannot reasonably accept.

20.2 Rawls on Unequal Liberty

This discussion may shed light on a puzzle about Rawls's doctrine of the equal basic liberties. The puzzle, which, for all the attention given to Rawls's texts, seems to have gone unmentioned, concerns the fact that Rawls's paradigm of unequal liberty is a ban on a minority religion (1971, sec. 33). To be sure, one might object to this ban simply on the grounds that it unjustifiably reduces everyone's liberty. No one is permitted to practice the banned religion. As an unjustified reduction in everyone's liberty, it would be ruled out by the "greatest extent" part of Rawls's first principle. The puzzle is why Rawls should describe a ban on a minority religion as an inequality in liberty, which is ruled out by the "equal" part of the first principle. What does it have to do with inequality? After all, the ban on the minority religion removes the same option from everyone's menu, like the prohibition of alcohol or perjury. Granted, it unjustifiably reduces everyone's liberty. But, again, it appears to reduce everyone's liberty equally. So why treat it as the paradigm of, specifically, unequal liberty?

One might reply that, if we take it as given that some people are adherents of the banned religion, the ban does not remove the same option from everyone's menu. It removes from some, but not from others, the option of "the religion to which I adhere." One difficulty with this reply, however, is that the same could be said of the prohibition of alcohol or perjury. Another difficulty with this reply is that Rawls explicitly rules it out. For Rawls insists that when evaluating whether people have been given their just shares, we should view people as free: as not bound by, or identified with, any religion or other conception of the good. Insofar as a person is viewed as free, there is no particular religion to which that person adheres. Rawls (1975) clarifies this in his reply to Nagel (1973). Nagel observes that a society that realized justice as fairness would not be neutral among conceptions of the good, since it would likely be a society in which some conceptions flourished and others did not. Rawls replied that while the theory was not neutral among conceptions, it was nonetheless fair to persons, viewed as free. For any given conception, it ensured that no person had (unfairly) greater opportunity to pursue successfully that conception than any other person—even if it did not ensure that each person would have the same opportunity to pursue successfully some conception as that same person would have to pursue another conception. I am inclined to agree with Rawls on this point. In evaluating whether someone's situation is better or worse, we should view them as free: as not associated with any particular choice, judgment, or so on. But then a ban on a minority religion, while perhaps unjustifiably restrictive for everyone, does not treat anyone, viewed as free, unequally. Structurally, a ban on a minority religion is no different from a ban on alcohol or perjury. It restricts everyone's liberty in the same way, removing the same choice equally from everyone's menu.

So, the puzzle remains. Whether or not the ban is justified, why does it seem so natural to understand the objection as one that has to do with inequality? The discussion of the previous section suggests an answer. The ban on a single religion would imply a disparity of consideration. The ban would effect a kind of hierarchy between those who are and those who are not socially identified with the banned choice. That is what it has to do with equality. Perhaps this is why a ban on a minority religion suggests itself so naturally to Rawls, and to us, as a paradigm of unequal liberty.

20.3 Self-Sovereignty

Our positive conjecture, however, is limited. There are other such interventions, which do not mark an underclass, that liberals would likely still find objectionable—at least liberals of the pure, not merely pragmatic sort with whom we have been traveling in the previous chapter and this one. Consider a system that steers people toward good career or relationship "matches." In principle, everyone's options might be pared back equally. For example, each astrological sign might be banned from dating exactly one other sign. Or, to take an example put to me by Jon Quong, consider a homogenous, puritanical society in which all agree that sex outside marriage is bad. Even in such a society, criminal penalties for fornication might seem intuitively illiberal, despite there being no nonpuritans to suffer any disparity of consideration. If this is so, then complaints against these illiberal but egalitarian interventions must be explained by something other than the claims of inferiority that are the focus of this book.

In this section, I explore what would seem to be needed to explain these complaints. It requires giving still freer rein to moral-philosophical speculation than the book already does, and even so it comes up short. I return to the speculation from Section 8.3 that one enjoys a certain kind of social standing, self-sovereignty, insofar as de facto authorities, whether individual or collective, do not command one. This social standing differs from the social standing of noninferiority with which this book is principally concerned. This is why self-sovereignty might promise to mop up the counterexamples of illiberal but egalitarian intervention with which this section began, such as steering toward good matches and the homogenous Puritans. Although no individual is related to any other individual as an inferior, each individual is still subject to the commands of a collective de facto authority, and each individual has a complaint about that.

Self-sovereignty would thus support a right against commands from a de facto authority. But it seems that we would then have to suppose, further, that this right against commands, like the right against force, is to enjoy adequate control over subjection to such commands—"adequate" as balanced against the burdens others would have to bear to provide one with greater control. Then analogues to the Avoidance (Section 2.7) and Responsibility (Section 19.4) Principles would follow. Now, while we may avoid, at least by exercising a right of exit, subjection to the commands of some de facto authorities, such as churches in a liberal order, we cannot avoid subjection to the commands of the state; it is inescapable. This is so even if the state, as with the Omittites, wields no force or, as in Our Trusting Future, makes no threats. So, the idea of a right against commands threatens to prohibit all the state's commands, even its liberal commands. What we would have to say, it seems, is that, while enjoying no control over subjection to the state's liberal commands, we still enjoy adequate control, given the burdens others would have to bear to provide us with further control. However, we would have to say, we do not enjoy adequate control over the state's illiberal commands, or rather its commands to desist from capital C Choices, for the reasons that support the Responsibility Principle. For leaving people free from those commands would not burden others unfairly, since others could already enjoy the benefits that those commands would bring simply by choosing appropriately. Whether these are plausible things to say is a further question.

This claim to self-sovereignty, or this right against commands, might seem, on its own, to prohibit too little. Just as it would permit, plausibly, state funding for the arts, insofar as such funding does not command anything but merely makes options available, it would also permit, implausibly, parallel funding for a specific church. And it would permit state advice to stay away from the Order since that is simply advice, not command. In the present dialectical context, however, neither is a problem. The right against commands can be supplemented by the previous section's account, based in claims against inferiority, which would prohibit such funding and advice. The more serious problem, to my mind, is that this right against commands may prohibit too much. It would prohibit, rigoristically, means interventions in Choices that took the form of commands, such as, for instance, sin taxes on cigarettes. And, left to itself, this right against commands would imply, implausibly, that such means interventions are objectionable to the same extent and for the same reasons as parallel end interventions, such as sin taxes on religious articles.

IV

Contrasts

In this part, we return to a question that was asked in Chapter 7: Are there really claims against inferiority? Few would deny that there are "complaints," to put it mildly, against extreme cases of bondage or caste. However, some may deny that those complaints are against relations of inferiority as such. They are, instead, complaints against, for instance, what republicans call "domination." Others, such as "luck egalitarians," may agree that "equality," somehow understood, is an important consideration, and they may agree that it is distinct from interests in improvement and rights against invasion. But they may contend that equality, on the relevant understanding, is different from the absence of relations of inferiority. This part reviews further arguments of this form: that there are valid complaints in conceptual space roughly where we purport to have found complaints against inferiority but that these valid complaints are not complaints against inferiority as such.

21

Being No Worse Off

At least in the Anglophone political philosophy of the past few decades, the word "equality" suggests a principle of distributive justice, to the effect that everyone should have the same amount of something. In spite of the otherwise egalitarian tenor of this book, this idea of equality, as a principle of distributive justice, plays no role in it. To the extent that something like distributive justice enters into the framework of this book, it is a matter of how some agent, Benny, is to trade off the interest of some patient, Indy, in some improvement against the interest of another patient, Altra, in some other improvement, when Benny must triage between those improvements. Again, Indy's improvement interest itself is noncomparative. How well off Altra is, or what Benny does for Altra, does not, in itself, affect whether Indy's improvement interest is satisfied. What counts as a fair trade-off among improvement interests, I suggested, is prioritarian rather than egalitarian. Other things equal, Benny has stronger reason to give Indy an improvement than to give Altra the same improvement when Indy is worse off than Altra. But it is not an unfair trade-off to improve things for Altra when one can't improve things for Indy, even if that increases inequality.

However, some believe distributive justice or injustice plays a different role. I have in mind here the "egalitarian" part of the "luck egalitarianism" of philosophers such as Cohen and Temkin. According to this view, justice and injustice are properties of states of affairs, and the relevant principle of distributive justice is egalitarian. Just states of affairs are those where people have equal amounts of something. States of affairs where people have unequal amounts of something are unjust.

21.1 Cosmic Fairness

More specifically, one might analyze this view, which I call the "Theory of Cosmic Fairness," as consisting in the following tenets.

- "Agent Independence": A distributive state of affairs—that some people have this and others have that—can be cosmically unfair to Altra, whether or not it results from what any agent does (Temkin 1993, 12–13; G. Cohen 2008, 153–155, 314).
- "Directedness": Restating Agent-Independence with a different emphasis, a distributive state of affairs can be cosmically unfair *to Altra*, whether or not it results from what any agent does.
- "Bare Comparison": More specifically, it is cosmically unfair to Altra for Altra to be worse off than Indy for reasons that are not due to their choices.

This last clause leaves open whether the Theory of Cosmic Fairness is "luckist." It is luckist if it is not cosmically unfair for Altra to be worse off than Indy for reasons that are due to their choices.

- "Normativity": The fact that it is cosmically unfair to Altra for Altra to be worse off than Indy is a reason for Benny to mitigate it.

Of course, once Benny can do something to mitigate cosmic unfairness, it then becomes the case that if Benny refrains from doing it, the cosmic unfairness does result from something that someone has done. The cosmic unfairness, going forward, results from Benny's refraining from mitigating it.

- "Patient Universality": The fact that it is cosmically unfair to Altra for Altra to be worse off than Indy in no way depends on Altra's and Indy's relations to one another, such as their belonging to the same society or epoch.
- "Agent Universality": The fact that it is cosmically unfair to Altra for Altra to be worse off than Indy, which gives Benny a reason to mitigate it, in no way depends on any special feature of Benny's situation, such as his relationships to Altra or Indy, other than simply that Benny is able to mitigate the unfairness.

Agent and Patient Universality follow simply from the generality of Bare Comparison. According to Bare Comparison, what matters is merely that Altra has less than Indy (in ways not due to their choices). No further relation between Altra and Indy needs to be involved. And no restriction is implied on who has a reason to do something about it.

Benny's reason to mitigate cosmic unfairness to Altra is distinct from Benny's reason to improve Altra's situation. In particular, Benny's reason to mitigate cosmic unfairness to Altra, unlike Benny's reason to improve Altra's situation, can be a reason for Benny to refrain from improving Indy's situation because this would make Indy's situation better than Altra's. This is so even if improving Indy's situation came at no cost to Altra because, let us suppose, Benny cannot do anything to affect Altra. By contrast, Benny's reason to improve Altra's situation is not a reason to refrain from improving Indy's situation. And Benny's reason to improve Indy's situation is a reason against refraining from improving Indy's situation. In sum, mitigating cosmic unfairness sometimes argues against inequality-increasing weak Pareto improvements.

This is not to deny that Benny might have reasons, rooted in Altra's claims against inferiority, that weigh against such inequality-increasing weak Pareto improvements to Indy. I have discussed several such claims that Altra might have. For one thing, Benny's improving things for Indy but not for Altra might violate Equal Treatment by Officials. Benny, while wielding superior power and authority over Indy and Altra, gives something to Indy but not to Altra, with no justifying difference between them.

However, this reason against certain inequality-increasing weak Pareto improvements differs from the reason to mitigate cosmic unfairness. In contrast to Agent Independence, Altra's complaint is only against what someone (i.e., Benny) does, not against a state of affairs that comes to pass through no agent's doings. In contrast to Agent Universality, Altra's complaint depends on Altra's being subject to Benny's superior power and authority. If Altra is not subject to Benny's superior power and authority, then Altra has no such complaint. In contrast to Patient Universality, Altra's complaint depends on Indy's also being subject to Benny. And, finally, Altra's complaint against Benny's inequality-increasing weak Pareto improvement to Indy's situation has a different basis. It is rooted in Altra's claims against inferiority, rather than in anyone's claims against cosmic unfairness.

Now, one might suggest that Agent Independence is a dispensable part of the Theory of Cosmic Fairness. As an alternative to Agent Independence, one could say that what is unfair to Altra is not that she has less than Indy but instead that some agent, such as Benny, fails properly to respond to her objection to having less than Indy. But what, on this suggestion, accounts for Altra's objection to having less than Indy, which Benny disregards? It's neither an interest of Altra's in improvement nor a claim of Altra's against inferiority. It would seem, instead, to be an objection to suffering the unfairness of having less than Indy. But that seems to presuppose that it is unfair to Altra to have less than Indy, whether or not there is a Benny who can do, or could have done, anything about it (Temkin 1993, 21n3).

One might also suggest that Directedness is dispensable. It is not cosmically unfair to Altra that she has less than Indy. It is instead cosmically unfair, period. It is simply a respect in which that state of affairs is impersonally bad. Altra has no more complaint about it than anyone else has—or, more to the point, no one has a complaint about it. It is simply a way the world is worse than it could be, just as the world is worse than it could be if there is less biodiversity (Munoz-Dardé 2005, 260, 266, 273; Anderson 2010a). However, Temkin (1993, 19) and G. Cohen (2008, 157–158) do describe it, at least at times, as unfair *to Altra* that she has less than Indy. And it is with good reason that they describe it this way. The idea that cosmic unfairness is impersonally bad, even if it isn't unfairness to anyone, is far less compelling. Indeed, it seems more like a fetish for a certain pattern than a concern of any moral seriousness.

So, Agent Independence and Directedness seem indispensable to the Theory of Cosmic Fairness. However, one might worry that Agent Independence and Directedness are incompatible, which would mean that the Theory of Cosmic Fairness must be incoherent. What can it mean to say that having less is unfair to Altra unless it means that Altra, in particular, has a complaint about it?[1] But how can Altra have a complaint that isn't addressed to anyone (Anderson 2010a, 9)? This seems to me a good question, and it isn't clear to me what answer can be given.[2] But let us allow this to pass. Grant, for the sake of argument, that Agent Independence and Directedness are compatible.

Even so, the Theory of Cosmic Fairness seems implausible, so long as that idea, and only that idea, is kept in focus. One sees this most clearly when one considers the full generality of Bare Comparison and its implication, Patient Universality. According to Patient Universality, the relevant comparison can be among people living in different times and places. No matter how distant they may be from one another, it is unfair for Altra to have less than Indy. Mitigating cosmic unfairness would thus be a reason against improving things for future generations, even in ways that cost us nothing. For refraining from improving things for posterity would avoid the consequence that our descendants, unfairly, had more than our ancestors. The thought that there is any reason (even if outweighed) against leaving a better world for posterity seems hard to credit.

Whatever plausibility the Theory of Cosmic Fairness has, I think, it borrows from other ideas. One of these is the perfectly credible idea that it is not fair to Altra that she is worse off than Indy. But it doesn't follow that it is unfair to her. What I would say is that fairness simply doesn't apply. Likewise, it isn't fair to Altra that the atomic number of carbon is six. But it's not unfair either. Fairness just doesn't apply. Similarly, it is not the case that Altra deserves to have less than Indy. But it doesn't follow that it is the case that Altra does deserve to have as much as Indy. Desert just doesn't apply. Similarly, it might be said that it is "morally arbitrary," in the sense that it has no moral justification, that Altra is worse off than Indy (G. Cohen 2008, 160, 172). But it doesn't follow that it is morally unjustified that Altra is worse off than Indy: that no justification is forthcoming when one is called for. Since it is just a brute state of affairs, rather than something someone has done, moral justification isn't called for in the first place.

To this, the Theorist of Cosmic Fairness might reply: "Imagine Indy enjoys some natural fortune that eludes Altra or Altra suffers some natural misfortune that Indy escapes. Can you deny that it is bad for Altra to be so unlucky?" (compare Temkin 1993, 21–22). I don't deny, as seems tautologous, that it would have been better for Altra to have enjoyed the good fortune or escaped the misfortune. She would then have been better off, in absolute terms, than she in fact is. But is it bad for her to be worse off, in comparative terms, than Indy actually is (living on a different planet, millennia apart . . .)? That's far less clear. Is it somehow less of a misfortune for her if, as it turns out, there was no Indy and she was always alone in the universe?

Of course, if one personifies "Fate," with her restless hand on the wheel, one can make sense of Altra's having a complaint involving not just the fact that she is worse off than she could have been but instead the fact that she is worse off than Indy in fact is. As Temkin stokes our intuitions, the person in Altra's position "has been treated unkindly by Fate . . . she has not been treated (by Fate) as the equal of her peers but has, as it were, been treated as less than the equal of her peers" (Temkin 1993, 21). Granted, if Fate is imagined as an agent who has the power to improve Altra's situation, in a way that would not be unfair to Indy, but stingily refuses, then Altra has a complaint—to wit, an improvement complaint—against Fate. Or if Fate is made an agent who, while holding sway over Indy and Altra, plays favorites, thus violating Equal Treatment by Officials, then Altra has a complaint—to wit, a complaint against inferiority—against Fate for a violation of Least Discretion. But such personifications can't legitimately support the idea that it is unfair to Altra to be worse off than Indy. This is for the pedestrian reason that Fortuna, as depicted in frescos and engravings, does not exist. So, what else can support the Theory of Cosmic Fairness?

The Theorist of Cosmic Fairness might point out that we would expect Altra, upon learning of Indy's escape from the natural misfortune, to think "Why me?" where this means something like, "If someone had to suffer that, why was it I, rather than Indy?" Common though this thought may be, it isn't clear that it makes sense, much less that a moral theory should be beholden to it. In what sense did anyone "have to" suffer that? Perhaps the more sensible thought is, "Why did that have to happen to me—or to anyone?" At any rate, both "whys" are, of course, rhetorical. There is no "reason" for either occurrence—either for the natural misfortune befalling one person rather than another or for its befalling anyone—and neither was fair. But, again, it does not follow that either occurrence was unfair.

Needless to say, it is regrettable that the natural misfortune happened to Altra, as it would be regrettable that it happened to anyone. It is a misfortune, after all. (Again, though, I doubt that it is more regrettable because there was an Indy to whom it didn't happen.) And if anyone can improve Altra's situation, they have, as a result of the misfortune, even stronger reason to do so than they otherwise would have had. And if they disregard that reason, that's cause not only for regret but also for resentment and guilt. But, beyond that, I don't think there is anything more to say.

21.2 Solidarity, Fraternity, Community

The Theory of Cosmic Fairness, if it were sound, would offer one putative comparative complaint against inequality-increasing weak Pareto improvements: that is, against making Indy's situation better than Altra's, even when it does not come at Altra's absolute expense. This would be the complaint that it is cosmically unfair to Altra for her to have less than Indy. Claims against inferiority account for, in certain contexts, another comparative complaint against inequality-increasing weak Pareto improvements. Again, if Benny is an official to whom Indy and Altra are subject, then Altra may have a complaint, stemming from Equal Treatment by Officials, against Benny's improving Indy's situation when Benny does not do the same for Altra. In the present section, I note a third kind of comparative reason that might at least weigh against inequality-increasing weak Pareto improvements: what might be called "solidaristic refusals." My main aim, by drawing contrasts with solidaristic refusals, is to sharpen our focus on cosmic unfairness and claims against inferiority. There is much more to be said about solidaristic refusals, and I only make a start here.

If Indy has a relationship of a certain kind with Altra, Indy might, "in solidarity with" Altra, refuse improvements in which Altra cannot share. Such relationships include those among members of trade unions, or musketeer trios, or prisoners of war. Typically, they are organized around a common struggle or danger. And typically the improvement that one member refuses consists in some relief from the common struggle or danger.

The point of such a solidaristic refusal, I suggest, following Feinberg (1968, 677) and Zhao (2019), is to reject the separation that would come from the improvement. This is how the refusal expresses, or constitutes, solidarity. By refusing an improvement in his own situation that Altra would not share, Indy binds his fate to hers, thereby forging a kind of unity with Altra. As the musketeer slogan goes, "All for one, and one for all." This means that the point of a solidaristic refusal is not to refuse a superiority over Altra that might come from the improvement. After all, the improvement that Indy enjoys might be privately enjoyed in a way that does not contribute to any superiority over Altra. My idée fixe about claims against inferiority is not so fixe that I don't recognize this. The point of solidaristic refusal is to reject separation, rather than superiority.

Nor is the point of such a solidaristic refusal to avoid the cosmic unfairness to Altra that would come from the improvement. However, the intuitive appeal of solidaristic refusal is sometimes mistakenly attributed to cosmic fairness. This is another instance of the Theory of Cosmic Fairness borrowing its plausibility from other ideas. As supposed evidence in favor of the Theory of Cosmic Fairness, for example, G. Cohen describes a case in which Jane, member of a heretofore equal society, is the beneficiary of some nondivisible, nonshareable manna. Rather than enjoy her bounty, in which others cannot share, she decides to destroy it (2008, 317–318; 2011, 229). Intuitively, Jane has some reason to undo this inequality-increasing weak Pareto improvement, and indeed, we might even admire her doing this. But what reason could she have, Cohen reasons, if not the reason to mitigate cosmic unfairness?

Well, the reason might instead be one of solidarity. And, indeed, this seems a more plausible interpretation of the case. First, Jane would not have anything like the same reason if she had no relationship with the others who were not so lucky: if she lived centuries after them. Second, if a third party were to intervene to destroy the manna over Jane's unwilling protests (with Jane crying out, "No! Every woman for herself!"), the equalization would not have the same value. In both these variants of the example, the equalization mitigates cosmic unfairness—the bare comparative fact that Jane has more than others—to precisely the same extent as in Cohen's original example. Why then do these equalizations, in contrast to Jane's destruction of the surplus manna in the original example, seem pointless? Perhaps because they, unlike Jane's sacrifice in the original, are not solidaristic refusals.

We might distinguish between more and less exacting demands of solidarity. The more exacting demands would be to refuse improvements that others do not share to the same extent. This would require strict equality among the relevant group. Less exacting variants, by contrast, would require refusing improvements that others do not share to some extent. In this light, the "comparative interpretation" of Rawls's difference principle might be seen as one of these less exacting variants. To explain, we need to distinguish three different difference principles (compare G. Cohen 2008, 17, 29, 157–158). The first difference principle simply says that things are to be distributed so that the worst off are as well off as possible. Once the worst off are as well off as possible, it is silent about making the better off still better off. This difference principle neither prohibits nor requires inequality-increasing weak Pareto improvements for those better off. The second difference principle, often referred to as "leximin" in social choice theory, says, once the worst off are as well off as possible, to make the next worst off as well off as possible, and then the next next worst off, and so on. This is, in effect, prioritarianism with infinite weight given, in any trade-off, to those worse off. This difference principle requires inequality-increasing weak Pareto improvements for the better off. Note that both these interpretations of the difference principle have the virtue, which Rawls argues utilitarianism lacks, of not sacrificing some people for the benefit of others (1971, 438; 1999, 124).

The third, comparative interpretation of the difference principle, which I am suggesting might be understood as a principle of solidaristic refusal, permits only such inequalities as make the worst off better off. This difference principle prohibits inequality-increasing weak Pareto improvements for the better off. For those improvements amount to a further inequality that does not make the worst off better off. This might seem puzzling. Why not make the better off still better off when this does not come at the expense of those worse off? Doesn't this comparative difference principle pointlessly sacrifice "efficiency" (or what G. Cohen calls "intelligent policy")? Doesn't the comparative difference principle thus betray, as Anderson (2010a, 17) argues, a tacit concession to the Theory of Cosmic Fairness? That is, doesn't it concede that it would be unfair for the better off to be still better off and that mitigating this unfairness counts in favor of the otherwise pointless sacrifice of efficiency?

We can now see that there is an alternative way to make sense of the prohibition on making the better off still better off. This is that the comparative difference principle might be a principle of solidaristic refusal. The better off refuse improvements in which the worst off cannot share. For this principle of solidaristic refusal, the relevant group, presumably, would be society as a whole, and the common struggle or danger would consist, perhaps, in the vagaries of disease and old age or the rough seas of the market.[3] If it were merely an accident that social institutions realized the comparative difference principle, then this fact might not count as, and so have the value of, a solidaristic refusal. But if it were part of the public culture that social institutions were designed to realize the comparative difference principle, so as to constitute a solidaristic refusal, then their doing what they were designed to do could count as a solidaristic refusal.

This conception of solidaristic refusal should be distinguished from a number of other ideas that travel under the labels of "solidarity" or "community" or "fraternity," only two of which I discuss here. First, "solidarity" (or "community" or "fraternity") can mean any feeling of special tie, loyalty, affection, association, shared values, and so on. It can include both more and less than solidarity, understood as binding one's fate to another in the face of a common danger or challenge. It can include more insofar as it can include ties that don't concern a common danger or challenge, such as ties of religion or ethnicity or nationality (Munoz-Dardé forthcoming). It can include less insofar as those ties can be expressed in ways other than by solidaristic refusals. Shelby's (2007, 67–70) list of the norms of group solidarity—identification, special concern, shared values, loyalty, and mutual trust—says nothing about solidaristic refusals.

To consider another instance, G. Cohen (2009, 34–36) discusses a kind of "community" that is threatened by economic inequalities (even inequalities that are cosmically fair because they result from option luck).[4] While this conception of community is never defined, it seems to consist in sharing similar experiences. Cohen's main example concerns the experience of the discomforts of public transit. Economic inequality threatens this community because economic inequality causes experiences to diverge. If Cohen's idea is that the relevant experiences are experiences of facing a common struggle or danger, then this notion of community may in fact be the notion of solidarity I have been describing. Indeed, Cohen speaks of the experience of shared "challenges" (35). If this is Cohen's understanding, however, then it is somewhat odd for him to write that "community is put under strain when large inequalities obtain" (34). For community, so understood, consists in the refusal to accept inequalities; it isn't something causally undermined by inequalities.

What might be causally undermined by inequalities is simply having the same experiences in general. If Cohen takes community to consist simply in having the same experiences, then community, so understood, differs from solidarity. It is true that a solidaristic refusal of an improvement that others can't share can contribute, in one way, to shared experience with others. The refusal can prevent the difference in experience that might result from the refused improvement. However, on the one hand, such a difference in experience might be avoided just as well by a third party's intervention to prevent an improvement to Indy's situation. And yet that third-party intervention would have no solidaristic value. And, on the other hand, significant differences in experience are compatible with solidaristic refusals. The union rep might refuse a pay raise her sisters wouldn't also get while spending the equal pay she does share with them to lead an altogether different private life. And this, in turn, raises a more general doubt that it is a forceful objection to economic inequality that it threatens community of this kind. After all, many other things besides economic inequality cause experiences to diverge. Consider gender, sexual orientation, labor specialization, religious and cultural diversity, the variety of pastimes, and so on. How compelling, then, is the reason to reduce this sort of heterogeneity? If it isn't very compelling, then how compelling is the reason to reduce economic inequality so as to reduce whatever heterogeneity results from that? And, assuming that there is already such noneconomic heterogeneity, how much additional partitioning of experiences does economic inequality introduce?[5] While there is more to be said about solidarity, I leave it there. For our purposes, what matters is to distinguish it from imagined or real comparative complaints of other kinds.

22

Relations of Equality

It might next be suggested that asymmetries of power and authority or disparities of regard even absent tempering factors, are not, in general, objectionable, as I have been suggesting.[1] They are not, in general, a bad. Instead, asymmetries or disparities matter only insofar as they are implicated in a failure to realize some specific good: namely, a relationship of a kind whose value depends on its being egalitarian (Scheffler 2015; Viehoff 2019).[2] Such relationships might include friendship or marriage.

On one version of this suggestion, asymmetries and disparities matter only insofar as they are an impediment to the specific good of, say, egalitarian friendship. But surely complaints against a relation of inferiority to someone amount to more than simply complaints against an impediment to an egalitarian friendship with them. Simply living in different times and places is also an impediment to a friendship, egalitarian or otherwise. But living at different times and places from people with whom one might have had an egalitarian friendship isn't, in general, objectionable or a cause for regret, at least not in the way asymmetries of power and authority and disparities of regard are.

A more plausible version of the suggestion is that when there is a not necessarily ideal form of relationship of a certain kind, such as a friendship, it calls for each participant to strive for an ideal form. This ideal form is constituted by, inter alia, egalitarian attitudes, dispositions, or practices that are incompatible with asymmetries or disparities. So, if there are asymmetries or disparities, then that indicates that one participant has not striven for the ideal form. Some other participant may have an objection about that failure to strive. This objection doesn't apply when mere distance in time or space prevents so much as a nonideal friendship from arising in the first place.

I don't doubt that some specific relationships do call on their participants to avoid asymmetries or disparities in this way. Friendship and marriage, as we have come to know them, aspire to an egalitarian form. However, I would maintain that there is also an independent, general objection to untempered asymmetries and disparities. For one thing, I suspect that the general claim against inferiority partly explains why friendship and marriage aspire to an egalitarian form. And I suspect even more strongly that the general claim against inferiority explains why cocitizenship aspires to an egalitarian form. This is, in fact, what I have argued. To recapitulate, I began by citing the general objection to untempered asymmetries and disparities. Next, I observed that where the state is concerned, the asymmetries and disparities are untempered; the state is inescapable, it wields final power and authority, and so forth. This, in turn, calls for secondary tempering factors such as Equal Influence, Equal Consideration, and Equal Citizenship. And these secondary tempering factors imply an egalitarian form of cocitizenship. I suppose, by contrast, that it could just be a brute fact that cocitizenship aspires to an egalitarian form, with no further explanation forthcoming. But that seems to me less plausible.

In any event, it seems that claims against inferiority can be raised in cases in which no specific, positive egalitarian relationship is in the offing. Consider two people with none of the other affinities necessary for a friendship or marriage. Asymmetries or disparities between them might still seem objectionable, and yet that cannot be because there is an incipient friendship or marriage between them whose aspiration to an egalitarian form someone is disregarding. Or, for good measure, consider an example from Viehoff (2019, 36): the asymmetric power a guardian might have over their child ward. This calls for the tempering factors of Impersonal Justification and Least Discretion. The guardian, for instance, would wrong the child in taking a bribe to enroll the child in one school rather than another. But this is not because, in so doing, the guardian would fail to realize some specific, positive egalitarian relationship, such as friendship or marriage, with the child. No such relationship is in the cards, so long as the child remains a child.[3]

23

Nondomination

In this chapter, I consider the possibility that what I have sought to analyze as complaints against inferiority are better understood as protests about what neo-Roman republicans call "domination" (Pettit 1997, 2012, 2014; Skinner 1998, 2002, 2008; Lovett 2010) or what scholars of Kant's legal and political philosophy call "dependence" (Ripstein 2009; Stilz 2009; Pallikkathayil 2010, 2017; Forst 2013). The paradigmatically troubling vignettes that republicans and Kantians analyze in terms of "domination" and "dependence"—the philosopher's fictions of the benevolent despot, the kindly slave master, the husband who keeps his wife in a gilded cage, the aristocrat given to noblesse oblige, and the colonial administrator who selflessly bears the "White man's burden"—look very similar to those I analyze in terms of relations of inferiority. How do these analyses differ, and why is my analysis to be preferred?

23.1 Domination and Inferiority

For Pettit, an agent, Powers, "dominates" an individual, Vic, just when Powers has the power to interfere in Vic's choices, with a preference as to how Vic chooses, that is "alien" and "arbitrary" with respect to Vic. Ripstein's "dependence" differs in two main respects. What matters for dependence is not quite interference in choice but instead the (nonconsensual) use or destruction of Vic's body or property. And what matters for dependence is not that the will is arbitrary with respect to Vic but instead that it is "private" or "unilateral." Let us consider a general formulation that tries to remain neutral on these differences. The objection is to domination, where Powers "dominates" Vic, let us now say, just when Powers is a will with the power to "encroach" on Vic, which will is alien with respect to Vic and either (i) arbitrary with respect to Vic or (ii) private or unilateral. To "encroach" on Vic is either (i) to interfere in Vic's choice, with a preference as to how Vic chooses, or (ii) to use or destroy Vic's body or property without Vic's consent.

On now to the differences between domination and relations of inferiority. On the one hand, domination is narrower than relations of inferiority. First, relations of inferiority consist not only in asymmetries of power but also in asymmetries of authority and disparities in regard.

Second, domination consists only in the power to encroach, whereas relations of inferiority may consist in asymmetries of power of other kinds. Powers might have power over Vic, such as to withhold goods, which does not use or destroy Vic's body or property. Once we are clear on what "interference in choice" could possibly be, we find that many cases of withholding goods do not involve the power to interfere in choice. As I argued in Part I, "interference" collapses either into invasion of body or property or into leaving someone's choice situation worse than they are entitled to from the interferer. Recall that we cannot say that just any effect on choice amounts to interference in choice. When an enslaved person abjectly begs for mercy from a sadistic and capricious master, the enslaved person affects the master's choice but presumably does not interfere in it. Note that this means that Boss's exploitative offer in Car Wash (Section 3.7) in no way interferes with Employee's choice. Boss does not invade Employee's body or property, and Boss does not leave Employee's choice situation worse than Employee is entitled to from Boss. And yet it seems like the sort of case that republicans would want to count as domination. Even by republicans' own lights, therefore, the official definition of the relevant sort of power, as a power to interfere in choice, seems too narrow.[1]

Finally, there is the further narrowing introduced by the phrase "with a preference as to how Vic chooses." Pettit suggests that if Powers is "indifferent to what [Vic] chooses," then Vic is not dominated (2014, 50; compare "vitiators" of choice, 2012, 38–39). This means that a sadistic jailer who flips a coin each night to decide whether to beat a prisoner, indifferent to how the prisoner has behaved in their cell, would not dominate the prisoner. Nor would Orwell's image of "a boot stamping on a human face forever" count as an emblem of domination. Again, even by republicans' own lights, the official definition of the relevant sort of power seems too narrow.

On the other hand, domination is, along two other dimensions, broader than relations of inferiority since it is present whenever Vic is exposed to an alien, arbitrary, or unilateral will's power of encroachment. First, domination is "Will Universal" in that there is no restriction on the sort of will that can dominate. The will need not be that of a superior individual. It might be the will of an equal or inferior individual. Or it might be the will of a collective or artificial person, with which comparisons of equality or inferiority make little sense. By contrast, inferiority is not Will Universal. A natural individual can stand in a relation of inferiority only to another superior natural individual. The fact that domination is Will Universal, whereas inferiority is not, makes it harder to escape domination than to escape inferiority. First, whereas one might escape relations of inferiority by having equal influence with other natural individuals over a collective will, one cannot thereby escape domination by the collective will itself. Second, whereas one might escape relations of inferiority by being subject to the asymmetric power and authority of an office, as opposed to a natural individual, one cannot escape domination by the artificial will of the office itself.

Second, domination is "Possibilist" in that it suffices for domination that the alien will can encroach. Once the will can encroach on you, you are dominated, no matter how the alien will might be disposed to restrain itself. This is so even if you can predict that the alien will will not, in fact, encroach. Since the only thing that holds them back is their arbitrary or unilateral will, you are dominated by them (Pettit 1997, 24–25; 2012, chap. 1.4; Ripstein 2009, 15, 36, 42–43). Inferiority is not, in the same sense, Possibilist. To be sure, my having asymmetric power and authority over you involves more than simply what I actually do to you but also what I can do to you; that much follows from what power and authority are. However, first, unexercised asymmetries of power make for inferiority only when there is endorsement of or submission to asymmetries of power, as argued in Section 5.2. This is why the neighbors of Kramer's (2008) "gentle giant," "G," while dominated by G according to the official definition, do not stand in relations of inferiority to G. G, as Kramer tells the tale, "loathes the idea of becoming a tyrant; his principal desire is to seclude himself altogether from his community. He does indeed depart therefrom, in order to reside in a cave among the nearby hills where he contentedly feeds off natural fruits and wildlife and where he spends his time in solitary reflection and reading and exercise"

(47). Second, my asymmetric power and authority over you, even when exercised, can be kept from constituting an objectionable relation of inferiority of you to me solely in virtue of what happens in the actual world, regardless of what happens in merely possible worlds. My superior power and authority may be, in fact, exercised in accordance with Impersonal Justification and Least Discretion, as discussed at greater length in Section 23.4.

I have drawn a number of distinctions between domination and inferiority. When we reread republican and Kantian discussions with these distinctions in mind, we find that inferiority often fits those discussions at least as well as, if not better than, domination as officially defined. For one thing, Pettit's (2012) general descriptions of nondomination frequently are just descriptions of the absence of inferiority: "The idea that citizens could enjoy this equal standing in their society, and not have to hang on the benevolence of their betters, became the signature theme in the long and powerful tradition of republican thought" (2012, 2, see also 11).[2]

Consider, next, the rhetoric that is used to characterize the objectionable relation: "domination," "mastery," "servitude," "subjection," and "despotism." As a matter of etymology and common usage, these don't mean "being exposed to another will." They mean something more specific, involving subordination to another person. That is, we understand what "domination," "mastery," "despotism," and so forth are, in the first instance, by reference to recognized forms of social hierarchy.

Now consider the paradigms used to elicit concern about being under the power of another. These are not cases of merely being exposed to the power of another will but instead cases of being subordinated to a superior individual in an established social structure. In addition to the examples listed at the beginning of this chapter, witness Pettit's (1997, viii, 5, 57; 2012, 1, 2, 7) examples: the priest and the seminarian, the creditor and the debtor, the clerk and the welfare dependent, the manager and the worker, the teacher and the pupil, the warden and the inmate.

To be sure, one might chafe at being under the power of not another individual but instead a group of individuals. But this should be understood in one of two ways. Either it expresses a concern about sentient encroachment, which we consider in the next section, or it is a concern about the superior power and authority of individuals as constituted by their greater influence over what the group does.

Granted, discussions sometimes work up to an instance of mutual domination among equals. Such is our condition, Kantians say, among even peaceful and benevolent coequal neighbors in a state of nature. But this is an extension, into a new context, of concepts we are expected to grasp first from recognized forms of social hierarchy. After all, when Ripstein (2009) seeks to tap anxiety about dependence or introduces independence as a "*compelling* normative" idea, he glosses it as "to be one's own master" (4), understood as: "to have no *other* master," "that no person be the master of another" (36). And this is unsurprising. To audiences not primed in the right way, "Let us have no masters" is a rousing political slogan. "Let us have no peaceful and benevolent coequal neighbors" is not.

Next, Pettit's (2012, 8, 82) test of nondomination—that one can "walk tall amongst others and look any in the eye," "not have to bow or scrape, toady or kowtow, fawn or flatter"—is not obviously a test of immunity to the power of others but instead a test of equal standing with others. Think of boxers eyeing one another before a bout.

Finally, there is the curious fact, which I return to later, that Pettit holds that democracy can free citizens from domination. But why should this be? Imagine a state that is perfectly democratic and externally compelled to be democratic. Even so, one is still dominated by the collective, democratic will. Democracy cannot offer relief from exposure to an alien will. What it can offer is not being subordinated to any other natural individual.

23.2 Domination and Encroachment

In sum, it often seems that what republicans describe as domination—exposure to an alien will—is more aptly analyzed in terms of a relation of inferiority—subordination to another natural individual or individuals within a social hierarchy. Why then don't republicans describe domination as simply a relation of inferiority to another natural individual? Why do they describe it as exposure to an alien will, subscribing to Will Universality?

It is, I believe, because republicans have confused the concern about relations of inferiority with a quite different set of concerns, with different sources, about sentient encroachment: invasion or interference by another will or wills. These concerns are Will Universal. Even if we cannot be inferior to collective or artificial wills, they can still encroach on us.

As I see things, these concerns about encroachment are of two kinds. First, there is a concern, which I have already acknowledged in this book, about violation of rights against invasion of your person and property. Moreover, you have a claim not only that your rights won't be invaded but that you can predict that your rights won't be invaded. Second, there is a concern about "interference in choice" that doesn't invade person or property. But what counts as "interference in choice"? The answer, I argued, is that *A* interferes in *B*'s choice just when *A* leaves *B*'s choice situation worse than *B* is entitled to from *A*. Thus, *B*'s complaint about *A*'s "interference in *B*'s choice" expresses *B*'s improvement complaint against *A*: that *A* could have left *B*'s choice situation better and was indeed required to. The complaint about interference is captured by the Choice Principle. Note, further, that you have a claim not only that others will observe the Choice Principle but also that you can predict that they will.

While these concerns about violation of rights against invasion and violations of the Choice Principle are Will Universal, they are not, I believe, Possibilist. What matters is whether, as you can predict, your rights are not actually invaded and whether, as you can predict, your choice situation is not made worse than you are entitled to. Indeed, as I explain later, the idea that our concerns about encroachment are Possibilist results from confusing these concerns with the concern about inferiority.

23.3 The Inescapability of Domination

I have been suggesting that we might better explain the motivating materials of republicans and Kantians in terms not of domination but instead of relations of inferiority to other individuals—or else a lack of reasonable confidence that other wills will not encroach on one. In this section, I suggest another reason to be wary of the Kantian-republican analysis in terms of domination. This is that, in addition to being a confusion of distinct concerns, and indeed because of being a confusion of distinct concerns, domination is unavoidable. Will Universality and Possibilism close off all avenues of escape.

Kantians and republicans tend to accept, plausibly enough, that we avoid being dominated by other individuals only if we live under a state. As Kant famously puts it, the state is necessary "however well disposed and right-loving human beings might be" (Kant 1797, 98). To set the stage for the argument for the necessity of the state, consider two reasons why, at least under certain contingent conditions, a just distribution of predictable nonencroachment might require the state. One reason is coordination. There are many just distributions of predictable nonencroachment. If each individual tries independently to realize one of these distributions, each is likely to try to realize a different distribution. For example, I may try to realize a distribution in which I work the land to the east of the creek and you work the land to the west, whereas you may try to realize a distribution in which I work the land to the west of the creek and you work the land to the east. This is likely to result in a worse distribution than if the state were to make some particular scheme salient. I may plow up the field you just planted. Another reason is assurance. I may not be able to predict that you will try to realize even a salient distribution. In order to enjoy a just distribution of predictable nonencroachment, each needs to be assured that the state stands ready to prevent others from invading.

The Kantian-republican argument goes further. Even in an ideal state of nature—where there is no problem of coordination and where a single, definite scheme strikes us all as natural—and no problem of assurance—where we know, in the way that we know of good neighbors, that they will not, in fact, encroach—we would still need the state. This is because, so long as we remain in a state of nature, other individuals retain their power of encroachment. Although they do not will encroachment, if their wills were to change, they would encroach. They dominate us (Stilz 2009, 56; Pettit 2012, 181–184; Pallikkathayil 2017). So, we need the state to deprive them of this power.[3]

If this is accepted, the question arises of how we are to avoid domination by the state. We are exposed to the state's power of encroachment. Why then aren't we dominated by the state? Suppose, by analogy, you are the slave of the kindly master. Now suppose he acquires a second slave. And suppose he makes it the case, by threats or barriers he controls, that neither of you can encroach on the other—as slave masters, kindly or not, are wont to do. How could that free you from domination by him?

Presumably, a properly constituted state is supposed to be different from this kindly master. But how different? For Kantians, for example, a properly constituted state is a "public" or "omnilateral" will, rather than a "private" or "unilateral" will. Suggestive words, but what exactly do they suggest?

One possibility is that, strictly speaking, the state isn't a will at all. However, the state makes decisions and takes actions in coordinated and structured ways. Why isn't that enough to make the state a will? Granted, one might argue that while we should be concerned about being under the power of individual wills, we should not be concerned about being under the power of collective wills, such as the state. But this would be to give up Will Universality and, more importantly, more or less concede that relations of inferiority are the underlying problem.

Pettit (2012, 160–166) pursues, in a different direction, the idea that in being exposed to the state, we are not exposed to a will in the relevant sense. He doesn't so much deny that the state is a will. Rather he emphasizes that no will is responsible for the fact that one lives under some state. Pettit is not denying, I take it, that there is some possible pattern of human action that would make it the case that I was not exposed to some state. His point is instead that if any particular state were to try, on its own, to bring about this pattern, it would fail. Another state would simply move in and take over. Thus, each state can honestly say to its citizens, "Nothing we might do would make any difference as to whether you are exposed to some state." Suppose this is true. It hardly seems to follow that the state doesn't thereby dominate its citizens. Compare taking captives at the fall of Troy. Each can honestly say to Hecuba, "If I don't dominate you, another Achaean will." True, but does it mean that Hecuba isn't dominated by whoever does take her captive?

One might next suggest that a properly constituted state won't invade except for the right sort of end. For Ripstein (2009, 192), a "public" will is one that acts with a "public purpose": that is, in order to achieve a condition of equal independence. So stated, this answer is uninformative. It defines "public" in terms of "independence"—a public will seeks (a condition of equal) independence—whereas "independence" is itself defined in terms of "public"—independence is exposure only to public wills (but not private wills). By contrast, if a "public purpose" is understood as a condition not of equal independence but instead of equal predictable nonencroachment by any will, public or private, then the suggestion is informative. But then the kindly slave master seems to be acting from a public purpose; he never invades the slaves, except to prevent them from encroaching on one another. Indeed, the same is true of my neighbors in the ideal state of nature. And the same would be true of my neighbor who takes it upon himself to improve local police protection, threatening to lock me in his basement if I don't contribute to his scheme and doing so when I refuse. Yet one would have expected Kantians to count these all as "private" wills. More generally, any reply of this form—that one is not dominated by a will so long as it actually exercises its power for the right ends—seems to give up on Possibilism: that is, to accept that what matters is how power is actually exercised.

Perhaps, then, a properly constituted state is a will that not only won't but also can't encroach except for the right sort of end. In his earlier work, Pettit (1997, 23, 55) understood an arbitrary will as a will that is not forced, in the exercise of its powers, to pursue a certain end: to track one's interests and ideas.[4] But what is the checking power? What is it that forces the state to pursue the right sort of end: that is, prevents it, if it should will encroachment for the wrong ends, from so encroaching? Surely no natural force holds it in check. And yet if the state is held in check by some other will, then why aren't we dominated by that will? Compare a master who controls whether one particularly strong slave will be constrained in his dealings with other slaves.

I shortly return to this problem for the checking-power proposal: namely, the problem of how there could be a checking power on the state that did not at the same time dominate us. However, let us set it aside for the moment. This is because Pettit's redefinition of "domination" in his later work seems, at least at first, to supersede the checking-power proposal. There Pettit replaces talk of an arbitrary will with a will that one does not control (2012, 57–58). When one controls the encroachment, the alien will is acting as one's servant, rather than as one's master, and so one is not dominated.[5] Thus, we are not dominated by a democratic state: a state that we, the People, control (2012, chap. 3.4; 2014, chap. 5).

But this seems a non sequitur. Our question is whether each of us is, as an individual, dominated by the state. And even in the most idealized democracy, I do not, as an individual, control the state's invasion. The most that can be said is that in the vanishingly unlikely case of a tie, my vote might be decisive. A tiny chance of decisiveness, however, can't free one from domination. Suppose a master, as a kind of cruel joke, informs his slave of the following plan. The master will toss a coin. If, but only if, it lands on its edge, the master will treat the slave in accord with the slave's stated preference. How is gaining the franchise any different? If, but only if, the votes of everyone else line up just the right way, one's vote will determine how the state treats one. If this tiny chance of decisiveness is not enough in the case of the slave, why should it be enough here?

Here one might stress that we must respect everyone's equal claims (Pettit 2012, 168). One might say, "Whatever control is given to you must be equally given to everyone else. Granted, you aren't given individual control, but you are given the closest thing compatible with giving the same to everyone." But, first, this does not address the basic problem: What is being distributed isn't control, and so it offers no relief from domination in the first place. It says, in effect, "Granted, you aren't given relief from domination, but you are given the closest thing to what you would need for relief from domination compatible with giving the same to everyone." Compare a doctor saying, "Granted, this fraction of a tablet won't lessen your symptoms, but it is the closest thing to what would be needed to lessen your symptoms compatible with giving the same to everyone." Second, let us assume that control is the only way to avoid domination and that only one or a few can enjoy control in any meaningful measure. In that case, we have a scarce, indivisible resource. The appropriate response to equally compelling interests in having the resource in that case presumably is a fair lottery. Thus, the appropriate response to equally compelling interests in control would seem to be not democracy but instead a lottery for dictatorship.

To be fair, Pettit doesn't say that we, as individuals, control the state. He says that, in a democracy, we have an equal share in the People's control over the state. This is more plausible but less relevant. If the People controls the state, then perhaps the People is not dominated by the state. And perhaps this assuages a concern about vicarious, collective subordination, discussed in Chapter 10: a concern that a group (such as the People) to which I belong not be dominated by another group (such as the state). But it doesn't mean that I am not dominated as an individual. It is still the case that the People, something I do not control, controls the state's invasion of me (Lovett 2019, 126).

If one adheres to the official, Will-Universalist definition of domination, therefore, it is altogether mysterious why democracy should be thought to free us, as individuals, from domination. By contrast, it is immediately clear why democracy would free us as individuals from subordination to any other individual. Thus, if the underlying anxiety is not about domination, but instead about inferiority, then it is clear how democracy addresses the anxiety. As far as domination is concerned, there is no difference between the coin-flipping master and an extension of the franchise. In both cases, one's degree of exposure to an uncontrolled alien will is exactly the same. Because of domination's Will Universalism, it makes no difference that the will is the People, rather than the master who leaves something to chance. As far as relations of inferiority are concerned, there is—as intuitively there seems to be—a significant difference. As the slave of a master, one stands in a relation of inferiority, whereas as a citizen with as much say as any other citizen, one does not. One might add that insofar as domination is concerned, being a dictator is preferable to enjoying Equal Influence, since being a dictator would free one from domination. By contrast, insofar as relations of inferiority are concerned, being a dictator is not preferable to enjoying Equal Influence.

If we assume I can escape domination only insofar as I control the would-be dominator, then the fact that the People control the state doesn't help me. But perhaps I can escape domination by the state even without controlling it. Perhaps it suffices that the state has no power to encroach, since if it did attempt to encroach, it would be checked by another body, namely the People. This is just to return to the proposal of a checking power on the state.

If we return to the checking-power proposal, then Pettit's redefinition of nonarbitrary power as power controlled by the would-be dominated turns out to be otiose. What matters is simply that the would-be dominating will lacks the power to encroach on me, whether I control it or not, because it would be checked by another checking power if it tried to encroach on me. Moreover, whether the checking power is the People also turns out to be irrelevant. What matters is simply that there is a checking power that is distinct from the will of the state. It might be "an effectively independent army, a group of moneyed supporters or even a foreign power" (Pettit 2012, 172).

Of course, this goes against what Pettit explicitly writes. In the passage I just quoted, Pettit is actually denying that the checking power can be "an effectively independent army, a group of moneyed supporters or even a foreign power." And in his most recent statements, he is explicit that the checking power must be the People: "What ensures, then, that the state does not compromise our freedom? The republican answer is: the fact that its interference is subject to popular control. We the people must control the state" (Lovett and Pettit 2019, 368). He continues, "If the abilities of the state to interfere in our choices are to be externally controlled, then it must be by the people themselves" (371).

In any event, if we return to the checking-power proposal, then we return to the problem we identified earlier with the checking-power proposal. Why aren't we then dominated by the checking power? Mustn't this checking power have the power to encroach on me? After all, if the checking power should will encroachment, then all it needs to do is lift its check on the state. The state will then encroach, acting as its agent or instrument. There are two responses to this problem. First, it might be said that the checking power, while not a natural force, might not be a will either. In that case, the checking power is not the sort of thing that can dominate. Indeed, Pettit and Lovett hold that, insofar as the checking power is the People, the People does not have a will. Second, the checking power, even if it is a will, might have the power only to check the state's encroachment but not to encroach itself, say, on some citizen, Vic.

To see how this might be, we need to say something about which the vast literature on republicanism says surprisingly little. When does a would-be dominator, Powers, have the power to encroach on Vic? The answer that seems most favorable to republicanism is what I will call the "Can Do Alone Test." Imagine that Powers were to will to encroach on Vic. Hold fixed, to the extent possible, everything else, including all other actual wills, besides Powers's. Then ask whether Powers encroaches on Vic. If so, then Powers has the power to encroach on Vic, otherwise not.[6]

On the Can Do Alone Test, whether the checking power has the power to encroach on Vic depends on whether the state it checks actually wills encroachment. If the state does not actually will encroachment, then the checking power has no power to encroach on Vic. Let the checking power will encroachment. Let it remove its check so as to bring it about. All the same, holding fixed the will of the state not to encroach, no encroachment will take place. So long as the state does not actually will encroachment and the checking power actually wills to resist any such encroachment, then neither has the power to encroach.

Still, there is a problem. If both the state and the checking power were to will encroachment, then they would succeed. Granted, there is no single will such that, if that will alone were to change, Vic would be encroached on. There is no "dyadic domination," as Simpson (2017) puts it. But there are two wills, the state and the checking power, such that, if both of those wills were to will encroachment, Vic would be encroached on. There might still be what Simpson calls "polyadic domination." For polyadic domination, the test of whether Vic is exposed to encroachment is the "Can Do Together Test." Imagine that every other will were to will to encroach on Vic. Hold fixed, to the extent possible, everything else. Then ask whether Vic is encroached on. If so, and if the other wills are alien and arbitrary, then Vic is polyadically dominated.

If we are supposed to be concerned about dyadic domination, why aren't we also supposed to be concerned about polyadic domination? To the extent that the concern about domination is a concern about exposure to sentient encroachment, it seems that we should consider not only exposure to a single will but also exposure to several wills.[7] Notice, however, that the very grammar of "domination" breaks down in the polyadic case. If we ask, "Who dominates?" in the case of polyadic domination, there is no answer. No individual will dominates since no individual will has the power to encroach. Nor does the plurality of wills jointly dominate since that plurality isn't itself a will, and only wills can dominate. The fact that, in this application, the grammar of domination unravels is, I suspect, symptomatic of the fact that republicanism has stitched, under the label of "domination," a concern about exposure to sentient encroachment with a distinct concern about being subordinated to a superior individual. In the case of subordination to a superior individual, like that of slave to master, there is a clear candidate for the dominator: that superior individual, the master. In the case of exposure to sentient encroachment, by contrast, there need not be any candidate for the dominator.

In any event, for their part, Pettit and Lovett appear to recognize polyadic domination. Now, since they do not accept that the People is a will, they do not accept the possibility of polyadic domination in a scenario in which both the state and the People will encroachment. However, they do accept the possibility of polyadic domination in a scenario in which every individual member of the People but Vic, each of whom does have a will, wills to encroach on Vic. That is, they apply the Can Do Together Test, and they seem to grant that if the test were positive—that if Vic were, in this counterfactual, encroached on—then Vic would be polyadically dominated.

However, Pettit and Lovett deny that the test in this case would be positive. The reason is that even if each citizen were to will encroachment on

Vic, they still would not know that this is what other citizens will, and so each citizen would be restrained from attempting to encroach on Vic by their fear—which, as it happens, is entirely false—that other citizens would oppose them.[8] In other words, Vic's protection in this scenario depends on universally mistaken fear on the part of everyone else that others will oppose them in encroaching on Vic when, in fact, they would willingly join in the encroachment.

One well wonders whether this is the sort of protection that ought to satisfy republicans. First, there is a question of whether such false fear even counts as an "external constraint." To be sure, accurate fear of failure if one tries to encroach does count as an external constraint. There is an external constraint—one will, in fact, fail—and one is just perceiving it (Pettit 1997, 23). But is misplaced fear of failure—when in fact no consequences will ensue and where there is no agency that is working to sustain a bluff—an external constraint? At that point, we seem to be saying that when the mere psychology of the would-be encroacher is one way, then it is external restraint, whereas when the mere psychology of the would-be encroacher is different, then it is only self-restraint. And this seems more or less the view that I go on to suggest: that what motivates the restraint makes the difference.

Second, there is a question of why this universally mistaken fear should protect Vic, at least for long. If everyone is out to get Vic, won't this eventually come to light? Of course, one could put a time limit on the Can Do Together Test. If the universal willing to encroach on Vic didn't result in encroachment within twenty-four hours, then Vic would not be dominated. But such a time limit seems unmotivated, insofar as the underlying concern is insulation from encroachment.

Once the possibility of polyadic domination is accepted, then domination is unavoidable. For we can ask, "If every other will—not simply every other individual citizen of your state, but every other will, corporate or artificial—were to will to encroach on you, would you be encroached on?" The answer seems quite plausibly to be yes. There is no chance of any checking power on this onslaught of wills, for every possible checking power has, by hypothesis, joined the onslaught.

To be sure, we do have valid concerns about sentient encroachment, whether by natural individuals or collective or artificial agents. As I have said, we have concerns that, as we can predict, other agents do not violate our rights against invasion and that, as we can predict, other agents do not leave our choice situations worse than we are entitled to from them. However, if we understand these concerns as subscribing to Possibilism—as concerns about being so much as exposed to the possibility of sentient encroachment, even if we know that the encroachment will never transpire—then there is no way for these concerns to be assuaged.

Republicans and Kantians might concede that there is no way to avoid domination. The sensible goal is to minimize it. I doubt that minimization will appeal to some Kantians, for whom a miss is as good as a mile in normative matters. And some republicans also appear to hold out the possibility of a state that would free us from domination, as opposed to merely reducing our net unfreedom (Pettit 2009, 40). In any event, it's not clear how this minimization of domination, even as a conceptual matter, is to be understood or why the state should be assumed to minimize domination. Crucially, how are we to trade off being subject to the numerous, less powerful wills of individuals, say, against being subject to the single, vastly more powerful will of the state? Granted, to turn Locke's famous metaphor ([1689] 1930, sec. 93) to a different purpose, we are much less likely to be treated badly under a single lion of the right kind than when surrounded by many polecats. But is it better or worse to be exposed to a single merely counterfactual lion or several merely counterfactual polecats? How are we even to think about it? It isn't simply that we lack a settled theory but moreover that we lack particular judgments to guide its construction.

23.4 Does Republican Philosophy Rest on a Mistake?

Why, then, do republicans understand the concerns about sentient encroachment in Possibilist terms? It comes, I think, from confusing the concern about sentient encroachment with the concern about being subordinated to another natural individual.

To begin with, subordination consists in asymmetries of power and authority. My having asymmetric power and authority over you is a matter of more than simply what I actually do to you but also of what I can do to you. That much follows from what power and authority are. However, my asymmetric power and authority over you can be kept from constituting an objectionable relation of inferiority of you to me solely in virtue of what happens in the actual world. If my power and authority are, in fact, exercised in accordance with Impersonal Justification and Least Discretion, then that may suffice. So, there are two mistakes here: First, the concern about sentient encroachment is confused with the concern about subordination. Second, it is assumed that objectionable subordination consists in the asymmetry of power itself, rather than in an asymmetry that is not actually regulated by Impersonal Justification and Least Discretion (or some other tempering factor).

Next, when we consider the tempering factor of Least Discretion, or rather the special case of the Duty to Exclude, then we can see another theory of error for Possibilism. The problem is that republicans misidentify the active ingredient in the examples they use to stimulate anxiety about domination. The standard examples of domination are, first, examples of being subordinated to a superior individual. Second, they are examples (with exceptions appearing sparingly and being passed over quickly [Pettit 2012, 63]) in which the dominator is said to refrain from invading you only because it's their "whim" (1997, 57), "mood" (1997, 5), "wish" (2014, 42), "caprice" (2012, 120), "pleasure" (1997, 54), personal "liking" (1997, 24), "grace and favour" (1997, 33), "affection" (2012, 59), or "indulgence and goodwill" (2014, xvi) or because you "ingratiate" yourself (1997, 69), "keep them happy" (1997, 88), have "soften[ed them] up" (2012, 65), seek their prior "permission" (2014, xv), or make them "warmed and charmed" (2014, 44). This is what gets our blood boiling and makes us feel that we are unfree, under the thumb of a dominator.

But what is it that gets our blood boiling? Republicans conclude that the significance of an expression such as "only because it pleases him" is that it implies there is some counterfactual world in which he doesn't treat you well: namely, a world in which it didn't please him. They take this to support Possibilism: that what's objectionable is mere counterfactual exposure to encroachment. The Duty to Exclude suggests a different way of interpreting the significance of "because it pleases him." That it pleases him is not a reason that serves any impersonal values that might plausibly justify his superior power. So, if he uses that power because it pleases him, then he's violating the Duty to Exclude. That—what's happening right here, in the actual world, not what might have happened in some counterfactual world—is the basis of your objection. In other words, the examples that are supposed to fuel Possibilism are explained by the Duty to Exclude.[9]

Boss's exploitative offer illustrates the explanatory value of attending to the reasons actually motivating the person with superior power. Recall that republicans presumably want to count Boss's exploitative offer as a case of dominating Employee. Although we puzzled over how republicans could count this as a case of domination, let us grant that it does so count. Can we then explain why Boss should refrain from making the offer? Possibilism makes this paradoxical. So long as Boss so much as has the power to make the offer to Employee, even if the thought of making it would never enter Boss's mind, what is objectionable already obtains. This means that Boss has no reason, at least as far as domination is concerned, to refrain from making the offer. For as soon as Boss can make the offer, he already dominates. Whether or not he then actually refrains from making the offer makes no difference to whether he dominates. Does Boss then have some further reason to refrain? Refraining doesn't improve the Employee's choice situation. Nor does it avoid a rights transgression. So, refraining does not avoid an "interference in choice" in either sense. Then what reason is there to refrain? And yet there does seem to be a significant reason to refrain.

The Duty to Exclude, by contrast, explains how actual exercises of power can wrong the person over whom power is exercised, which Possibilism makes mysterious. Boss's offer wrongs Employee because Boss uses his office for reasons that don't serve the impersonal reasons that justify that office. Boss thereby violates the Duty to Exclude. If instead the thought of making such an offer never enters into Boss's mind, then Boss does not use his office for those impersonal reasons. Boss doesn't violate the Duty to Exclude. No wonder that Employee has a complaint only when Boss actually makes the offer but not when Boss merely could make the offer. And so no wonder that Boss has a reason to refrain from actually making that offer: namely, Employee's complaint.

V

A Last Instance

Democracy

So far in the book, I have argued that interests in improvement and rights against invasion cannot explain a number of commonplace claims. In this part and the next, I consider one last commonplace claim: the claim to democracy. Once again, this claim cannot be explained by interests in improvement or rights against invasion—or, indeed, by other claims that are from time to time invoked to support democracy, such as a claim to have one's political preferences satisfied. It is explained instead by claims against inferiority.

24

Preliminaries

In speaking of this claim to democracy, I have in mind the following. Ordinary political discourse, at least in the West, at least in public fora, has rarely questioned that social decisions should ultimately be controlled by some principle of one person, one vote. As fierce as debates over law or policy may be, those debates have taken place against a background assumption that, in the end, the question will be resolved by such means. If the question is not decided by plebiscite, then it is decided by officials, or their appointees, elected through a process that respects some recognizable form of political equality. Indeed, these offices and processes may depend on a constitution that is itself open to popular amendment. An alternative form of rule, where political decisions would be entirely made by an unchosen class, whether defined by birth, virtue, or training, has not been seriously contemplated.

Even in political philosophy—which is, as to be expected, more reflective—a commitment to democracy, thus broadly understood, often outstrips any explicit justification. Sometimes it is just assumed that our task is to construct a political philosophy for a liberal democracy, where some principle of one person, one vote is, like the injustice of chattel slavery, a "fixed point." In *A Theory of Justice*, to take a signal example, Rawls (1971) unhesitatingly includes rights of political participation in the list of equal basic liberties. But why rights of political participation belong on the list, alongside liberty of conscience and free choice of occupation, is never made entirely clear. His discussion of these questions in sections 36 and 37 remains, at least to my mind, one of the darkest corners of that great book.

Perhaps, though, little needs to be said. Democracy has a straightforward justification or, indeed, justifications. There may be an instrumental case for democracy. At first glance, at least, it seems plausible that, at least over the long run, democracy better secures the public interest than the alternatives. Moreover, democracy may seem to have more intrinsic virtues. It is a particularly fitting response to persistent disagreement, it will be said. It treats people fairly. It does not insult them. It realizes a form of autonomy. It provides avenues for civic engagement. Indeed, where explicit justifications of democracy are offered—and there have been notable proposals in recent years—they typically rest, in the end, on one or more of these considerations. However, I doubt, as I argue in this part, that any of these considerations represents even a pro tanto justification of democracy of the right kind.

24.1 Defining the Terms

Let us say that a political decision is "democratically made" if and only if it is directly or indirectly democratically made. A political decision is "directly" democratically made when it was made by a process that gave everyone currently subject to it equal or both equal and positive, and formal or both formal and informal, opportunity for informed influence over it. A political decision is "indirectly" democratically made when it was made by, for the time being and for lack of something better, a "representative": an official, or official body, where the decision to have that official, or official body, make that decision was itself (directly or indirectly) democratically made and where the official, or official body, satisfies whatever other "standards of selection" and "standards of conduct" are implied by the values that justify democracy, beyond those that apply to all officials.

This initial formulation is just a starting point. It leaves a number of choices open that we might hope a justification of democracy would help us settle. A more permissive, "equal" conception requires only equal, but not necessarily positive, opportunity. It treats lotteries as no less democratic than voting. By contrast, a "positive" conception requires both equal and positive opportunity.

A more permissive, "formal" conception requires equality (or equality and some positive measure) of only formal opportunity. Suppose the relevant procedure is voting. Then formal equality requires, first, no unequal legal or structural barriers to acquiring relevant information or rationally influencing others' votes or the decisions of representatives. This would be violated, for example, by "viewpoint" restrictions on political speech or unequal restrictions on political association. Second, formal equality requires universal (adult) suffrage. This would be violated by property qualifications for the franchise, or a poll tax, or other prerequisites for voting that are unequally difficult or costly for some to meet. Such prerequisites include Jim Crow literacy tests and contemporary voter ID requirements (assuming, as seems overwhelmingly credible, that these do not protect against inequalities arising from fraud). Finally, formal equality requires equally weighted votes. This would be violated by the scheme of plural votes proposed by Mill ([1861] 2015, chap. 8). On this scheme, every citizen was to have at least one vote, but those with signs of superior intelligence were to have additional votes. Mill included as signs of superior intelligence a university degree and an occupation involving the supervision of others. A formal conception thus requires, by stipulation, many of the institutions typically associated with democracy. It requires not only universal suffrage and equally weighted votes but also, crucially, freedom of political speech and association. However, it is left open whether a formal conception requires other such institutions, such as majority rule or proportional representation. These issues are taken up in Part VI.

A less permissive, "informal" conception would require equality of informal opportunity as well. Informal opportunity consists roughly in the availability of resources, such as wealth and leisure, to apply to the legal or procedural structure to acquire information, to vote oneself, or to influence the votes of others (or the decisions of representatives).

We would also hope that a justification of democracy would inform us about which standards of selection and conduct representatives must satisfy. Standards of selection concern how individuals are chosen to become or remain representatives or members of representative bodies. Should they be elected, for example, or selected by lot? Standards of conduct concern how representatives should behave in office. Should they act as "delegates," seeking to satisfy the preferences of their constituents, or as "trustees," seeking to promote the public interest as they see it?

If that is, for now, what "democracy" means, what does it mean to justify it? To "justify" democracy, I suggest, is to answer one or more of the following three questions. First, the "Question of Institutions": Why should we want, establish, or maintain democratic institutions? Why do we, in general, have reason to try, over the long run, to make political decisions democratically? Second, the "Question of Authority": Why does the fact that a political decision was made democratically give others a complaint against me (perhaps answerable) if I fail to implement or comply with it? Finally, the "Question of Legitimacy": Why does the fact that a political decision was made democratically remove an objection that I would otherwise have to some relation of rule that the implementation of that decision involves? In other words, why is democracy a "legitimating condition"? Or, even if I still have an objection to its implementation, why might the fact that the decision was democratically made be at least a countervailing reason in favor of its implementation that weighs against my objection?

24.2 Three Interests in Democratic Decision-Making

To keep our bearings, we need to distinguish between three structurally different kinds of interest that an individual can have in a political decision: interests in correspondence, interests in influence, and substantive interests. One's interest in "correspondence" with respect to a decision is satisfied just when the decision is the one that matches one's choice or judgment. One's interest in "influence" with respect to a decision, by contrast, is satisfied to the extent that the decision is reached by a process that is positively sensitive to one's choice or judgment. On the one hand, one can enjoy correspondence without influence. For example, the dictator might impose the policy that, as it happens, one thinks best, even though he never asked one's opinion. On the other hand, one can enjoy influence without correspondence. One might be outvoted in a fair election.

Within the category of interests in influence, we can distinguish between interests in absolute influence and relative influence. One's interest in "absolute" influence is advanced to a greater degree insofar as a wider range of decisions is more sensitive to one's choice or judgment. On the one hand, a system of decision by lottery (in which the decision itself, as opposed to the opportunity to make it, is selected randomly) would not advance anyone's interest in absolute influence. On the other hand, one's interest in absolute influence is advanced to a greater degree as the electorate gets smaller (other things equal) since this increases one's share of influence over political decisions. The same happens as the state gets more powerful (other things equal) since this increases the scope of the political decisions that one influences.

One's "relative" interest in, say, no less influence, by contrast, is satisfied just to the extent that decisions are no less sensitive to one's choice or judgment than to anyone else's. A system of decision by lottery would guarantee that since it would not give anyone any absolute influence. And the size of the electorate and the power of the state would be immaterial.

Three forms of influence, each of which can be considered in absolute or relative terms, should be distinguished. One is "decisive" when, had one's choice or judgment been different, the decision would have been different. For example, under majority rule, one is decisive just when there is a tie or when one is a member of a majority that wins by a single vote. One has "control" over the decision if one's judgment or choice would be decisive over a wide range of changes in relevant conditions, including, especially, the choices and judgments of others. "Wide" is, of course, vague but will serve our purposes. An effective dictator, for example, has control over decisions. Some might say that one has influence only when one is decisive. But this hardly seems a conceptual truth. There is an intelligible notion of "contributory influence," which might be understood on the model of applying a vector of force that combines with other vectors to determine a result. The result is sensitive to this vector of force, and the vector remains the same in its magnitude and direction, no matter what other vectors are supplied (Goldman 1999). Images of placing equal weights on scales or applying equal tension to a rope in a game of tug-of-war suggest themselves.

Finally, I define "substantive interests" negatively. They are whatever interests in political decisions one might have that are not interests in correspondence or influence with respect to those decisions.

24.3 Substantive Interests

What is wrong with the simple, instrumental argument that democracy best serves substantive interests? For a bit more concreteness, let's suppose that the substantive interests in question are interests in improvement. Then the instrumental argument becomes that democracy best serves the public interest. On the one hand, democracy may be said to achieve this by identifying what would best serve the public interest. Perhaps more heads directly addressed to the question of which decisions best serve the public interest are better than one. Or perhaps, since each person is the best judge of her own interests, each should confine herself to the question, "Which decision would best serve my interests in improvement?" Democracy then aggregates answers to that question in such a way as to ensure the decision best promotes a fair distribution of the satisfaction of those interests in improvement. On the other hand, democracy may be said to serve interests in improvement by making institutions more efficient. Perhaps democracy is especially transparent or energizing. Perhaps it facilitates peaceful transfers of power or prevents descent into "extractive institutions" (Acemoglu and Robinson 2012).

If this is right, then we should accept the following:

> "Reliability Thesis": As things actually are, or could reasonably be expected to be, some democratic procedure of decision-making is more substantively reliable than any nondemocratic procedure. That is, assuming the relevant substantive interests are interests in improvement, there is some democratic procedure such that if people, in general, try, over the long run, to follow it, then the public interest will be better served than it would be if people were to try to follow any nondemocratic procedure.

The word "try" here is crucial. Tautologically, the procedure of implementing the decisions that would best serve the public interest would best serve the public interest. But given inevitable disagreement about which policies best serve the public interest, and the need for coordination in cases of underdetermination, it would be a recipe for gridlock if everyone tried to do this. It is very plausible that a procedure whose decisions were less ambiguous would better serve the public interest. And the Reliability Thesis claims that, among such less ambiguous procedures, some democratic procedures best serve the public interest.

Still, several problems remain. There is, first, the "Bridging Problem." This is the perennial difficulty with indirect or two-level theories, like rule utilitarianism. Why does it follow from the fact that it will have good effects if people, in general, try, over the long run, to follow some democratic procedure that any particular decision that might issue from that procedure is authoritative or legitimate? Suppose someone could better promote the public interest by disregarding the democratic decision. What reason does that person have against this? The Reliability Thesis may answer the Question of Institutions: whether to establish and sustain democratic institutions in general and over the long run. But it is less clear how it answers the Questions of Legitimacy and Authority, which have to do with the normative standing of particular decisions that issue from those institutions.

The second problem is that, even if it is only hypothetical (and admittedly clichéd), we can imagine that the will of a benevolent dictator or the calculations of a bureau of technocrats would be more substantively reliable. And yet there seems to be a familiar democratic objection to such arrangements. Some would say, more specifically, that democracy is a legitimating condition. Even if the state is substantively reliable, they feel, there remains some complaint against the state, unless the state is democratic. Perhaps this reaction is misplaced, but it is common.

Finally, people's democratic commitments often seem less contingent and more confident than they would be if they rested simply on the Reliability Thesis. This is particularly so when we consider not more abstract arguments for democracy as a whole but instead complaints that more specific institutional features—such as the filibuster or the Electoral College or gerrymandering—are undemocratic. Are these complaints based simply on empirical hypotheses that these particular features lead to substantively worse outcomes? As we return to in Section 28.2, those empirical hypotheses seem too qualified and unsure to account for the reflexive certainty of the complaints.

24.4 Resolving Disagreement

If, then, we can't justify democracy by appealing to substantive interests, then it seems we must appeal instead to interests in influence or interests in correspondence. Some, however, may say that this is too quick. They deny that we need to appeal to interests in correspondence or influence. It is enough simply to appeal to the phenomenon of disagreement. "You cannot just unilaterally implement the decision that best serves the public interest," the thought might run, "because people disagree about which decision does best serve the public interest. You would be begging the question."

Why does disagreement matter? To be sure, because of coordination failures or active conflict, one will often bring about worse results if one tries to implement a better decision (strictly speaking, one that, if all tried to implement it, would be better) than if one tries to implement a decision that most others agree with—in at least the minimal sense that they will in fact try to implement it. But, first, the decision that most others agree with in this thin sense need not have been arrived at democratically. They may, for example, just be habituated to follow where the strongman leads.[1] And, second, unilateral implementation need not always have worse results. One might have access to special levers, or choke points, that allow one to produce better results even when one goes against the collective tide. For example, one might be the strongman.

Alternatively, it might be argued that it is somehow unfair simply to implement a superior decision if others disagree that it is superior (Singer 1973; Waldron 2001; Estlund 2008; Christiano 2010; Shapiro 2012). Some worry that such arguments will be self-defeating. What if the appropriateness of the democratic procedure, or the very ban on controversial considerations, is also controversial (Christiano 1996, 2010 on Singer 1973; Estlund 2008, 60–61)? And some worry that lotteries might be fairer in such contexts than voting (Estlund 2008, 78–82). But the deeper problem comes earlier. What is unfair, in the first place, about implementing decisions that can be justified only by considerations with which others disagree? Presumably the unfairness would consist in not giving some interest, or claim, its due. But what interest? The decision that best serves the public interest, by definition, gives everyone's interests in improvement their due. So, it seems that it must be some interest in correspondence or influence that is not given its due. But then the question is what that interest is. Citing disagreement does nothing to advance our understanding.

25

The Negative Observation

Correspondence

What interests then justify democracy? We have narrowed our search to either an interest in correspondence, which is satisfied to the extent that decisions match one's choice or judgment, or an interest in influence, which is satisfied to the extent that the decisions are reached by a process that is positively sensitive to one's choice or judgment. In this chapter, we consider mainly arguments that the relevant interest is an interest in correspondence.

25.1 Securing Acceptance

As we saw in Section 2.1, consent and reasonable acceptability are often said to be legitimating conditions, which answer some objection to the state. That one isn't subjected to a political decision without one's consent is a kind of influence of one's choice over the decision. That one can reasonably accept a political decision is a kind of correspondence between the decision and one's attitudes. Perhaps, then, the interest in correspondence or influence that we are looking for is, so to speak, an interest in not being subjected to whatever is objectionable about the state, without consent or reasonable acceptability. The idea is not so much that influence or correspondence realizes some good (such as the good of a satisfied preference, which is the subject of the next section). The idea is rather that influence or correspondence answers an objection to what would otherwise be an evil. In Part I, we struggled to identify what the complaint against the state could be that was answered only by consent or reasonable acceptability. But let us assume, for the sake of argument, that there is such a complaint. Would democracy meet this complaint by securing consent or reasonable acceptability?

It is true that a certain kind of democracy, or equal influence over political decisions, is necessary and sufficient for securing consent: that is, for ensuring that no political decision is implemented without consent. This is that each individual has a veto over whether there is any political decision at all (Wolff 1970, chap. 2.1). But this rules out the vast majority of recognizably democratic procedures.

As for reasonable acceptability, democracy seems neither necessary nor sufficient for that. In principle, a decision that is not reached through democratic processes can have such a justification that everyone could accept it in the relevant sense. And the democratic decision, if any, on that occasion can lack such a justification (Estlund 2008, 92). Might one make a more contingent, instrumental argument: that democratic procedures are at least the most reliable route to securing reasonable acceptability (Valentini 2013)? Granted, the most reliable way to satisfy acceptability may well be to arrive at decisions on the basis of open debate in which those who will be subject to and those who will be involved in implementing those decisions offer one another public justifications. But this argues only for public debate of a certain kind. It does not imply that the final decisions informed by that public debate must be reached via equal opportunity to influence. They might be reached instead by a "consultation hierarchy," with autocrats using public debate as an indirect mechanism of consultation and subjects using it as a forum for the mutual display of commitment to the relevant acceptability principle.[1] The autocrats would review the public debate to test whether policies would be acceptable to the subjects consulted, choosing for implementation only among policies that do satisfy it and then reinforcing the message, already conveyed by the public debate itself, that the policies selected had such justifications.

25.2 Satisfying Preferences

Perhaps, then, we should view correspondence between attitudes and policies not as a way of answering an objection to what would otherwise be an evil but instead as a way of realizing a good. The "Satisfy Preferences Argument" makes the case as follows:

1. Each of us has a correspondence interest in the satisfaction of his or her policy preferences as such.[2] Put another way, it is somehow a

good thing for each of us when her policy preferences are satisfied, whatever those preferences might be.
2. As with other interests, such as interests in improvement, we should strive to satisfy each of our correspondence interests in a way that makes trade-offs among us fairly. After all, if it is a good for each of us to have her policy preferences satisfied, then we should try to give each of us as much of this good as we can, in a way that trades off among us fairly.
3. The best means to such a fair distribution of policy preference satisfaction is equal and positive opportunity for influence over political decisions.
4. Therefore, we should strive for equal and positive opportunity for influence over political decisions, which is just democracy.

The argument that a virtue of democratic institutions is more "responsive" policy often seems to be a special case of the Satisfy Preferences Argument. A policy is "responsive," at a given time, on a given question, insofar as it satisfies the majority if any (or, alternatively, plurality, Condorcet winner, etc.) of policy preferences at that time, on that question.

For two reasons, let us suppose that the nature of things somehow makes it the case that, for any given question of policy, there are only two alternatives. First, this simplifies the discussion. Second, it reinforces the point that my present objections to the Satisfy Preferences Argument are independent of results in social choice theory, such as Arrow's theorem, which is discussed in the next section. Since those results require more than two options, they can't be the problem with this argument.

And there are indeed problems with the Satisfy Preferences Argument, specifically with (1) and (3). Against (1), too briefly put, I doubt we have an interest in the satisfaction of our preferences as such. At most, our (informed) preferences are reliable indicators of what we have an interest in, just as our order from a menu is a reliable indicator of what we will enjoy eating. Moreover, even if we had an interest in the satisfaction of our preferences, it seems arbitrary to focus on distributing the satisfaction of political preferences in isolation from other preferences.

Furthermore, when a person's policy preferences conflict instrumentally, as they often will, how are we to say what satisfies those preferences overall?

Suppose Prefferson prefers policy *M* because he prefers policy *E* and mistakenly believes *M* is a means to *E* when *M* in fact undermines *E*. Does enacting *M* satisfy Prefferson's policy preferences or not? If we say no—that is, if we say that preferences for policy ends trump preferences for policy means—then why not conclude that Prefferson's preferences are satisfied just by satisfying his interests overall or, if he's public spirited, by realizing the public interest? After all, there is something to the Socratic thought that those are the "policy objectives" Prefferson ultimately prefers. If, on the other hand, we say yes—that policy *M*, "other things equal," satisfies Prefferson's preferences—then one despairs of saying what satisfies his preferences overall.

Something similar goes for conflict over time. Suppose that, in year 1, Prefferson prefers *P* in year 2, whereas, in year 2, Prefferson opposes *P* in year 2. Do both preferences count? Does each preference count just so long as it is held? Does the later preference override the earlier preference? Why? Because the later preference is better informed? But it needn't be.

And, in any event, why should it matter whether preferences are informed? To be sure, people who are anxious about unresponsive policy are often also anxious that even when policy is responsive, it is responsive to uninformed preferences (Gilens 2012, 12). But it's not clear why, on the present argument, it should matter whether the preferences that are satisfied are informed. Granted, uninformed preferences may be poor indicators of substantive interest, but that's a different issue.

Against (3), is equal and positive opportunity for influence over political decisions the best means to a fair distribution of the satisfaction of policy preferences? Wouldn't a fair distribution of the satisfaction of policy preferences involve something more like maximizing the satisfaction of the policy preferences of those with the least satisfaction over time—prioritarianism as applied to the satisfaction of policy preferences? Maximizing minimum satisfaction seems more in keeping with the idea of giving priority to meeting the claims of those whose claims are overall worse served. Is the idea, then, that if we follow something like majority rule, we will maximize minimum satisfaction: that everyone will get what she wants a fair share of the time?

First, persistent minorities, who are consistently outvoted, do not get their preferences satisfied a fair share of the time. Now, one might reply that this only reveals the limitations of majority rule. And, indeed, people concerned about persistent minorities often suggest alternatives to majority rule, such as proportionality. If 67 percent prefer policy Major—say, that all the songs at the prom be country and western—and 33 percent prefer alternative policy Minor—say, that all the songs at the prom be urban contemporary—then, where possible, we should aim for a policy that somehow goes 67 percent of the way to satisfying Major and 33 percent of the way to satisfying Minor—say, making 67 percent of the songs country and western and 33 percent of the songs urban contemporary. But proportionality does not maximize minimum satisfaction either. If we were to maximize minimum satisfaction, then that would argue for a fifty-fifty split between policies Major and Minor, regardless of the number supporting either policy (so long as at least one person supported each policy).

Second, there is the frequent observation that fulfillment of interests in correspondence, whatever they are, may well come in degrees. Alternatives to majority rule may allow for greater expressions of intensity of preference. But again, these will be at best imperfect measures. Yet one might think, to the extent that one enters empathetically into a mindset concerned with the satisfaction of preferences, that intensity ought to bear on whether the distribution of preference satisfaction is fair.

Third, there are two routes to seeing to it that policy matches Prefferson's preferences. Either policy can adjust to his preferences or he can adjust his preferences to policy. If Prudence gave Prefferson the second route, furnishing him with sound, accessible arguments to revise his preferences, why should he continue to have a claim on Prudence to give him the first route: namely, adjusting policy? Who bears what responsibility for satisfying his interest in correspondence? Only others? Or can he be asked to do his part too? Even if policy is not responsive to his preferences, Prudence might say, this isn't unfair to him. She did *her* part. At that point, why is the fact that his correspondence interest goes unsatisfied, even if regrettable, not his (as Scanlon [1998, chap. 6] puts it, "substantive") responsibility?

Fourth, this view has somewhat puzzling implications for the conditions of selection of representatives. The conditions of conduct—that is, the standards of behavior representatives ought to satisfy—that it suggests are straightforward enough: that representatives should strive to satisfy policy preferences in a fair way. And indeed, it is often suggested that the chief conduct condition on representatives is precisely "agent responsiveness": that representatives strive to realize policy responsiveness—that is, to satisfy those policy preferences that enjoy a majority. I return to this in Section 27.7. The present question is why, if satisfying policy preferences should govern conduct, it shouldn't also govern selection. That is, shouldn't that representative be selected who will best satisfy policy preferences? But there is no guarantee that elections will select such representatives. The candidate preferred by a majority may not be the candidate who will best satisfy their policy preferences. This is so even if we count their preferences for candidates as one policy preference among others. In sum, there is a surprisingly weak connection between electoral democracy and the goal of satisfying policy preferences.

Finally, anxiety about unresponsive policy is often joined with anxiety that even when policy satisfies preference, policy may not be caused by preference (Gilens 2012, 66–69). But why should causality matter for the satisfaction of preferences as such? As Gilens and Page (2014, 572–573) caution, their "evidence does *not* indicate that . . . the average citizen always loses out"; indeed, "ordinary citizens," while impotent, "often win." Granted, we need some mechanism to reveal what people's attitudes are in order to know which decision will correspond with those attitudes. However, this mechanism of revelation need not involve any influence over the outcome. The fact that I voted for a decision is an indicator that my attitudes are favorable toward it, that I abstained is an indicator that my attitudes are less favorable toward it, and that I voted for some alternative is an indicator that my attitudes are less favorable toward it still. But, in principle, other indicators may be as good. My sibling's vote, for example, might be at least as reliable an indicator of my attitudes as my vote. Similarly, an appropriately selected statistical sample of voters might be at least as reliable an indicator of attitudes in the population as a tally of all votes. If so, then a system that allowed my sibling to virtually represent me or consulted only the votes of a statistical sample might be no worse a means to a fair distribution of correspondence-interest satisfaction (Brighouse 1996, 120; Estlund 2008, 76–78).

This concern for causality—that policy should match people's attitudes because people have those attitudes—seems to gesture toward a democratic ideal not of correspondence but instead of influence: not of satisfying the People's policy preferences but instead of ensuring the People's control over policy. Influence, as opposed to correspondence, is the topic of the following chapter.

25.3 Two Interpretations of Arrow's Theorem

Before I end this chapter on correspondence, however, it is worth saying something of the significance of Arrow's theorem (1963), for two reasons. First, some, most notably Riker (1982), have viewed Arrow's theorem as fatal to received justifications of democracy. Second, the discussion has a lesson, about the idea of a collective will, on which later points will depend.

Arrow's theorem says, to put it very informally, that there is no method for aggregating (three or more) individuals' rankings of (three or more) options into a collective ranking of those options where that method satisfies:

- Unanimity: If every individual prefers *x* to *y*, then *x* is collectively preferred to *y*.
- Nondictatorship: There is no individual such that when that individual prefers *x* to *y*, *x* is collectively preferred to *y* no matter what others prefer.
- Independence of Irrelevant Alternatives: The collective ranking of *x* and *y* depends only on how individuals rank *x* and *y*.
- Ordering: The collective ranking is complete and transitive.

There are at least two lessons of Arrow's theorem, depending on what the aggregation method is supposed to do. On one interpretation, the aggregation method is meant to serve the Satisfy Preferences Argument. The aggregation method is supposed to give us a ranking of outcomes according to how fairly (or otherwise desirably) they distribute preference satisfaction. On this interpretation, Unanimity, at least, has a natural rationale. If everyone prefers *x* to *y*, then presumably the occurrence of *x* would better distribute preference satisfaction than the occurrence of *y*. On this interpretation, what Arrow's theorem shows is that we cannot completely and transitively order options in terms of which better distribute preference satisfaction. This would put the Satisfy Preferences Argument in doubt.

However, the basic framework of Arrow's theorem, where the individual inputs are ordinal rankings, already limits what we can say about the satisfaction of preferences. What can we say about satisfaction of individual A's preferences if *x* occurs rather than *y*? The most we can say is either that person A's preferences will be better satisfied (if A prefers *x* to *y*), worse satisfied (if A prefers *y* to *x*), or equally well satisfied (if A is indifferent). We cannot say how much better A's preferences will be satisfied if *x* occurs rather than *y*. Nor can we compare the degree of preference satisfaction that A enjoys if *x* occurs against the degree that B enjoys if *x* occurs. If we deny such comparability, however, then straightaway one wonders how, when individuals' preferences conflict—when A prefers *x* to *y*, whereas B prefers *y* to *x*—there could be a fact of the matter whether *x* distributes preference satisfaction better than *y*, worse than *y*, or just as well as *y*. And if there is no fact of the matter, it seems immediate that we can't have a complete ordering of outcomes. Granted, we would now have a rationale for Nondictatorship. For dictatorship implies that when the dictator prefers *x* to *y* whereas someone else prefers *y* to *x*, there is a fact of the matter: namely, that *x* distributes preference satisfaction better than *y*. But by the same token, Arrow's theorem might seem like overkill; we already knew we couldn't order many outcomes. In any event, the lesson of Arrow's theorem would seem to be that if we want to pursue the Satisfy Preferences Argument, we will need richer information about preference satisfaction.

More generally, it seems that we need richer comparisons of how people fare in order to say anything much in a normative register about politics at all. Riker serves as ad hominem illustration. Riker denies interpersonal comparisons (1982, 111). But he believes there is a positive case for democracy: "liberalism." According to liberalism, democracy, by making it possible to vote officials out of office, tends to protect people from certain bads, such as "oppression" (242–243). But even in what we would describe as an oppressive regime, of the sort that Riker thinks democracy guards against, some people, namely the oppressors, avoid the bad of oppression. So, Riker's argument must be that liberalism better distributes of freedom from oppression. But to speak of better or worse distributions of freedom from oppression, it seems we need fairly rich comparisons of freedom from oppression.

On the other interpretation, the aggregation method is supposed to constitute a collective will. It is supposed to tell us, given only the preferences of individuals, what the will of the group is. The lesson of Arrow's theorem is then that there is no way to constitute a collective will. This is the lesson Riker (1982, 238–239) draws. "Populist" justifications of democracy, which assume there is a will of the People, rest on a false assumption.

Why should we accept Arrow's conditions on a principle of group will constitution? Ordering has a clear rationale. At the limit, an incoherent individual will is not a will at all. However, insofar as the other conditions are conditions of fairness to individuals, as Riker sometimes describes them, it is not entirely clear why they should be conditions on the constitution of a collective will. Compare my individual will. Suppose my individual will is what results from the aggregation of various constituents: for example, my superego, my ego, and the cacophony of desires making up my id. It is not clear why my individual will, in order to be my will, must be "fair" to these constituents, whatever that would mean. Indeed, one wonders whether Riker isn't simply confusing the idea of fairly distributing preference satisfaction with the idea of constituting a collective will.

In any event, it is far from clear why Independence of Irrelevant Alternatives should be a requirement on constituting a collective will. For one thing, it rules out Borda counts.[3] Yet, offhand, it isn't clear why the ordering delivered by Borda count couldn't constitute the collective will. And once again it isn't clear why the individual constituents of the collective will should be restricted to ordinal rankings. Why not allow for intensity of preference? If we relax Independence of Irrelevant Alternatives and allow richer structures of preference, then there are multiple candidates for the will of the People.

This very point may support, by different means, the thesis that Riker takes to be supported by Arrow's theorem: that there is no way to aggregate individual preference orders into a collective preference order that can lay claim to being the will of the People. The thought is not, as Riker's appeal to Arrow's theorem would have it, that there are zero candidates for the will of the People. The support comes instead from the opposite problem. Once we grant that the Independence of Irrelevant Alternatives is not necessary to deliver the will of the People, and once we allow for richer structures of preference, then there are simply too many candidates for the will of the People. How would one decide among them? With what right do we identify the will of the People with preferences aggregated by majority rule, say, rather than preferences aggregated by Borda count? Again, the idea of the will of the People seems too shapeless to settle the issue.[4]

By contrast, the question of what counts as the will of the People has more determinacy when we are given not simply a bare assemblage of individual preferences (or other mental states) but instead a decision-making process that people have actually coordinated on and executed. The fact that people actually coordinated on and executed a particular candidate decision-making process might justify the claim that the upshot of that particular decision-making process, among all the other abstract possibilities, represents the will of the People. But what people actually coordinate on and execute isn't something read off their individual preferences—read off what each, in the privacy of his own mind, prefers. It is instead a matter of what people actually intend and do and what they take others to intend and do. The quest for the right method for aggregating preferences—the one that constitutes the true will of the people—presupposes that it is something distinct from the decision process that people actually coordinate on and execute. For the point of identifying the right method for aggregating preferences is, it seems, to have a standard against which to evaluate the decision processes that people actually coordinate on and execute. The underlying assumption is that people ought to coordinate on and execute the decision-making process that delivers the outcome that would be selected by the best method for aggregating preferences.

This conclusion, that there is no will of the People given merely by the bare assemblage of individual preferences, might well tell against some justifications of democracy: namely, justifications that require that there be a will of the People. In the next chapter, we encounter the idea that while no individual agent can enjoy much positive influence or be decisive, the People as a collective agent can enjoy significant positive influence or be decisive. This may require that the People have a will. But many proposed justifications of democracy do not require that there be a will of the People. The Satisfy Preferences Argument, for example, does not require it. It requires only a way of fairly distributing people's interests in the satisfaction of their preferences. A fair distribution of preference satisfaction need not be a collective will.

26

The Negative Observation

Influence

In the previous chapter, I argued against proposals that the interest justifying democracy is an interest in correspondence, which is satisfied to the extent that decisions match one's choice or judgment. In this chapter, I consider proposals that the interest justifying democracy is an interest in influence, which is satisfied to the extent that decisions are reached by a process that is positively sensitive to one's choice or judgment.

26.1 Absolute Decisiveness or Control

We can rule out an interest in absolute decisiveness or control over political decisions on structural grounds, without even inquiring into its basis. Even if there is some interest in absolute decisiveness over political decisions, democracy extremely rarely satisfies it. Moreover, even in those singular cases in which one does enjoy decisiveness, one can hardly be said to enjoy control. One's decisiveness depends, precariously, on the choices of many others. Indeed, if individuals had interests in control, then that would seem to argue not for democracy but instead for a lottery for control. That would seem the appropriate way to distribute a scarce, indivisible resource among people with equal interests in it.

Here, as at similar junctures in democratic theory, one might be tempted to appeal to the collective. Although democracy does not give individuals some good (here, absolute decisiveness or control), it does give the collective—the People—that good. One worry about this, discussed in the previous chapter, is that there may be no fact of the matter about whether the People enjoy control because there is no fact of the matter about what the People's will is.

I now press a different difficulty. I assume that the justification of democracy must rest on the interests of individuals. This follows not only from the general view that it is the interests of individuals that fundamentally matter but also from more specific intuitions underlying, for example, the Question of Authority. Intuitively, other individuals have a claim on me to implement the democratic decision. I would be wronging those individuals in failing to do so. The difficulty, then, is, first, that it is obscure what individual interest is served by a collective's enjoying control. And, second, even assuming that some individual interest is served by a collective's enjoying control, it is not clear why the collective must be democratic.

To illustrate, suppose the suggestion is that when one identifies with a collective to which one belongs, one, as an individual, somehow vicariously enjoys the goods the collective enjoys. Not an easy thought. But even if we think it, it's not clear why it argues for democracy, since it's not clear why one must identify with a democratic collective. People actually identify with collectives organized around ruling families and charismatic dictators. Or perhaps the suggestion is that, whether or not one identifies with the collective, one is a member of the collective and so vicariously enjoys the goods it enjoys, only if one in fact has equal influence? But it is not clear why equal influence should be a necessary condition of membership. And if it is a necessary condition of membership, then it becomes obscure why anyone deprived of it should care. If I lack equal influence, the thought runs, I am not a member. But if I am not a member, why care whether I lack equal influence? After all, I do not care particularly whether I have equal influence with individual Egyptians over the government of Egypt. And a sufficient reason for this is that I am not Egyptian.

26.2 Positive Influence as a Means to Political Activity

So, our search seems to have narrowed to some interest in relative or absolute contributory influence or relative decisiveness. But what might this be? There are two general, structural objections to an appeal to an interest in absolute influence. First, if what citizens have reason to value is absolute influence, an increase in the size of the electorate (unless offset by an increase in the power or reach of political decisions) reduces the value each citizen enjoys. But this is absurd. Population growth does not, as a kind of arithmetical truth, threaten what each of us cares about, insofar as we care about democratic rights.[1] Second, positive influence argues against lotteries. But is it clear in cases where we know we can't do better than lottery that something is lost if we don't have positive influence? If one of us must be drafted, to consider an example to which we return in Section 27.2, is it obvious that we should vote on whom it will be?

Setting aside these general, structural objections, what might the interest in absolute influence be? As we saw in Section 1.5, the value of many activities depends on their flowing from the agent's choices, which in turn flow from her informed, autonomous judgment. Accordingly, we have an interest in such influence as a means to these activities. Such choice-dependent activities include expression, religious observance, personal relationships, marriage, the bearing and rearing of children, work, and, more ambitiously, living one's life as a whole. Taking up this last possibility, one might argue that one has an interest in being the author of one's own life, which requires that one likewise be the author of certain central features of it, such as one's career or choice of spouse. One such feature, one might less plausibly continue, is the political decisions to which one is subject.[2] The difficulty is that this would seem to require control over political decisions. After all, if one merely shared contributory influence with millions of other people over other aspects of one's life—such as one's choice of career or spouse—one would hardly count as the author of one's life.

Instead of seeing control over political decisions as a prerequisite for a kind of global autonomy, one might instead suggest, less grandiosely, that some influence over political decisions is part of one particular choice-dependent activity. It might be said that alongside other choice-dependent activities, such as expression and religious observance, we should count (blandly put) "political activity." This is the activity of freely forming one's convictions (often by confrontation with the reasoning and convictions of others) and knowingly bringing those convictions to bear on political decisions (often by trying to get others to change their convictions) by participating in the procedure by which political decisions are reached and subsequently implemented. This is what Constant described as "the liberty of the ancients"—or at least the "pleasure" brought by the exercise of that liberty ([1819] 1988, 316).

We should pause for a paragraph to distinguish political activity, which constitutively requires influence, from "political reflection": the activity of merely reflecting on what political decisions should be or, more abstractly, on justice itself. Political reflection, crucially, does not require influence. Indeed, reflection on justice is largely reflection on decisions over which we have no influence because they are historical, insulated from popular influence, or both. (Consider reflection in civics classes or law schools on the justice or injustice of US Supreme Court decisions reached prior to the expansions of the franchise brought about by the Fifteenth and Nineteenth Amendments.) For precisely this reason, I find it unpromising to appeal to the value, instrumental or noninstrumental, of political reflection to justify democracy, as some appear to have done. For instance, Rawls (2001a, 45) appeals, in this way, to citizens' interest in the "adequate development and full exercise" of their capacity for a sense of justice, and Christiano (2010) appeals to what he calls the "interest in learning the truth about justice." Even if one has less political influence than others, one can enjoy as much opportunity for political reflection, provided that one has the same access to relevant resources, such as education, information, argument, and time.[3]

Returning to political activity, thus distinguished from political reflection, J. Cohen (1999, 406–407; see also 2001, 72–73) suggests that the case is "analogous to a central point that figure[s] in the case for private liberties," such as freedom of conscience. He continues, "A characteristic feature of different philosophies of life is that they each give us strong reasons for seeking to shape our political-social environment: for exercising responsible judgment about the proper conduct of collective life. . . . Common ground among these competing, reasonable philosophies is that citizens sometimes have substantial, sometimes compelling reasons for addressing public affairs." In a similar vein, R. Dworkin (2002, 202–203) suggests that we should make "it possible for [each person] to treat politics as an extension of his moral life." In his words, "Just as someone denied opportunity to worship according to his or her own lights is denied a foundational part of religious life, so someone denied opportunity to bear witness to his concern for justice, as he understands what the concern requires, finds his political agency stultified. . . . But the demands of agency go beyond expression and commitment. We do not engage in politics as moral agents unless we sense that what we do can make a difference, and an adequate political process must strive, against formidable obstacles, to preserve that potential power for everyone."

If we have an interest in political activity, then we have an interest in some positive, absolute influence over political decisions, as a constituent of such activity. Here we can distinguish two different interpretations of the interest in political activity. On the first, "individualist" interpretation, which Cohen's and Dworkin's remarks most naturally suggest, the interest is in bringing one's individual convictions to bear on political decisions, just as one might bring one's individual convictions to bear on one's personal religious practice, expression, or associative choices. The point is to have one's "moral life extended" through, or see the imprint of one's convictions in, political decisions.

On the second, "collective" interpretation, the interest is instead in participating in an intrinsically valuable, usually collective, activity of making political decisions: the joint project of the People's self-government, say. In participating in that activity, one will be bringing one's convictions to bear on political decisions, but that is not the point of participating. The point, instead, is just to play one's part in a valuable, collective activity, as one might play on a team, perform in an orchestra, or paint one's part of a joint mural. What sort of influence is required for political activity? While Dworkin suggests that it requires decisiveness ("making a difference"), mere contributory influence might well be enough, especially on the collective interpretation.

In general, others have a claim on us to provide them with opportunity, justly distributed, to pursue other choice-dependent activities, such as religious observance, expression, and association. (As we saw in Section 1.5, if an interest of ours supports a claim on others, it's usually not a claim to the actual satisfaction of the interest but instead a claim to a fairly distributed opportunity to satisfy it: to a suitable choice situation.) Presumably this is part of the argument for familiar liberties of conscience, expression, and association. Since political activity is a choice-dependent activity relevantly like these, perhaps others likewise have claims to improvement that we provide them with opportunity, justly distributed, to pursue political activity. How do we provide them with this? The answer might seem to be by seeing to it that decisions are made by positive democratic procedures, implementing those decisions, and bearing their effects. That way, everyone has opportunity, fairly distributed, to bring their convictions to bear on actual political decisions. But then democracy would be justified.

There are, however, three problems with this line of argument. The first is that it gives us no grounds to distinguish between opportunity for political activity qua citizen and opportunity for political activity qua official. The second problem is that it does not explain why opportunity for influence should be equal. The final problem is that others' interest in choice-dependent activities does not, as this argument requires, give them a claim on us to lend ourselves in that way to those activities.

I discuss the second and third problems in the next two sections. In what remains of this section, I discuss the first problem. Presumably, we think everyone qua citizen should have equal opportunity for political activity in a much more demanding sense—standing equal availability of the activity (as with religious observance)—whereas we think everyone qua official should have equal (or fair?) opportunity for political activity in a much weaker sense—equal chances, given a certain level of aptitude, in competition with others, as with other careers (Section 17.1). But what justifies treating these forms of political activity differently? Surely, just as contributing to a grassroots effort for the election of a candidate, as one citizen among others, is a valuable activity, so too is working for the passage of legislation as a successful candidate. Without a principled distinction, we seem pressed either to assimilate opportunity qua citizen to opportunity qua official, which would license fair competition for voting credentials, or to assimilate opportunity qua official to opportunity qua citizen, which would seem to rule out representative institutions.

26.3 Must Means to Political Activity Be Equal?

Having raised this problem, however, I now set it aside and focus exclusively on opportunity qua citizen. The second problem we face is a structural problem for any interest in absolute influence. If we have an interest in absolute influence, then why not distribute opportunity for influence unequally so long as this increases the opportunity of the worst off? Why suppose that a fair distribution of opportunity to satisfy interests in political activity is an equal distribution of opportunity to influence political decisions?

Start with informal opportunity. A fair distribution of informal opportunity for religious practice does not require equal informal opportunity for religious practice. Against a backdrop of an otherwise just distribution of wealth, for example, it is not objectionable for some group to have greater informal opportunity for pilgrimages than another group. By analogy, it would seem, a fair distribution of informal opportunity to satisfy the interest in political activity need not be an equal distribution of informal opportunity to influence political decisions.

It's tempting to reply that political activity, unlike religious activity, is a zero-sum game: it is "competitive" in the sense that one person's condition can be improved only if another person's condition is worsened (Rawls 1993, 328; Brighouse 1996, 132; 1997, 165). If unequal informal opportunity for religious activity is fair, it is only because that inequality works to the advantage of the worst off, perhaps by increasing their informal opportunity for religious activity. Unequal informal opportunity for political activity, however, can never increase the informal opportunity for political activity of the worst off.[4]

Why should this be? Suppose that, from a benchmark of equality, giving some people better informal opportunity for political activity than others have would lead to an overall increase in wealth and leisure. This possibility, in the present context, is not some abstract curiosity. It is precisely the trade-off we face if we accept, for the sake of argument, that some nondemocratic procedure, such as Mill's plural voting scheme, might be more substantively reliable. Presumably, this increase in wealth and leisure could be redistributed to those with the least of such resources. This might increase their informal opportunity for political activity.[5]

The argument that it could not increase their informal opportunity for political activity—the implicit reasoning behind the idea of the zero-sum game—rests on a confusion. Perhaps it can be argued that from a benchmark of equality, increasing Big's informal opportunity for political activity to a greater extent than Little's will reduce the conditional probability of Little's political goals (e.g., the enactment of Little's preferred policy, achieving correspondence) if Little engages in political activity. But it does not follow from this that Little's informal opportunity for political activity is thereby reduced. First, even if the conditional chances of correspondence if Little engages in political activity are reduced, Little may have more chance to satisfy the condition if he so wishes—to engage in political activity if he chooses to—in the first place. For example, from a benchmark of equality, we might increase both Big's and Little's leisure time to devote to civic affairs but increase Big's to a greater extent. Even if this means that correspondence is less likely if Little devotes himself to civic affairs, it may be the case that Little is more able to devote himself to civic affairs. It is not obvious that this should mean a net decrease in his informal opportunity for political activity.

Second, realizing a political goal, important though it may be for other (e.g., substantive) interests, may not be crucial for satisfying the interest in political activity. Political activity arguably is a matter of participating in the process in a way that is guided by one's convictions. Its value does not turn on the outcome. Perhaps it is enough merely to have contributory influence over the decision: to fight the (as one sees it) good fight or play one's part in the decision-making process. To risk a trivializing analogy, suppose I lose one tennis partner and gain another, more skilled tennis partner. My chances of winning are lower. But are my chances of realizing the values of playing lower?

Setting aside inequality in informal opportunity, inequality in formal opportunity for political activity (such as Mill's plural voting scheme) can also increase the formal opportunity for political activity of the worst off: as it were, the "absolute weight" of their vote. Granted, with other choice-dependent activities, it hard to see how this can occur. How, by giving less formal opportunity for religious practice to some, can we increase their absolute formal opportunity for religious practice? But political activity is special in this respect. If nondemocratic procedures are substantively more reliable, then they might increase the reach and power of the state. By increasing the reach and power of the state, they broaden the range of political decisions that the worst off can influence. This, by definition, increases the extent of their formal opportunity for political activity. New ways of bringing their convictions to bear on political arrangements become possible that before were not (Christiano 2010, 104–106; Brighouse 1997, 166–167).

26.4 Must We Lend Ourselves to Political Activity?

The final problem is this. What would be required of us to provide others with the opportunity to engage in political activity is categorically different from what can reasonably be required of us to provide others with—to use analogies suggested by the individualist interpretation—the opportunity to practice their religion or speak their mind or—to use analogies suggested by the collective interpretation—the opportunity to pursue other valuable collective activities, such as team sports or orchestras, with willing participants. Providing others with the opportunity to engage in political activity requires, distinctively, that we become active or passive instruments of that activity: that we carry out or bear the resulting political decisions so as to consummate that activity. It seems doubtful that others' interest in other choice-dependent activities gives them a claim on us to lend ourselves in that way to those activities, even when our doing so is required for their pursuit of those activities. In order that someone has the opportunity to practice his religion, for example, he may have a claim on me to avoid interfering with that observance, to cede to him a fair share of resources that he might use for his observance, and to tolerate the effects of his observance on the character of our shared culture. But it's less clear that he has a claim on me to become an active or passive instrument of his religious observance. If nine Jewish men need a tenth, it is not as though they have a claim on me to make their minyan. The same is true if—to use analogies better suited to the collective interpretation—eight players need a ninth for their ball game or three musicians need a fourth for their quartet. So why do others' interests in specifically political activity, by contrast, give them a claim on us to lend ourselves to that activity, when this is not the case for any other choice-dependent activity?

One answer is that political activity is simply more important or central than other choice-dependent activities, in such a way as to give others, in this unique case, a claim on us to lend ourselves to it that they elsewhere lack. I cannot rule this possibility out, but I have my doubts. Many people quite reasonably find at least as much meaning in lives organized around family, professional, artistic, or religious activities as around political activity. Another answer is that while there might be a social world in which no one is conscripted into anyone else's choice-dependent activities, there is no realistic possibility of a social world in which no one is conscripted into anyone else's political activity. Assuming that it would be a disaster to have a procedure, such as a lottery, in which decisions are influenced by no one, we will be lending ourselves to someone's political activity. And if someone's interest in political activity will be satisfied, one might argue, then fairness requires that everyone's interest in political activity be satisfied. Yet fairness requires this only if the reason for giving that person the opportunity to engage in political activity is her interest in it. Fairness does not require it if the reason is something else entirely: if her having the opportunity is just a by-product. Suppose, for example, that while everyone has an interest in chopping down a tree, no one's interest is sufficient in itself to entitle him to an opportunity to chop down a tree. Nevertheless, the health of the forest requires that exactly one tree be chopped down, and by Forrester in particular, who will do it the right way. As a kind of by-product, Forrester will have the opportunity to satisfy his interest in chopping down a tree. But it hardly follows that everyone with the same interest must have the opportunity to chop down a tree. Similarly, even though their personal interests in it are insufficient to justify it, perhaps a phalanx of technocrats must be allowed to rule because that would produce the substantively best results. As a result, those technocrats will be able to satisfy their interest in political activity, just as Forrester will satisfy his interest in chopping. But it hardly follows that everyone with the same interest must have the same opportunity if, as we are allowed to suppose, their having that opportunity will produce substantively worse results.

To be sure, this is not to deny that people have genuine interests in political activity. When people participate in elections, for example, they are not simply aiming to achieve a result that's good for all but also pursuing a meaningful activity, in part constituted by their exercise of influence. Nor is it to deny that there are ways of providing people with some elements of opportunity for political activity that do not require becoming active or passive instruments of that activity. Suppose that other elements of democratic decision-making are already in place: that is, everyone stands ready to implement and bear democratic decisions. Then my giving someone access to and resources to make use of the democratic forum, for example, may be a way of giving them opportunity for political activity without lending myself to it. It may be analogous to providing others with the opportunity to proselytize (for example, space in airport terminals) in the religious case without somehow becoming an instrument of their religious practice. But this point does nothing to explain why I should stand ready to implement and bear democratic decisions in the first place when a substantively better, nondemocratic procedure was available.

At this point, one might be tempted to insist that people just do have an interest in influence over decisions that affect their interests. In addition to having the tautologous interest in their interests' being positively affected, people also have an interest in being able to influence decisions that affect their interests, independently of whether this influence positively affects their interests. This interest is not situated in a broader, independently recognized pattern of values. For example, it is not to be assimilated to interests in choice-dependent activities or explained in expressive terms. It is basic and sui generis. This would give us a straightforward justification of democracy. Since political decisions to which one is subject tend to affect one's interests, the interest in influence over decisions that affect one's interests would imply an interest in influence over political decisions. One might have hoped to say more about this interest, to situate it among other familiar interests. But perhaps this is all one can say.

In any event, the suggestion overgeneralizes wildly. Many nonpolitical decisions, in businesses, families, and churches, affect our interests. Yet we do not feel the same pressure for democratic decision-making in such contexts. Moreover, many decisions that seem strictly private and personal can affect the interests of others. I might be crushed if you refuse my nephew's marriage proposal or Christ as your personal savior. Does it follow that I should have a vote over whether you do?

One might blunt the edge of this objection by arguing that one's interest in influence over a decision is proportional to its effects on one's interests (Brighouse and Fleurbaey 2010). Since your private decisions are likely to affect your interests more significantly than mine, you should have a greater say. But, still, is it plausible that I should have any say at all over whether you marry my nephew or accept the Gospel? Moreover, if we blunt the objection in this way, then we cannot explain democracy, understood as equal opportunity to influence political decisions, in terms of an interest in influence over what affects one's interests. For few political decisions do affect everyone's interests equally. Of course, one might avoid this problem by insisting that people have a basic, sui generis interest in equal and positive influence over specifically political decisions. But that answer offers no articulate justification of democracy at all. It just posits an interest in positive democracy as such.

26.5 The Expressive Significance of Relative Influence

In any event, the meagerness of the kind of absolute influence over political decisions that even positive democratic procedures give any one of us may lead us to conclude that influence matters only as a symbol. More ambitiously, one might claim that to deny Virginia Louisa Minor absolute influence is to express a negative judgment about her. Decision by lottery would somehow demean us all. Less ambitiously, and more plausibly, the claim would be that to deny Minor as much influence as others have is to express a negative judgment about her. The relevant interest would be in relative influence. If someone is to have influence, then everyone should have equal influence, lest the inequality convey, or be taken to convey, something disparaging about those with less. It is Minor's opportunity, not actual influence, that matters, simply because others don't insult her if she chooses not to exercise an opportunity that she nonetheless has.

This expressive approach raises three questions: "What insult?" That is, what is the content of the negative judgment? "What objection?" That is, why is it objectionable? "Why democracy?" That is, why is democracy the only or best way to avoid it?

Begin with the "What insult?" question. One might suggest that the negative judgment is that Minor's interests of kind *K* (e.g., improvement interests) are less important than others' *K*-interests. Yet what expresses this judgment, one might have thought, is a procedure that serves her *K*-interests less well. And such procedures are already open to objection on that count: namely, that they serve her *K*-interests less well. While this insult may add, well, insult to this underlying injury, it can't explain why ills not already open to that objection are ills. Put another way, if the objection is to the judgment that interests in improvement are less important (Beitz 1989, 110; R. Dworkin 2002, 200), then it is hostage to the instrumental argument considered earlier (Arneson 2010, 35).

Next one might say that the insult is that the target's basic, native capacity for commonsense judgment about political matters is inferior. This makes the answer to the "What objection?" question plain enough. It might even be said to strike at the target's very moral personality (R. Dworkin 1996, 28; Waldron 2001, 238–239; Christiano 1996, 74; 2010, 93; Richardson 2002, 62–63). It is especially objectionable, in the way characteristic of discrimination, discussed in Chapter 13, when this alleged inferiority is attributed to gender or race.

But this answer to the "What insult?" question makes the "Why democracy?" question hard to answer. The traditional arguments for property qualifications and Mill's case for plural voting say nothing about anyone's basic or native capacities. Instead, they speak to lacking relevant experience or education, occupying positions in society that make one susceptible to distorting pressures, or lacking the kind of stake in public affairs that fixes the mind soberly on the long term.

Well, one might say, the insult is simply that the target would make inferior political decisions to those of someone else, for whatever reason, whether native or not. But then the "What objection?" question becomes unanswerable. Messages to the effect that one person will make a worse political decision than someone else are pervasive in our culture, without seeming, as a rule, objectionable. Such messages are sent by ordinary disagreements over policy, deference to endorsements by newspapers and unions, debates over qualifications for office, differential grades in high school civics classes, and the selective hiring of political commentators.

In any event, even if we had an answer to the "What objection?" question, the "Why democracy?" question would still loom. To begin with, there are any number of grounds for denying a person equal formal opportunity other than that they would make worse decisions. It might simply cost too much to get her to the polls, or print ballots she can read, or add enough benches to the town hall. Or, if we take a current conservative argument at its face value, weaker identification requirements would expose us to the scourge of voter fraud. Moreover, we can deny suffrage to a certain person on no grounds at all—and so a fortiori not on the grounds that her decision-making is inferior. We can permanently disenfranchise people at random: what we might call "suffrage by lottery" (Wall 2007; Estlund 2008, 182; Arneson 2009).

When it comes to informal opportunity, such arguments are not mere philosopher's hypotheticals. They are voiced by public officials. The line of recent Supreme Court decisions striking down limits on campaign finance and expenditure may well express an objectionable lack of concern about the inferior informal influence of all but the 1 percent. But these decisions cannot plausibly be taken to express the judgment that the 99 percent are inferior decision-makers—only that the proposed restraints of political speech are intolerable. Moreover, other deprivations of or failures to protect equal influence are neither intentional nor manifest to anyone (at least prior to painstaking research).

It might be said that we have overlooked an obvious answer to the "What insult?" question: the insult is that those with less or no influence are not equal citizens or full members of the political community (Beitz 1989, 158; R. Dworkin 2002, 187). But this is either implausible or unhelpful. At one extreme, we can view equal opportunity for influence as a purely arbitrary symbol of citizenship (somehow otherwise conceived): a mere historical accident.[6] But this is hard to credit. For one thing, it makes it a mystery why people have strived, and do strive, for equal influence in societies in which it had not, or has not, already acquired the status of an emblem of equal citizenship or membership. Why, for example, would it have been absurd to expect the women's suffrage movement to have been satisfied by the US Supreme Court's declaration in *Minor v. Happersett,* 88 US 162 (1875), that, although it implied nothing about their rights to political influence, women were without question as much citizens as men (Brighouse 1996, 122)? And it would make the case for democracy implausibly precarious. Why not a concerted public information campaign to replace the vote with another, less consequential symbol: perhaps a flag sent to each citizen on his or her eighteenth birthday?

Distancing ourselves from this absurd extreme, we can argue, more plausibly, that, first, there is a particular conception of citizenship or membership that we have reason to value (whether or not it currently prevails) and, second, that on that conception, it is explicable why a deprivation of influence would express that those deprived are not equally citizens or members. But then it is not clear that we are making any progress. Suppose we try to articulate a conception of citizenship that does not yet build in entitlement to influence but is such that a denial of influence would naturally express or be taken to express a denial of citizenship so conceived. We are, I think, more or less fated to recapitulate our earlier answers to the "What insult?" question. Is a citizen or member someone whose substantive interests are just as important? Then this is, in effect, our first answer: that the insult is that substantive interests are not as important. Is a citizen or member instead a competent decision maker? And so on.

27

The Positive Conjecture

Equal Influence

We turn the page on the negative observation: that the commonplace claim to democracy cannot be explained by interests in improvement, rights against invasion, or an alleged interest in the satisfaction of preferences. Now we turn to the positive conjecture. The justification of democracy rests on the secondary, vertical tempering factor of Equal Influence, which is satisfied insofar as any individual who is subject to superior untempered power and authority has as much opportunity as any other individual for informed, autonomous influence over decisions about how that power and authority are to be exercised. Insofar as I have as much opportunity for informed, autonomous influence over the decisions regulating the power and authority as anyone else, there's no one to whom I can point and say, because that individual had greater influence, I, in being subjected to that power and authority, am subordinated to that individual's superior power and authority. Granted, I have far less influence than the collective that wields the superior power and authority. But that collective is not another natural person, with whom a question of equality would arise.

27.1 Equal Influence

What is equal opportunity to influence a decision? Note, first, that it is a matter of influence, not correspondence. So long as one enjoys equal influence, whether or not one enjoys correspondence does not, in itself, bear on whether one stands in relations of inferiority to others. Second, what matters is one's equal relative influence, not the absolute extent of one's influence. The fact that one does not have influence over the decision does not put one under the power and authority of another if no one else has influence over it either.

Third, what matters is retained opportunity for influence, not its exercise. The reason for the focus on opportunity is not, as with the interest in political activity, that my political activity has value only if it is guided by my own convictions. Indeed, the present view is silent on whether my exercise has any value at all. Nor is the reason for the focus on opportunity that asking me to pitch in is a reasonable way to divvy up the labor of servicing my needs. It's instead that if you and I have, and will continue to have, the same opportunity to influence the decisions to which we are subject, then the fact that I refrain from exercising it on occasion does not somehow subordinate me to you. It is important, however, that my opportunity to influence is retained over time. It isn't enough that I consented in the past to permanently divest myself of a say. And it isn't enough that, once upon a time, you happened to win a lottery. This is why a denial of suffrage by lottery would still be problematic, even though it would not express that anyone was an inferior decision-maker or that anyone's substantive interests were less worthy of concern.

Fourth, what matters is, specifically, equality of opportunity for informed influence. Suppose an asymmetry in influence over a decision would threaten a relation of inferiority between us. It scarcely defuses the threat that while both of us can, in a suitably objective sense, influence the decision, I know how to influence it in accord with my judgments but you do not: your attempts at influence are, from your perspective, more or less random. To take an extreme case, a disparity of knowledge of this kind could be what makes you my slave; I know the code that unlocks your chains, whereas you can only enter numbers at random. The point is not that giving you as much information as I have will lead us to make a better decision—although it may well do that too. The point is instead that, whether or not it leads to a better decision, it helps remedy the imbalance in power between us.

Fifth, what matters is equal opportunity not only for informed influence but also for autonomous influence: influence knowingly in accord with judgments that are themselves reached by free reflection on what one takes to be relevant reasons. It scarcely defuses the threat of inferiority if I can manipulate the judgments that underlie your vote.

Finally, when people enjoy equal opportunity for influence, this will often be because some people, who in some sense have greater "natural" power, cede equal opportunity for influence to others. This is compatible with

Equal Influence. However, it is important what form the ceding of equal opportunity takes. If it is a condescending gift or a matter of personal discretion, then Least Discretion would be violated (Section 23.4).

27.2 Equal, Not Positive, Opportunity

How might we ensure equal opportunity for informed, autonomous influence over political decisions? One possibility, already broached in passing, is to ensure that no individual has any opportunity for influence over those decisions. In principle, political decisions might be made by someone, but not by someone with whom any of us, who are subject to the decision, has ongoing social relations. In that case, that person's greater opportunity to influence decisions would not threaten relations of inferiority. At first glance, though, it may be obscure how this could occur. Rule by a colonial power will not fit the bill, since only the narrowest conception of social relations would deny that there are social relations between colony and metropole. However, if one looks across time, rather than space, then the phenomenon comes to seem pervasive. To a great extent, the accumulated body of law to which we are subject was made by those no longer living. In this way, we are subject to political decisions of the dead. Now, perhaps we have the sort of ongoing social relations with the dead that make avoiding relations of inferiority with them an object of concern. But perhaps not. On this view, Thomas Jefferson's suggestion, in his letter to James Madison of September 6, 1789, that every generation should draw up its own constitution, on the grounds that "'the Earth belongs in usufruct to the living'; that the dead have neither powers nor rights over it," would be not simply unworkable in practice (as the more reliably earthbound Madison tactfully observed in his reply of February 4, 1790) but also wrongheaded even as a matter of theory. The basic point is this. If our concern were for correspondence, or some kind of absolute influence, then Jefferson's proposal would be the obvious ideal. By contrast, as far as claims against inferiority are concerned, perhaps there is no objection to rule by the "dead hand of the past": where all are committed to following whatever law may have been bequeathed to us, just as we might all be committed to following whatever law a majority of us chose. At least it is an open question. And if there is no such objection, then this may be one respect in which human mortality is not entirely to be regretted. It offers us intelligent decision-making without the threat of social hierarchy.

Indeed, one might wonder whether we must even wait for the intelligent decision maker to pass away. Perhaps we need only wait for them to pass out of power. Suppose August is subject to a decision that April alone made months ago. Now, however, April has no more power to change the decision than August has. They are equally powerless to change it. Does August now stand in a relation of subordination to April? Perhaps not. Perhaps, if no one now wields greater influence over a decision, then that decision satisfies Equal Influence now, even if the decision was made in the past in a way that did not satisfy Equal Influence.[1] That is, April might have had reason, at the time of making the decision, to make it in a way that was compatible with Equal Influence, such as by giving August an equal say in its making. But if April does not, and if she is later dispossessed of the special power to change the decision and no one else has any greater power to change the decision, then perhaps the decision satisfies Equal Influence henceforth. If this is right, then it might shed fresh light on the puzzle about why the massive body of old law that present lawmakers, whether courts or legislatures, have neither made nor actively reaffirmed (such as by refraining from repealing it) continues to have authority (Tuck 2015, 259). Suppose that the present lawmakers do not actively reaffirm the whole body of old law because they cannot. Then that body of old law has whatever authority stems from Equal Influence, simply because it is, at present, not a decision over which anyone now has greater opportunity for influence.

The difficulty, of course, is that this inheritance of past decisions, as rich as it may be, is neither perfectly prescient nor perfectly self-interpreting. Decisions may be substantively unreliable, and conflicting interpretations may lead to coordination failures, with ensuing substantive losses. New decisions will need to be made, and old decisions will have to be disambiguated. This can be done without giving any of us any opportunity for influence, such as by lottery, or it can be done by giving each of us some positive but equal opportunity for influence, such as by voting. This gives a simple answer to at least the Question of Institutions from Section 24.1: Why should we want, establish, or maintain democratic institutions? The answer is that democratic institutions realize Equal Influence.

Needless to say, this does not rule out other arguments that appeal to something other than Equal Influence for positive procedures over merely equal procedures, such as lotteries. One argument is simply instrumental: that, as things actually are or could reasonably be expected to be, some positive equal procedures are more substantively reliable than any nonpositive procedures that give equal opportunity for influence. Alternatively, one might suggest that there are noninstrumental reasons for positive influence. In Chapter 26, however, I explained my pessimism about several proposed noninstrumental reasons for positive influence.

Moreover, the idea that there is, in all cases, a standing noninstrumental argument for positive influence sits ill with some intuitions. For instance, there is the intuition that, when it comes to deciding who is to be conscripted into an unwelcome task, a fair lottery is better than a vote. A lottery fully satisfies the substantive claims of each—namely, that each should have the highest chance of avoiding conscription compatibly with fairness to others—whereas a vote only introduces the possibility of substantive unfairness (for example, that voters gang up on a salient or disliked candidate). If we insist there is always a noninstrumental argument for positive procedures—that some important value of "self-governance" always argues in favor of a vote—then we need to explain why, in this and similar cases, that value is overridden in favor of a lottery.

In Section 8.9, however, I suggested a different argument in favor of positive influence. This is that positive democratic procedures are one way of giving substance to the horizontal factor of Equal Citizenship. In order for positive influence to give substance to Equal Citizenship, however, there need not be positive influence in all cases, only in a significant range. And there are other ways of giving substance to Equal Citizenship without positive influence at all: namely, by showing positive consideration. In Section 27.4, I suggest a further argument in favor of positive influence over, specifically, the selection of the highest officials.

27.3 Explaining Authority and Legitimacy

Moving beyond the Question of Institutions, how do we answer the Question of Authority? Why does the fact that a political decision was made democratically give others an objection, or even a complaint, if I fail to implement or comply with it? The answer is that if I were to disregard the democratic decision, then I would be depriving others of equal opportunity to influence this very decision.

For influence over the decision, in the sense relevant in this context, is not simply influence over what gets engraved on tablets or printed in registers; it is influence over what is actually done. The point is that in disregarding the democratic decision, I would be depriving others of equal influence. This is so even if I myself don't somehow treat them as inferiors to me, in particular.

How, next, do we answer the Question of Legitimacy? Recall that there are two ways of understanding the Question of Legitimacy. The first asks: Why does the fact that a political decision was made democratically remove my pro tanto objection against its implementation, which involves some relation of rule? In other words, why might democracy be a legitimating condition, as Section 2.1 observed that consent or reasonable acceptability is often said to be? On this first interpretation of the Question of Legitimacy, the problem to be solved is not that there is a deficit of positive reasons to implement the decision but instead that I have an objection against some relation of rule that would be involved in implementation.

As I suggested in Section 8.1, the complaint against the state is a complaint against the relations of inferiority involved in subjection to political decisions. And if that is the complaint, then Equal Influence is one of the things that answer it, for the reasons already explained. In other words, it makes perfect sense that Equal Influence should be seen as a legitimating condition if the very thing that raises the problem of legitimation is the asymmetry of power and authority that the state involves. The answer to the Question of Legitimacy, so interpreted, is straightforward.

There was, however, another interpretation of the Question of Legitimacy. Even if the fact that the decision was democratically made does not remove my objection against its implementation, why might it constitute a positive reason that weighs against that objection? The answer to the Question of Legitimacy, understood in this second way, is just the flip side of the answer to the Question of Authority. If I, as agent, have positive reason to implement democratic decisions, then so do others. And their reasons weigh against my objections as patient. Note that this reason might obtain even if other positive reasons to implement democratic decisions are lacking because of, say, the Duty/Directive Gap of Section 2.6.

Consider, now, two objections. First, some may object that others are not deprived of equal influence when I refuse to implement a decision that others are implementing, provided that I believe anyone else may refuse as I do. If I have greater influence than others, this is only due to their own voluntary choice. But this objection requires that anyone's refusal would have influence comparable to my refusal. This is unlikely where there is any significant division of labor in the implementation of the decision.

The second objection is as follows: What if, as is generally the case, there is more than one formal procedure that gives equal opportunity for influence? Suppose, as I argue in Section 29.1, that plurality rule and majority rule for changes to the status quo are both "a priori equal" procedures, which provide equal opportunity for influence. Suppose that people have voted on the question of change or stasis on the expectation, based on law or custom, that a change will be made only if there is a majority for that change. The votes come in, and a plurality, but not a majority, is in favor of the change. Suppose Offe were to let plurality rule settle the matter—instead of, as expected, majority rule—and Offe were to implement the change. There is an intuition, which I share, that Offe would be acting, in some sense, undemocratically. But why should this be, if plurality rule no less than majority rule gives equal opportunity for influence?

There may be two reasons for this. First, people debated and voted expecting that majority rule would decide the matter. If it was only Offe who was informed that plurality rule would or might decide the matter, then Offe actually had greater opportunity for informed influence than others had. In other words, a certain degree of prior coordination about which decision procedure will be followed is typically necessary for equal opportunity for informed influence. I return to this point in Section 30.8.

It might be, however, that the idea of abandoning majority rule occurred to Offe only after the polls closed. This brings us to a second response. If law or custom has established that a particular a priori equal procedure will be used, then that decision itself may enjoy democratic authority, either because it was reached in a way that gave equal opportunity for influence or because it was a decision made by those no longer in power. For Offe to decide to adopt some other procedure is a personal imposition.

27.4 Is Representation Compatible with Equal Influence?

How is Equal Influence compatible with "representative democracy" or, as I said earlier, "indirectly" democratically made decisions? We might well begin by asking how Equal Influence is compatible even with "direct democracy." Even in a direct democracy, imagining that such a thing were possible, there would be offices, such as clerk and peace officer, that are not held by everyone. And those who hold such offices wield, by definition, decision-making powers that others lack, thereby wielding asymmetric power and authority. Perhaps such offices are tempered, to some extent, by Impersonal Justification and Least Discretion. But how are they tempered by Equal Influence? After all, the officeholder has exclusive opportunity to influence the decisions their office makes. The rough answer is that the asymmetric power and authority of the office are tempered by Equal Influence, at least to some extent, insofar as the office is controlled by a decision-making body that those subject to the office have equal opportunity to influence. This is because of the phenomenon of Supersession, which I now explain. Together, Equal Influence and Supersession are a way of instantiating the tempering factor of Downward Equalization.

Suppose that Hyman has asymmetric power and authority over Loman, a slave. However, Hyman's asymmetric power and authority are controlled by a third party, Ultima. For instance, Hyman was freely chosen by Ultima, does nothing but carry out Ultima's highly specified orders, and can be removed by Ultima at any time. Indeed, we might imagine that Hyman is himself a slave who has simply been picked out by Ultima to order other slaves around today. Then it seems that Loman's subordination is not so much to Hyman as to Ultima. We might be tempted to say that this is because the asymmetric power and authority are ultimately not so much Hyman's as Ultima's or because Hyman is acting as Ultima's agent, proxy, delegate, or representative.[2] But these may be simply restatements of what we have already described. In that case, they don't provide any deeper explanation.

Generalizing somewhat, suppose that Hyman has asymmetric power or authority in comparison with Loman (either over Loman or over others) in virtue of Hyman's greater opportunity to influence the decisions of a decider, Beta. This might be because Beta just is the natural person Hyman, because Beta is an office that Hyman occupies, or because Beta is a group of which Hyman, but not Loman, is a member. Suppose further that a decider, Alpha, controls Beta. Then, to the extent that Alpha controls Beta, Loman's subordination is not so much to Hyman as to whichever natural individuals have the opportunity to influence Alpha, to the extent that they have opportunity to influence Alpha. Call this general phenomenon, in which one is, as it were, subordinated to those who control one's subordinators, "Supersession."

To see its bearing on Equal Influence, suppose that when we look to see who has the opportunity to influence Alpha, we find that Loman has no less opportunity to influence Alpha than anyone else has. Then, we might say, there is no one to whom Loman is more subordinated than he is to himself. And so, we might say, there is no one to whom Loman is subordinated. One such possibility is that Loman has the exclusive opportunity to influence Alpha. This would explain why the principal need not be subordinated to the agent in principal-agent arrangements in which the agent has decision-making powers that the principal lacks. Think of a seventeenth-century dynast (our Alpha in this case) sending their diplomat (our Beta in this case) to this or that foreign court to negotiate treaties and alliances. Although the diplomat has special powers to negotiate that affect the dynast's interests, the dynast can suitably control the diplomat so that the dynast is not subordinated to the diplomat. Another such possibility, which is the one that most interests us, is that Loman has equal opportunity with every other citizen to influence Alpha, with Alpha still controlling Beta. In that case, Loman's subjection to Beta is tempered by a combination of Equal Influence and Supersession.

More generally, let Hyman have asymmetric power or authority in comparison with Loman, either over Loman or over others, in virtue of Hyman's greater opportunity to influence the decisions of a decider, Beta. This asymmetric power or authority will be tempered to a greater degree, first, as a decider, Alpha, controls Beta to a greater degree and, second, as the ratio of Hyman's opportunity to influence the decisions of Alpha to Loman's opportunity is smaller—perhaps to the point that Loman has equal or greater opportunity to influence the decisions of Alpha.

When does Alpha "control" Beta, and to a greater degree? We can distinguish three kinds of control Alpha may have over Beta. First, there is "directive control," which Alpha enjoys to a greater degree (i) to the extent that Beta merely specifies, applies, executes, and prioritizes Alpha's directives; (ii) to the extent that less discretion is left to Beta about how to do so; and (iii) to the extent that Alpha can issue Beta new directives at shorter intervals. Beta's activities under (i) include not only specifying vague decisions, applying those decisions to particulars, and choosing means to execute decisions but also, importantly, prioritizing the execution of different decisions under conditions of uncertainty. For example, Alpha may have directed Beta to achieve *A* and *B*, leaving Beta to decide whether it is worth it to lower the chances of *A* slightly in order to increase the chances of *B* significantly. Second, there is "occupancy control," which Alpha enjoys to a greater degree (i) to the extent that Alpha decides who has influence over Beta's decisions by, say, occupying the office Beta or being a member of the body Beta and (ii) to the extent that Alpha can decide this at shorter intervals. Note that this might be a relevant form of control over Beta, even if it does not translate into influence over the content of Beta's decisions. Finally, there is "regulative control," which Alpha enjoys to a greater degree (i) to the extent that, if Beta makes independent decisions, which do not merely specify or execute Alpha's decisions, Alpha can constrain or overrule those decisions and (ii) to the extent that Alpha can do this sooner after those decisions are made, with the limit being constraining the decisions from the start.

The thought, then, is that the asymmetric power and authority of officials over individual members of the People are tempered, at least to some degree, insofar as those officials are ultimately controlled, at least to some degree, by the People as a collective body. This gives positive, as opposed to merely equal, influence a distinctive role to play in the selection of officials. Suppose the decision to implement some policy directly, such as that we all break camp and move west, was made by lottery, with equal, but not positive, influence. Then, in virtue of being subjected to this decision, we are not subordinated to the superior power and authority of anyone else. But things look different when we are confronted with an official who enjoys special decision-making powers. Why aren't we, in virtue of being subjected to his decision, subordinated to him? Our reply is that it is because, at least in part, his decisions are sufficiently controlled by a body, the People, whose decisions we each have equal opportunity to influence. However, control requires that the body, the People, have positive influence over the official. And it is hard to see how the People can have positive influence unless individual members of the People have positive influence. This case for positive influence does not rest on a positive value of the People's governing themselves, let alone of an individual's governing herself. Instead, the case for positive influence rests on avoiding relations of inferiority to officials, which the People's controlling officials helps achieve.

Return now to the contrast between direct and representative democracy. Let us suppose that, in both direct and representative democracy, there is a decision-making body, the People, such that each natural person has equal opportunity to influence what the People decide. And let us suppose that, in both direct and representative democracy, the People sit at the top of the decision-making hierarchy, controlling the highest officials, who control other officials. Then one difference between direct and representative democracy is that, in a direct democracy, the People not only sit at the top of the hierarchy but also, as it were, occupy positions further down the hierarchy. Decisions that in a representative democracy would be made by officials are, in a direct democracy, instead made by the People themselves. The handoff from the People to officials, as it were, happens at a lower level of the hierarchy in a direct democracy. This difference, however, may not be so significant. The logic of Supersession would seem to make the most pressing question the question of who has influence over the top of the hierarchy.

The most pressing question, then, is whether the People in a representative democracy do sit at the top of the decision-making hierarchy. On the contrary, it might be said that the People have only occupancy control, not directive or regulative control, over the highest reaches of the official decision-making hierarchy. After all, if we look at the role of the People in the institutional structure of representative democracy, we find that that role is limited to periodically selecting who will occupy the highest offices, such as those of the legislature and the chief executive. Once selected, however, the highest officials, or highest collective bodies of officials, make their own decisions, without any direction or regulation from the People. The People may decide who will make the decisions, but the People do not decide which decisions they will make. This does little to temper the asymmetric power and authority of officials over individual members of the People.

Against this, I argue that, under certain conditions, elections are decisions not only about who will occupy which offices but also about what those who occupy those offices will do: decisions about which directives the highest officials (and bodies) are to follow once in office. I assume that when individual members of a collective take themselves to be voting on a given question, then the outcome of the vote can be seen as the collective's deciding that question. Thus, if individuals take themselves exclusively to be voting on the question of who will occupy an office, and nothing more, then the outcome of the vote is simply the collective's deciding who will occupy that office. However, under certain conditions, we can interpret the question being decided as not only who is to occupy the office but also what they are to do once in the office.

The first of these conditions is that there is a sufficient range of candidates and parties on offer. Second, voters vote for candidates and parties on the basis of what voters expect these candidates and parties will seek to do in office, and candidates and parties compete for votes by trying to influence these expectations. Third, information is available to voters about what the candidates and parties will seek to do in office, which takes the form not only of explicit campaign promises and party platforms but also personal biographies and party histories, among other things. Fourth, voters are in a position to form autonomous opinions about what the candidates and parties will seek to do in office. Fifth, in competing for votes, candidates and parties not only seek to inform voters about what they will do in office but also revise their plans for what they will do in office in order to appeal to voters. This means that voters' judgments have at least a kind of passive influence over what sort of plans they are presented with. Even if voters do not initiate new plans themselves, new plans are initiated by candidates and parties in an effort to appeal to voters' judgment. Thus far, these conditions seem largely in keeping with Schumpeter's "truer to life" definition of democracy as "that institutional arrangement for arriving at political decisions in which individuals acquire the power to decide by means of a competitive struggle for the people's vote" (1942, 269) and in which the initiative comes from the candidates and parties, not from voters themselves. However, we can add, as a further condition, that it is open to voters to have more active influence by participating in intraparty activities, as well as by working with other movements or organizations to bring concerns to the attention of candidates and parties. There is a role to be played here by a well-functioning, informal public sphere (Habermas 1996)—if not to facilitate joint deliberation as such, at least to satisfy the conditions listed. There is also a potential role to be played by more regimented institutions, such as randomly selected or self-selecting citizens' commissions, which, by voicing concerns, setting agendas, or drafting proposals, formally "structure the informal public sphere" (Landemore 2021, 77).

Under such conditions, it would be misleading to say that the People merely select who will occupy the highest offices or merely "consent" to their occupying them (Landemore 2020, 83–85). Granted, those are the only options explicitly presented to them on the ballot. However, given the further conditions we are imagining, those options are, at the same time, options of what highest officials (and bodies) will seek to do. One doesn't vote just for a candidate or a party but also for a platform in the broadest sense. Thus, the People can be seen as deciding which directives, broadly defined, the highest officials (and bodies) are to specify, apply, execute, and prioritize. This suggests that the People do have at least some measure of directive control over the highest offices (and bodies). As to whether these conditions are satisfied in the real world, a key question, to which I return in Chapter 32, is whether voters can be seen as voting on the basis of what they expect candidates and parties to try to do in office.

The People may well issue a directive about what highest officials are to do, it might be replied, but issuing a directive does not suffice for directive control. Highest officials must be constrained to follow the directive. The question, however, is what sort of constraint this must be. My view, discussed earlier in Section 27.1, is that it is sufficient constraint that the highest officials see themselves as duty bound to follow the directives, as a way of respecting Equal Influence, and act accordingly. As I discuss shortly, it is a conduct condition on officials that they act in such a way as to permit the People, through elections, to exert directive control over them. Of course, there is no guarantee, in practice, that officials will see themselves in this way and so no guarantee that the People will exert directive control. But that tells us what we already knew: namely, that whether democratic values are realized depends on how elected officials behave.

There is no denying that in direct democracy, where laws and executive orders are made by the People, no question of control over highest officials even arises, and so no question of sufficient control. And if the People are permanently in session, rather than simply constituted at elections, and are always overseeing what lower officials there are, then the People exercise greater control over those officials: the People can issue more specific directives or regulate the officials' decisions and can do so at shorter intervals. So, in representative democracy the asymmetric power and authority of officials are less fully tempered by Equal Influence than in direct democracy. That much must be granted. The question is whether the asymmetric power and authority of officials might be sufficiently tempered such that, in combination with other tempering factors such as Impersonal Justification and Least Discretion, our relations to those officials do not constitute relations of inferiority.

Here is it worth noting that certain secondary tempering factors apply particularly to the highest officials in a representative system, such as legislators and chief executives. First, Equal Application tends to be satisfied by the highest officials, since the highest officials (or the bodies of which they are a part) tend to make decisions that apply to all citizens, including themselves. By contrast, judges tend to make decisions that apply only to certain others, such as a decision that this parent must pay child support. Second, citizens are not in general Upwardly Unaccountable to the highest officials. Obedience is not understood to be owed to the highest officials, not even in their official capacities, as obedience might be understood to be owed to a judge or police officer, at least in their official capacities. Finally, insofar as highest officials stand for reelection, not being reelected is itself a form of Downward Accountability.

27.5 Bankers and Judges

We have been assuming a simplistic, chain-of-command model. However, in representative democracies, there are typically officials and official bodies who aren't elected but don't take directives from the highest elected officials and indeed are supposed to be insulated from "the political process." There are officials and official bodies, such as high courts and central banks, that wield significant power and authority but seem to stand outside the decision-making hierarchy described here. Unlike highest officials, such as legislators and chief executives, they are not directly elected by the People and so cannot be said to specify, apply, execute, and prioritize their directives. Unlike other officials, they do not specify, apply, execute, and prioritize the directives of the highest officials.

How then are the asymmetric power and authority of such "independent officials" and bodies tempered, if and when they are? First, the highest officials (and bodies) still exercise occupancy control over independent officials (and bodies). Second, in so doing, they may also exercise directive control in the way in which the People, by exercising occupancy control over independent officials (and bodies), exercise directive control. That is, highest officials (and bodies) may appoint independent officials with an eye to what they are likely to seek to do in office. It might be objected that such occupancy control, and directive control via occupancy control, is limited because of the length of terms that independent officials hold. But perhaps this is just a good argument that their terms should be shorter.

Finally, independent officials are constrained in their decision-making powers. Central banks have a narrow, specified remit over monetary policy to carry out a directive to balance inflation and unemployment. Courts are constrained, first, in that they can only respond to cases brought to them. Second, they are constrained by existing law, which they are not free to rewrite, in how they dispose of those cases. As Hart (1992, 273) observes, "not only are the judge's powers subject to many constraints *narrowing his choice* from which a legislature may be quite free, but since the judge's powers are exercised only to dispose of particular instant cases he cannot use these to introduce large-scale reforms or new codes. So his powers are *interstitial* as well as subject to many substantive constraints."

What are we to say when a constitutional court strikes down a statute as unconstitutional? Imagine, as a stylized case, that we have inherited a constitution that assigns review powers to a constitutional court. Decisions of the court can be, in effect, overruled by amending the constitution, but that requires a two-thirds majority in a referendum. First, it should be noted that the court here exercises only regulative, not directive, control. Second, it may only impose a higher supermajority requirement. It is not an objection on grounds of Equal Influence that the constitutional court thwarts the will of the majority by, in effect, imposing a supermajority requirement on the passage of the statute, if, as I argue in Section 29.1, Equal Influence is as content with supermajoritarian requirements as with majoritarian ones. It may, however, be a perfectly valid objection, indeed one with which I am increasingly sympathetic, on grounds of substantive reliability.

27.6 Selection Conditions: Election over Sortition

Should the selection of higher officials and bodies be by election or, as some have suggested, random, by sortition (Guerrero 2014; López-Guerra 2014; Landemore 2020)? There is, of course, the empirical question of whether elections select better officials than sortition: officials who bring about substantively better results. There are reasons from the armchair, at least, to question the assumption that sortition must select worse officials. To begin with, what makes an office effective in bringing about substantively good results may simply be, first, that it assigns responsibility to some specific person or body to make a decision—thus avoiding a kind of tragedy of the commons—and, second, that it provides that person or body appropriate resources—above all, freedom from other cares and distractions—to make the decision. Even if election tends to select people with distinctive traits, whereas sortition has no similar tendency, distinctive traits may be of little importance. Moreover, greater diversity and descriptive representation in a decision-making body, at least under certain conditions, and other things equal, may improve decision-making (Landemore 2013). If sortition leads to more diverse and descriptively representative officials than elections, then sortition might thereby lead to better decisions.

Setting aside the empirical question, Equal Influence might seem at first to favor neither election over sortition nor sortition over election. In both election and sortition, all enjoy equal opportunity to influence who occupies the highest offices or bodies: equal and positive opportunity in the case of election and merely equal opportunity in the case of sortition. However, in Section 27.4 I argued that when elections meet certain conditions, voters do not simply decide which candidates and parties will occupy the highest offices and bodies but moreover, in so doing, decide on directives that the highest officials and bodies are to specify and execute. Under elections, the People, by exercising occupancy control, also exercise some measure of directive control. To the extent that they do, the People can be seen as sitting at the top of the official hierarchy. Under sortition, by contrast, the People exercise no control over officials, not even occupancy control, let alone directive control. Under sortition, the People cannot be seen as sitting at the top of the official hierarchy. Instead, at the top of the official hierarchy are simply those individuals, whoever they are, who are selected by sortition.[3]

For this reason, election would seem to reconcile government with equality, or at least noninferiority, better than does sortition. This is to disagree with the classical view, as Aristotle reports it at *Politics* IV.9 1294b6, according to which sortition was the more egalitarian constitution, or at least that "it seems democratic for officials to be chosen by lot, and oligarchic by election" (2017, 96). This disagreement might give us pause. Have we failed to take the measure of some countervailing respect in which sortition reconciles government with equality better than does election?

Sortition might seem to avoid a disparity of esteem for political judgment that election introduces. At times, this is what Manin (1997) seems to have in mind when he suggests that modern election is "inegalitarian," "aristocratic," or "oligarchic" in a way in which classical sortition was not. However, it is not clear why substituting election for sortition should introduce a disparity of esteem for political judgment that would not have existed before. For one thing, all that Manin appears to show is that elected officials will tend to be viewed by voters as salient or distinctive in some way, not necessarily as having better political judgment. As Manin concedes, a voter's judgment that one candidate for election is "superior" might consist simply in that voter's judgment that the candidate is "more like me" (140–141). For another thing, differential esteem for political judgment seems perfectly available under sortition, even if it doesn't find expression in voting. People might hope that Jones and not Smith wins the lottery or that last year's winner did a better job than this year's winner is doing. And even if election does introduce a disparity of esteem that would not have existed under sortition, that need not amount to an objectionable relation of inferiority if the disparity was merited.

Next, it might be said that sortition is closer to rotation (Landemore 2020, xvii, 89–90; 2021, 79). First, if the aim of rotation is to distribute the holding of offices equally, then it cannot achieve this if the ratio of citizens to offices is too high. Second, I argued in Section 8.8 against rotation as a tempering factor. Finally, elections with term limits would, in any event, achieve rotation as well as sortition.

It might be replied that, even if sortition cannot distribute the holding of office equally, it nevertheless distributes chances for holding office equally. By contrast, "elections will systematically close off access to power to people who are too ordinary to stand out in the eyes of other citizens" (Landemore 2020, 89, attributing a similar point to Manin 1997). Why might noninferiority argue for equal chances for holding office? Suppose that, despite the tempering factors, citizens who are subject to offices will stand in lingering, objectionable relations of inferiority to those who hold offices. Holding office, for as long as one holds it, is temporary relief from those relations of inferiority. Since only some can enjoy this temporary relief, it is an indivisible good. So, as with other indivisible goods, the fair way to distribute it is by a lottery. This is what sortition accomplishes. The trouble is that, if what I argued earlier is correct, sortition at the same time removes one of the tempering factors on the relation of officials to those subject to them: namely, that the People enjoy some measure of occupancy and directive control over officials through elections. So sortition, while offering more equal chances of relief from a bad, nonetheless makes the bad worse for those who do not receive relief. This seems a poor trade-off.[4]

27.7 Conduct Conditions: Collective Decisions, Not Aggregated Preferences

How should the highest officials (taking these to include members of the highest official bodies) conduct themselves in office? Impersonal Justification still implies that highest officials, like all officials, should, in executing their offices, follow the decision-making processes that, against the background of other offices, best serve impersonal reasons, such as the public interest. Which processes these are is a difficult, empirical matter. Consider the traditional question of whether members of legislative assemblies should act as "trustees," deciding on the basis of their judgment of what best serves the public interest (as Burke [[1774] 2015] famously argued), or as "delegates," deciding on the basis of their judgment of what will best satisfy the directives or preferences of their constituents. One can imagine arguments for both sides: that they best serve the public interest when they act as trustees, pursuing the public interest directly, and that they best serve the public interest when they act as delegates, pursuing it indirectly by a kind of invisible hand.

This is just to consider what Impersonal Justification implies for the conduct of the highest officials. What does Equal Influence imply? We saw earlier that Equal Influence requires that the highest officials should behave so as to make it possible for elections to be the giving of directives. In order for the People to exercise directive control over the highest officials (and bodies), voters must be in a position to predict what candidates and parties would seek to do in office if elected. Only then can a vote for a candidate or party be, at the same time, a vote on the directives that highest officials (and bodies) are to specify and execute. This requires, first, providing information before election on the basis of which people form expectations and, second, as a conduct condition, seeking to do, once in office, what the electorate had reason to expect, given the information available to the electorate at the time of the election, they would seek to do if elected.[5] The information available to the electorate includes not only, or even primarily, the formal platforms adopted at party conventions or promises made on the campaign trail, which may be known to be, at least in part, ritualized posturing. As any reasonable person can appreciate, highest officials will need to exercise judgment in the face of unforeseen emergencies, opposition, new information, changed conditions, proposed bargains, trade-offs among objectives, shifts in the attention of others, and much else. Combinatorial explosion would await any attempt to formulate, let alone communicate, a complete hypothetical plan for every possible constellation of factors (which is in part why a lottery to determine which directives highest officials are to pursue is unrealistic). Evaluating what a given candidate or party will do in office is instead largely a matter of knowing what the candidate or party is like: their values, priorities, worldview, perception of threats, sources of information and advice, risk aversion, adaptability, and much else. Evidence of this comes from not only what they say they will do but also what they have done in the past and the company they keep.

Equal Influence also implies, by a different route, a similar conduct condition. If candidates and party leadership are themselves part of the electorate, then they should have no better information at the time of the election about how they themselves will conduct themselves in office than is available to voters at large. Either candidates and parties should not hide anything at the time of the election, or, if they do hide something, they should conduct themselves in office as someone from whom it was hidden had reason to expect they would act. Otherwise, those candidates or party members would enjoy greater opportunity for informed influence in the election than other voters.

Why not say that highest officials should strive, even after they are in office, to satisfy the current preferences of the electorate, rather than to conduct themselves as the electorate had reason to expect at the time of the election? Such highest officials would be "agent responsive," insofar as they strove to achieve what in Section 25.2 I called "policy responsiveness": to see to it that the policy preferences presently held by a majority (or plurality, etc.) are satisfied. In Section 25.2, we considered, and rejected, an instrumental argument for agent responsiveness: the Satisfy Preferences Argument. This argument held that individuals have an interest in the satisfaction of policy preferences as such and that agent responsiveness is a means to policy responsiveness, which just is a fair distribution of the satisfaction of those policy preferences. Here we consider a different, constitutive argument for agent responsiveness. In order for the highest officials to be properly under the direction of the citizenry as a whole, they must strive to satisfy the People's preferences. This new argument for agent responsiveness indeed remedies one of the shortcomings of the earlier, instrumental Satisfy Preferences Argument. The Satisfy Preferences Argument could not explain why it should matter whether preferences causally influence policy. After all, a satisfied preference is a satisfied preference, whether or not it brings about its own satisfaction. The present argument, by contrast, offers more of an explanation of why it matters that preferences causally influence policy. If the highest officials are not satisfying the People's preferences because they are the People's preferences, then they are not taking direction from the People. Nevertheless, like the Satisfy Preferences Argument, the present argument for agent-responsiveness does not imply that the highest officials must be elected or selected in any other particular way. So long as the highest officials, however selected, seek to satisfy preferences, the highest officials take direction from the People.

Does this constitutive argument for agent responsiveness succeed? Is agent responsiveness a conduct condition? To begin with, it is not obvious that, in order for Beta to be properly under the direction of Alpha, Beta must seek to satisfy the current preferences of Alpha, as opposed to following Alpha's last stated directions. Suppose Beta has been sent with instructions but knows that Alpha's mood will change in a week's time. It is not obvious that Beta is properly under the direction of Alpha only if Beta caters to Alpha's changed mood rather than carries out the instructions. More generally, it is not obvious that, in order for the highest officials to be properly under the direction of the People as the highest body, the highest officials must satisfy the current preferences of the People, as opposed to the decision of the People in the election.

But there is a deeper problem with the idea that highest officials are under the direction of the People, understood as constituting the highest body, insofar as the highest officials strive to satisfy the People's preferences. It is unclear how we are to identify what the People as a whole prefer: the will of the People. This new argument for agent responsiveness faces a problem that the earlier Satisfy Preferences Argument avoided. As observed in Section 25.3, the Satisfy Preferences Argument does not require a conception of what the People, understood as a collective, prefer: a conception of the will of the People. It requires only a principle telling us how to trade off the satisfaction of one person's interest in policy-preference satisfaction against another's. The present argument for agent-responsiveness, by contrast, does require a conception of the will of the People, which exercises directive control. And, as observed earlier, if all we have is the raw profile of policy preferences of the various members of the People at any given time, it is not clear that we can identify a determinate will of the People about how highest officials are to act. There seem to be too many candidates for the will of the People. On what grounds can we say that the will of the People is given by the preferences of a majority, as opposed to a plurality or one or another supermajority threshold? By contrast, if there is actual, deliberate coordination on some decision-making procedure, as there is in a formal election, then the result of the procedure can count as the will of the People. The fact of actual coordination and execution distinguishes that process from all the other abstract possibilities.

VI

A Democracy Too Lenient and Too Demanding?

The vertical tempering factor of Equal Influence requires democracy of some kind. But of what kind? This part asks this question—What kind of democracy?—from two perspectives. One is the perspective of institutional designers. If it were up to us, what sort of "democratic" features should we build into institutions? The other perspective is that of institutional critics. Why, if at all, should we be dismayed by reports of "undemocratic" features of existing institutions?

The answers to this question, we will find, exhibit two opposed tendencies, each of which may be discomfiting in a different way. On the one hand, formally, Equal Influence, on its own, constrains less than one might have thought. From the perspective of institutional designers, this permissiveness may be welcome. It gives us great freedom in institutional design, letting us fill in the rest simply by considerations of the public interest. From the perspective of institutional critics, however, this formal permissiveness may be deflating. For it may give us no grounds to criticize certain ills as intrinsically undemocratic. On the other hand, informally, Equal Influence constrains more than one might have thought. To be sure, it gives us grounds to criticize certain ills as undemocratic. However, it may also seem overwhelmingly demanding.

28

Pathologies of American Democracy

As I take up, in what follows, the second of our two perspectives—that of institutional critics—I have in mind some of the ills from which, it is said, democracy in the contemporary United States suffers.[1] This chapter describes what these ills are and indicates the limitations of familiar appeals to results and responsiveness in explaining why the ills are ills.

28.1 The Ills

This section simply enumerates some of the real or alleged ills of democracy in the contemporary United States.

Vote suppression: Certain barriers make voting costly or difficult—at the limit, impossible. They are higher, often by design, for certain ages, races, ethnicities, and income levels. Examples are voter ID laws, limits on early voting and late registration, long wait times at polling places, and disenfranchisement for certain criminal convictions. Such measures appeared to resurge after, first, the 2010 election gave Republicans control of many state legislatures and, second, *Shelby County v. Holder* (570 US 529 2013) weakened the prophylactics the Voting Rights Act of 1965 had set against such barriers.[2]

Formally disproportionate representation: The ratio of one district's representation—understood as its voting power in the relevant body (e.g., the size of its Senate delegation)—to its population is greater than that of another district (e.g., Wyoming vs. California or Puerto Rico or the District of Columbia).

Substantively disproportionate representation: The share of representation (e.g., representatives preferred by White people but not Black people) of some relevant group in the relevant body (e.g., a state's congressional delegation) is greater than the share of relevant constituents in that group (e.g., voters in the state who cast ballots for White-but-not-Black preferred representatives).

Status quo bias: Changing policy is harder than keeping it.[3] Some status quo bias is due to supermajority requirements. Some such requirements are recent developments, with no constitutional basis, such as the filibuster.[4] Some status quo bias is due instead to the difficulty of reaching agreement among different bodies, often controlled by different parties ("gridlock"), or reaching agreement among factions within parties over which leadership has diminished influence (Hacker and Pierson 2010, 2016; Gilens 2012; Pildes 2014; Mann and Ornstein 2016).[5] And some status quo bias seems endemic to centralized decision-making. Changing policy simply demands more of scarce resources, such as time and attention (Baumgartner et al., 2009).

Persistent minorities: A more or less fixed group is reliably outvoted. Often when this is so, elections are uncompetitive and reliably won by large margins.

Gerrymandering: Districts are drawn so as to advantage a particular incumbent or group (and not as a remedy for some objectionable disadvantage) (Daley 2016; Wang 2016). Some substantive disproportionality is due to gerrymandering, as when, for example, Republicans draw a few districts in which Democrats will win by huge margins and many (still equipopulous) districts in which Republicans will win by smaller but still comfortable margins. However, some substantive disproportionality has other causes, such as "clustering" or "natural gerrymandering": that Democrats, on average, reside closer to one another than do Republicans. Similarly, some persistent minorities result from gerrymandering, as when a Democratic incumbent sees to it that her own district contains a reliable majority of Democratic voters. But not all persistent minorities result from gerrymandering.

Polarization: This includes a number of interrelated trends, which I describe in very rough terms. First, greater proportions of elites, if not the mass public, support more extreme policies, or overlap on fewer policies, than they have in the past. Second, the parties—or at least their elected officials, leadership, and more engaged members—are further from one another and exhibit less overlap. (Note that the second sort of polarization might occur without the first if members were simply "sorting" themselves into parties that matched their static ideologies, rather than changing their ideologies themselves.) These changes appear to be asymmetric, with most of the change coming simply from the right moving further right (Mann and Ornstein 2016; McCarty 2019, 42–43). Among other causes may be the realignment of the White South toward the Republican Party after 1964 (McCarty 2019, chap. 5). Third, there is greater sorting into parties along lines of race, religion, geography, and personality traits (Mason 2018; Klein 2020, 3). Finally, there is evidence of increased antipathy, or at least increased willingness to express antipathy, toward members of the opposing party (Lelkes 2016).

Money in campaigns: More money is spent on elections and referenda, while restrictions on campaign finance and expenditure, as well as systems of public funding, have been struck down, weakened, or opted out of.

Special interests: Interest groups, often via professional lobbyists, have, in some sense, excessive access to or influence over the decisions of officials. Moreover, the decline of private-sector unions has changed which interests have access or influence.

Gilens's findings: Let us say that policy is more "Gilens responsive" to a group at a time to the extent that an increase in the proportion of that group preferring at that time that a policy be adopted increases the probability that it is later adopted. Gilens (2012) finds that not only is federal policy more Gilens responsive to the affluent than to other groups, but it is not at all Gilens responsive to the nonaffluent when preferences diverge from the affluent. What's more, the fact that policy is more Gilens responsive to the affluent appears not to be much explained by education, information, voting, or contact with officials. The culprit may simply be that the affluent donate more money to campaigns (Gilens 2012, chap. 8; Bartels 2016, 257–268).

Arbitrary voting: Negatively, Achen and Bartels (2016) argue that votes tend not to be influenced by voters' policy preferences, "ideology," or ("real" or "perceived") interests. Positively, they argue that votes are systematically influenced by the three factors: (A) myopic retrospection: the rate of income growth in last two quarters before the election; (B) partisan affiliation: membership in a formal political party; and (C) group identity: belonging to a race, gender, ethnicity, or religion.

I don't expect this list of ills to get high marks for taxonomical hygiene. Some of the ills are hard to distinguish, even in theory, from one another. Even when they can be distinguished in theory, they amplify one another in practice. For example, money in campaigns may contribute to disparities in Gilens responsiveness. Polarization puts agreement out of reach, which in turn exacerbates status quo bias. At the same time, it's also worth noting that some of these ills appear to mitigate others in ways that those sounding the alarm don't always note. For example, to the extent that myopic retrospection holds, shouldn't we expect that differences in campaign spending won't influence elections simply because we shouldn't expect such differences to affect the rate of income growth? Similarly, to the extent that group identity and party affiliation are as insulated from persuasion as Achen and Bartels (2016) suggest, and to the extent that people vote on the basis of group identity and party affiliation, shouldn't we expect voting to be less sensitive to campaign spending? For these reasons, it's a bit puzzling why Achen and Bartels (2016, 327) stress limiting money in campaigns as a chief remedy for the arbitrary voting behavior they identify.

I ignore some other ills often mentioned in the same breath. In part, this is from (too rare) mercy for my reader. The list is already overly long. In part, these other ills have less to do with those specific aspects of democracy that are this book's focus. For instance, the benefits of political order (simply in terms of what I call in the following "better results"), even in nondemocratic regimes, derive from its being known that people will follow certain procedures that resolve disagreement and achieve coordination without excessive cost (e.g., bloodshed or soaring bond rates). These procedures are bound to outrun explicit codification, requiring some shared understanding of things that just aren't done. Much of the anxiety about status quo bias and polarization in the reports I have in mind—and it is anxiety that I share—is anxiety that old understandings have decayed and new understandings either have not taken root or carry needless risk. Whereas once it went without saying that one didn't take hostages—a depopulated judiciary, default on the federal debt—it is becoming routine (Hacker and Pierson 2016; Mann and Ornstein 2016).

28.2 Beyond Results

Are these ills alleged of democracy ills simply because they have worse results? It is, after all, very common to complain that this or that allegedly "undemocratic" feature of institutions leads to worse results, where "better results" consist of what I earlier described as the better satisfaction of substantive interests or, more specifically, the better realization of the public interest.

To be sure, describing the ills concretely, taking things as they are, and sighting the near horizon, I agree that some of the ills are ills because the ills have led, and can be predicted to lead, to worse results. But I think this for, in some sense, partisan reasons. The simple fact is that many of the ills enhance the power of the political right. Voter suppression and disproportionate representation favor Republicans. So too may money in campaigns and myopic retrospection (Bartels 2016, chap. 3). And Republican control of the levers of power (at least since the exit of "big state" progressives like Nixon) has had significantly worse outcomes than Democratic control would have had and increasingly worse outcomes as polarization has intensified.

However, the worse results in question are typically thought to be less partisan. The ills are supposed to have "systemic" effects that all can agree, more or less regardless of party, are worse. The partisan tone of the previous paragraph no doubt struck some readers as out of place in academic writing. And that's just the point. The concerns about democracy are typically assumed to be independent of the fortunes of one's favored party or policies. That's why the partisan tone of the previous paragraph seems so out of place.

As common as these complaints are, they are very difficult to assess. It isn't just that the data are scanty, as controlled experiments are impossible and natural experiments few and far between. It's not clear, in most cases, how the hypothesis is even being framed. How specifically is the allegedly undemocratic feature described? Which alternatives to that feature are considered for comparison? What background is held fixed? How long is the "long run" over which the undemocratic feature is hypothesized to work its mischief? When do we call "time!" and tote up the scores of the system with that feature and the alternatives without it?

This is some reason to doubt that the complaints about such ills all rest on the belief that they lead to worse results. The empirical hypotheses seem too qualified and uncertain to account for the unqualified, reflexive character of many of the complaints. A further reason for doubt is that complaints about worse systemic results seem like complaints that everyone has, whereas complaints about at least some of the ills, such as about persistent minorities, seem like complaints that only some, such as the minorities, have. A final reason for doubt is that complaints about the ills are explicitly framed in terms of values other than worse systematic results, such as procedural fairness or political equality.

28.3 Beyond Responsive Policy

Are the ills ills, then, because they reflect, or bring it about, that policy is insufficiently responsive?[6] Policy is "more responsive" at a time, let us say, simply to the extent that, on each given policy question, the policy preferred by a majority (or plurality, etc.) of the electorate at that time obtains.

Unresponsive policy is indeed implicated in many of the listed ills. Had suppressed votes been cast, they might have brought about policy responsive to the preferences of morally relevant electorate: namely, an electorate including the suppressed. Status quo bias thwarts responsiveness when a majority prefers a change in policy. By diminishing the representation of the majority, disproportionality makes it less likely that the majority's preferred policies are enacted. Polarization and lack of competition push policies further from the center, where, arguably, most preferences lie. If outspending the opposition improves the chances that a favored candidate or proposition wins, then outspending majorities may thwart majority preferences. And if candidates so much as believe that outspending the opposition improves their chances, they may be induced not to support, or even to oppose, the majority's preferred policy in order to attract such spending. If special interests influence policy, and if special interests oppose majority preferences (Gilens and Page 2014, 570), then this again may thwart majority preferences. If policy is more Gilens responsive to the affluent, and if the affluent are fewer, then this may make policy less responsive in the present sense. Arbitrary voting dampens responsiveness in referenda and doubly in elections. If people do not vote on the basis of their policy preferences, then they are not only less likely to elect officials predisposed to pursue policies that they prefer but also less likely to pressure those officials, by the threat of removal, to pursue such policies.

The question, however, is why unresponsive policy is a problem. First, lack of responsiveness might, of course, lead to worse results. However, this would just take us back to the previous section. And, in any event, it is uncertain, as an empirical claim, that lack of responsiveness does lead to worse results. As I started to read Gilens (2012), for example, my reaction was, "Yikes! Surely things would be better if policy were more responsive to the preferences of the nonaffluent."[7] But thinking about it more, I was less sure. Granted, Gilens presents evidence that greater Gilens responsiveness to nonaffluent preferences would lead to, say, a higher minimum wage. But he also presents evidence that it would lead to more restrictive abortion policy. (Whether one views these as worse results, of course, will depend on one's point of view.) And was I implicitly thinking that things would be better if policy was more Gilens responsive to the electorate as a whole? Not at all clear. Since the middle of the twentieth century, Gilens responsiveness to the electorate as a whole has been lowest with Lyndon Johnson's domestic policy (due in no small part to opposition to immigration reform) and highest in the first George W. Bush administration (Gilens 2012, chap. 7). In a similar vein, Bartels (2016, chap. 6) notes that unresponsive political elites long held the line against majority preferences for estate tax repeal.

Is, then, lack of responsiveness a problem in itself because people have in an interest in the satisfaction of policy preferences as such? We already considered and rejected this possibility in Section 25.2. Or is responsiveness a conduct condition on certain officials? We considered and rejected this possibility in Section 27.7.

29

The Permissiveness of Formal Equality

This chapter asks what Equal Influence requires of formal procedures. Formal procedures, roughly speaking, govern both the electoral system (the casting and counting of ballots in elections and referenda) and parliamentary procedure (how representatives, if any, reach final decisions). Formal procedures abstract from informal access to information and ability to persuade others. The key conclusion of this chapter is that Equal Influence, in many cases, requires very little of formal procedures. When it comes to formal procedures, Equal Influence constrains less than one might have thought.

29.1 A Priori Equality

Equal Influence requires equal opportunity for informed, autonomous influence. But how exactly is the relevant influence to be understood? I suggest that influence is best interpreted as what I earlier called "contributory" influence. This is the sort of influence one can have even if one is not decisive: the sort of influence illustrated by applying tension to the rope in a game of tug-of-war or adding weight to one side of scales.

How should contributory influence be measured? Bloodless though it sounds, I suggest that by *X*-ing, I exercise equal contributory influence over a decision just when my *X*-ing has "equal a priori chances of being decisive over the decision": that is, has equal chances of being decisive on the assumption that no pattern of *X*-ing by others is more likely than any other pattern. If, as it were, the weights are equally heavy, then everyone should have the same chance of tipping the scales, assuming that no placement of other weights is more likely than any other placement. One's "a priori chances" are one's chances assuming that every pattern of other votes is just as likely as any other pattern. Thus, on this measure, I and you have equal influence over an outcome just when my vote and your vote would have equal chances of being decisive over the outcome, assuming that no pattern of other votes is more or less likely than any other pattern. An equivalent measure would be a priori chances of success conditional on voting. One enjoys "success" when one's choice enjoys both influence and correspondence: that is, when one voted for an outcome and it obtained. Let us call these equivalent measures "a priori equality."[1] As anemic as a priori equality may seem, it would explain at least two of the ills listed in Section 28.1. Voter suppression and formally disproportionate representation violate a priori equality.

What I am suggesting, to be clear, is that formal procedures should realize equal a priori chances of decisiveness as the natural measure of equal contributory influence. I am not suggesting that voting rules should realize a priori chances of decisiveness because what most fundamentally matters to each individual is equal actual decisiveness. That suggestion would invite the reply: "If what matters is equal decisiveness, then why should anyone care about equal chances of decisiveness under the utterly artificial and unrealistic assumption that no pattern of votes is more likely than any other? What we should seek to realize is equal actual decisiveness: that, given how everyone actually votes, either everyone is decisive or no one is."

Of course, one might argue on independent grounds that equal actual decisiveness is what we should seek to realize: that it represents a better interpretation of equal influence than equal contributory influence. It might seem to be somehow more realistic, more attentive to the facts on the ground. In one way, however, this alternative interpretation makes no difference. As things are, electoral systems that realize equal a priori chances also realize equal actual decisiveness because they almost never leave anyone decisive. Lee (2001, 128) expresses a common but mistaken view in writing: "Under 'one person, one vote,' individuals who are constantly in the voting minority do indeed have an equality of potential influence, in the sense that, independent of knowledge of the constellation of interests among voters, they would be seen as just as likely to cast the deciding vote as anyone else. But, given the particular constellation of interests among voters that results in certain individuals being constantly in the voting minority, the actual influence of those individuals is clearly not equal." (See also Beitz 1989, 10–11.) On the contrary, under "one person, one vote," what Lee calls "actual influence"—what I call "actual decisiveness"—is almost always equally zero. One person's vote almost never makes a difference, whether she is in the minority or the majority. It is true that the satisfaction of interests in correspondence, if there are any, will be unequal. Those in the majority will have those interests satisfied, while those in the minority will not. And it is likely that the satisfaction of substantive interests will also be unequal. But those are different questions.

In another way, however, the interpretation makes a difference, for the worse. Many systems that realize equal actual decisiveness do not realize equal a priori chances. With selective disenfranchisement—or with plural voting, in which some have additional votes—no one is almost ever decisive either. For example, even if the schooled were to have two votes each to the unschooled's one, it would still almost always be the case that no one, schooled or unschooled, was ever decisive, since it is almost as rare for vote tallies to differ by one or two votes as it is for them to differ by only one. So, according to the actual decisiveness interpretation, equal opportunity for influence would still be realized, counterintuitively, in these cases. This is one reason for favoring the a priori interpretation.

There is another reason why equal actual decisiveness seems untenable as an interpretation of equal opportunity for influence exercised by voting. It violates the following:

> "Compossibility Principle": Equal opportunity for *X*-ing should not be understood in such a way that whether equal opportunity for *X*-ing obtains among individuals depends on how any of those individuals exercises the opportunity to *X*.

The basic thought is that what we have reason to provide equally is opportunity for influence, not what actually results from the exercise of that opportunity, given how others exercise their like opportunities. For instance, it shouldn't be a violation of your equal opportunity for a job that, if I exercise my like opportunity and apply for it, I decrease your chances for it. It should not be a reason for or against applying that I would thereby deprive you of equal opportunity.

Similarly, there seems no reason to equalize, for each of us, something, such as decisiveness, that depends on how the rest of us actually vote.

Suppose that the yeas are two and the nays are one, abstracting from my vote. If I vote yea or nay, then decisiveness will be equal, since no one or everyone will be decisive. But if I abstain, then decisiveness will be unequal. The yeas, but not the nays, would have been decisive. It seems implausible that this is a reason for me to vote yea or nay: that whether or not people enjoy political equality in this scenario turns on how I cast my vote.

Finally, one might suggest that the measure of equal influence should reflect not what actually happens but instead what is likely to happen. What should be equalized is not actual decisiveness but instead "ex ante decisiveness": the epistemic probability of being decisive, given what the relevant evidence suggests about how others will vote. Setting aside the new difficulty of saying whose evidence (Nate Cohn's? Karl Rove's?) when (a week before the election? the eve of the election?) determines whether you have equal influence, it's not clear how the shift to the ex ante perspective helps. So long as the epistemic probability converges to the long-run frequency, precisely the same institutions satisfy the imperatives "Equalize ex ante decisiveness!" and "Equalize actual decisiveness over time!"

As an alternative measure of equal influence, one might propose equal actual success, where one is successful when one enjoys both influence and correspondence. And, indeed, people generally care more about being successful than they care about being decisive: about whether what they voted for prevailed than about whether it prevailed by a single vote. However, it remains odd to suggest, and a violation of the Compossibility Principle, that all of us have reason to equalize for each of us something, like success, that depends on how the rest of us actually vote. And even if success does matter, it would add little to our discussion. For so long as I exercise opportunity for influence, I succeed just when my preferences are satisfied.[2] Given that, the imperative "Equalize success!" recommends much the same as the imperative "Equalize preference satisfaction!" which we already considered in Section 25.2.[3]

29.2 Majority Rule

A priori equality—each person being decisive in the same number of possible "profiles" of votes—does not imply "neutrality" among decisions: that, for any two decisions, each is produced by the same number of profiles of votes (May 1952). So, it does not rule out supermajority requirements, against the common view that political equality somehow demands majority rule. Supermajority requirements give everyone equal a priori chances at decisiveness. But supermajority requirements are not neutral. Fewer profiles produce a change than reproduce the status quo.

However, it is often said that such rules are incompatible with political equality. Thus, Jones (1983, 160) writes: "To allow the will of the minority to prevail would be to give greater weight to the vote of each member of the minority than to the vote of each member of the majority, thus violating political equality." But why should this be? Doesn't everybody's vote have equal weight under a supermajority rule? Even with supermajority requirements, for any given decision, every person has the same opportunity to influence the adoption of that decision as has any other person—even if the (equally enjoyed) opportunity to influence the adoption of that decision is greater or less than the (equally enjoyed) opportunity to influence the adoption of some other decision. Such a rule gives people equal opportunity to influence decisions even though it is not neutral among decisions. Presumably, what matters for relations of equality among people is that people have equal opportunity to influence decisions, not that decisions have equal opportunity of being made.

Jones's thought must be: "Such a rule does not give people equal opportunity for influence. For, holding fixed the decisions people favor, the rule gives some people greater opportunity to influence the adoption of the decision they favor than it will give others to influence the adoption of the decision they favor."

There are, however, two reasons to resist this reply. First, where an interest in a choice-dependent activity, in the sense introduced in Section 1.5, is at stake, there are at least the makings of a complaint that it is harder for A to satisfy that interest given A's actual attitudes than it is for B to satisfy that interest given B's actual attitudes (Patten 2014). After all, one engages in a choice-dependent activity only insofar as one's actual attitudes guide one. (For example, with respect to freedom of movement, Wander may have less opportunity to exercise it guided by his desire to go greater distances than Homebody has to exercise it guided by his desire to go shorter distances. In such a case, Wander might protest that Wander's interest in the liberty is not as well satisfied as Homebody's interest in the liberty.) Where relations of equality are concerned, by contrast, what ultimately matters is not some choice-dependent activity that one pursues by exercising an opportunity but instead a relation that one stands in to others by having an (equal) opportunity. Recall that it would be satisfied equally well by one's having no opportunity for exercise at all—so long as no one else had any influence either. So, there aren't even the makings of such a complaint.

Second, when we consider, for the purposes of a broadly liberal political morality, how to meet people's equal claims, it seems appropriate to view them as free: as not bound by or identified with any particular choice, judgment, or outlook. So conceived, there are no grounds for saying that the rule treats them differently. Recall the debate between Nagel and Rawls discussed in Section 20.2. Nagel (1973) observed that a well-ordered society, as described by Rawls (1975), was not neutral among conceptions of the good, since it might be a society in which some conceptions flourished and others did not. Rawls replied that while the theory was not neutral among conceptions, it was nonetheless fair to persons, viewed as free. For any given conception, it ensured that no person had (unfairly) greater opportunity to pursue successfully that conception than any other person—even if it did not ensure that each person would have the same opportunity to pursue successfully some conceptions as that person would have to pursue another conception. As we saw, Rawls's response might seem to permit banning everyone's practice of, say, one religion but not other religions. After all, while not neutral among faiths, the ban might seem fair to persons viewed as free from the faith they actually have. But, as we also saw, there are other objections to such a ban. It may limit everyone's opportunity (whether or not they are drawn to it) to no good effect. And insofar as people (even the unobservant) are socially identified by religion, banning a faith, even if it did not limit opportunities in an objectionable way, would tend to stigmatize those identified with it as an underclass, as we saw in Section 20.1.

Neither objection, however, applies, in general, to supermajority requirements. First, such requirements may be to some good effect. Second, while people may be socially identified to some extent as conservatives and progressives, they are not, I take it, socially identified as supporters of keeping whatever the (possibly highly progressive) present policy happens to be and supporters of (possibly extremely reactionary) changes to the present policy.

Thus, in principle, even unanimity requirements to depart from the status quo decision are compatible with Equal Influence. The choice among such systems will rest on other, principally substantive, considerations. Presumably, the concern for substantive reliability will sometimes favor and sometimes oppose neutrality, depending on the kinds of decisions being made. For certain questions of policy, interests in stability and resistance to passing temptations may argue for supermajorities (as with, say, constitutional amendments), or special conditions may make consociational structures particularly desirable. On other questions of policy, simple majorities may tend to produce better results by making representatives more responsive and accountable. So, in response to blanket objections to status quo bias, we have to say, somewhat deflatingly, that it all depends.

29.3 Equal Populations

In most respects, as we have seen, a priori equality may seem too permissive. In one respect, however, a priori equality may seem too restrictive. Under a district system, a priori equality requires that a district's representation be proportional to its population. However, the US Senate apportions two senators to each state, regardless of population. This violates Equal Influence. It might also be expected to lead to a violation of Equal Consideration, with, for example, greater federal funding per capita going to residents of less populous states. For either reason or both reasons, this in turn violates Equal Citizenship. So far, this seems reasonable enough. After all, many do see the Senate as being at odds with what political equality, given a clean constitutional slate, would recommend. What may seem a little much, however, is the suggestion that underlying the objections that residents of California have to this structure of representation is a concern that they are somehow thereby subordinated to residents of Wyoming.

There are a number of confounding factors, however. First, people are free to change their state of residence, and they do with considerable frequency. Second, there is the fact that with respect to other indices, such as income and cultural influence, Californians are relatively advantaged. Finally, when two unequally populated groups reach joint decisions, giving equal influence to each group threatens relations of inferiority (of any given member of the more populous group to any given member of the less populous group) less to the extent that the groups approximate independent, sovereign states (as opposed to groups within a single, sovereign state).

One explanation for this may simply be that there is not the same density of relations across members of different sovereign states. Another explanation may be the countervailing force of the vicarious concern, discussed in Chapter 10, about the subordination of one's group to other relevant groups. Intuitively, although again I do not propose a theory of this here, a sovereign state has some claim to equality with other sovereign states, regardless of population. And sovereign states do seem like relevant groups: that is, natural foci of this vicarious concern. There is palpable tension in the apology "Yes, of course, I view your state, Mexico, as subordinate to mine, the United States, but take no offense! I otherwise don't view you as subordinate to me."

Whatever explains it, this confounding factor means that the more closely the relevant districts approximate independent, sovereign states, the less it will threaten relations of inferiority to accord those districts equal influence over joint decisions. Thus, the one-nation, one-vote structure of the UN General Assembly seems less inappropriate than, say, malapportioned congressional districts in Alabama or Tennessee before the judicial reapportionment revolution of the 1960s, districts that had no history as independent, sovereign states. And the latter, in turn, seem less inappropriate than a system that explicitly gave a nonterritorial professional bloc and (a vastly more numerous) nonprofessional bloc equal representation.

The US Senate, then, is apt to seem an intermediate case, largely because it was established at a time when the former colonies were, more or less, independent, sovereign polities. This history is responsible for the vexed, federal character of the US Constitution: a compromise, contested at times by war, between a union of sovereign states and a union of citizens under a national government. To the extent that the federal model correctly applies to the United States—to the extent that it is closer to the General Assembly than to Alabama congressional districts in the 1950s—some form of equal representation of states would be natural. To be sure, I do not mean to defend federalism. On the contrary, it seems to me an irredeemably anachronistic doctrine that enjoys only selective and opportunistic advocacy. The point is simply that, in light of the influence that federalism still exercises over Americans' political self-conception, we should not expect to find in the US Senate particularly clear or telling counterexamples. The same, I suspect, goes for similar federal structures in other national legislatures.

29.4 Proportional Representation

Does Equal Influence require proportional representation, at least where seats in a legislative assembly are at issue? "Proportional representation" can mean quite different things. "Multiparty proportionality" requires that a party's representation in an assembly be proportional to preferences for that party's representatives. This conception is perhaps best realized by party list systems. In such systems, roughly, parties draw up lists of candidates, and the number of candidates from each party's list elected to the assembly is proportional to the number of votes cast for that party. "Nonpartisan proportionality" requires that each representative be associated with a distinct, equinumerous set of constituents who preferred that candidate to some alternative. This conception is perhaps best achieved by single transferrable vote. In such systems, voters rank the various candidates. If a candidate is top ranked by a certain quota of voters, that candidate is elected. Any surplus votes for that candidate are then distributed to the not-yet-elected candidate ranked next highest on those ballots. Alternatively, or in addition, the candidate who is ranked highest on the fewest number of ballots is eliminated, with those votes being distributed to the candidate ranked next highest on those ballots. The process continues until all the seats are filled. "Two-party proportionality" is more closely approximated as the division of seats in the assembly between the two major parties more closely approximates the division of support for those two major parties in the electorate. "Majority proportionality" requires that a party have a majority in the assembly when a majority of the votes cast were for its representatives.

In a district system, each district controls a certain number of seats, voters within the district vote for a particular candidate to occupy a particular seat, and the candidate with a majority or plurality of votes for that seat is elected. In district systems, there is a natural tendency for every seat to be held by a member of one or the other of two major parties. This tendency thwarts multiparty or nonpartisan proportionality. Preferences for candidates who do not belong to either of the two major parties will enjoy no representation in the assembly. So, in practice, district systems can at best realize two-party or majority proportionality. It is sometimes suggested, as a kind of reductio, that if representation by party must be proportional, as multiparty, two-party, and majority proportionality require, then, absurdly, representation by every affiliation must also be proportional. However, it doesn't seem arbitrary to single out party affiliations as special, since parties are expressly organized to advance a policy platform by electing representatives.

In any event, a priori equality does not require proportionality on any of these interpretations. To be sure, there are arguments that political equality is incompatible with district systems. Political equality, it might be said, requires "anonymity": that two profiles of votes should deliver the same outcome if we swap the party support of any two voters. Anonymity rules out district systems. For example, if we swap the opposing votes of a voter, Ty, in a tied district and a voter, Lopside, in a far-from-tied district, then we change the outcome (Christiano 1996, 234; Still 1981, 382; Bartholdi et al., 2020). However, it's unclear what Lopside's objection to this could be if not unequal decisiveness. And we already rejected equal decisiveness as a measure of political equality in Section 29.1. And even if anonymity did rule out multidistrict systems, it still would not require multiparty, nonpartisan, or two-party proportionality. Anonymity is compatible with a winner-take-all system, in which, for each seat in the assembly, all voters vote for a particular candidate for that seat. That might be expected to result in the party with majority support controlling every seat in the assembly.

Are there other reasons, besides Equal Influence, to care about proportionality, on any of these interpretations? It might be said that proportionality leads to more responsive policy. Setting aside doubts that we should care about responsive policy, these interpretations of proportionality bear an uncertain relationship to responsiveness. For example, two-party proportional representation need not lead to more responsive policy. First, so long as majority proportionality is already satisfied, more two-party proportional representation has no effect on party control. Second, so long as representatives for a given party hold similar views, it will have no effect on the range of views advanced in the assembly. It might be said that individuals have an interest that their preferred party enjoys greater representation in the assembly for its own sake. But an interest in greater representation in itself seems fetishistic. Moreover, as we saw in Section 25.2, if a fair distribution of the satisfaction of such preferences is maximizing minimum satisfaction, then it would argue not for multiparty, two-party, or majority proportionality but instead for an even division among all the parties that enjoy any support whatsoever. If, for example, there were only two parties (each enjoying support by at least one individual), then there should be a fifty-fifty split between the two parties in the assembly, no matter what the division of support was. That is what would maximize the minimum satisfaction of any individual. Alternatively, one might argue that proportional representation is important in itself. It is important, it might be said, that an assembly should reflect the electorate in miniature. But it is unclear why that should be important in itself.

Of course, there may be substantive reasons to favor systems that allow for multiparty or nonpartisan proportionality over district systems. Perhaps these systems give greater voice to the interests of dispersed minorities that would otherwise be submerged or make the assembly an image in miniature of the electorate as a whole, leading to substantively better decisions. On the other hand, there may be substantive reasons to favor district systems. Perhaps they give greater voice to distinctive regional interests that would otherwise be submerged, leading to substantively better decisions. Perhaps district systems, by making representatives more closely bound to specific, geographical constituencies, facilitate communication between constituents and representatives, leading to substantively better decisions. Or perhaps district systems lead to more stable governments, leading to substantively better decisions. The argument for stability might be that since district systems tend toward only two major parties, they compel the formation of coalitions before, rather than after, elections, which makes control over the assembly after elections smoother.

29.5 Persistent Minorities

One might object that the permissiveness of a priori equality is unacceptably complacent about "persistent minorities": more or less stable groups whose members are consistently outvoted. This is to assume that persistent minorities are cause for concern. But why should they be?

One concern is obvious and, in the real world, of the utmost seriousness. The existence of persistent minorities can be expected to lead to outcomes that are substantively bad—and bad, in particular, because they disadvantage members of those minorities. When it is said that under polarization, minority group interests are not represented, the root concern is often just that outcomes will tend to treat members of those groups—the people with those interests—badly in substantive terms (Beitz 1989, chap. 7).

However, suppose—departing, in a diagnostic spirit, from the real world—that the outcomes are substantively correct. Members of the minority are, in fact, treated fairly, at least with respect to their substantive interests. Is there still some objection? It may be objected that members of the minority do not enjoy correspondence or preference satisfaction. But we have already considered this. It may also be objected that members of persistent minorities do not enjoy equal influence (Still 1981, 379–380; Beitz 1989, 14; Buchanan 2004, 361). But insofar as they have equal a priori chances, they have equal contributory influence. And, as we saw, they will almost always have equal actual decisiveness because almost no one, including any member of the majority, is ever decisive. It is common to dramatize the special complaint of members of persistent minorities by saying that their vote made no difference: that the outcome would have been the same no matter what they had done. But members of persistent majorities can almost always make the same complaint as members of persistent minorities: that the outcome would have been the same no matter what they had done.

Some further grounds for special complaint may remain, however. First, it remains the case that the majority as a group enjoys decisiveness—indeed, insofar as the polarization persists, control—whereas the minority as a group does not. And, in fairness, this is often how the point is put. So perhaps there is an objection about vicarious, collective subordination, of the sort discussed in Chapter 10. The members of the persistent minority might have reason to object that their group is subordinated to the majority, in virtue of the majority's control over political decisions. Next, the fact that voters are sorted by their membership in some historically subordinated group, whether or not this makes them persistent minorities, may also, depending on the context and when the sorting is not remedial, contribute to a disparity of regard. The objection to it is like other objections to discrimination. The other possible complaint is not against the presence of a persistent minority as such. It is instead against the manipulation of formal procedures that often attends a persistent minority: where voting rules are changed or districts are gerrymandered to favor a specific person, group, or party. Take Guinier's (1994, 75) example in which a board responded to the election of a member from an ethnic minority by replacing a requirement for certain motions from a single member's say to two members' say, effectively depriving the new board member of the power to make such motions. Indeed, much of Guinier's concern about persistent minorities seems to be with "switching" (7) or "rigging" (8) the process to favor a particular group. We return to this possibility in Section 30.8.

30

Gerrymandering

A Case Study of Permissiveness

In the last chapter, we saw that Equal Influence can be deflatingly permissive about formal procedures. The present chapter illustrates this point, using gerrymandering as a case study. Although, in the end, we do identify some objections to gerrymandering, the search is more involved than one might have expected because of the permissiveness of Equal Influence with regard to formal procedures.

30.1 Defining "Gerrymandering"

In contrast to other pathologies of American democracy, gerrymandering has few public advocates. Few openly contend that it is good thing or even that measures to curb it would be bad. By contrast, many contend that unfettered, private spending on campaigns is a good thing. It informs voters, and measures to curb it would violate freedom of political speech. And many contend, even if disingenuously, that voter ID requirements are a good thing. They prevent fraud. The closest anyone comes to openly arguing in favor of gerrymandering is that there's no workable legal test of whether districts have been gerrymandered or that gerrymandering does not violate any constitutionally guaranteed right. This defensive posture reflects a "visceral reaction" (Alexander and Prakash 2008) that gerrymandering is objectionable: unfair, undemocratic, or at any rate fishy. But how so?

Let me begin by defining some terms. Gerrymandering is a problem only in "district systems," where, as I call it, a "superdistrict's" voters are sorted into districts. Typically, the districts are associated with territories, with a district's voters being just those who primarily reside in the territory. Each district independently elects by majority (to fix ideas) a "delegation of district representatives" to the "superdistrict assembly." The superdistrict assembly then makes decisions by majority (again to fix ideas) for the superdistrict as a whole. District systems tend to divide representatives between two major parties.

Some district systems do not give each voter equal voting power (more later on how this is to be understood) across the superdistrict, either because some voters have greater voting power within a district or because the share of the voting power of a district's delegation to the assembly is not proportional to the district's share of population in the superdistrict. In the United States, the Senate and, albeit to a lesser degree, the House and the Electoral College give some districts—that is, states—greater voting power. However, since the reapportionment cases of the 1960s, it has been harder to bring this objection against congressional districts within a given state. Those cases found, roughly, a constitutional requirement that states' congressional districts have equal populations, against a background assumption that each congressional representative has the same voting power as any other.

A district system that gives every citizen equal voting power, however, can still suffer from gerrymandering. Let us provisionally define "gerrymandering" as drawing districts with the intent, based on a belief about how people are likely to vote, to bring about certain electoral outcomes. One way to gerrymander is to "pack" the other party's voters in a smaller number of districts, thereby giving one's party smaller, but still reliable, majorities in a greater number of other districts. Another way to gerrymander is to "crack" the other party's voters evenly across all the districts, thereby ensuring that they constitute a majority in none.

This definition of gerrymandering may not cut, as it were, at the moral joints. In particular, intent may not matter morally. Even without any intent to bring about electoral outcomes, compactness and contiguity criteria—along with the fact that Democratic voters are more likely to reside in more densely populated areas, say—may naturally "pack" Democrats into fewer districts with the same result as an intentional gerrymander. Some scholars suggest that such "clustering" or "natural gerrymanders" are no less objectionable (Wang 2016; Beitz 2018).

Gerrymanders can aim for different kinds of "electoral outcomes": (1) "district representation": who represents the district in the assembly; (2) "group representation": how many representatives of a given party or group are in the assembly; (3) "party control": which party controls the assembly; and (4) "policy": what laws, policies, and so forth the assembly enacts.

Gerrymanders come in three main varieties, distinguished in part by the electoral outcomes they seek. (1) "Racial gerrymanders" obstruct outcomes favored by a racial minority. Remedies typically aim to increase group representation by candidates from or favored by the racial minority. (2) "Incumbent-protection gerrymanders" aim for district representation by the incumbent. (3) "Partisan gerrymanders" aim for party control (or at least greater group representation by a particular party) as a means to policy.

30.2 Results

What, then, is wrong with gerrymandering? One answer is that gerrymandering has bad results. To be sure, I think that partisan gerrymandering, in particular, led to worse results for most of the 2010s. But to a great extent, I think this for partisan reasons. It led to Republican control of Congress until 2018. Compounding this, the creation of safe Republican seats led to worse representatives. With safe seats, the only real electoral pressure is the Republican primary, and Republican primary voters support worse policies than Republicans, let alone the electorate, as a whole. If I left it at this, my objection to gerrymandering would be uncomfortably close to the recent defense of gerrymandering by North Carolina representative David Lewis: "I think electing Republicans is better than electing Democrats. So I drew this map to help foster what I think is better for the country."[1] Moreover, in both popular and academic discourse, the objections to gerrymandering tend to be at least superficially nonpartisan.

True, one can take a broader view and argue that gerrymandering leads to systemically worse results that don't depend on the policies of the gerrymandering party. Still, as common as arguments of this kind are—that some putatively undemocratic feature of institutions leads to systemically worse results in the long run—I find them exceedingly hard to evaluate, as I noted in Section 28.2. It's not just that the data are so scanty. It's hard to know how even to frame the hypotheses. How generally is the feature specified? Which alternatives count as relevant? Which other conditions are held fixed? How long is the "long run"?

At any rate, I am going to bracket whether gerrymandering has bad systemic results and then ask whether any further objection to gerrymandering remains. Many people seem to think a further objection does remain. First, when people say why they object to gerrymandering, they often don't say anything about results but instead contend, for instance, that gerrymandering wastes or dilutes votes, which is unfair, or anyway a bad thing, in itself. Second, even when people don't say why they object to gerrymandering, the immediacy, certainty, and heat of their objections suggest that those objections do not rest on evaluation of qualified, empirical predictions about systemic effects. It seems hard to explain the outcry against gerrymandering as simply reflecting a social-scientific hypothesis about what is required for optimal long-term results. Finally, when people object to racial or partisan gerrymandering, their objection often seems to be partial: on behalf of only part of the electorate, such as Black or Democratic voters.[2] But systemic defects don't seem partial in this way. If anyone has an objection to them, everyone does.

30.3 Responsiveness

What, then, is the objection to gerrymandering? Perhaps that it makes policy insufficiently responsive to the superdistrict. Gerrymandering seems most to threaten responsiveness when it violates Majority Proportionality: that is, when a party with a minority of support in the superdistrict nonetheless enjoys party control. This already suggests one limitation of this appeal to responsive policy. While partisan gerrymandering may lead to violations of Majority Proportionality, there is less reason to expect that racial and incumbent gerrymanders do.

At any rate, in Section 25.2 I raised doubts that policy should be responsive. I won't rehearse all the points made there. But recall at least the point that a fair distribution would seem to involve maximizing the satisfaction of the policy preferences of those with the least satisfaction over time. To simplify, suppose one's policy preferences are satisfied to the extent that one's own party, in a two-party district system, holds a greater share of legislative seats. Then, assuming there is at least one voter in each party, a fifty-fifty split in the legislature would maximize minimum preference satisfaction. A shift to fifty-one to forty-nine, by contrast, would reduce the minimum from fifty to forty-nine. Note that this is true even if 99 percent of voters support one party and 1 percent of voters support the other. Rather than indicate some problem with partisan gerrymandering, therefore, the appeal to interests in preference satisfaction seems to argue for continual partisan gerrymandering in favor of the minority party.

A further difficulty arises if we say that not only the satisfaction of preferences for policy but also the satisfaction of preferences for district representation matter. Then Democratic voters "packed" into a district are more likely to see their preference that their district have a Democratic representative satisfied, whereas Democratic voters "cracked" into districts are less likely to see their preference satisfied. It seems odd, however, to think that "packed" voters lack a complaint that "cracked" voters have.

30.4 Equal Influence and A Priori Equality

Setting aside results and preferences, one might argue that gerrymandering distributes influence over political decisions unequally. It violates Equal Influence. When is one's opportunity for influence as a voter, as opposed to an official or persuader of other voters, equal (provided one has equal access to relevant information)? As I argued in Section 29.1, it is when voters enjoy a priori equality, where you and I enjoy a priori equality with respect to an outcome just when my vote and your vote would have equal chances of being decisive over the outcome, assuming that no pattern of other votes is more or less likely than any other pattern. A priori equality is violated by malapportionment, plural voting, and less than universal suffrage. But a priori equality isn't violated by gerrymandering. So if a priori equality is the right measure of equal influence, gerrymandering does not violate Equal Influence.

Why not say instead that the right measure of equal influence requires, instead, equal actual decisiveness? I won't rehearse the arguments against this proposal, arguments given in Section 29.1. But note that it's hard to see how the objection to gerrymandering could be that it distributes actual decisiveness unequally. For actual decisiveness is almost always equal, except in rare cases in which the outcome turns on a single vote. One way to minimize inequalities in actual decisiveness, then, would be to minimize outcomes decided by a single vote. It might be said that this is done by making districts less "competitive": that is, reducing the difference in vote share between winner and second-place finisher. But this is precisely what packing generally does. Indeed, a frequent complaint about gerrymandering is precisely that it makes districts less competitive. I suppose one could say that the objection is only to cracking, which makes districts more competitive.

But again, it seems odd that cracked voters should have an objection that packed voters lack.

Why not say that what should be equalized is not actual decisiveness but instead "ex ante decisiveness," the epistemic probability of being decisive given what the relevant evidence suggests about how others will vote? Again, as noted in section 29.1, so long as the epistemic probability converges to the long-run frequency, precisely the same institutions satisfy the imperatives "Equalize ex ante decisiveness!" and "Equalize actual decisiveness over time!"

Might there be something else, equality of which gerrymandering objectionably disturbs? The "efficiency gap" measure of partisan gerrymandering suggests the answer: the equality of "nonwasted" votes (Stephanopoulos and McGhee 2015). The number of nonwasted votes in a set of elections is the sum of the minimum number of votes, in each election, required to elect the successful candidate. Note, however, that this is not equalization among individuals but instead among parties. Indeed, if my vote is successful but not decisive, then there's no fact of the matter whether it was or was not wasted: whether or not my vote belongs to "the" set of votes that was just enough to elect the candidate. The reason to care about the efficiency gap, if there is one, has to do with neutrality among parties, which we consider in Section 30.6.

30.5 Two-Party Proportionality

Proportional representation is often invoked in defense of gerrymandering, in the following way:

1. Gerrymandering is objectionable only insofar as it departs from proportional representation.
2. So, gerrymandering is objectionable only if proportional representation is required.
3. If a district system is permissible, then proportional representation is not required (since any district system is bound to depart from proportional representation).
4. So, if a district system is permissible, gerrymandering is not objectionable (McGann et al. 2016, 42–43).

However, one might accept (1) but reject (2). One might grant that a nonpartisan-proportional or party-proportional system is not required, since the best district system is no worse than the best nonpartisan-proportional or party-proportional system. Still, one might argue, district systems that are more two-party proportional are better than district systems that are less two-party proportional. The objection to gerrymandering is precisely that it makes district systems less two-party proportional than necessary to achieve the benefits of a district system. As Beitz (2018) argues, "The effect of partisan gerrymandering is to impose an unjustifiably large share of the costs of [a district system] on those whom it disadvantages."

The question, then, is what is good about two-party-proportional representation, apart from better results or responsiveness. What are the "costs" to which Beitz refers? He suggests that "voters are less likely . . . to have a representative in the legislature whose political commitments track their own reasonably closely" (344). This brings us back to the topic of preferences. Now, however, what matters is not the satisfaction of one's preferences for policy but instead minimizing the "distance" between one's policy preferences and the policy preferences of the closest representative in the legislature. Suppose the *A* party, with 51 percent of the vote, controls sixty seats, whereas the *B* party, with 49 percent of the vote, controls forty seats. Beitz's suggestion seems to be that if instead the split was more two-party proportional, say fifty-one seats to forty-nine, the maximal distance any voter must suffer would be reduced.

Setting aside why minimizing the maximum distance should matter, why think that making the split more two-party proportional would minimize the maximum distance? Perhaps we are to suppose that (i) no *A* representative is closer to any *B* voter than some *B* representative (and vice versa), (ii) the greater the number of *B* representatives, the greater the range of *B*-voter preferences represented by someone in the legislature (and vice versa), and (iii) the spread of *B*-voter preferences is just as wide as the spread of *A*-voter preferences. For example, there might be 200 evenly spaced points in *A*-voter space each occupied by the same number of *A* voters (and vice versa). Each successive *A* representative elected to the legislature then occupies the midpoint of the widest gap between any two adjacent *A* voters. Thus, the first *A* representative is at point 100, the second at 50, the third at 150, the fourth at 25, and so on. Assuming all this, it is then true that moving from a sixty-to-forty to a fifty-one-to-forty-nine split would reduce the maximum distance between any voter and the closest representative. But this has nothing to do with two-party proportionality. It simply reflects the fact that, under the assumptions, whatever the distribution of the votes, the maximum distance is minimized by approaching a fifty-fifty split. If the *A* party had 60 percent of the vote, moving from a sixty-to-forty split to a far less two-party-proportional fifty-one-to-forty-nine split would still reduce the maximum distance.

Perhaps, then, the idea is that even if the spread of possible *B*-voter preferences is as wide as the spread of possible *A*-voter preferences, the ratio of the spread of actual *A*-party preferences held by some voter to the spread of actual *B*-party preferences is proportional to the ratio of votes for the *A* party to votes for the *B* party. But why think that this is generally true? Suppose there are 10,000 distinct points in *B*-voter space. One might expect that with, say, 40,000 *B* voters, at least one voter actually holds each possible *B*-voter preference. That's enough to argue for a fifty-fifty split, even if there are 60,000 *A* voters.

30.6 Majority Proportionality

I noted earlier that partisan gerrymandering, if not racial or incumbent gerrymandering, threatens majority proportionality. Granted, district systems cannot guarantee majority proportionality. But given a district system, one might complain that gerrymandering makes majority proportionality less likely than necessary.

But why accept majority proportionality? One argument is just by analogy.

1. Members of the majority have an objection about departures from majority rule by district voters over district representation.
2. Members of the majority have an objection about departures from majority rule by representatives over policy.
3. Departures from majority rule by superdistrict voters over party control are sufficiently like either of these other departures.
4. Therefore, members of the majority have an objection about departures from majority rule by superdistrict voters over party control.

As a psychological explanation of why many protest partisan gerrymandering, this has a certain verisimilitude. People find it objectionable just because it's similar to violations of majority rule that people find objectionable.

But how does it fare as a normative explanation of why, if at all, partisan gerrymandering is, on reflection, objectionable? Is there a more principled case for majority rule? Some might argue for majority rule on the grounds that it leads to better results or the satisfaction of preferences. But we have already considered those possibilities. Is there some more intrinsic democratic reason in favor of majority rule? The standard answer is that majority rule is entailed by neutrality between outcomes. Indeed, the nub of complaints about "partisan asymmetry," the "efficiency gap," and "mean-median difference" (Wang 2016) seems to be neutrality between parties, which seems a special case of neutrality between outcomes where the outcomes are party representation.

But why accept neutrality between outcomes? Again, there may be a case to be made for equal influence among people. But that doesn't require neutrality between outcomes, as I argued in Section 29.2. "However," one might protest, "partisan gerrymandering that violates majority proportionality does treat people unequally; it favors (say) Republicans over Democrats. For example, Democrats may need 60 percent of the vote to gain control over the assembly, whereas Republicans need only 40 percent." But this isn't so. Partisan gerrymandering doesn't exploit any rule that says that Democrats need 60 percent of the vote to gain partisan control over the assembly whereas Republicans need only 40 percent. Instead, it exploits control over the districting process gained by winning earlier elections. Had Democrats won those earlier elections, they would now need only 40 percent of the vote. The bias is a kind of lagged advantage to the winners of earlier elections. And that just looks like favoring the status quo.

30.7 Racial Gerrymandering and Discrimination

The objection to racial gerrymanders might seem obvious; they are wrongful discrimination. But, on closer inspection, two challenges come into focus. First, we need a conception of wrongfully discriminating against a group that does not require giving members of that group less of some good than members of another group. For we have yet to identify a good that gerrymandering gives people less of: an "impact," as it were, that might be "disparate." As we have seen, merely being assigned to one district rather than another does not unfairly deprive you of a valuable opportunity.

As I argued in Chapter 13, however, discrimination consists in disparities of regard, which need not involve the lesser provision of some good. Perhaps a disparity in regard might take the form of an effort to thwart electoral preferences. Perhaps that is, in itself, hostile or adversarial treatment. This objection to racial gerrymandering would then depend on intention to whatever extent that disparities of regard depend on intention. Natural racial gerrymanders, at least if they were understood to be natural, might not be objectionable in the same way.[3]

The second challenge is to identify which groups, when treated in those ways, are wrongfully discriminated against. If there are any such groups, presumably racial groups are among them. Racial groups are more or less defined by a history of group subordination, of a kind that involved far more than simply thwarting electoral preferences by gerrymandering schemes. But if we grant this, why not also say that partisan gerrymandering is wrongful discrimination against political party, just as racial gerrymandering is wrongful discrimination against race? To be sure, it might be wrong, say, to refuse to hire someone because of their party ID. But, first, it's not clear whether what makes this wrong, when it is wrong, is simply refusing to hire someone for an improper reason (which would violate the Duty to Exclude) or whether refusing to hire someone because of their party ID, like refusing to hire someone because of their race, is wrong in a distinctive, further way. And, second, one doubts that it can be wrongful discrimination, in general, to try to thwart the electoral preferences of members of the opposing political party—let alone simply to try to improve the electoral fortunes of one's own political party.

To be sure, racial gerrymanders might also be objectionable because they have independently objectionable effects. The effect might be that policy unfairly disserves the substantive interests of minorities. Or it might be that there are no, or disproportionately few, representatives from a racial group. Or it might be that a racial group is consistently outvoted, that it is a persistent minority in the sense discussed in Section 29.5. Note that even if the racial group has representatives, it might still be outvoted on questions of policy in the assembly.[4] Offhand, there seems no more reason to expect these effects from intentional than from natural gerrymanders.

If we have identified an objection to racial gerrymandering, we still have not identified an objection to incumbent-protection or partisan gerrymandering. We turn now to three such objections. First, such forms of gerrymandering may exploit asymmetric influence and so deprive some of equal informed influence. Second, such forms of gerrymandering may involve official corruption: a violation of the Duty to Exclude. And finally, such forms of gerrymandering may space elections too far apart, weakening the People's control of officials.

30.8 Equal Influence and Asymmetric Information

Consider an example meant to be illustrative of a certain kind of partisan gerrymandering. The letter of the law says that an election can be held on the first or second day of the month, at the discretion of the election commissioner. However, elections have always been held on the second, and few even realize that the first is a legal possibility. The election commissioner, a partisan of the Fête Party, holds the election on the first, informing only members of his own party. When the members of the opposing Fiesta Party are confronted on the second with the fait accompli, they would seem to have a complaint. Their complaint isn't that elections on the second somehow have better long-term results or are intrinsically more democratic than elections on the first. The complaint is that they, the members of the Fiesta Party, weren't informed, whereas members of the Fête Party were informed, about when the election would be.

But why is that grounds for complaint? An answer lies in Equal Influence: that citizens have a complaint about being deprived of equal opportunity for informed, autonomous influence over political decisions. The adjective "informed" is key. Citizens must have equal opportunity to know what the decision-making procedure is. This is not to say that you were deprived of equal opportunity simply because you do not in fact know what the procedure is. For others may have led you to water and done all that could be expected of them to put you in a position to know. But if you form reasonable but false expectations about what the procedure is—or even if you formed false and unreasonable expectations but it would have been cheap and easy for others to correct the mistake—then you may well have been deprived of equal influence.

On an admittedly extremely stylized depiction, Republican gerrymandering around 2010 redistricting bears some comparison to machinations of the Fête commissioner. Democrats assumed that everyone was complying with the rules of the more restrained "Traditional Contest," according to which the partisan makeup of Congress is largely determined by elections of representatives every two years. They understood that control of state governments might result in some gerrymanders but that these would be kept within traditional bounds. Republicans, by contrast, had no plan to comply with the rules of the Traditional Contest. Instead, they were complying with the rules of a fewer-holds-barred "Lagged Contest," where the partisan makeup of Congress is determined mainly by elections of state governments every decade. That is, the Republican REDMAP project systematically targeted elections of state governments in 2010 in order to gerrymander to an unprecedented extent. Democrats falsely believed that both sides were competing in the Traditional Contest, and this was a reasonable belief—or, at any rate, cheap and easy for Republicans to correct. Democrats might complain that they were deprived of equal opportunity for influence. It was as though Republicans knew, but withheld from Democrats, when the "real" election—that is, the one that would determine the partisan composition of states' congressional delegations—would take place.

Of course, it's a further question what relation this stylized depiction bears to the reality. A REDMAP-er might well reply: "Don't blame us! You should have known better!" As the architect of REDMAP, Chris Jankowski, puts it: "There's people who play on the other team who should do their job" (Daley 2016, 75). He has a point. Karl Rove, for instance, made no secret of what was afoot (xvii). On the other hand, students in high school civics courses and applicants for citizenship are certainly encouraged in the impression that everyone plays the Traditional Contest: that members of Congress are elected directly every two years, not that the party composition of the state's congressional delegation is determined by whatever state government happens to be in power at the time of redistricting. And even politically savvy actors, while aware that full-tilt gerrymandering was legally possible, seem to have assumed that the other side would not push things to the edge of legal possibility. Daley (2016) describes REDMAP as a "secret plan" and a "surprise" and reports shock from old hands, such as North Carolina congressman David Price: "This is not same-old, same-old. This has been taken to an extreme" (41). McGann et al. (2016, 14) describe *Vieth v. Jubelirer,* 541 US 267 (2004) as an "unnoticed revolution" in partisan gerrymandering, explaining in some detail why it went "unnoticed" even by otherwise well-informed observers.[5]

This objection to partisan gerrymandering, I am suggesting, might be an objection to depriving some of equal opportunity for informed, autonomous influence over decisions by depriving them of opportunity to be informed about the decision-making procedure that others in the system will follow. It's hard to see how natural gerrymanders—pure demographic shifts against randomly drawn maps meeting contiguity and compactness constraints—would give rise to such an objection because it is hard to see how this would involve anyone's exploiting asymmetric information.

This objection to partisan gerrymandering depends, as we have seen, on which decision-making procedures it is reasonable for participants to expect other participants to follow. And what is reasonable to expect depends on contingencies of history and context. If it was common knowledge that everyone played the Lagged Contest, this objection simply would not apply. If we all get used to gerrymandering, in other words, it will cease to be objectionable, at least on these grounds.

If this seems counterintuitive, notice that gerrymandering is a special case of a more general category: selecting a particular a priori equal procedure from among other a priori equal procedures that, given the predicted distribution of electoral sentiment, will favor a particular outcome. Such selection needn't involve drawing districts. For example, an incumbent might replace majority rule with plurality rule for fear that the presently divided opposition would otherwise unite in a runoff. Or a party may call for elections now in the summer, when their poll numbers are soaring, rather than later in the winter, when they may have regressed. We might call this "temporal gerrymandering." If this is objectionable, surely it isn't because some deep principle of democracy, independent of some complicated, empirical argument about long-run systemic effects, favors majority rule with runoff over plurality rule—much less summer elections over winter elections. It seems more plausible that the objection has to do with deviating from the established or accepted a priori equal procedure: the procedure that it was reasonable to expect others to follow. By contrast, when it is established or accepted that parties will select among a priori equal procedures to favor themselves, no one seems to call foul. Temporal gerrymandering in some parliamentary systems (such as the UK prior to the Fixed-Term Parliaments Act of 2011), for example, is a matter of course. Everyone knows that everyone else is playing a lagged game, in which the governing party has an advantage in when it calls elections.

30.9 Corruption

I have asked, so far, whether the objection to gerrymandering is to how it distributes influence among voters. Might the objection be instead to how it distributes influence between the official in charge of districting, Gerry, and ordinary citizens? This would resonate with the complaint that "voters should choose their representatives, not the other way around" (Berman 2005). But two doubts arise straightaway. First, there would presumably be no objection to Gerry's greater influence if he had used it to district without gerrymandering. Second, I suspect that many gerrymanders that seem objectionable when performed by officials would still seem objectionable if (cutting out the middleman) they were effected by direct plebiscite.

Perhaps there might be an objection if Gerry uses his greater influence corruptly, in a way that violates the Duty to Exclude. Whether Gerry's gerrymandering violates the Duty to Exclude depends on whether the reasons for which Gerry gerrymandered serve the impersonal reasons that justify Gerry's office. If Gerry is a legislator, then offhand one might expect that reasons of policy do serve the values that justify his office. If legislatures serve any impersonal reasons, they presumably serve them by legislators being sensitive to reasons of policy. This makes it harder to pin the charge of corruption on partisan gerrymanders, which may well be made for reasons of policy. The North Carolina state representative quoted earlier has a point.

It is harder, but not necessarily impossible. One might distinguish between two offices that Gerry holds: legislator-on-matters-of-districting and legislator-on-other-matters. And one might argue that even if the office of legislator-on-other-matters serves impersonal reasons when the legislator acts for reasons of policy, the office of legislator-on-matters-of-districting does not. So, partisan gerrymandering, even when influenced by policy, can violate the Duty to Exclude. Now, assuming that "serving impersonal reasons" here means "having good results," the argument that partisan gerrymandering is corrupt would have to presuppose a prior argument that partisan gerrymandering leads to bad results. However, the complaint at issue would not be about the bad results themselves but instead about Gerry's specific violation of the Duty to Exclude. This violation would wrong all those who are subject to the gerrymander, even Gerry's copartisans. But perhaps we can explain the appearance that his copartisans are not wronged by appeal to the fact that they will see themselves to have been benefitted or at least see their preferences to have been satisfied.

In any event, when incumbent Gerry indulges in an incumbent-protection gerrymander, as opposed to a partisan gerrymander, then his reason may well be to get reelected even at the expense of policy. To protect their seats, incumbents often strike deals with incumbents of the other party, which opposes their policies. Drawing the maps merely to get oneself reelected, damn the policy consequences, seems far less likely to serve the values that justify the office of legislator. It seems more like feathering one's nest.

Insofar as the objection to gerrymandering is an objection to a violation of the Duty to Exclude, it depends on intent. Suppose that Gerry in fact gerrymandered a district map in a way that violated the Duty to Exclude. If Gerry had drawn the same map, but not for reasons that do not serve impersonal values—if Gerry had simply applied some randomizing procedure—then it would not have violated the Duty to Exclude.

30.10 Frequency of Elections

One final objection to gerrymandering, which is perhaps the most serious, is that it simply makes elections too infrequent. True, it's not clear that partisan gerrymandering makes districts' elections of their representatives less frequent. Some claim that partisan gerrymandering of congressional districts replaces the direct election of representatives every two years with an indirect election, via the election of the state government that controls districting, every ten years. But what partisan gerrymandering seems more clearly to do is instead to make the party composition of the state's congressional delegation indirectly determined every ten years. Each district's election of its representative still occurs directly, every two years. Indeed, partisan gerrymandering might be superimposed on term limits.

There is more plausibility, however, in the claim that incumbent-protection gerrymandering makes the district's election of its representative insufficiently frequent. Consider an extreme analogy: once elected by a majority, a representative can unilaterally change the vote threshold for reelection to be safely below a poll of likely support. This seems close to electing representatives for terms that extend as long as the representative chooses. This does seem like an intrinsic, democratic objection, at least to incumbent-protection gerrymanders. Recall, from Section 27.4, that the People's occupancy control over officials weakens as elections become less frequent. There may be debate about how frequent elections must be for occupancy control to be adequate, but presumably representatives should not have the power to give themselves life terms. Strictly speaking, this objection does not depend on any intent to gerrymander. If, improbably, a series of randomly drawn districts in effect gave a life term to some incumbent, then this would be objectionable on the same grounds: that it made elections too infrequent.

This, in turn, suggests that partisan gerrymandering may be objectionable for similar reasons. Granted, partisan gerrymandering may not make districts' elections of their representatives less frequent. But if what representatives do in office is largely determined by their party affiliation, then it is the choice of party, rather than the choice of individual officials, that determines what officials do in office. So, directive control, which is control over what officials do in office, ultimately depends on control over which party takes power. And directive control, like occupancy control, weakens as elections become less frequent. If the partisan composition of congressional delegations is determined by state governments every ten years, then, in effect, the elections for party control take place every ten years instead of every two. There is already the question of whether this interval is too long for the People to have adequate directive control. But the darker worry in the United States in the present moment is that because of the gerrymandering of state legislatures, the partisan composition of congressional delegations may be determined by one party indefinitely. With that, and with the geographical tilt in favor of the Republican Party in the Senate and Electoral College, we risk entering a period of one-party rule. And that represents another threat to the People's directive control. The People do not have control over policy when only one option is presented to them. This seems an objection that each of us has, even if some of us may welcome the policies the single party pursues.

31

The Demandingness of Informal Equality

If Equal Influence demands deflatingly little of formal procedures, it demands a great deal, perhaps impossibly much, of informal conditions, or so this chapter suggests. Recall that informal opportunity consists roughly in the availability of resources, such as wealth and leisure, to apply to the legal or procedural structure to acquire information or influence the votes of others or the decisions of officials.

31.1 Money and Time

As far as Equal Influence is concerned, inequalities in informal conditions are no less threatening than inequalities in formal procedures. This is not to deny that there may be other reasons to be concerned about formal inequalities. For instance, insofar as formal inequalities involve more direct relations to the state, they may be violations of Equal Consideration in a way informal inequalities would not be. When the state denies someone an equal vote, the state is directly withholding a privilege from them, like issuing a prohibition on travel. When the state merely facilitates an economic structure that leaves someone else with greater leisure time to devote to civic affairs, the state is not directly withholding anything. The point is that, as far as Equal Influence, as opposed to Equal Consideration, is concerned, influence is influence, whether formal or informal.

To be sure, an unequal distribution of time or money does not immediately entail an unequal distribution of informal opportunity for influence. It depends on whether inequality in time and money can be converted into inequality in influence. In theory, diminishing returns to time and money might set in quickly, above a low threshold, so that disparities in time and money could not be converted into disparities in influence. However, unless the nonaffluent are systematically choosing not to exercise informal opportunity that they have, for example, Gilens's findings suggest that informal opportunity for influence is not distributed fairly or equally among affluent and nonaffluent citizens. Similarly, the money lavished on campaigns, as well as the extensive lobbying efforts of special interests, suggest that many close to the action believe money can be converted into influence, either over voters or over officials. Moreover, so long as officials so much as believe that campaign spending influences voters, that may suffice to make it the case that campaign contributions do in fact influence officials.

If inequalities in leisure and wealth can be converted into inequalities in informal influence, then equal opportunity for informal influence would require either preventing the conversion or reducing the inequalities in leisure and wealth itself. A challenge, to put it mildly. On the other hand, reducing at least unfair inequalities in leisure and wealth is something we already have reason to do.

How could we ensure equality of informal opportunity for influence? One answer would be a lottery. For example, the system might give each person a vote, with the decision being made by a lottery giving equal weight to each (sufficiently) distinct policy option that received at least one vote. Here money spent convincing others to vote for one's preferred option would not bring any advantage over simply casting a vote for it oneself.

It is less clear that sortition, the random selection of officials, as opposed to lottery, the random selection of policy options, would solve this problem, contrary to what Guerrero (2014) suggests. For money and time can be spent to influence those who might be selected by sortition. It might seem that no one would spend money or time on that, since it would be so obviously wasted. What are the chances that an advertisement, say, would influence the particular person who happened to be selected? The answer is that they are the same chances that an advertisement would influence the deciding vote on a referendum or ballot initiative. And, as residents of states such as California know, much money and time are spent in campaigns to influence the deciding vote on referenda and initiatives.

Let us assume, however, that the loss of other goods, such as substantive reliability, that would result from a lottery, if such a thing were even conceivable, would be too much to bear. Then measures must be taken to assure equality of informal opportunity for influence compatible with positive influence.

31.2 Judgment Dependence

There is, of course, the practical problem of how to achieve such equality of informal influence. There is a limit to what philosophy, of the present variety, can say on that score. However, there is a more immediate theoretical objection to the very idea of equal opportunity for informal influence. And this is a philosophical question.

The objection rests on the intuition that it matters what form informal influence takes. Granted, it may be objectionable if Expert has more opportunity than Crank to make his case to Hearer because of factors that do not depend on Hearer's autonomous judgment: his free reflection on what he takes to be relevant reasons. For example, it may be objectionable that Expert, but not Crank, has access to a printing press. But it hardly seems objectionable that Expert has a greater capacity to affect Hearer's vote simply because Hearer will, upon free reflection, take the considerations that Expert offers to be better reasons. The "Difference Intuition," to give it a name, is that while "judgment-independent" inequalities in opportunity for informal influence may be problematic, "judgment-dependent" inequalities—which merely result from the influenced person exercising his judgment—certainly are not. But, the objection runs, an account like ours, which requires equality of opportunity for influence as such, cannot draw this distinction and so cannot account for the Difference Intuition (R. Dworkin 2002, 195).

One might, at first, be tempted by a theory of error for the Difference Intuition. It is not that judgment-dependent inequalities are less objectionable but instead that measures to eliminate them are more objectionable: incompatible, for example, with freedom of expression. But this seems to me misguided. The tension with freedom of expression is less severe if the measures take the form of subsidies or simply moral encouragement (for example, not to allow oneself to be influenced by opinions that one finds convincing), rather than restrictions. Still, such moral encouragement seems misplaced (R. Dworkin 2002, 197–198). The Difference Intuition ought to be taken at face value.

However, I believe our account can explain the Difference Intuition—or rather, it gets the explanation for free since this distinction is built into any evaluation of a distribution of opportunity (e.g., as fair or unfair, equal or unequal). Set aside political influence for the moment and consider a fair distribution of opportunity for religious practice, composed of religious liberty and means to make use of it. While a fair distribution may be upset by judgment-independent factors, it is not upset by judgment-dependent factors, such as others' not sharing your faith. That is, fair opportunity to pursue one's religious convictions should not be understood in such a way that, simply because there are not enough people persuaded by my faith, leaving me without the quorum required for its rites, I am deprived of fair opportunity to pursue my religious convictions. For my inability to muster that quorum results from what surely counts as others' exercise of their opportunity to pursue their religious convictions: their refusal to be persuaded by my faith. In other words, the very project of evaluating opportunity to pursue one's religious convictions seems to require us, first, to distinguish between inequalities that result simply from others' pursuing their own convictions—from their exercising like opportunity—and inequalities that have independent sources, such as political persecution or an unjust distribution of leisure. And it requires us, second, to view only the latter as threatening the acceptability of the distribution.

Recall the Compossibility Principle of Section 29.1, which says that equal opportunity for *X*-ing should be understood in such a way that whether it obtains among individuals does not depend on how one of those individuals exercises the opportunity to *X*. For example, it seems wrong to say that whether or not you and I enjoy equal opportunity for some job depends on whether I apply for it. Am I supposed to refrain from applying so as not to deprive you of equal opportunity?

Similarly—returning to the case of political influence—Crank cannot claim that, simply because Hearer concludes that his arguments don't hold water, she has deprived him of equal opportunity for influence. For the alleged deprivation of Crank's equal opportunity results simply from Hearer's exercising the opportunity to do what surely counts as her (Hearer's) exercise of her like opportunity: namely, opportunity to influence political decisions on the basis of her autonomous judgment, on the basis of what she, on free reflection, takes to be relevant reasons. And if Hearer's disregarding Crank's reasons in this way does not deprive Crank of equal opportunity, then there is no reason to avoid so depriving her by disregarding her reasons.

In sum, the very idea of equality of opportunity requires us to distinguish between judgment-dependent and judgment-independent inequalities and to see the latter, but not the former, as compromising that equality of opportunity. There is, then, no special embarrassment here for the idea of equal opportunity for political influence. There's just a distinction we make whenever we evaluate a distribution of opportunity.

The distinction between judgment-dependent and judgment-independent influence may explain why certain media endorsements do not constitute an objectionable inequality of influence. That is, it may provide a response to the view of the majority in *Citizens United v. Federal Election Commission,* 558 US 310 (2010) that the media exception of section 441b of BCRA was "all but an admission of the invalidity of the antidistortion rationale" (i.e., that "immense aggregations of wealth" by corporations might influence policy in ways that "have little or no correlation to the public's support" (*Austin v. Michigan Chamber of Commerce,* 494 US 652 [1990]). Suppose that people seek out the opinion page in the *Daily Grey* based on an assessment of *Grey*'s reliability, judgment, congenial worldview, and so forth on political questions. To the extent that the influence of *Grey*'s opinion page depends, in this way, on readers' prior judgment that *Grey* has worthwhile things to say on political questions (Lowenstein 1985, 846), that influence seems more judgment dependent. By contrast, to the extent that the *Red Network*'s influence results from *Red*'s interleaving sports and entertainment programming, or the only local news broadcast with partisan editorials, it seems more judgment independent. Someone who merely wants to see the highlights from the game or tomorrow's weather has not chosen to seek out what *Red* has to say on political matters.

However, some are tempted by the view that it's not a problem when some citizens can spend more money to influence other voters, since voters in the end can, by their equal votes, ratify or reject those attempts at influence. A problem arises only when money is used to influence elected officials directly. That short-circuits the democratic process (Thompson 1995, 113–115; Lessig 2011, 160–162; 2015, 58–60, 150–152) since voters cannot ratify or reject those attempts to directly influence elected officials (Pevnick 2016, 68–69).

Yet this view seems unstable. For it seems that voters can ratify or reject these attempts to directly influence officials, at least when the attempts take the form of campaign contributions, as opposed to outright bribes. If contributions are disclosed, then voters can reject them by refusing to reelect the official. Or voters can reject them by making the contributions worthless: by refusing to be influenced by what the contributions can buy. Thus, if we say that equality of votes somehow nullifies inequality of indirect influence on other voters by campaign spending, then, by the same logic, we should say that equality of votes likewise nullifies inequality of direct influence on officials by campaign contributions. Either both are problems or neither is.

Now, I agree that it is implausible to suppose voters can reject these attempts to directly influence officials by campaign contributions. How are voters supposed to "refuse to be influenced" by what campaign contributions can buy? For example, suppose a few wealthy donors, by controlling the "money primary," determine which candidates ever to come to voters' attention. How can one "refuse to be influenced" by the fact that one is kept in ignorance of the alternatives? But this is just the point. We cannot rely merely on equality of votes to nullify inequality of indirect influence on other voters. This is why we cannot rely merely on equality of votes to nullify inequality of direct influence on officials via campaign contributions.

31.3 The Diversity of Objections to Money in Politics

Since the 1970s the US Supreme Court has held that to regulate political money is to regulate constitutionally protected political speech. And the only valid rationale for that is combatting corruption or its appearance. Finding no substantial connection to corruption, the court has thus struck down restrictions on campaign expenditures as opposed to contributions (*Buckley v. Valeo,* 424 US 1 [1976]), on contributions to referenda as opposed to candidate elections (*First National Bank of Boston v. Bellotti,* 435 US 765 [1978]), on contributions to groups that engage in expenditures uncoordinated with campaigns (*SpeechNow.org v. FEC,* 389 US App. DC 424, 599 F.3d 686 [2010]), and on total contributions to different campaigns by a single donor (*McCutcheon v. FEC,* 572 US 185 [2014]). Indeed, it's not clear why, in consistency, the court shouldn't go further and lift the ban on the activities just listed by foreign entities (*Bluman v. FEC,* Dist. Court DC, 800 F. Supp. 2d 281 [2011]). In sum, the debate over campaign finance reform has become largely a debate over the meaning of "corruption." Skeptics of reform insist on a narrow construal, no doubt gratified by the suggestion in *Citizens United v. Federal Election Commission,* 558 US 310 (2010) that corruption can only be quid pro quo and cannot consist in the purchase of access alone.

Advocates of reform, by contrast, urge us to develop an expansive, systemic conception of corruption not only to vindicate the constitutionality of campaign finance reform but also to understand the manifest deformation of American government by political money. This new conception, they insist, must recognize that corruption is a matter of structural forces and not a matter of personal impropriety. We must not assume that corruption is only the sort of thing that might be depicted in a Gilded Age cartoon, à la Thomas Nast or Joseph Keppler, with bloated pols with dollar-signed sacks. In this spirit, Thompson (1995) and Lessig (2011, 2015) propose new conceptions of "institutional" and "dependence" corruption, respectively.

I suggested in Section 11.4 that the closest thing to a distinctive objection to corruption is an objection to violations of the Duty to Exclude. Is this support for a new conception or comfort to the old? The contrast between old and new conceptions is too elusive to be certain. I imagine that advocates of a new conception might welcome the conclusions that the distinctive objection to corruption can be leveled at acts that are not quid pro quo, that are habitual or unaware, and that are motivated not by money but instead by political advantage, gratitude, loyalty, or even a high-minded cause. Moreover, many of the measures the court has struck down or viewed with suspicion can perfectly well be justified as prophylactics against violations of the Duty to Exclude, even on our restricted, railroad-era conception. Why not worry that some legislators will act in office so as to attract or repay uncoordinated expenditures on grounds that don't serve impersonal reasons?

In any event, if some such expansive conception is an effective legal strategy, I yield to it and wish it well. But insofar as the question is one of conceptual hygiene—a question perhaps best left for esoteric moralists—I worry that these expansive conceptions suppress relevant distinctions (Hasen 2016). No doubt violations of the Duty to Exclude are one problem of money in politics. But there are others. First, money in politics can disserve the public interest in diverse ways. It can lead to bad decisions. It can lead to waste (not least the waste of politicians' time fundraising). Second, money in politics can deprive aspirants of fair opportunity to hold elected office. This is just a special case of a more general improvement complaint, not special to politics: that no form of employment should be closed to one simply because one isn't rich. Third, money in politics can result in unequal informal opportunity for influence. This need not involve any violation of the Duty to Exclude. A candidate might just passively benefit from lopsided uncoordinated expenditures. A final objection to money in politics is that it can lead to a violation of Equal Treatment (compare Thompson 1995, 80–84). It's sometimes said, by way of defense, that money buys only access, not results. But buying access is already a violation of Equal Treatment by the State. It's one thing for a legislator to stop taking calls from constituents. There are only so many hours in the day. But it's another to stop taking calls from some constituents while still taking calls from donors.

I worry, therefore, that these new conceptions merely affix the label "corruption" to ills that are already independently intelligible and that have no organic connection to inflammatory emblems of corruption such as bribery and nepotism. For instance, Lessig (2011, 8; 2015, 4) all but identifies "dependence corruption," at least when applied to legislatures, with policy (Dawood 2014) that is not responsive to the policy preferences of the majority at any given time but instead is responsive to ("dependent on") something else. But such dependence can occur for a host of reasons that have nothing to do with corruption on any recognizable use of the term. A supermajority requirement, for example, also makes policy less responsive to the majority and so, of necessity, more responsive to something else, such as rural minorities. (Compare Wu 2018, 58.)

Among the pathologies of the current regime of money in politics, therefore, are not only violations of the Duty to Exclude but also of Equal Influence and Equal Treatment by the State. These are all violations of tempering factors meant to tame the asymmetries among persons threatened by the final, inescapable, and vastly superior power and authority of the state. If this is right, then not only corruption but also other of these pathologies of the current regime of campaign finance and lobbying are pathologies for the same underlying reason. And if that is so, then it seems incoherent, at least when sounded at the right philosophical depth, to view only one of them as calling for a remedy. That is, from the standpoint of moral philosophy, if not constitutional law, the court's position, or at least the position a lay observer could be forgiven for ascribing to the court, looks unstable: namely, that corruption is the only pathology of the current regime of campaign finance and lobbying serious enough to treat.

31.4 Information and Organization

Equal Influence requires equal opportunity to knowingly influence political decisions in line with one's judgments. Hence, unequal access to information about how to influence political decisions in line with one's judgments is itself a form of unequal opportunity for influence (Rawls 1971, sec. 36; Singer 1973; Christiano 1996, chap. 3; Dahl 1998, 86).[1]

The practical challenge of inequalities of money and leisure may seem dwarfed by the challenge posed by disparities in access to information. Even under an ideal distribution of wealth and leisure, the mere division of labor would seem to militate against equal access to information, or at least information relevant to a given policy question (Schumpeter 1942; Downs 1957). Those in a given industry, for example, will surely have greater access to information about existing regulation in that industry, possible alternatives, and their likely effects. It's what they do all day. While it's true that greater access to information relevant to a particular policy does not necessarily mean greater access to information relevant to policy overall, it would be a happy coincidence if differences in access to information relevant to particular policies were perfectly offsetting.

In addition to the practical challenge, there is also a conceptual challenge. What matters is not simply having access to as much information as others. More information might be distracting, paralyzing, or at least irrelevant. Simply increasing the throughput of stories on Hillary Clinton's email management might be like a document dump in discovery. One wants to say that what matters is having access to information that puts one in as good a position to exercise informed influence as others are in. But how is this to be understood?

Perhaps the severity of these challenges detracts from the plausibility of the ideal that puts the challenge to us. But if not, the ideal supplies a further reason for a vigorous and able press, guided by a sense of proportion. The role of the fourth estate is not just to inform members of the public in absolute terms, as it were. It is also, by so doing, to close the relative gap between the public and those in the know (there being no option of, and obvious costs to, the cognoscenti "leveling down" by somehow unlearning what they know).

If that weren't enough, one worries about still another challenge: the relative difficulty of organizing with others on one side of a policy question, of exercising formal opportunities for political association. In some cases, these advantages in organizational capacity are due to more time, money, or information (Schattschneider 1960, chap. 2). We have, in effect, already considered that. If, for instance, advantages in money undermine equal opportunity for influence, so too do advantages in organization that result from advantages in money. Astroturf is yet one more thing money can buy. However, there are independent organizational advantages: independent, that is, of time, money, and information. First, there is the organizational advantage that comes from simply having fewer actors to coordinate than the opposing side has, thus having an easier collective action problem to solve. Roughly speaking, the greater the number of actors who will benefit from a nonexcludable good that their latent political organization might bring about, the more likely they are to seek to free ride: to enjoy the good without contributing to the organization. Second, there is the potential for harnessing for political purposes organizations that were established for nonpolitical purposes. Here a key piece of organizational structure is the control of goods, such as insurance coverage, journal subscriptions, or jobs in a closed shop, from which nonmembers can be excluded, which provides a mechanism to overcome collective action problems. Both points were famously made by Olson (1965, chap. 6).

Finally, even where numbers are similar, the very structure of the policy dispute may make it easier for one side to organize. When the costs to group *A* of policy *P* are salient to *A* and are perceived by members of *A* to be concentrated and certain, whereas the benefits to *B* of *P* are less salient, more diffuse, and less certain, we might sooner expect *A* to organize in opposition to *P* than *B* to organize in support of *P*. And this difference in salience can be reinforced in turn by the simple fact that opposition to *P* coalesces around a clear and easily policed rule, such as "No new restrictions on firearms" or "No new taxes," whereas *P* is just one of many possible departures from such a rule that are competing against one another for support. For example, the power of the NRA, at least for much of its lifetime, wasn't simply due to the largesse of wealthy individual donors or gun manufacturers. Much of its funding came from a grassroots membership, which it, moreover, very effectively mobilized to vote against candidates who so much as entertained gun-control legislation.

If, for any of these independent reasons, *A* finds it easier to organize, do *A*'s members have greater opportunity for influence? Or should we instead chalk up the difference to their greater willingness to use their opportunities, lamentable as this may be? I am not sure. But if we count it as an inequality in opportunity for influence, then it adds a distinctively political case for strengthening both labor unions and antitrust enforcement. There is already an economic argument for unions; they are needed as a counterweight to the monopsony power of employers (which drives wages too low from the perspective of both workers and consumers). Moreover, organized labor may be necessary to moderate the asymmetries of power and de facto authority of owners and managers over workers within the firm. But there may also be a distinctively political argument for the state's facilitating the organization of labor: namely, that insofar as employees otherwise face greater difficulty than employers in organizing politically, employees need help to enjoy equal opportunity for political influence. Similarly, there is a political case for reinvigorated antitrust enforcement, beyond the economic argument that industrial concentration stifles innovation and raises prices. The fewer businesses there are in a particular industry, the easier it is for those businesses to overcome the collective action problem (Wu 2018). If business interests already have organizational advantages, then reducing industry concentration would at least avoid compounding them. Note that this argument makes more sense on a view, like ours, that is concerned with equalizing opportunity for influence than on a view that is concerned with increasing absolute opportunity for influence. If instead the concern was, say, with maximizing opportunities for political participation, then policies that made it harder for business interests to organize would seem already to have a strike against them.

32

Arbitrary Voting

In this chapter, I consider the view, prevalent among political scientists, that voting behavior is somehow "arbitrary." In what sense, I ask, is voting behavior arbitrary? And if voting behavior is arbitrary, what implications does it have for our justification of democracy, such as it is?

32.1 The Case against the Folk Theory

It is a prevalent view among political scientists that voting behavior is arbitrary, in a way that would surprise and disconcert laypeople who are otherwise well informed about politics. I consider Achen and Bartels (2016), which has been much discussed, as representative of this sort of view. While I do not question the empirical soundness of the findings they survey, I do raise some questions about whether their findings support their headline claims—and indeed about how their headline claims are even to be understood.

Achen and Bartels criticize what they call the "folk theory," which assumes that policy preferences, ideology, and interests account for voter behavior. The stronger version of the folk theory, which often seems like a strawman, assumes that voters' preferences are for specific policies, such as raising the federal minimum wage to $10.25. The weaker version, by contrast, recognizes preferences for a broader range of political outcomes. So, it allows that people may not vote on specific policies but instead may vote on broad ideological principles or may vote "retrospectively" on the basis of past results. Since people vote in some such way, the folk theory concludes, all we need for well-functioning democracy is to give everyone an equal vote. Whereas the stronger version insists that people vote directly on policy, via referenda or initiatives, the weaker version is content to give party leaders and elected officials wide discretion. So, we can take arbitrary voting behavior to be, negatively, voting behavior that does not conform to either version of the folk theory.

If the folk theory is wrong, then how do people vote? Positively, Achen and Bartels argue that votes are influenced by three systematic factors:[1] (A) myopic retrospection: the rate of income growth in last two quarters before the election; (B) partisan affiliation: membership in a formal political party; and (C) group identity: belonging to a race, gender, ethnicity, or religion.

One might wonder why their positive claims—say, that votes are determined by partisan affiliation—should be taken to support, or even be thought consistent with, their negative claims, that votes are not determined by policy preferences, ideology, or interest. In particular, one might wonder why we should contrast a vote for one's party with a vote for one's policy preferences, ideology, or interest. Granted, the party's stance may diverge from one's policy preferences, ideology, or interests in this particular, or here and now. But supporting the party, despite that, seems a reasonable strategy for advancing one's policy preferences, ideology, and interests in general, or over the long run. Voting for the party that by and large supports your prior policy preferences seems a reasonable way to go about satisfying them. True, some of the platform's fine print might not be your ideal, but grown-ups realize that politics requires coalition building and tactical sacrifice. Moreover, one's party's support for a particular policy may provide one with evidence that the policy aligns with one's preferences, ideology, or interests, given that the party usually supports policies that so align. However, Achen and Bartels (2016) present evidence that people vote for their party not on such instrumental or evidentiary grounds but instead because their party affiliation influences their (i) beliefs about economic and social conditions and the effects of (even recent) policy, (ii) beliefs about which policies the parties support, and (iii) broader preferences for policy (285). Voters who know more in other respects may actually be more susceptible to such influences since they also know the party line better (Bartels 2016, 130–131).

Why then do people affiliate with the parties they do? In some cases, it is just a vestige of some earlier myopic retrospection. For example, a person may have voted for Roosevelt in 1936 because things were looking up that year and then continued voting for Democrats for years after from sheer force of habit. In some cases, it is just the way one was brought up. But mostly people affiliate with parties because people identify with some racial, gender, ethnic, religious, regional, or class group, and they see that party as the party of that group.

32.2 Why Arbitrary Voting Matters

Why, if at all, should that matter? One might worry about unresponsive policy. However, much of Achen and Bartels's discussion of arbitrary voting doesn't say anything about whether policy is responsive to preferences for policy. Instead, it says that preferences for policy are themselves determined by group identification and party indoctrination. But if what matters is satisfying policy preferences as such, then it should not matter where those preferences came from.

Next, one might worry that arbitrary voting leads to substantively worse results. But what exactly is the worry, and what is supposed to follow from it? One line of thought might run: "Let's take voting behavior as a given. It turns out that it is arbitrary. Therefore, some relevant alternative procedure in which voting has (in some sense) less influence over policy than it has now would lead to better outcomes." But then why assume this? To paraphrase Churchill, what faith do we have that some alternative would fare better?[2]

Another view might be: "Let's take it as given that voting influences policy as it does. Therefore, if voting was less arbitrary, outcomes would be better." Granted, it's hard to see how less myopic retrospection—voting on the basis of income growth not over the last two quarters but instead over, say, the last twelve—could produce worse results. But why assume a higher correlation of votes with specific policy preferences and a lower correlation of votes with party affiliation would lead to better results—especially if parties help craft informed, coherent, workable packages of policy?

Moreover, why assume that less arbitrary voting is a relevant alternative? After all, it is not clear that less arbitrary voting is something a suitable "we" could bring about, at tolerable cost. Among the sources of arbitrariness may well be deep-seated tendencies in the human psyche: to trust people like ourselves, to be distracted by salience, to shun cognitive dissonance, to gravitate toward confirming or reassuring evidence, and so on. Guarding against these tendencies often requires intensive training, structure, and reinforcement, even in highly focused, regimented, professional contexts. Why be optimistic about the returns to similar efforts in the all-things-considered, freewheeling, unblushingly amateur context of voting?

Of course, even if it's not possible, without prohibitive cost, for the relevant "us" to do anything about how an arbitrary voter, Arby, votes, it might still be possible, without prohibitive cost, for Arby to do something about it. If so, things might be better if Arby did something about it. (Indeed, Arby may wrong the rest of us by not doing something about it.) But is this to say more than that the world would be better if people were better: to ink one more entry in the long ledger of the wages of human frailty?

We turn now from responsiveness and substantive results to Equal Influence. At first, it might seem that Equal Influence is not compromised by arbitrary voting. Arbitrary voting has to do only with how people exercise their opportunities for influence, not what opportunities they have to exercise. Equal Influence, by contrast, is a matter of the opportunities themselves, not how they are exercised. However, arbitrary voting does threaten the idea that the People exercise directive control over officials via elections. That requires that votes for candidates and parties can be understood as votes for what those candidates and parties will do in office. And that may seem to be threatened by arbitrary voting.

32.3 Is Voting Arbitrary?

Is voting then arbitrary? Central to Achen and Bartels's account of arbitrary voting is the idea of group identification, which is supposed to drive party affiliation. It's not entirely clear, however, what it means, in their view, to identify with a group. Achen and Bartels (2016) suggest that it is to see a group as "central" to one's "self-concept" (228). But this definition isn't met by the illustration they offer, in the very next paragraph, of a Northern Irish atheist who is presumed to have a group identity as a Protestant or Catholic, even though, evidently, this is not important to his "self-concept" (even as an "emotional attachment that transcend[s] thinking").

The "realignment" of White southerners to the Republican party perhaps best exemplifies Achen and Bartels's view of how group identification drives party affiliation. The folk theory imagines that voters were saying to themselves: "I oppose policies of racial integration. Republicans are now more likely than Democrats to oppose such policies. So, I will vote Republican."

But, according to Achen and Bartels, not even abstract racial animus, let alone specific policies, had much to do with it. Instead, voters just began seeing Republicans as the party of White southerners. The soliloquy, if it could have been consciously expressed, would have gone: "I identify as a White southerner. Nowadays the Republicans are the sort of party that a White southerner votes for. So, I will vote Republican." Nothing more would be forthcoming about why White southerners should vote Republican. They just do.

This does leave it mysterious why the Republican party started, around the 1960s, to be viewed as the party of White southerners, if there was no association with the interests, policy preferences, or ideology of White southerners. And, on closer inspection, the folk theory may cover even this example. If White southerners viewed the sort of party that a White southerner votes for as the party of White supremacy, as Achen and Bartels grant, then were they not affiliating with a party on the basis of an "ideology" (252)? White supremacy is an ideology and indeed brings with it a number of policy preferences.

At any rate, the folk theory covers reasonably well the other examples Achen and Bartels adduce to show that group identification explains party affiliation. Consider their observation that women's party affiliations have been more responsive than men's to the parties' stances on abortion. Achen and Bartels speculate, plausibly enough, that because women's interests are more affected by abortion policy, they have stronger, more settled preferences about it. True, one can say that women have these stronger, more settled preferences because they are members of the group "women" (206). But, first, can't one say this whenever policy affects interests? It is because creditors are members of the group "creditors," for example, that they want low inflation. This point bears emphasis. To claim that "identifying with a group" drives voting behavior offers no alternative to the folk theory if the relevant group is simply the group of people with such and such an interest, policy preference, or ideology.[3] Second, what matters is not that womanhood is "central" to anyone's "self-concept" but simply that women are more affected by the policy. Finally, even if group identification drives these policy preferences, still those policy preferences drive party affiliation and voting, just as the folk theory would have it.

One might take a similar view of Achen and Bartels's cases of racial and religious groups affiliating with parties that were more "favorable" and less "antagonistic" to them. Even if Jews in the 1930s had few opinions about specific policies, they might have preferred that the interests of Jews be protected. And they might have assumed that because Democrats were more welcoming of Jews, Democrats would do a better job of that. Granted, expressing less hostility toward a group or putting one of its members forward as a candidate for office does not guarantee the party will act in the best interest of that group. But the only evidence that Achen and Bartels cite supports the reliability of such proxies. Even factoring in the risks of pandering and "identity fraud," it seems sensible enough for a member of such a group to expect an official from the same group (309), or at least an official or party that openly expresses less hostility to that group (238), to be less hostile to that person's policy preferences, interests, and ideology—all the more so if, reasonably enough, that person's policy preferences, interests, and ideology partly consist in broader social and political treatment of members of her group as equals.

In sum, Achen and Bartels's examples are broadly consistent with the "folk" idea that people affiliate with the parties they do because they independently believe those parties will satisfy their political preferences. Granted, some of these preferences are not for specific policies and are often shaped by group membership (although sometimes only because group membership implies certain interests). And granted, many such preferences, such as those of a racist or nativist or sexist variety, may well be immoral, self-destructive, and yet, for all that, overwhelmingly powerful. But it is not clear that theorists, let alone the folk, deny any of these points. So, it is not clear that Achen and Bartels's evidence supports their conclusions.

Indeed, strange as it may at first sound, there are a priori grounds for skepticism about explaining voting behavior by appeal to group identity in a way that bypasses interests, policy preferences, or ideology. To be sure, one can observe that people who identify with certain groups tend to vote for certain parties. But that, in itself, is not an explanation of why they vote for those parties, let alone an explanation in competition with the folk theory. For an explanation, one needs to describe some intelligible psychological mechanism by which group identification leads to voting behavior but that bypasses perceived interests, policy preferences, or ideology. And this is harder than it looks. As we saw, Achen and Bartels's best case, that of the White southerner, doesn't fit the bill, by their own lights.

I can think of two broad possibilities for such an intelligible psychological mechanism. First, the act of voting a certain way might be incompatible with one's group identity, but in a way divorced from any connections to interests, policy preferences, or ideology. Consider that there are some things that people feel they cannot do because they identify as a member of a group, even though this has no bearing on how they view their interests, policy preferences, or ideology. For instance, many men of my generation, both gay and straight, could not bring themselves to wear a dress or makeup, even though they in no way think less of other men wearing dresses or makeup and even though this has no bearing on their interests, policy preferences, and ideology. Now imagine a party called the "Vote Like a Girl Party." Certain men might wish the Vote Like a Girl Party and its platform well. They might harbor no doubts about the capability of women to hold elected office or positions of authority over men. They just might not be able to vote for the party because voting for it would be, for them, like wearing a dress. So that's one schema. But one wonders whether any real-life cases fit it. For example, the actual reservations voters have about candidates who are women, because they are women, are linked to views that women aren't up to the job (and so would not serve interests) or shouldn't hold positions of power and authority (as a matter of ideology). Another case of this general kind would be that of a voter who feels the candidate looks down on, has insulted, or has taken for granted the voter's group. As a matter of spite or healthy self-respect, the voter might feel unable to vote for the candidate. However, one imagines that in real-life cases, the candidate's attitudes will also be taken as evidence of a lack of concern or understanding for members of one's group that does implicate interests.

Second, group identity might drive electoral preferences that have no connection to interests, policy preferences, or ideology. One might want a candidate from one's high school, hometown, or favorite sports team to win, even though one does not believe they would better serve one's interests, policy preferences, or ideology than their opponent. One's motivation might be local pride or being a fan of a particular team. As social identity theory indicates, merely being categorized as a member of an otherwise arbitrary group can lead one to favor it (Ellemers and Haslam 2012). Perhaps some people are motivated in this way to vote for someone from their gender, race, religion, or ethnicity. But in the case of these less trivial group identifications, one imagines will be more to it, which will implicate interests, policy preferences, and ideology. One imagines that Black Democratic voters who were specially motivated to vote for Obama thought that whether or not Obama was more likely than Clinton to pursue policies of racial justice, the very fact of his election would have a salutary effect on how Black people viewed themselves and were viewed by others, and that such views themselves would, in the long run, work against racist structures still so prevalent in the United States.

Conclusion

Not So Much Liberty As Noninferiority

Modern political philosophers stretch their canvases on various framings of liberty and equality. There is, first, the question of which conception of liberty we should espouse. The liberty of the ancients or the moderns (Constant [1819] 1988)? Positive liberty or negative (Berlin [1958] 1997)? Then there is a corresponding question of which conception of equality earns our fealty. A distributive conception or a relational one? Next there is the supposed contest between liberty and equality. Partisans of liberty insist that liberty may not be sacrificed to equality (Narveson 2010), while champions of equality hold up equality, not liberty, as the "sovereign virtue" (R. Dworkin 2002). Against these hedgehog pronouncements, those of a more foxlike persuasion doubt that there is a general answer to the question of whether liberty or equality holds sway. Tragic conflicts are inevitable in a world not made to contain everything (Berlin [1958] 1997, 197; Williams 2005, chap. 9). And then there are those who question whether there is a conflict between liberty and equality at all. Perhaps the alleged conflict of liberty and equality is really a conflict of the liberties of the haves against the liberties of the have-nots (G. Cohen 1995; Sterba 2010). No doubt much, including the question of whether there is one debate here or several, turns on how the terms are defined.

Where does this book stand with respect to this tradition? To a first approximation, my overarching framework recognizes two understandings of liberty and one of equality. On one understanding of liberty, one is free insofar as one has the opportunity to live a worthwhile life. Or, at least, that is why being free matters. If so, then claims to liberty are just claims to improvement.[1] On another understanding, one is free insofar as one is not invaded, whether or not invasion might improve one's condition. If so, then claims to liberty are just rights against invasion. Our conception of equality is the absence of relations of inferiority. Claims to equality are claims to noninferiority—or, more simply, claims against inferiority.

In a pluralist spirit, I see these as distinct claims, which can conflict, although the conflicts are not always to be found where other theorists suppose. Rights against invasion, for example, stand in the way of uses of violence that might bring about a better distribution of opportunity to live a worthwhile life—albeit not, as I argued, in the way of state imposition. Claims against inferiority, to take another example, may militate against distributions of opportunity that would be otherwise fair. With the foxes, I have not tried to order these claims by stringency, to say that one claim takes, in general, priority over the others.

What I have sought to do in this book, however, is to focus our attention, negatively, on the limits of what our two conceptions of freedom can explain and, positively, on what our conception of equality might explain. My negative observation has been that, to a greater extent than is recognized, our concerns about society and politics, captured in our commonplace claims, are not concerns of freedom, in either of these senses. This is so even when they seem to advance under one or another device of freedom. The problem of justifying the state, for example, or at least the more than minimal state, is typically billed as the problem of reconciling the state with the freedom of the individual.

My positive conjecture has been that these commonplace claims are instead claims against inferiority. To a greater extent than we have articulated to ourselves, our political thinking is driven by concerns not so much about freedom as about inferiority. My train of thought in the book thus amounts to a kind of slow-motion, anti-libertarian judo—where "libertarian" is now meant to cover not only enthusiasts for rights against invasion but also enthusiasts for any conception of individual liberty. If you press hard enough on worries about the state's encroachment on the individual, I have argued, you end up in a posture not so much of defense of personal liberty as opposition to social hierarchy.

To a first approximation, I said, we can view our three main building blocks—claims to improvement, rights against invasion, and claims against inferiority—as representing two conceptions of liberty and a conception of equality, respectively. But one might, with equal justice, say that all three are conceptions of liberty. Granted, the sort of freedom pressed by claims against inferiority isn't freedom understood as being resourced to chart a life according to your choices or of being insulated from invasion by others. Instead, it is freedom understood as having no other individual as master, of being subordinate to no one. It is *liberté* understood so as to make *liberté,* égalité, *fraternité* a kind of conceptual "stutter" or disfluency.

If we admit this conception of freedom as having no master, however, we need to fortify ourselves against a temptation to conflate it with freedom of other kinds. Such conflations are tempting, in part, because the limitations of the one notion of freedom can be obscured by substituting, when convenient, the other notion. And it is tempting, in part, because it seems to yield a kind of master value, which could somehow shoulder the whole weight of a political philosophy. I suspect that the republican's notion of nondomination is born of such a conflation: a conflation of freedom as having no master with freedom as being insulated from actual invasion. The result is a conception of freedom as insulation from so much as potential invasion. And that, I have argued, is impossible to realize, so long as we live with others.

I have also touched on, in passing, yet another conception of freedom, besides the opportunity to live a worthwhile life and insulation from invasion: positive self-rule. One enjoys freedom of this kind when the political decisions under which one lives are one's own decisions. Perhaps that means correspondence: that the political decisions are ones that you prefer. Or perhaps it means, more than this, success: that this correspondence results from the positive influence of your choices. Or perhaps it means that the content of the political decisions is such that, in obeying them, you serve only your own reasons (see Section 8.3).

Here, too, there is a danger of conflation. The conflation this time is of freedom as noninferiority with freedom as self-rule: the conflation of having no master with having oneself as master. Rousseau's *Social Contract,* as I read it, is built on the fault line of this very conflation. On the one hand, Rousseau hopes that rule by the general will will be rule by no other particular individual. Since all have equal influence over the formation of the general will, in being subjected to it, they are not subordinated to any other individual; "each, giving himself to all, gives himself to no one" (chacun se donnant à tous ne se donne à personne, bk. 1, chap. 6). On the other hand, Rousseau also hopes that rule by the general will will realize positive self-rule for each person: understood as "obedience to the law one has prescribed to oneself" (bk. 1, chap. 8). Rousseau's climactic phrase "obey only himself" (n'obéisse . . . qu'à lui-même, bk. 1, chap. 6) is one among many passages that yoke the two aspirations together: the (here literally expressed) aim of not being subordinate to any other person—to obey no one else—with the (here at least implicated) aim of positively ruling oneself—to obey oneself. These are also conflated by Berlin in his account of positive liberty. For instance, he suggests that the attainment of positive liberty might be expressed by the slogans, "'I am my own master'; 'I am slave to no man'" ([1958] 1997, 204), as though these expressed one and the same thought.

Rousseau and Berlin are yoking together two very different beasts that shouldn't be expected to plow the same furrow. The fact that some decision fails to be yours—and so does not realize self-rule—is still compatible with its succeeding in not being any more someone else's—and so freeing one from inferiority.[2] Decisions by lottery offer perhaps the clearest examples. Decisions by lottery are not one's own because they are no one's. But, for that very reason, they are no more the decisions of any other individual. However, the same can be said of decisions by vote, or other procedures, so long as all have equal opportunity to influence the outcome.

I see no way, barring sleight of hand, that we can have our own will as rule while living under political decisions. Unless one is a dictator, political decisions are not one's own, as an individual. But, as I have suggested, I'm less pessimistic—as a matter of theory, although not, of course, of practice—that being subjected to political decisions might count as being ruled over by no one else, at least to such an untempered extent that one would have a complaint against inferiority. Not freedom as self-rule, but instead freedom from any other's rule over oneself, so understood, may be the most we can, even in principle, hope for. Or at very least, there is the basic structural point that it is harder to avoid heteronomy—understood as subjection to the power and authority of a will that isn't one's own, whether that of a superior, an inferior, an equal, or none of these; whether that of a natural or artificial being; whether that of an individual or a collective—than it is to avoid inferiority—understood as subjection to the superior power and authority of a natural individual. It is harder simply because there is more to avoid.

I close with replies to two imagined critics. The first lays a charge of co-optation: "Objections to hierarchical relations, asymmetries of power, and suchlike have long been at the center of protests against the oppression of the working class, women, people of color, the colonized, and so forth. Appropriating these ideas, you then claim that all that is needed to address them is . . . wait for it . . . precisely the formal structures of bourgeois liberalism that we already know are laughably inadequate protections against such oppression! The 'very Eden,' as Marx ([1867] 1978, 343) had it, 'of the innate rights of man.'"

To begin with, I have not claimed that such structures are all that is needed. So, I agree that they are, on their own, inadequate protections. I have argued that they are part, but only part, of what is required to address relations of inferiority. If the critic were to go further and argue that any such structures, however supplemented, must be instruments of oppression, then we would indeed disagree.

I also invite the critic to consider the "revolutionary potential" of the book's claim that in order to make sense of a host of liberal, even libertarian, ideas, one must see relations of inferiority as a problem to be addressed. To embrace those seemingly minimal, abstract, "formal" ideas, such as that officials should treat like cases alike, is, if the book is right, to be committed to many of the maximal, concrete, "substantive" protests voiced by feminists or Marxists. One can't consistently worry about the state's encroachment on the rugged individual, for example, without also worrying about imbalances of power between husband and wife or the hierarchical authority of employer over employee. The concerns that underlie them are continuous.

The second critic, if somehow they should have had the patience to read this far, finds all this talk of "equality" utterly lacking in historical consciousness. "It blows out of all proportion," they might say, "the opportunistic rhetoric of certain coalitions of social classes in the North Atlantic at the end of the eighteenth century." Or something like that.

Perhaps some concerns for liberty have such shallow historical roots. But I suspect that this concern about relations of equality may reach deeper into the history, or even the natural history, of our species (Tomasello 2016, 162). It is hard to see how our earliest hunter-gatherer ancestors could have so much as entertained the idea of liberty, in the specific senses of "being the author of one's life," or pursuing one's "life plan," or one's "conception of the good," or choosing among meaningfully different options in how to live one's life. And should one of our ancestors have somehow entertained it, she would have had nothing to apply it to. What was to be done, presumably, was what everyone did, and what everyone had done, for as long as anyone could remember (Tomasello 2016, 97). To be sure, our earliest ancestors must have expressed ample creativity in play, dance, gossip, storytelling, and much else. But when it came to what a contemporary philosopher might call a "life plan," it would seem that there was just one of those, if you were a woman, and another, single life plan if you were a man, except perhaps for doing double duty as a shaman.

While liberty, in that sense that preoccupies contemporary philosophers, was not a concern, equality nevertheless seems to have been. There is reason to believe that our ancestors were fiercely vigilant in maintaining relations of equality, at least among adult men. People who got it into their heads to upset the balance were teased, ostracized, or killed (Boehm 2001). What was intolerable, it seems, was not the absence of another option about what to do. That was a given. The question of what was to be done had only one answer. What was intolerable was, instead, another person setting himself up as the one to tell you to do it (Graeber and Wengrow 2021, 133). This was among the reasons, one imagines, why the birth of enduring hierarchy was no easy delivery: why it had to be midwifed by the coordinated manipulation of superstition and the control, by violence, of food stores.

If we take the longest historical view, the question that we have been exploring comes to seem not a recent, adventitious preoccupation. Instead, it comes to seem one of the first questions of politics: If complex, large-scale society—if, in one sense of the word, civilization—requires a differentiation of roles and a concentration of power and authority, can it be reconciled with the equality of standing that was guarded so jealously before?[3] It is a question that one imagines those on the margins of the first kingdoms and empires must have asked themselves, in that uneasy season between when they first grasped the strange, new terms of life on offer and when they fled beyond the hinterlands or were compelled, by force of arms or lack of alternatives, to accept those terms. The aim of this book has been to suggest that we philosophers bring this question into more explicit reflection. Whether it has made any progress in answering it is another story.

Notes

Introduction: A Negative Observation and a Positive Conjecture

1. While Graeber and Wengrow (2021) might seem at first to dismiss this assertion as myth, the details of their view seem largely in keeping with it. Consider how they themselves describe the hierarchies that they claim that authors such as Boehm have overlooked. These hierarchies were "dismantled" on a "regular"—and so presumably predictable—"basis" (115). The "eminence and subservience" that they involved were treated "as temporary expedients, or even the pomp and circumstance of some kind of grand seasonal theater" or as "just playing games" (115). They were not "permanent and intractable systems of inequality" (119). And these hierarchies existed for only "most of the last 40,000 or so years" (112).

2. To be sure, to stylize Rawls's theory as a view about what it would take to meet claims to improvement is to abstract away a great deal. There is no place within his system for the idea that the bare fact that I can improve your situation tends to support your having a claim on me to improve it. The closest thing in Rawls to that idea is considerably more qualified and restricted. To begin with, Rawls's question of how to distribute social primary goods arises only among fellow members of a particular society, whose cooperation has produced those goods. Moreover, the duty on individuals with respect to the distribution of primary goods is not to distribute them directly but instead to foster and support institutions that distribute them. However, these qualifications and restrictions tend to strengthen, rather than weaken, my point in the text. If resources that are less qualified and restricted than those that Rawls offers are not enough to explain what we seek to explain, then a fortiori Rawls's more qualified and restricted resources will not be enough. There are also two broader differences in focus between Rawls's theory of justice and the framework that this book adopts. First, the idea of a claim against an agent to act in some way, while central in my thinking, is not particularly central in Rawls. This is curious, since whatever else we know of injustice, we know that those who suffer it have, on that ground, a complaint against it. Second, I avoid the word "justice," which of course is the centerpiece of Rawls's political philosophy. So long as we are clear about the various claims that individuals have, it is not clear to me what turns on whether those claims can be said to represent claims of justice. However, I do acknowledge that there is an important question of how to fairly trade off interests in improvement.

3. In effect, this book tries to do for contemporary political philosophy what Allen (2014) does for the Declaration of Independence.

1. The Received Materials: Improvement and Invasion

1. There may be cases in which Indy has a claim on Benny to act for certain reasons (or at least not to act for certain reasons). This will be the case, for example, with the Duty to Exclude, introduced in Section 11.4. That is, when we take the grounding focus, we see that part of what Indy has an interest in is precisely that Benny act for certain reasons. And when we take the guiding focus, we see that part of how Benny is to guide his action is to act for those reasons. In such cases, therefore, even when we take the grounding or guiding focus, we see that Benny fails to meet a claim of Indy insofar as he acts or does not act for those reasons.

2. To say that Benny failed to improve Altra's situation is typically understood to presuppose that had Benny made a different choice, Altra would still have existed. More generally, Indy's improvement complaint might also be answered by saying that had a different choice been made, someone would have been saved from a worse fate (Kolodny 2022). Since these complications are beyond our concerns in this book, I assume that any trade-offs are among people who will exist no matter what we choose.

3. The luckist position is one of several tenets of what has been called "luck egalitarianism." In its canonical form, luck egalitarianism holds the following (G. Cohen 2008, 93; Temkin 1993, 12). First, states of affairs can be unfair to individuals, even if they were not brought about or sustained by any agent's choice. Second, agents have reason to mitigate the unfairness of those states of affairs when they can. Third, states of affairs are unfair to individuals roughly insofar as those individuals are worse off than others in some respect. (I say more about these first three components in Section 21.1.) More specifically, it is unfair to individuals that they should be worse off than others when this does not result from their choices, when it is bad brute luck. However, finally, it is not unfair to them when it does result from their choices, when it is option luck. So when they are worse off for such reasons, they do not have a claim on others to mitigate it. This last tenet is more or less the luckist position described in the text.

In later work, however, Cohen (2011, chap. 6) seems to reverse his stance on this last tenet. There he appears to hold that, when inequality is due to option luck, it is unfair to Indy. (The fact that Indy made a choice may affect other reasons Benny has, Cohen suggests, but it does not affect the reason supplied by the unfairness of Indy's having less than Altra.) I also reject this revised view—that inequalities resulting from option luck are always unfair—just as I reject the original tenet—that inequalities resulting from option luck are never unfair. As argued in the text, it depends on the particulars of the case.

4. If there is no relevant agent, then the reasons that underlie rights against invasion cannot be at issue, since those reasons, as we will see, concern other agents: they are reasons to want to control how other agents treat one.

2. Is the Claim against the State's Force?

1. Simmons (2000, 137) stresses the difficulty of accounting for the state's "right to use coercion" or to "direct and enforce," absent consent. Narveson (2010, 123) cites "coercion," "threaten[ing] punishments or other invasions," and "forcibly imposing on persons." Nozick's (1974, ix) chief complaint against a more than minimal state is that it "will violate persons' rights not to be forced to do certain things," including "to aid others." Rawls, as we have seen, argues that the state's "exercise of political power" must meet a special condition because it is "coercive power," "us[ing] force in upholding its laws" (Rawls 1993, 136–137). Larmore (1999, 605–608) and Nagel (1991, chap. 14) likewise see force and coercion as raising this special condition. As we have seen, R. Dworkin (1986, 191) views the primary "puzzle of legitimacy" as a puzzle about the justification of "coercion," "enforcing," and "using force." See also Huemer (2013, chap. 1), who is especially clear on these issues. As Edmundson (1998, 90) summarizes such positions: "The coercive nature of law not only renders the state presumptively illegitimate, it sets the bar of legitimacy at a higher level than is normally necessary for the legitimacy of individual or concerted private activity."

2. Some forms of restitution can't be counted as forward-looking defense. If I destroy your property, there's nothing left to defend. Instead, I am required to pay you compensation. However, getting me to pay that compensation is not best thought of as a fourth category, a further way of enforcing the original directive not to destroy your property. Instead, I'm now under a new directive: namely, to compensate you for your destroyed property. This requirement can, in turn, be enforced in one of the three ways distinguished in the text: threatening me if I violate it, directly preventing me from violating it (e.g., by garnishing my wages), or imposing a deterrent if I defy the threat.

3. The Natural Duty Argument is suggested by Quong (2011, chap. 4) and Wellman (1996, 2005). Waldron (1993) argues for something like (4), following, but does not discuss the enforcement of directives.

It is a little puzzling that Quong suggests the Natural Duty Argument. The Natural Duty Argument is supposed to justify the state without appeal to a legitimating condition. Yet Quong holds that the state does need to meet a legitimating condition of public justification.

Wellman (1996, 219n13) claims that his argument for the permissibility of state coercion does not rest on anything like Duty Permits Force. Instead, the claims of the target to be free from coercion are simply "outweighed" in cases of emergency rescue. But this seems inadequate. The examples Wellman uses to motivate the claim of "outweighing" appear to be either (temporarily) commandeering someone's property or issuing (as opposed to following through on) threats. But what is presently at issue is something different: following through on a threat with force on someone's person. And it's not intuitive that the Force Constraint is overcome merely because an emergency rescue is underway. After all, our motivating case, of toppling Uno to save Duo and Trio, was an emergency rescue.

4. Simmons (2005, 192), who affirms "the natural right of all persons to enforce morality (by coercion, if necessary)," may accept Duty Permits Force. But Nozick (1974, 91–93) does not.

5. Narveson (2010, 158–159) accepts Duty Permits Force but rejects a natural Duty to Improve. Simmons (2000, 137), by contrast, accepts a natural Duty to Improve.

6. Compare Murphy's (2014, 130) "basic structural point."

7. See Nozick (1974, 6); R. Dworkin (1986, 191; 2011, 319–320); Klosko (2005, 49–50); Quong (2011, 115). This is why Dworkin holds, as noted earlier, that justified coercion requires a "community of principle": justified coercion requires political obligations, which in turn require a community of principle. Force Requires Duty also appears to be an implicit premise in the argument that the state wrongs us by enforcing prohibitions on private enforcement (Nozick 1974, 24; Simmons 2000, 156). Since there is no natural duty to refrain from private enforcement, the argument runs, the state violates Force Requires Duty in enforcing its directives to refrain from private enforcement.

There is a different principle in the vicinity of Force Requires Duty, put forward by Tadros (2011): namely, that the Force Constraint is lifted only when the target has a duty to bear the costs the force imposes or would have such a duty in an otherwise similar situation where there was something the target could actively do so as to bear those costs. I find this view, while ingenious, ultimately undermotivated and overly constraining.

8. Granted, Raz (1986, 104, 148) stresses that the fact we do not have a general duty to obey "even laws which the government is justified in making" does not mean the state is not justified in using force or coercion to "enforce moral duties on those who are inclined to disregard them." Presumably, by "moral duties," Raz means duties of autonomy that people have independent of any duty to obey the law. See also Raz (1990a, 15).

9. I don't claim this interest in control explains why the Force Constraint has a deontological or agent-relative character. After all, when we refrain from using force on Uno to save a greater number from force, the greater number might ask why their interests in control do not outweigh Uno's interest. Why certain kinds of interests should give rise to deontological constraints is a difficult question. My claim is only that this interest in control is among them.

10. The Avoidance Principle captures, I think, the defensible part of a "rights forfeiture" theory of punishment. See Goldman (1979); Morris (1991); Simmons

(1991); Kershnar (2002); Wellman (2009, 2012). However, this account differs from rights forfeiture theories in a number of respects. First, the account doesn't imply, as most rights forfeiture theories of punishment maintain, that one forfeits a right only by violating a right, which is more or less Force Requires Duty. Second, this account does not, a fortiori, imply a strict equivalence between the right violated and the right forfeited (which is what leads to Goldman's [1979] "paradox"). "Proportionality" is explained in the way described at the end of Section 2.3. Third, this account also doesn't imply, as do some rights forfeiture theories, that if Flintstone violates a right, then others can, for any purpose, violate (or rather do what would otherwise count as violating) the same right of Flintstone. It does not imply, for example, that if a sadist secretly inflicts pain on Flintstone without knowing that Flintstone is a violator, then the sadist does not violate his rights. The Force Constraint is lifted only for uses of force, such as deterrence, that provide others with goods that are sufficiently important to justify Flintstone's reduced control over others' uses of force. Uses of force in secret and for private satisfaction don't provide others with such goods. Finally, the Avoidance Principle offers a justification for the "forfeiture of rights," which rights forfeiture theories tend to leave mysterious. The justification, to put it in terms congenial to the rights forfeiture theory, is that just as one can "waive rights" through one's choices, so too can one "forfeit rights" through one's choices, when the costs to others of greater "immunity to the loss of rights" would unfairly burden them. "Waiver" and "forfeiture" are different answers, in different contexts, to the same basic question: What sort of control over how others treat one is it fair to expect when balanced against the costs others must bear to provide one with such control?

Simmons (1991, 335) similarly appeals to fairness to explain why the Force Constraint is lifted in Flintstone's case, although, I think, in the wrong way. "To extend such privileges to those who break the rules," he argues, "would seem to involve serious and straightforward unfairness to those who limit their own liberty by obeying the rules." The thought appears to be that, if others bear burdens to respect the Force Constraint but you don't bear them, then they are permitted to compensate themselves, and so equalize the burdens, by not respecting the Force Constraint toward you. How does this compensate them? Presumably by providing them with deterrent protection. The trouble is that unequal burdens borne in respecting the Force Constraint can arise even if no one has violated the Force Constraint. In such a case, Simmons's argument would seem to license scapegoating to equalize burdens. In short, this seems the wrong way to think about fairness in this context. The relevant question of fairness is how to balance the interests that the Force Constraint is meant to protect against the interests that would be disadvantaged by more extensive protection. The Avoidance Principle does this directly.

11. For other criticism of Force Requires Duty, see De Marneffe 2005, 130; 2010, 76; Tadros 2016, chap. 6, although his doubts seem prompted by exceptional cases.

12. Indeed, on this view, deterrents may be permissible even when the state is not ideally directive. Even if the current set of directives is suboptimal, the stern message sent by following through—"If you violate one of these directives, then you will suffer the deterrent"—may have better effects than the lax message sent by not following through—"If you violate one of these directives, then you may not suffer the deterrent." While, by definition, there are patterns of conduct better than general compliance with the suboptimal directives, there may also be worse patterns of conduct. And the lax message may only encourage such worse patterns. Assuming that people have had adequate opportunity to comply with the suboptimal directives, the Deontological Complaint might be answered. Of course, the state should replace its suboptimal directives with optimal ones. Indeed, it may be acting impermissibly in not doing so. The point is that if the state has not yet done so, the message sent by its not following through on the threats it has made may be worse than its following through. Paradoxically put, it may be permissible for the state to impose deterrents for violations of directives that it has impermissibly issued and that it is permissible for individuals to violate. This suggests, incidentally, that relaxing the assumption that the state is an ideal enforcer makes the Deontological Complaint harder to answer than does relaxing the assumption that its directives are ideal.

13. This point is easily obscured by confusing the threat to punish Flintstone, which aims to prevent Flintstone's use of force and so might be justified by Vic's interest in being free from Flintstone's force, with following through on the threat after Flintstone's violation, which does not defend against his violation. (Although Quinn [1985] argues that what justifies the threat justifies following through, I don't think the argument succeeds.) So, for good measure, further suppose that Flintstone was not even deterred by our threat. In that case, not even the threat to Flintstone was justified by Vic's interest in defending against Flintstone's force, since it did nothing to serve that interest. All the same, following through on the threat serves Vic's interest in deterring Dieter.

14. To my knowledge, Boonin (2008, chap. 5, especially sec. 5.11) offers the most resourceful defense of replacing our system of punishment with a system of restitution against, among other things, the objection that it would provide insufficient deterrence. However, Boonin relies heavily on the idea that a violator owes restitution to third parties for encouraging others to violate. But what encourages others is not the violation itself but instead the fact that the violator isn't brought to justice. So, to apply Boonin's approach to our current discussion would amount to including as part of Flintstone's force negative effects resulting from changes in others' behavior resulting from Flintstone's not suffering a deterrent. But this would make even State Imposition compatible with Strong Libertarianism, since imposing a deterrent on Violet protects us from Violet's force in the same sense: from negative effects resulting from changes in others' behavior resulting from Violet's not suffering a deterrent.

4. Last Attempts

1. The difference, it might be replied, is that when I move my foot from here to there, you are not "taking orders from" or "being bossed around" by me, as an inferior by a superior. The duty is "not deliberately imposed by one human being on another with the aim of subjecting another to a duty" (Raz 1990a, 16). If so, then this would be a step in the direction of an explanation in terms of claims against inferiority.

2. Raz (1994) suggests that a claim to the "right to impose obligations on . . . subjects" is constitutive of a legal system. I find this far from obvious (compare Murphy 2014, 86, 115–116). It may be constitutive of the state that it claims, or presupposes, a permission to issue and enforce directives (which may suffice for Raz's jurisprudential purposes). Similarly, Williams (2005, 6) suggests that it is not the state's coercion, but rather its claim that the coerced ought to comply, that triggers what he calls the "basic legitimation demand."

3. We might also include commandeerings of private property; dispositions of public property, such as public land, buildings, and equipment; or, more abstractly, things done with "our flag" or in "our name."

5. Relations of Inferiority

1. Specifically, relational egalitarianism is often presented as a rival to luck egalitarianism. Briefly put, luck egalitarianism is the Theory of Cosmic Fairness—that it is unfair for Altra to be worse off than Indy for reasons that are not due to their choices—with the luckist addendum that it is not cosmically unfair for Altra to be worse off than Indy for reasons that are due to their choices: that is, for reasons that are due solely to "option luck." To be sure, I reject the two main tenets of luck egalitarianism. In Section 21.1, I reject the Theory of Cosmic Unfairness. And in Section 1.5, I reject the luckist addendum that no one can complain of what results from option luck. That said, it is no part of my positive conjecture that this conjecture must somehow be a competitor to luck egalitarianism (compare Tomlin 2015; Lippert-Rasmussen 2018).

2. I labor to find in Anderson's work, suggestive though it is, any stable, explicit analysis of what social inequality (or whatever it is that relational egalitarians by definition oppose) comes to. Whereas I have sought to distinguish relations of inferiority from deprivations of improvements and invasions, Anderson doesn't distinguish social inequality from other, more familiarly theorized, ills. First, she identifies social inequality (perhaps following Young [1990]) with "oppression" (Anderson 1999, 289), "exploitation," "marginalization," and the infliction of "violence upon others" (313). But these evils aren't necessary for relations of inferiority. In the Half-Warm Society of Section 13.1, for example, no one is visited by exploitation or unjustified violence. And in Hierarcadia of Section 7.3, no one is marginalized, if "marginalized" means "pushed onto the margins" or "lacking a

recognized place in society" (compare Young 1990, 53–55). Nor are these evils sufficient for relations of inferiority. "Unjustified violence," for example, is possible, and objectionable, even among people who do not share a society or when inflicted by an inferior on a superior. And even where these evils are implicated in relations of inferiority, there are distinct improvement and invasion complaints against them. To be sure, there are improvement and invasion complaints against unjustified violence. Second, Anderson suggests that the objection to social inequality is to hierarchies based on judgments of superior "intrinsic worth"; "natural" or unchosen distinctions, such as "family membership, inherited social status, race, ethnicity, gender, or genes"; and a denial that "all competent adults are equally moral agents" (1999, 312). While these may be sufficient for relations of inferiority—insofar as they involve an unmerited disparity of regard—none is necessary. Indeed, even Anderson's primary target—the sort of social inequality that might result from implementing luck egalitarianism—needn't, in all forms, make judgments of "intrinsic" worth or appeal to "natural" statuses. Finally, Anderson cites "domination" as a component of social inequality, which she seems to understand in something like Pettit's terms ("they do not live at the mercy of others' wills," 315). But, as I discuss in Chapter 23, this confuses the object of analysis.

3. Compare G. Cohen's (2013, 200) discussion of the cynical scout.

4. This is not to deny that one may stand in a relation of inferiority to each of several individuals in virtue of the asymmetric power and authority they each enjoy in virtue of their membership in a collective, as when a family collectively "owns" a slave.

5. Contrast the republican idea, discussed in Chapter 23, that natural persons have an objection to being exposed to alien wills. Since that idea doesn't concern equal standing, it needn't be symmetrical. I can have an objection to being exposed to the alien will of the state without the state having an objection to being exposed to me or any other objections on its own behalf. I owe a special debt to Adam Lovett for clarifying discussion of these points.

6. This implies that Hyman's power over Loman need not be "social power" in the sense defined by Abizadeh (forthcoming), as power that effects outcomes either despite the resistance of or with the assistance of others. In another sense of "social," the power is social, however, insofar as the outcome effected by Hyman's power is something that happens to another person, Loman.

7. This is another illustration of how Hyman's power over Loman need not be a power to overcome Loman's resistance. When Loman obeys Hyman out of habit, Hyman has authority over Loman, and so power over Loman, but possibly no power to overcome Loman's resistance, should Loman choose not to act out of habit.

8. For a case involving authority rather than power, suppose my neighbor, Stentor, is the only person whose voice carries sufficiently to solve certain coordination problems. Stentor has greater de facto authority over me than I have over him.

9. I am indebted to unpublished work by Jake Zuehl.

10. Compare Ridgeway (2019, 28, 48), who gives a fascinating analysis of the intricate dynamics of status-based deference, in which a key role is played by the reactions of, in my terms, a fourth-party observer, Quatro, of Miro's greater deference to Hyman than to Loman.

11. I sense something of this tendency, to reduce hierarchies to disparities of regard, in Viehoff (2019), Motchoulski (2021), and Van Wietmarschen (2021). In particular, Van Wietmarschen suggests that social hierarchy is a matter, if not of regard, then of valuing persons. However, I worry that this leaves out hierarchies constituted by asymmetries of power and manages to count hierarchies constituted by asymmetries of authority only by stretching the meaning of "valuing a person" in a way that makes the claim to unity and simplicity superficial.

12. Against this, Viehoff (2019, 12) writes: "When we think, for instance, of the sense in which the servant is 'below' the lord of the manor, we do *not* just mean that, *within their particular relationship,* the servant is subordinate." But the very appropriateness of the word "subordinate" indicates that there is a sense in which the servant is "below" the lord in virtue of being, well, that lord's servant.

13. Bell and Wang (2020) press similar questions.

14. Thus becoming what the Random Acts of Kindness Foundation calls a "Raktivist."

15. Paradoxically, perhaps, the better off Hyman leaves Loman relative to Loman's other options, the greater the costs of exit and so the less escapable the asymmetry.

16. So this is not a form of what Lippert-Rasmussen (2018, 7) calls "luck relational egalitarianism."

17. Letting hiring decisions be influenced by discriminatory "reaction qualifications," for example, or using gender to predict traits, such as aptitude for military education, that are correlated with gender only because of prior gender discrimination, may be, if not participating in, then acquiescing in, such a disparity of consideration.

6. Disparities of Regard

1. "An unequal society will have strong conventions of deference to and perhaps flattery of superiors, which presumably do not deceive the well placed into thinking their subordinates admire them, except with the aid of self-deception" (Nagel 2002, 10).

2. For this reason, I find Runciman's "maxim" of social equality, "free inequality of praise, no inequality of respect" (1967, 221), too hasty.

3. It is also worth keeping in mind that two comparative appraisals of qualities or achievements can differ without either being mistaken. There can be indeterminacies and matters of taste.

4. The use of phrases such as "violations of respect" (Fourie 2015, 93) to describe Loman's objection tends to obscure this distinction.

5. An Oxfordian, for whom I had held the door rather too long, in his opinion, once chastised me for being "exceedingly civil."

6. For a fuller account of social norms, see Brennan et al. (2016). I resist Van Wietmarschen's (2021) suggestion that social hierarchies, at least in the sense that interests us, consist in social expectations. If certain asymmetries in power and authority, or certain disparities of regard, are objectionable, they are objectionable whether they are sustained by social expectations or some other mechanism, such as brute force.

7. In Chapter 20, I discuss another subspecies of a disparity of consideration, which results from condemning choices with which members of a group are identified.

8. I'm indebted here to discussion with Tony Rook.

9. The distinction between consideration of persons and esteem for particular qualities and achievements is indebted to Runciman's (1967) distinction between "respect" and "praise." Runciman forthrightly avoids a positive definition of inequalities in respect, proposing instead to understand them as inequalities in "status" that cannot be interpreted as inequalities in praise. However, I suspect that a more positive characterization of "respect," or, in my terms, consideration for persons, may be needed to maintain the distinction between an unobjectionable disparity of praise, or esteem, for a particular quality or achievement and an objectionable disparity of respect, or consideration, for a particular basing trait. Runciman also suggests, mistakenly in my view, that praise, but not respect, is necessarily positional, so that, in all contexts, to praise a second person is to diminish the praise given to the first person. It is true that praise requires a comparison, but the comparison could be to a possible quality or achievement, rather than to the actual quality or achievement of another person. If the whole class excels and everyone earns an A, then I might praise all of them for that remarkable achievement.

This distinction between consideration of persons and esteem for particular qualities and achievements is likewise indebted to Darwall's (1977) distinction between recognition respect and appraisal respect for a person. Consideration, like recognition respect, bears on practical deliberation in a way appraisal respect need not, and the appropriateness of consideration, like recognition respect, rarely depends on variable traits, whereas the appropriateness of esteem, like appraisal respect, does. However, the distinctions differ in other ways. For one thing, recognition respect involves sincerity in a way consideration does not (40–41). For another, appraisal respect is only for dispositions to act on reasons, or for what depends on such dispositions, whereas there can be esteem for qualities and achievement that are not, or do not depend on, dispositions to act on reasons.

7. Reductive Gambits

1. There is certainly some affinity between claims to social bases of self-respect and claims against inferiority. The affinity is strongest where Rawls suggests that the social bases of self-respect are (at least partly) secured by equal public standing. The affinity seems weaker, though, elsewhere. Rawls includes among the social bases of self-respect having one's talents appreciated (1971, sec. 67), which, as we saw in Chapter 6, is compatible with a disparity of consideration. And Rawls includes not being sacrificed for the benefit of others already better off (sec. 29), against which there is already an improvement complaint: namely, a complaint against having one's interests unfairly traded off against the interests of others.

2. As Baldwin (1963, 88) writes: "There are too many things we do not wish to know about ourselves. People are not, for example, terribly anxious to be equal (equal, after all, to what and to whom?) but they love the idea of being superior. And this human truth has an especially grinding force here [in America], where identity is almost impossible to achieve and people are perpetually attempting to find their feet on the shifting sands of status."

8. The State and the Secondary Tempering Factors

1. As Raz writes, "There is a problem in submitting to the rule even of an enlightened benevolent other. . . . It is not the problem of abdicating one's responsibility for one's actions, of forgoing one's autonomy. It is a problem of the relations between one person and another. We have views of what interpersonal relations are morally acceptable. One-sided submission to the will of an authority seems to violate these precepts" (1990a, 16).

2. In this respect, the title I gave to two of the articles from which this book derives, "Rule over None," was misleading. If, by some "ruling over others," we mean that some people but not others will make certain decisions, including decisions about how people are to behave, that the others (and perhaps the decision maker themselves) will then follow, whether from duty or coercion or habit or custom or acceptance of salient coordination points or whatever, then some will "rule over others" even in the most direct democracy conceivable. Even if all laws are made by plebiscite, still the application of those laws by officers of the peace, say, will involve some "ruling over others." The open question is whether ruling in this sense—some making decisions for others (as well, perhaps, as for themselves)—no matter what other conditions are satisfied, suffices to make the relationship between the ruler and others an objectionably hierarchical relationship.

3. Why not say that there is just one simple tempering factor? There is no objection to asymmetric power and authority just when they are "justified." If "*X* is justified" just means "*X* is such that there is no objection to it," then this is an unhelpful tautology. Presumably the idea is that the presence of a justification of a

certain kind relevantly changes the asymmetric power and authority so that those relations no longer have the same objectionable character. But this leaves us with several questions. First, what kind of justification? The fact that your being under my power and authority might serve the needs of my children is a justification. It appeals to genuine reasons—namely, agent-relative reasons that I, but not you, have to serve the needs of my children—and it shows how these reasons would be served by what is to be justified—namely, your being under my power and authority. But presumably this isn't a justification of the right kind. Second, why does a justification of the right kind, whatever it is, change the asymmetric power and authority in such a way as to make them less objectionable, as opposed to providing reasons that might outweigh the objection? Note that Impersonal Justification gives answers to both these questions. Finally, why can't there be other tempering factors that change the character of asymmetric power and authority in ways that don't depend on how the power and authority are justified?

4. It might seem odd to count Equal Citizenship as a secondary factor since it realizes the primary factor of Egalitarian Relationship. Still, it is called for to address relations of inferiority that are not tempered through an independently obtaining primary tempering factor. Equal Citizenship is called for because Egalitarian Relationship does not otherwise obtain.

5. Likewise, it seems implausibly broad to suggest there is an objection against exposure to alien power since we are inevitably exposed to alien power. See the discussion of republicanism in Chapter 23.

6. I assume here that there is not an intermediate objection—to being subject to superior de facto authority, whether or not that of another natural individual—on the grounds that concerns about superiority are concerns about relations among natural individuals. See Section 5.1.

7. Young (1990, chap. 4) criticizes the "distinction between public, impersonal roles in which the ideal of impartiality and formal reason applies, on the one hand, and private, personal relations which have a different moral structure" (97). One criticism is that justification by impersonal reasons is insensitive to particularities of interest, projects, and relationships. This criticism does not touch the present understanding of justification by impersonal reasons. Your particular interests, projects, and relationships are still there when they are thought of as someone's rather than yours. Another criticism is that it "helps to justify hierarchical decisionmaking structures" (97). This criticism does apply to the present understanding of justification by impersonal reasons. But I don't see it as a criticism.

8. I find myself tempted to add, "giving equal weight to everyone's interests." But this addition is empty. So long as I give proper weight to everyone's interests qua someone's and do not give weight to personal reasons, then I will give, as a kind of by-product, equal weight to everyone's interests.

9. Compare Raz (1990a, 8). This view may be broader than Raz's (2019) view that the proper purposes of government are the interests of the governed. Raz

qualifies that this should be understood broadly to include "their moral interests" (7). But if, by "moral interests," Raz means interests in fulfilling their duties, then this will still be narrower since not all government actions that promote impersonal values are actions that help subjects fulfill their duty to promote impersonal values. It is also worth noting that Raz does not explain why anyone has any objection to government action that does not serve the interests of the governed. At one point he seems to suggest that it is a constitutive truth about "the very nature of government" (7). But it's not clear why such a constitutive truth should ground a complaint. Why should anyone have a complaint about the mere fact that what would otherwise count as a government acts in a way that precludes it from counting as a government?

10. Ripstein seems to suggest that the difference between acting for public purposes and acting, corruptly, for private purposes can be shown to depend only on external conduct, not on attitudes (2009, 193–194). For the reasons given in Section 11.4, I doubt this can be done. I agree, though, that "alienated" officials, who "do not care about the law or justice, but only about doing their jobs and collecting their pay," need not violate the Duty to Exclude. For the explanation, see Section 12.2. For some other contrasts with Ripstein's framework, see Section 23.1.

11. I was helped in thinking through this by some unpublished work by Kathryn Joyce.

12. There is an emerging literature on a person's right to an explanation of decisions that affect them, which is partly prompted by the growth of automated decision-making. Tellingly, these discussions tend to assume that the right is held not against all decision makers (such as the romantic interest who declines the offer of a date) but instead only against those who wield superior power and authority, especially within an institutional hierarchy (Vredenburgh 2021; Lazar unpublished manuscript).

13. Avoiding disparities of regard may also require that Hyman is held accountable for his actions by those affected by them. If Loman is held accountable for his actions by those who are affected by them, then there will be a disparity of regard if Hyman is not also held accountable for his actions by those who are affected by them.

14. For Rawls, this equal status matters, in turn, because it supports the social bases of self-respect, which matters, in turn, because the social bases of self-respect are important means to pursuing one's life plan. See Section 7.2.

9. The State and the Firm

1. Note that this point undercuts a common fallback from the firm-state parallel-case argument, which might be called the "firm-municipality parallel-case argument." While it is granted that the firm differs from the national state, this fallback argument maintains that the firm nevertheless does not differ from a

municipality. Thus, so long as democracy is required at the level of the municipality, it is likewise required of the firm. While the worker may be able to exit the firm in a way the worker cannot exit the (national) state, it is said, the worker is similarly able to exit the municipality (Dahl 1985, 114). Or while the firm differs from the state in being regulated by it and subject to it as a higher court of appeal, it is said, the municipality likewise differs from the state in being regulated by it and subject to it as a higher court of appeal (González-Ricoy 2019, 681). But if the objection to the state is to its enforcement, then the firm-municipality parallel-case argument may fare no better than the firm-state parallel-case argument. For, arguably, municipalities, such as have local police departments, courts, and criminal statutes, are involved in enforcement. So perhaps one should no more expect that what goes for the municipality should go for the firm than one should expect that what goes for the state should go for the firm.

2. It is illuminating here to revisit G. Cohen's definition of slave, serf, and proletarian as "subordinate producers." Cohen recognizes that it is not sufficient for one's being a proletarian, or presumably having the complaints typical of being a proletarian, that one owns all of one's labor but none of the means of production (1978, 69). That might be true of a well-paid, intuitively nonproletarian, self-employed architect who rents the necessary equipment for each project. A further necessary condition is that one is a "subordinate" with a "superior." Cohen takes this to mean that (i) one produces for others who do not produce for one; (ii) "within the production process [one is] commonly subject to the authority of the superior, who is not subject to [one's] authority"; and (iii) one "tends to be poorer than" the superior. But what bears most or all of the weight of the term "subordinate" is, as this account emphasizes, (ii) the subjection to authority within the production process. After all, regarding (i), teachers produce lessons for pupils who do not produce for them without being their subordinates. (And as Cohen writes: "To the extent that there is reciprocity [i.e., that (i) does not hold], there is some justice in the subordination, but not a lack of subordination," 70.) And, regarding (iii), a poorer person of a past century need not be subordinate to a richer person of this century (although the poorer person might have improvement complaints if their poverty was the result of excessive saving whose fruits were enjoyed by the people of this century).

3. For independent reasons, one might doubt that everything that is required of the state should be required of the firm within the state. States are required to respect the civil liberties of their citizens. But firms are not, plausibly, required to respect the same civil liberties of their employees, in the sense of not disciplining them for exercising those same civil liberties at work. So, it is not clear that it is a valid complaint against the firm, as Anderson appears to assume it is, that firms "impose controls on workers that are unconstitutional for democratic states to impose on citizens who are not convicts or in the military" (2017, 63). The most obvious example is free choice of occupation itself. I shouldn't lose US citizenship

if I choose to be a dog walker rather than a mouse impersonator, but surely Chuck E. Cheese's can exile me for that choice. But there are other examples. Consider Tsuruda's insight that "it would seem to violate the freedom of speech for the state to ban all discriminatory speech, yet prohibiting a wide range of discriminatory speech in the paid workplace is surely a requirement of justice" (2020, 334n98).

4. Even where production is separable, however, evaluating and incentivizing productivity may be better done by a boss, Williamson observes, simply because it is easier to evaluate and incentivize productivity on the job than at the hiring stage itself (Williamson 1973, 322).

5. Alchian and Demsetz argue that this is not a hierarchical arrangement, as opposed to a continual renegotiation of labor contracts within a market. But it is hard to see how, in practice, a hierarchical arrangement would be avoided, as Anderson (2017, 55) observes. (Her subsequent criticism that Alchian and Demsetz somehow overlook the theory of the firm [56], though, seems unfair. It would seem they are simply offering a theory of firm different from Coase's.)

11. Claims against Corruption: The Negative Observation

1. While the primary wrongdoer is the corrupt official, others, such as bribers, can also commit related wrongs. For example, offering bribes may abet the official in acting corruptly or gain unfair advantage over others.

2. Compare Raz's (2019) parable of Rex, who orders "the purchase of a very expensive diamond ring for his lover." As Raz observes, "he cannot be said to have acted arbitrarily, that is, in indifference to reason," since his reason "is a good reason between lovers" (6–7).

Another way to bring out the contrast, nicely suggested to me by Daniel Viehoff, is to note that the sort of personal reasons that make it permissible for a civilian not to seek or to refuse to accept or relinquish an office (e.g., your child would not get piano lessons) don't make it permissible for the same person, once in the office, to make official decisions that disserve the public interest (e.g., diverting school resources from higher priorities so that your child gets piano lessons).

3. For this reason, Murphy's (2014, 138) mostly "instrumental" account of the duty of officials to obey the law seems to me at best incomplete. He is surely right that when one finds oneself behind the wheel of an office, disobedience has graver consequences for the public interest than most private actions. But this leaves unexplained the further fact that in official decisions, private interests have no, or little, weight against the public interest, whereas in private decisions, private interests do have weight against the public interest.

4. Nagel (1979, 80) suggests this although later observes that it "fails to explain why the *content* of public obligations differs systematically from that of private ones," and, in particular, in virtue of "a stricter requirement of impartiality" (82).

5. Sharing "insider" information about how one is likely to exercise an office might be another use of an office that is not an exercise of it.

6. So, the Duty to Exclude is, in effect, a source of exclusionary reasons in addition to those Raz (1990b) lists.

12. Claims against Corruption: The Positive Conjecture

1. The Duty to Exclude applies only to offices that Offe presently occupies. So, candidate Candi does not violate the Duty to Exclude to run for office from personal ambition, even if Candi knows there are already equally qualified candidates in the race.

2. This justification of lotteries is a special case of what Stone (2011) calls the "sanitizing" function of lotteries.

3. The applicable federal laws in the United States governing bribery reflect at least two different dimensions of "quid-pro-quo-ness": how specific the official act and how definite the agreement to perform it. A conviction is less likely if the official only vaguely agrees to help the briber when she can, or agrees only to give some, perhaps not dispositive, weight to the favor in deciding whether to perform the act (Lowenstein 2004).

4. Compare Raz (1977, 220): "Since it is universally believed that it is wrong to use public powers for private ends any such use is in itself an instance of arbitrary use of power."

5. Perhaps it is even possible for officials not merely to exclude reasons but also to treat certain considerations as positive reasons, to give them weight in favor of the decision, from motives other than appreciation of the force of those reasons. The disaffected official might be like the psychopath who doesn't sincerely feel the force of moral reasons but knows how to mimic the decision, in any given case, that would be reached by someone who did feel their force and who mimics the decision from motives of prudence or the mere force of routine.

6. Likewise, Boss would wrong Employee by announcing without conditioning. In "Akratic Car Wash," Boss can't control himself. He hasn't said anything to Employee. But if Employee were somehow to volunteer to wash his car, the flush of power would lead Boss to stop the firing. Realizing this about himself, Boss tells Employee about it.

7. Note that while Bell and Wang (2020) are skeptical of democracy, at least for contemporary China, at least when understood as "competitive elections at the top," they appear to take it as given that rulers should not be partial or corrupt (78, 81–84).

13. Claims against Discrimination

1. If this occurred in competitive contexts, then the pattern of differential treatment would worsen the opportunities of the left-handed in absolute terms.

But let us suppose it does not occur in competitive contexts, only in noncompetitive contexts. For more on competition, see Chapter 17.

2. Compare Lippert-Rasmussen (2014) on "social salience."

14. Claims to Equal Treatment

1. In Westen (1982), one finds suggestions of this kind. But it is somewhat unclear because Westen at times seems to recognize "comparative rights," which would support equal treatment complaints.

2. Nagel (1979, 84) writes: "There is no comparable right of self-indulgence or favoritism for public officials or institutions vis-à-vis the individuals with whom they deal. Perhaps the most significant action-centered feature of public morality is a special requirement to treat people in the relevant population equally. Public policies and actions have to be more impartial than private ones, since they usually employ a monopoly of certain kinds of power and since there is no reason in their case to leave room for the personal attachments and inclinations that shape individual lives." Granted, insofar as the person who occupies an office has a personal life outside of that office, they cannot complain that they have no outlet for their partiality. But this doesn't explain why others have objections if they are partial in their offices. Or suppose they are "married" to their office and so have no such outlet. Why the "monopoly of certain kinds of power" should imply equal treatment is also mysterious, unless the thought is, along the lines we propose, that superior power must be constrained by Least Discretion and so by Equal Treatment by Officials.

3. For doubts about Scanlon's explanation of this pattern, see Kolodny (2019).

4. Other such special relationships might be said to be those between trade unions or musketeer trios, organized around a common struggle or danger. Members should refuse to favor themselves, even when this would not come at other members' expense. The phenomenon in these cases, however, seems to me different from equal treatment. It is a matter of "solidarity," as I discuss in Section 21.2.

5. The ideas of treating like cases alike and treating like people alike are often run together (Hart 1992, 160–162; Westen 1982). However, as I note in the text, they are quite different ideas, with different bases.

15. Claims to the Rule of Law

1. Bingham (2010, chap. 4) uses a violation of Equal Treatment to illustrate the violation of the element of the rule of law that he calls "law not discretion." This suggests implicit agreement that Equal Treatment is explained by Least Discretion.

2. In a recent revision of his earlier account of the rule of law, Raz (2019, 8) suggests, roughly, that the core of the rule of law consists in government acting "with the manifest intention to serve the interests of the governed." As I noted in Section 8.4, this is very close to what I call Impersonal Justification.

16. Claims to Equal Liberty

1. This is compatible with the fact that the concern for the social bases of self-respect plays a role in justifying the principles that regulate the distribution of other goods. The parties choose the principles they do in part because of how they support the social bases of self-respect.

2. And as G. Cohen (2008) stresses, "only insofar as it benefits," as opposed to "so long as it does not disbenefit," itself expresses a comparative, egalitarian idea. The former idea, but not the latter, prohibits inequality-increasing weak Pareto improvements, in which the better off are made better off but the worse off remain as they were. I return to this point in Section 21.2.

3. Rawls's first argument for the priority of liberty is that at a sufficiently advanced stage of development, first, certain pursuits are simply more important than other pursuits and, second, any increase in liberty, no matter how small, is always a better means to those privileged pursuits than any increase in money, no matter how great. In special cases, this may be true. Perhaps, within many religious traditions, simple prayer—which requires only the forbearance of others—takes priority over temple construction—which requires money. But, as many note, it hardly seems true in general.

Rawls's second argument is not so much for the priority of liberty as for the priority of, specifically, equal liberty. If people have equal liberty, and if equal liberty takes priority over the distribution of other goods, then people enjoy a kind of equal status. As I noted in Section 8.9, I am very sympathetic to the structure of the argument.

4. G. Cohen (2011, 188–189) suggests two other possible differences between "state" and "business" provision of freedom. One is that the businesses, but not the state, are distributing scarce goods. But police protection is also in limited supply. Indeed, so too are many legal permissions; only so many can do the permitted act before the cost becomes prohibitive. The other possible difference is that the "prohibition" of an act can be an "insult to" or "diminution of" "status" in a way the refusal to give a gift or accept an exchange on certain terms is not (191–192). I explore something like this in Section 20.3.

17. Claims to Equality of Opportunity

1. One way of reading Rawls (1999, 73)—"the reasons for requiring open positions are not solely, or even primarily, those of efficiency"—is simply as a reminder that workers' position complaints (and, as we will soon discuss, their selection complaints) must be given their due weight.

2. Although the terms "competition" and "competitive" often appear in discussions of equality of opportunity (e.g., Daniels 1978, 217; Arneson 1999, 77; 2013c, 316), these terms aren't defined, they aren't consistently applied, and their significance, if any, isn't explained.

3. Here I set aside the possibility that Arbeit might have complaints that Arbeit was led to expect the position would go to the best qualified or that Arbeit would find the job more rewarding than Boulot. The traits of Arbeit that make it the case that he would find the job more rewarding may overlap, to some degree, with the traits that make Arbeit more qualified for it. But they are not, in general, the same.

4. It is not clear how far Scanlon's concern is, or is exclusively, a concern about being "treated as an individual," as opposed to a member of a statistical class. If, in general, graduates of university A really do tend to be better prepared than graduates of university B, would it disregard the reason that Scanlon has in mind to use that as a "proxy"? The concern may be instead about whether the process seeks out factors that have some "rational" or "explicable" connection to qualifications. The fact people who like "curly fries" on Facebook score higher on IQ tests (Kosinski et al. 2013), even if no less statistical, might seem more problematic. What the problem is, however, is another question.

5. As Scanlon (2018) cautions us, the additional education might not mean White has greater college potential. Suppose the additional education means White can place out of some required first-semester courses. However, a study has shown that placing out of the first semester does not predict higher achievement at the end of four years. In that case, there is still a violation of Equal Potential, not in the additional high-school education but instead in the sensitivity of college admissions to it. And Blue has an improvement complaint about this. However, in the example in the text, we are supposing that, as a result of the additional high school education, White does in fact have greater potential and college admissions is simply registering this.

6. One might object: "But if White simply makes use of his opportunity when Blue does not, then White also reduces Blue's chances. Surely that isn't distributively unfair." The reply is contained in the objection. Blue doesn't have less opportunity; Blue just doesn't make use of it. This is related to the Compossibility Principle, discussed in Section 29.1.

19. Claims against Illiberal Interventions: The Negative Observation

1. Of course, "liberalism" connotes more. There is freedom of thought and expression, which, in ways both manifest and elusive, seems categorically different from freedom of action. (We protect public advocacy of crime, for example, in a way we do not countenance its conspiracy, attempt, facilitation, or commission.) There are rights to participate in democratic processes. And there are procedural safeguards, such as the right to a fair trial.

2. I assume that the strongest case in favor of such illiberal interventions, and so the case to be addressed, is that those interventions would improve choice situations and not, for instance, that they would reduce the incidence of actions that are somehow independently immoral.

3. Another candidate for such an intermediate formula is Rawls's (1971, 1993) "list of liberties" or his even more abstract specification of "the two moral powers of citizens." Neither takes us very far beyond our particular judgments. While Rawls identifies, and to some extent prioritizes, certain abstractly conceived valuable activities that illiberal interventions might impair, he doesn't provide much guidance beyond that on the question of which choices are "protected" from which sorts of "interventions."

4. And it protects even less if we replace "choices that don't (themselves, nonconsensually) harm others" with "choices such that intervening in them does not protect others from harm."

5. Fees and taxes tend to differ from penalties and fines in that they (i) don't condemn the activity, (ii) are insensitive to the intent of the activity, (iii) do not increase abruptly when the activity crosses some threshold, and (iv) do not increase with repetition (Cooter 1984; Cooter and Siegel 2012).

6. These further libertarian commitments, however, have further implications for liberal protections if Force Requires Duty is assumed: that (absent consent) the Force Constraint is lifted only where a duty is, or would be, violated. Libertarians who hold that Pitt can, by voluntary choice, make it permissible for Norton to kill Pitt in gladiatorial combat or hold him in slavery will then hold that it is wrong to use force to prevent Norton from killing Pitt in gladiatorial combat or recovering him as a fugitive slave because Norton has no duty to act otherwise.

7. Some philosophers who accept all these claims sometimes suggest they are related in a different way: not that the prohibition on illiberal interventions follows from the right against what one cannot accept but instead that the case for the right against what one cannot accept depends on prior acceptance of the prohibition on illiberal interventions. Views of this kind are not to our present purpose, since they assume, rather than explain, what we are trying to explain. For example, Freeman (2007, 218–219) suggests that a violation of the right against what one cannot accept is wrong because it "borders on a violation of liberty of conscience" (compare Tadros 2016, 137). Similarly, Quong (2011, 291) suggests that one counts as "reasonable" only if one is committed to certain liberal ideas, which include, or at least independently justify, a prohibition on illiberal interventions (183). But then to motivate the right against what one cannot reasonably accept, it seems, we must first independently motivate these liberal ideas. For why insist that the problematic treatment must accepted by "reasonable" people, understood as people who accept those liberal ideas, unless there is some prior case to be made for those liberal ideas?

8. As mentioned in the previous endnote, Quong (2011, 185) understands "unreasonable" in a third way as simply not accepting specific liberal ideas. A utilitarian might be "unreasonable" in this sense without being epistemically or morally unreasonable. It is less clear, though, why being "unreasonable" in this third sense should similarly limit what one can ask of others.

9. See Quong's Puritans in Section 20.3. It seems implausibly constraining to require grounds compatible with any reasonable commitments that someone might hold (J. Cohen 2009, 234).

10. Gaus seems to take this to imply that "coercing" Prudie is impermissible unless it is "publicly justified" (2003; 2009, 89; 2011, sec. 17.3) (though he acknowledges at times a "blameless liberty" to coerce even without public justification [2011, sec. 22.3.b; 2014]). It's obscure why this is since one can "coerce" Prudie without presupposing that she has a duty to do otherwise. Gaus must be assuming, first, that Prudie's coercer presupposes something like Force Requires Duty, namely that coercing Prudie to do something is permissible only if Prudie has a duty to do otherwise, and, second, that Prudie's coercer presupposes that their own coercion of Prudie is permissible.

11. One might, I suppose, suggest that reasonable acceptability is a vertical tempering factor on asymmetries of power and authority. Indeed, something like this is at times casually suggested. For example, "one person cannot rightly wield power over another unless they can justify the exercise of that power to the person over whom it is exercised" (Quong 2011, 2). Perhaps the idea would be that the asymmetric power and authority are not that of a superior because they are in fact one's own power and authority, insofar as they are justified only by reasons one could reasonably accept. This would be structurally similar to the suggestion of Section 8.3 that what would otherwise be alien authority is not if it only commands one to do what serves one's own reasons.

20. Claims against Illiberal Interventions: The Positive Conjecture

1. Raz (2001) suggests that paternalistic coercion assigns the coerced second-class status. This in turn undermines trust, without which, he argues, paternalistic coercion is subject to objection (see Section 3.6). In effect, I follow Raz but propose cutting out the middleman. Assigning second-class status, it would seem, is objectionable in itself. We needn't go on to argue that it vitiates the defense against a different objection: namely, paternalistic coercion without trust. Moreover, I suggest, what assigns second-class status is not coercion, which I have argued is anyway elusive, but condemning choices with which some are identified. Compare Wall and Klosko (2003); Wall (2005); Christiano (2006); Nussbaum (2011); and, especially, Eisgruber and Sager (2007).

21. Being No Worse Off

1. A similar problem arises for the later G. Cohen's (2011, 133) treatment of unequal outcomes that result from voluntary gambles. On the one hand, departing from the "luckist" line of his earlier work, he suggests that such an unequal outcome is an unjust outcome and so presumably an outcome that is unjust to the loser of the gamble. On the other hand, he wants to say that it is an unequal

outcome about which no one can complain because the loser, who otherwise would have had a complaint, waived their complaint by choosing to gamble. Again, it is hard to see what it means to say that the outcome is unjust to the loser if not that the loser has some complaint about it (and a complaint that others don't similarly have).

2. Temkin seems to respond (1993, 21n3) by suggesting that what it means to say it is unfair to Altra is not that she has a complaint, in particular, but instead that it is bad for her, in particular. However, the idea that it is bad for her, in particular, is hard to square with the view, which Temkin also seems to hold, that inequality-increasing weak Pareto improvements are so much as possible: that improving Indy's situation over Altra's need not be worse for Altra (12). For, if it is bad for Altra for Indy to be better off than Altra, then improving Indy's situation over Altra's makes Altra worse off.

3. Indeed, there are suggestions of this in Rawls's discussions of how the difference principle embodies "fraternity" (1971, 90–91). "Reciprocity" in Rawls, however, seems a different idea: "to respond in kind to what others do for (or to) us" (2001, 127). For illuminating discussion, to which this section is greatly indebted, see Munoz-Dardé (2018).

4. This is to be distinguished from two other conceptions of community in G. Cohen's work: "justificatory community," which consists in being able to "comprehensively" justify social arrangements to others (2008, chap. 1), and a conception of "community" that is constituted by the valuing of doing for others and their doing for you, as opposed to simply wanting, strategically, to extract from them certain goods and services (2009, 39).

5. There might, however, be an instrumental worry about specifically economic heterogeneity. If the needs of the less affluent are to be met, then the more affluent must be motivated to do things for the less affluent (or at very least be motivated to refrain from doing things to the less affluent). Insofar as the affluent are insulated from the experience of the deprivations of the poor, they may be less motivated (Satz 2017, 18).

22. Relations of Equality

1. Wolff (2015, 2019) and Sangiovanni (2017) similarly emphasize the bad of treating as an inferior, rather than the good of equality.

2. However, elsewhere Viehoff (2017, 293) seems to suggest that equal power can be ("nonderivatively") justified only on the grounds that it avoids the "distinctive bad" of unequal power, not on the grounds that it is a positive good constituted by our having equal power.

3. As it happens, Viehoff sees this as a counterexample to my view that untempered asymmetries of power and authority present a problem in general. But, for the reasons given in the text, it seems to me to support that view.

23. Nondomination

1. Pettit would presumably resist using the Choice Principle to define interference in choice since he favors an "entirely unmoralized" (1997, 54) notion of interference. I worry, among other things, that this will leave Pettit without any principled or defensible distinction between "offers," "bribes," and "rewards," on the one hand, which don't interfere because they don't make an option worse (1997, 52; 2012, 52; 2014, 35), and "threats," on the other hand, which do interfere because they do make an option worse. But "worse" relative to what? To the actual status quo? To "default expectations" (2012, 73)? Does this mean that while Powers's continued withholding of assistance that only Powers can provide, as Vic's requests become more and more desperate and abasing, cannot count as actual interference and so not as domination, continued assistance that might be subsequently withdrawn, which would count as interference, does count as domination (2012, 73; 2014, 48)? In any event, if we change the case so that Boss is offering to rescind Employee's firing, then, even relative to the actual status quo and default expectations, this improves Employee's options and so does not, in an unmoralized sense, interfere.

2. Compare also Pettit's assertion, without explanation, that the "republican approach strongly supports expressive egalitarianism" (2014, 80).

3. Ripstein (2009, 173), however, does not make (or does not read Kant as making) this argument for the necessity of the state. Once we have set aside issues of coordination and assurance, he seems to suggest, the only remaining problem concerns the acquisition of property: namely, that in a state of nature, acquisition amounts to one person unilaterally putting others under enforceable obligations. In fact, one wonders whether, despite Ripstein's invocations of the kindly slave master and the republican tradition, he needs to understand dependence in such a way that dependence is implied by the mere possibility of relevant kinds of treatment by a unilateral will. Ripstein's arguments might not change much if he held that one is dependent only insofar as one is actually treated by a unilateral will in those ways.

4. Although Pettit's account of nonarbitrariness is "substantive," requiring being forced to a certain end, the arguments in the text apply as well to a "procedural" account, such as Lovett's, which requires simply being forced, to whatever end.

5. A further difficulty is that both of Pettit's definitions of "arbitrary" make even the most appropriate direction of some people over others in, say, the workplace count as arbitrary. Suppose we say a will is arbitrary with respect to someone insofar as it is a will that is not forced to track that person's interests and ideas. In general, workplace directives don't track the interests of the worker. If they track interests, they are those of the client or firm. The package needs to be delivered, the report needs to be filed, the patient needs a new IV, and so forth. If the question is what is in the interests of the worker, the answer presumably would be not to have to work at all. As his bumper sticker tells us, he'd rather be fishing. So even the most appropriate direction by bosses of workers counts as arbitrary

(Anderson 2019, 200). Suppose instead we say that a will is "arbitrary" with respect to someone insofar as it is a will they do not control. Again, even the most appropriate direction by bosses of workers counts as arbitrary, unless there is workplace democracy parallel to state democracy (and, as I go on to suggest, not even then).

6. At times, the literature may suggest the "Can Do With Impunity Test": if Powers were to encroach, Powers would not be punished. But why should Vic care whether Powers would be punished after the accomplished fact of Powers's encroachment if Vic's concern is being proof from encroachment? Of course, the fear of punishment may be why Powers won't will to exercise the power of encroachment that Powers nonetheless has, but domination concerns what Powers can't do, not what Powers won't do. Alternatively, Kantians may favor a "Can Permissibly Do Test": if Powers were to encroach, Powers would act impermissibly. But this seems to define away the possibility of domination. Even if Powers were to hold Vic in empirical slavery, Powers would still not dominate Vic. This is because it would continue to be the case that, if Powers encroached on Vic, Powers would act impermissibly.

7. The republican cannot say that the probability that a single alien will will change is higher than that plural alien wills will change. Probability isn't to the point, and in any event, the probabilities might be reversed.

8. Pettit and Lovett suggest this in reply to Simpson's claim that if the People can check the state, the People can also encroach on an individual, Vic. Pettit and Lovett argue that the People would come together to check the state if it misbehaved because they could count on others joining with them but that individual members of the People would not encroach, even if they all willed encroachment, because they would falsely believe they would not be supported.

9. It is worth revisiting a worry raised back in Section 8.7. There might be military officers, say, who could, if they had a mind to do so, ignore civilian control. However, these military officers are disposed to respect civilian control precisely because they respect Equal Influence. Equal Influence, I claimed, is still secured thereby. I imagine that a republican reading that might have thought it just isn't good enough: "Imagine that the Praetorian Prefect refrains from asserting his greater raw power over us, and grants us equal 'power' in decision-making, as a condescending gift, to bestow or withdraw at his pleasure. Surely that would invite the sort of complaint that you interpret as a complaint against 'relations of inferiority' and I interpret as a complaint against domination." But I have already explained why there would be a complaint in such a case. If the Prefect is granting us equal influence as a condescending gift, which is his to bestow or withdraw at his pleasure, then he is violating the Duty to Exclude.

24. Preliminaries

1. Or as Wollheim (1962, 83) and Barry and Øverland (2011, 113) imagine, they may be implementing a decision they only mistakenly think is the democratic one.

25. The Negative Observation: Correspondence

1. In the sense coined by Rawls (2001b) and anticipated in Rawls (1971, sec. 36) as the "forum of delegates" from which the executive "discerns the movements of public sentiment."

2. I interpret the "interest in being at home in the world" of Christiano (2010, 92, 226–227) as having a similar structure, as is strongly suggested by the claim that its satisfaction is what persistent minorities are deprived of.

3. Informally, Borda counts work as follows. Assuming three options, each option gets three points for each individual who ranks it first, two points for each who ranks it second, and one point for each who ranks it third. The options are then collectively ordered by their point total.

4. Indeed, at some points, Riker's reasoning seems to be that there are too many candidates, rather than too few (1982, 234).

26. The Negative Observation: Influence

1. The contrary proposition has its advocates, however. See Constant ([1819] 1988, 316); Dahl (1989, 204–205); and Rousseau ([1762] 1997, sec. 3.1), where Rousseau concludes "the larger the State, the less the liberty."

2. Shapiro (2012) suggests that democracies "give expression to, and create opportunities for the exercise of, the individual's autonomous capacities," where "autonomy" is understood as "the power to control one's life." My criticism here owes much to Christiano (1996, chap. 1).

3. It might be said that if one has less influence, then one will not have the same access. This is because people who aim to sway votes will have less incentive to provide one with access. This is questionable even as it stands, given the difficulty of restricting access to resources for political reflection to only those with influence. The disenfranchised, for example, can no more easily escape televised campaign advertisements during election season than registered voters. This argument thus raises no barrier to selective disenfranchisement, so long as the relevant resource providers cannot cheaply exclude the disenfranchised from the provision of resources to the enfranchised. In any event, even where this particular incentive is absent, the same access can still be provided to those with less influence through other channels. Nothing stands in the way of providing the same education and leisure time to those with no, or less weighty, votes.

4. A different reply, which stresses the more collective understanding of political activity, might be that unless opportunity for influence is distributed equally among us, we do not constitute a self-governing collective. But why? If a collective with an inegalitarian structure (e.g., orchestra, plural voting electorate) can decide and do other things, why can't it decide that it is to do things and then do them? What more is required for a collective to govern itself?

5. Estlund (2000) and Pevnick (2016) discuss another such trade-off. Restricting money in campaigns, in an effort to equalize influence, may impede the dissemination of information, which may thereby worsen the opportunity for informed influence of those with the least such opportunity. Perhaps. But, as Estlund grants, that's a significant "may." Increasing the throughput of accurate reports about, say, a certain official's use of a private email server might only distract people from more important things or engrave a vague impression of disqualifying misconduct.

6. R. Dworkin (2002, 201), for example, comes very close to suggesting it is a historical accident that we reject Mill's plural voting scheme.

27. The Positive Conjecture: Equal Influence

1. Consider Viehoff's (2019) example of a tribesman who happens to find himself with a fortuitous opportunity to negotiate a treaty with his tribe's neighbors and then returns to his own tribe with the treaty a fait accompli. Although all in the tribe now live under his unilateral decision, it does not seem as though they live under any objectionable relation of inferiority to him. Perhaps this is because the accidental ambassador is now just as powerless as any other tribesman to change the treaty. Our view of the case might be different if the other tribe refused to negotiate through anyone but him, making him the master of the tribe's foreign policy going forward. It is also worth noting that the accidental ambassador satisfies Equal Application. He is as much subject to the treaty as anyone else.

2. Although I use the phrase "representative democracy," I believe the language of "representation" encourages investigations that distract from or obscure what seem to me the central moral-philosophical questions. I have in mind investigations, which otherwise have much to teach us, of what the concept of representation is, as in Pitkin (1967) and Rehfeld (2006), or of how the concept of representation has been historically understood, as in Manin (1997).

What is a "representative" supposed to be? Is a "representative" simply a member of a legislative assembly? That seems the implicit paradigm in Pitkin (1967) and Manin (1997). But this seems too narrow. More or less the same questions of political morality concern officials within democratic institutions who are not members of legislative assemblies, such as the president of the United States.

Is a representative then an "elected official"? This might seem to be suggested by Manin's view that election is the distinguishing characteristic of the historical formation he calls "representative government." But this doesn't seem right either. For one thing, the pope is elected, but it isn't clear that he is a "representative" in the relevant sense (at least not of the College of Cardinals). For another thing, when Manin invites us to be puzzled about why, in the eighteenth century, election came to occupy the role once occupied by sortition in antiquity, he presupposes that there is some genus of official of which "representative" is just one species, a species distinguished by the differentia of "elected." After all, Manin is inviting us to be struck by the seeming arbitrariness of an exclusive focus on that particular species, to the neglect of the rest of the genus. Why, by the eighteenth century, had it come to seem as if that type of official, who in antiquity might have been chosen by lot, now had to be elected? But then it seems to me that that unstated genus is just that of what we call below "highest officials."

Is a "representative," as Rehfeld (2006) proposes, "someone in a role whose function is, in part, to 'stand in for' someone to a certain audience"? As an account of English usage, Rehfeld makes a persuasive case. However, as Rehfeld intends, this concept of "representative" has nothing in particular to do with democracy. It is both broader and narrower than what interests democratic theorists. It is broader since it includes sales agents and defense attorneys in nonpolitical contexts. But it is narrower since it does not include chief executives, who do not, in general, apart from foreign policy, stand in for anyone to a certain audience. Nor is it clear that members of legislative assemblies stand in for anyone to a certain audience. Perhaps members of legislative assemblies in a district system stand in for their districts to the audience of the other members. But can the same be said of members of legislative assemblies in party list systems? Note also that not everyone who is "authorized to act on someone's behalf," such as a doctor, is a representative, since what they are authorized to do may not involve standing in for someone to an audience.

3. There are two other reasons for favoring elections over sortition. First, elections provide all citizens with positive influence, whereas sortition provides positive influence only to those who are selected. Insofar as there is an argument, based in Equal Citizenship, for positive influence, this supports elections over sortition. Second, standing for reelection is itself a form of Downward Accountability that has no analogue in sortition. Not being reelected is a way of being held accountable. Simply not being selected by lot for another term is not.

4. For contemporary readers, some of the intuitive egalitarian appeal of sortition may be borrowed from the intuitive egalitarian appeal of citizens' assemblies or commissions. However, the egalitarian appeal of citizens' commissions—the idea, say, that they are more egalitarian than elected legislatures—may not derive solely, or even primarily, from the fact that their membership is randomly selected. It may instead derive from the fact that they, first, merely identify concerns, place items on the agenda, or shape proposals, with final decisions being made by referenda or elected officials. In that case, they might be viewed as formal structurings of the public sphere. Second, citizens' commissions are typically short lived, with their members soon stepping down from their offices. Finally, the commissions, like judges and central bankers, typically address only some specified question (see Guerrero [2014], who assumes that sortition would select members of commissions addressing some single issue).

Note that a proliferation of short-lived, single-issue citizens' commissions would have drawbacks, at least if they had the power to make final decisions. The centralization of decision-making power in highest officials facilitates Downward Accountability. If citizens are upset with the state of things, they can hold those higher officials—few in number and, especially where there are elections, well known—accountable. By contrast, if highest officials are replaced by myriad short-lived citizens' commissions, each with its own narrow remit, a given citizen may have little idea where the buck stops.

5. There is, of course, the further question of how to incentivize such behavior from highest officials. Here I merely offer two remarks, from the armchair, about the usual suggestion: that we incentivize highest officials by threatening not to reelect them. The first remark is that, if this were so, it would imply there is no incentive in a system of term limits or when an official prefers not to stand for election again. The second remark is that there may be significant selection pressures toward highest officials who will do what they gave others to believe they would do, even when this makes no difference to their chances of reelection. Highest officials who are less likely to advance the party platform even when it makes no difference to their chances of reelection, for example, may be less likely to ascend to party leadership. (Compare Mansbridge [2009] on a "selection model" of political representation.)

28. Pathologies of American Democracy

1. This part of the book was mostly written before Donald Trump's refusal to accept the results of the 2020 election and mobilization of an armed insurrection. All the ills I discuss, needless to say, pale in comparison to that.

2. The decision struck down the act's "coverage formula" for "preclearance," which specified that certain states and localities, due to histories of discrimination, needed prior federal approval for changes in voting rules.

3. "Nominal" policy, that is. Keeping "nominal" policy may well mean "real" changes. The purchasing power of the minimum wage may erode, or temporary tax cuts may expire.

4. A filibuster in effect requires sixty senators, out of a chamber of one hundred, to agree to end debate on most bills and some appointments. Use of, or anticipation of, filibusters has become much more common over the past few decades.

5. Arguably due to term limits, loss of control over committee assignments, and avenues for fundraising that bypass party leadership.

6. Note that the fact that policy is not responsive does not imply that policy does not depend on which party holds office or that elections don't matter. Even if the policies enacted by Democrats and Republicans are equally unresponsive to citizen preferences, they may still differ markedly. There's more than one way to ignore the People.

7. A view Gilens both encourages and discourages, sometimes in the same paragraph (2012, 3).

29. The Permissiveness of Formal Equality

1. This is in the spirit of Shapley and Shubik (1954). Forceful criticisms of the use of the Shapley-Shubik index for other purposes, such as Barry (1980), do not apply to the present, limited application of their basic idea. Compare also what Bartholdi et al. (2020) call "equity."

2. If the success that matters is one's vote both influencing and corresponding to the outcome, then one has a standing reason to change one's vote to be on the winning side. And one has reason to change one's vote to realize the right distribution of success. Both seem odd.

3. However, a concern for success would explain one thing that was left unexplained by the argument of Section 25.2: why it should matter that preferences cause policy. One is successful only when one's preferences are satisfied as the result of one's own influence.

30. Gerrymandering: A Case Study of Permissiveness

1. As quoted in the District Court Memorandum Opinion in *Rucho v. Common Cause*, No. 18-422, 588 US ___ (2019).

2. For example, Kennedy's concurring opinion in *Vieth v. Jubelirer*, 541 US 267 (2004) suggested that partisan gerrymandering violates freedom of speech since officials impose burdens on members of the disfavored party for their prior support of it. This argument presupposes that gerrymandering imposes special burdens on the disfavored party. This is why I don't consider this free speech objection independently in the text: namely, that it presupposes that gerrymandering imposes some special burden. As we will see, it's hard enough to identify what this special burden is. And once we have identified what it is, we have already identified an objection to gerrymandering.

3. It would thus be hard to explain the 1982 amendment to section 2 of the Voting Rights Act, requiring only discriminatory outcomes, not discriminatory intent, other than as an "evidentiary dragnet."

4. The creation of majority-minority districts can increase the representation of the minority. But this may not improve, and indeed may worsen, the prospects of control by the party or the pursuit of policies favored by the minority.

5. I have been discussing an asymmetry of information between Republican party operatives and Democratic party operatives. But even once the Democratic party wised up, there would still be another asymmetry of information: between the politically informed, who knew the party composition of the delegation was fixed every ten years, and the less informed but still reasonably knowledgeable civics-class graduate or citizenship-exam examinee, who believed it was up for reevaluation every two years. (Compare McGann et al. [2016, 192] on "transparency.") If less informed voters have an objection on these grounds, however, then

less informed voters of the gerrymandering party would also have this objection. This might not make sense of the feeling that they lack an objection that members of the other party have. But this might be explained by the fact that members of the gerrymandering party will see themselves to have been benefitted or at least see their preferences to have been satisfied.

31. The Demandingness of Informal Equality

1. Note that access to information seems to presuppose at least some actual information. You don't have access to information if you don't know that you can acquire it or that it's worth acquiring.

32. Arbitrary Voting

1. Achen and Bartels also note some less systematic influences on voting: sundry events that elected officials cannot plausibly be thought to control, such as droughts and shark attacks; unjustifiable fears about the effects of policy (such as of fluoridated drinking water); and superficial differences in framing or effects of policy (such as whether voters' personal finances are worsened via higher taxes or higher insurance premia).

2. Granted, the discovery that people vote arbitrarily reveals that arguments of the form, "Given that people don't vote arbitrarily, the alternative would not lead to better outcomes," rest on a false premise. But that's a more limited point.

3. The same tendency shows up in many other discussions of how identity drives political behavior. For example, consider Klein (2020, xxii): "Much that happens in political campaigns is best understood as a struggle over which identities voters will inhabit come Election Day: Will they feel like workers exploited by their bosses . . . as parents worried about the climate their children inhabit?" What are we overlooking if we instead describe the struggle as being over which questions of interest, policy, or ideology will be most salient to voters come Election Day: better pay, action on climate, etc.?

Conclusion

1. It is worth recalling here that claims to improvement are, in the main, claims to improved choice situations. And many concerns that might find expression as concerns about "freedom" are concerns about ways in which choice situations can be made better or worse. In general, one's choice situation can be better insofar as it enables one to pursue choice-dependent activities, which are possible or valuable only insofar as they flow from one's own autonomous choices or judgments (Section 1.5). More specifically, an otherwise good option may lack value because of an adverse value-of-compliance effect: (i) because the option is pursued from motivations corrupted by ulterior penalties or rewards; (ii) because the option is

not "selected" from an adequate range of alternatives; (iii) because the option is not pursued with "independence," in Raz's terms, since one is coerced, strictly speaking, into it; or (iv) because the option is not one's own achievement, as Dworkin suggests, since one is end steered toward the option, on the grounds that a certain way of life is good or bad (Section 19.3). In any of these ways, the value of an otherwise good option can be compromised, which can in turn make the choice situation worse.

2. As Raz writes, "Even if democratic power is the most extensive power over myself and others I can have, without claiming for myself more than others can have, it is not the most extensive power I can have over myself. It still involves submission to the will of others" (1990a, 3–4).

3. It is a question at least coeval with what Williams singles out as the "'first' political question": the "Hobbesian" question of how to secure "order, protection, safety, trust, and the conditions of cooperation" (2005, 3).

References

Abizadeh, Arash. 2008. "Democratic Theory and Border Coercion: No Right to Unilaterally Control Your Own Borders." *Political Theory* 36:37–65.

———. Forthcoming. "The Grammar of Social Power: Power-to, Power-with, Power-despite, and Power-over." *Political Studies.*

Acemoglu, Daren, and James Robinson. 2012. *Why Nations Fail.* New York: Crown.

Achen, Christopher, and Larry Bartels. 2016. *Democracy for Realists.* Princeton, NJ: Princeton University Press.

Alchian, Armen, and Harold Demsetz. 1972. "Production, Information Costs, and Economic Organization." *American Economic Review* 62:777–795.

Alexander, Larry. 1992. "What Makes Wrongful Discrimination Wrong? Biases, Preferences, Stereotypes, and Proxies." *University of Pennsylvania Law Review* 141:149–219.

———. 2016. "Is Wrongful Discrimination Really Wrong?" University of San Diego Legal Studies Research Paper.

Alexander, Larry, and Saikrishna Prakash. 2008. "Tempest in an Empty Teapot: Why the Constitution Does Not Regulate Gerrymandering." *William and Mary Law Review* 50:1–62.

Allen, Danielle. 2014. *Our Declaration: A Reading of the Declaration of Independence in Defense of Equality.* New York: Liverlight.

Anderson, Cameron, John Angus, D. Hildreth, and Laura Howland. 2015. "Is the Desire for Status a Fundamental Human Motive? A Review of the Empirical Literature." *Psychological Bulletin* 141:574–601.

Anderson, Elizabeth. 1999. "What Is the Point of Equality?" *Ethics* 109:287–337.

———. 2010a. "The Fundamental Disagreements between Luck Egalitarians and Relational Egalitarians." *Canadian Journal of Philosophy* 40:1–23.

———. 2010b. *The Imperative of Integration.* Princeton, NJ: Princeton University Press.

———. 2017. *Private Government.* Princeton, NJ: Princeton University Press.

———. 2019. "Workplace Government and Republican Theory." In *Republicanism and the Future of Democracy,* edited by Yiftah Elazar and Geneviève Rousselière, 189–206. Cambridge: Cambridge University Press.

Anderson, Scott. 2011. "On the Immorality of Threatening." *Ratio* 24:229–242.

Aristotle. 2017. *Politics*. Translated by C. D. C. Reeve. Indianapolis, IN: Hackett.

Arneson, Richard. 1989. "Paternalism, Utility, and Fairness." *Revue Internationale de Philosophie* 170:409–423.

———. 1999. "Against Rawlsian Equality of Opportunity." *Philosophical Studies* 93:77–112.

———. 2005. "Joel Feinberg and the Justification of Hard Paternalism." *Legal Theory* 11:259–284.

———. 2009. "The Supposed Right to a Democratic Say." In *Contemporary Debates in Political Philosophy*, edited by John Christman and Thomas Christiano, 197–212. Oxford: Oxford University Press.

———. 2010. "Democratic Equality and Relating as Equals." Supplement, *Canadian Journal of Philosophy* 36:25–52.

———. 2013a. "Discrimination, Disparate Impact, and Theories of Justice." In *Philosophical Foundations of Discrimination Law*, edited by Deborah Hellman and Sophia Moreau, 87–111. Oxford: Oxford University Press.

———. 2013b. "The Enforcement of Morals Revisited." *Criminal Law and Philosophy* 7:435–454.

———. 2013c. "Equality of Opportunity: Derivative Not Fundamental." *Journal of Social Philosophy* 44:316–330.

———. 2013d. "Paternalism and the Principle of Fairness." In *Paternalism: Theory and Practice*, edited by Christian Coons and Michael Weber, 134–156. Cambridge: Cambridge University Press.

———. 2014. "Political Liberalism, Religious Liberty, and Religious Establishment." In *The Role of Religion in Human Rights Discourse*, edited by Hanoch Dagan, Shahar Lifshitz, and Yedidia Z. Stern, 117–144. Jerusalem: Israel Democracy Institute.

Arrow, Kenneth. 1963. *Social Choice and Individual Values*. New Haven, CT: Yale University Press.

Baldwin, James. 1963. *The Fire Next Time*. New York: Dial.

Barry, Brian. 1980. "Is It Better to Be Powerful or Lucky?: Parts 1 and 2." *Political Studies* 28:183–194, 338–352.

Barry, Christian, and Gerhard Øverland. 2011. "Do Democratic Societies Have a Right to Do Wrong?" *Journal of Social Philosophy* 42:111–131.

Bartels, Larry. 2016. *Unequal Democracy*. 2nd ed. Princeton, NJ: Princeton University Press.

Bartholdi, Laurent, Wade Hann-Caruthers, Maya Josyula, Omer Tamuz, and Leeat Yariv. 2020. "Equitable Voting Rules." ArXiv. Revised August 29, 2020. https://arxiv.org/abs/1811.01227.

Baumgartner, Frank, Jeffrey Berry, Marie Hojnacki, David Kimball, and Beth Leech. 2009. *Lobbying and Policy Change*. Chicago: University of Chicago Press.

Beeghly, Erin. 2018. "Failing to Treat Persons as Individuals." *Ergo* 26:687–711.

Beerbohm, Eric. 2012. *In Our Name*. Princeton, NJ: Princeton University Press.

Beitz, Charles. 1989. *Political Equality.* Princeton, NJ: Princeton University Press.
———. 2018. "How Is Partisan Gerrymandering Unfair?" *Philosophy and Public Affairs* 46:323–358.
Bell, Daniel, and Wang Pei. 2020. *Just Hierarchy.* Princeton, NJ: Princeton University Press.
Berlin, Isaiah. 1956. "Equality." *Proceedings of the Aristotelian Society* 56:301–326.
———. (1958) 1997. "Two Concepts of Liberty." In *The Proper Study of Mankind,* 191–242. New York: Farrar, Straus and Giroux.
Berman, Mitchell. 1998. "The Evidentiary Theory of Blackmail: Taking Motives Seriously." *University of Chicago Law Review* 65:795–878.
———. 2002. "The Normative Functions of Coercion Claims." *Legal Theory* 8:45–89.
———. 2005. "Managing Gerrymandering." *University of Texas Law Review* 83:781–854.
———. 2011. "Blackmail." In *The Oxford Handbook on the Philosophy of Criminal Law,* edited by John Deigh and David Dolinko, 37–106. Oxford: Oxford University Press.
Bingham, Tom. 2010. *The Rule of Law.* London: Penguin.
Bird, Colin. 2014. "Coercion and Public Justification." *Politics, Philosophy, Economics* 13:189–214.
Blake, Michael. 2001. "Distributive Justice, State Coercion, and Autonomy." *Philosophy and Public Affairs* 30:257–296.
Boehm, Christopher. 2001. *Hierarchy in the Forest.* Cambridge, MA: Harvard University Press.
Boonin, David. 2008. *The Problem of Punishment.* Cambridge: Cambridge University Press.
Bowles, Samuel, and Herbert Gintis. 1993. "A Political and Economic Case for the Democratic Enterprise." *Economics and Philosophy* 9:75–100.
Boxill, Bernard. 1992. *Blacks and Social Justice.* Lanham, MD: Rowman and Littlefield.
Brennan, Geoffrey, Lina Eriksson, Robert E. Goodin, and Nicholas Southwood. 2016. *Explaining Norms.* Oxford: Oxford University Press.
Brighouse, Harry. 1996. "Egalitarianism and Equal Availability of Political Influence." *Journal of Political Philosophy* 4:118–141.
———. 1997. "Political Equality in Justice as Fairness." *Philosophical Studies* 86:155–184.
Brighouse, Harry, and Marc Fleurbaey. 2010. "Democracy and Proportionality." *Journal of Political Philosophy* 18:137–155.
Buchanan, Allen. 2004. *Justice, Legitimacy, and Self-Determination.* Oxford: Oxford University Press.
Burke, Edmund.(1774) 2015. "Speech at the Conclusion of the Poll at Bristol." In *Reflections on the Revolution in France and Other Writings,* edited by Jesse Norman, 147–153. New York: Knopf.

Cheng, Joey, and Jessica Tracy. 2014. "Toward a Unified Science of Hierarchy: Dominance and Prestige Are Two Fundamental Pathways to Human Social Rank." In *The Psychology of Social Status,* edited by Joey Cheng, Jessica Tracy, and Cameron Anderson, 3–27. New York: Springer.

Cholbi, Michael. 2017. "Paternalism and Our Rational Powers." *Mind* 126: 123–153.

Christiano, Thomas. 1996. *Rule of the Many.* Boulder, CO: Westview.

———. 2006. "Does Religious Toleration Make Any Sense?" In *Contemporary Debates in Social Philosophy,* edited by Laurence Thomas, 171–191. Oxford: Blackwell.

———. 2010. *Constitution of Equality.* Oxford: Oxford University Press.

Coase, R. H. 1937. "The Nature of the Firm." *Economica* 4:386–405.

Cohen, G. A. 1978. *Karl Marx's Theory of History: A Defence.* Princeton, NJ: Princeton University Press.

———. 1995. *Self-Ownership, Freedom, and Equality.* Cambridge: Cambridge University Press.

———. 2008. *Rescuing Justice and Inequality.* Cambridge, MA: Harvard University Press.

———. 2009. *Why Not Socialism?* Princeton, NJ: Princeton University Press.

———. 2011. *On the Currency of Egalitarian Justice.* Princeton, NJ: Princeton University Press.

———. 2013. *Finding Oneself in the Other.* Princeton, NJ: Princeton University Press.

Cohen, Joshua. 1989. "The Economic Basis of Deliberative Democracy." *Social Philosophy & Policy* 6:25–50.

———. 1997. "The Natural Goodness of Humanity." In *Reclaiming the History of Ethics: Essays for John Rawls,* edited by Andrews Reath, Barbara Herman, and Christine Korsgaard, 102–139. Cambridge: Cambridge University Press.

———. 1999. "Reflections on Habermas on Democracy." *Ratio Juris* 12:386–416.

———. 2001. "Money, Politics, and Political Equality." In *Fact and Value,* edited by Alex Byrne, Robert Stalnaker, and Ralph Wedgwood, 47–80. Cambridge, MA: MIT Press.

———. 2009. *Philosophy, Politics, Democracy.* Cambridge, MA: Harvard University Press.

Conly, Sarah. 2013. *Against Autonomy.* Cambridge: Cambridge University Press.

Constant, Benjamin. (1819) 1988. "The Liberty of the Ancients Compared with That of the Moderns." In *Constant: Political Writings,* edited by Biancamaria Fontana, 307–328. Cambridge: Cambridge University Press.

Coons, Christian, and Michael Weber, eds. 2013. *Paternalism: Theory and Practice.* Cambridge: Cambridge University Press.

Cooter, Robert. 1984. "Prices and Sanctions." *Columbia Law Review* 84:1523–1560.

Cooter, Robert, and Neil Siegel. 2012. "Not the Power to Destroy: An Effects Theory of the Tax Power." *Virginia Law Review* 98:1195–1253.
Cornell, Nicolas. 2015. "A Third Theory of Paternalism." *Michigan Law Review* 113:1295–1336.
Dahl, Robert A. 1985. *A Preface to Economic Democracy.* Berkeley: University of California Press.
———. 1989. *Democracy and Its Critics.* New Haven, CT: Yale University Press.
———. 1998. *On Democracy.* New Haven, CT: Yale University Press.
Daley, David. 2016. *Ratf**ked: The True Story Behind the Secret Plan to Steal America's Democracy.* New York: Liverlight.
Daniels, Norman. 1978. "Merit and Meritocracy." *Philosophy and Public Affairs* 7:206–223.
Darwall, Stephen. 1977. "Two Kinds of Respect." *Ethics* 88:36–49.
Dawood, Yasmin. 2014. "Classifying Corruption." *Duke Journal of Constitutional Law and Policy* 9:103–133.
De Marneffe, Peter. 2010. *Liberalism and Prostitution.* Oxford: Oxford University Press.
De Waal, Frans. 2007. *Chimpanzee Politics.* Baltimore, MD: Johns Hopkins.
Downs, Anthony. 1957. *An Economic Theory of Democracy.* New York: Harper and Row.
Dworkin, Gerald. 1972. "Paternalism." *The Monist* 56:64–84.
Dworkin, Ronald. 1986. *Law's Empire.* Cambridge, MA: Harvard University Press.
———. 1996. *Freedom's Law.* Oxford: Oxford University Press.
———. 2002. *Sovereign Virtue.* Cambridge, MA: Harvard University Press.
———. 2011. *Justice for Hedgehogs.* Cambridge, MA: Harvard University Press.
Edmundson, William A. 1998. *Three Anarchical Fallacies.* Cambridge: Cambridge University Press.
Eidelson, Benjamin. 2013. "Treating People as Individuals." In *Philosophical Foundations of Discrimination Law,* edited by Deborah Hellman and Sophia Moreau, 203–227. Oxford: Oxford University Press.
———. 2015. *Discrimination and Disrespect.* Oxford: Oxford University Press.
Eisgruber, Christopher, and Lawrence Sager. 2007. *Religious Freedom and the Constitution.* Cambridge, MA: Harvard University Press.
Ekins, Richard. 2012. "Equal Protection and Social Meaning." *American Journal of Jurisprudence* 57:21–48.
Elazar, Yiftah, and Geneviève Rousselière, eds. 2019. *Republicanism and the Future of Democracy.* Cambridge: Cambridge University Press.
Ellemers, Naomi, and S. Alexander Haslam. 2012. "Social Identity Theory." In *Handbook of Theories of Social Psychology,* vol. 2, edited by Paul A. M. Van Lange, Arie W. Kruglanski, and E. Tory Higgins, 379–398. Thousand Oaks, CA: Sage.

Estlund, David. 2000. "Political Quality." *Social Philosophy and Policy* 17:127–160.
———. 2008. *Democratic Authority.* Princeton, NJ: Princeton University Press.
———. 2019. *Utopophobia.* Princeton, NJ: Princeton University Press.
Fanon, Frantz. 1952. *Black Skin, White Masks.* Translated by Charles Lam Markmann. New York: Grove.
Feinberg, Joel. 1968. "Collective Responsibility." *Journal of Philosophy* 65:674–688.
———. 1984. *The Moral Limits of the Criminal Law.* Vol. 1, *Harm to Others.* Oxford: Oxford University Press.
———. 1986. *The Moral Limits of the Criminal Law.* Vol. 3, *Harm to Self.* Oxford: Oxford University Press.
Fishkin, Joseph. 2014. *Bottlenecks.* Oxford: Oxford University Press.
Flannery, Kent, and Joyce Marcus. 2012. *The Creation of Inequality.* Cambridge, MA: Harvard University Press.
Foot, Philippa. 2002. "The Problem of Abortion and the Doctrine of Double Effect." In *Virtues and Vices,* 19–32. Oxford: Oxford University Press.
Forst, Rainer. 2013. "A Kantian Republican Conception of Justice as Nondomination." In *Republican Democracy,* edited by Andreas Niederberger and Philipp Schink, 154–168. Edinburgh: Edinburgh University Press.
Fourie, Carina. 2015. "To Praise and to Scorn: The Problems of Inequalities of Esteem for Social Egalitarianism." In *Social Equality: Essays on What It Means to Be Equals,* edited by Carina Fourie, Fabian Schuppert, and Ivo Wallimann-Helmer, 87–106. Oxford: Oxford University Press.
Fourie, Carina, Fabian Schuppert, and Ivo Wallimann-Helmer, eds. 2015. *Social Equality: Essays on What It Means to Be Equals.* Oxford: Oxford University Press.
Freeman, Samuel. 2007. *Justice and the Social Contract: Essays on Rawlsian Political Philosophy.* Oxford: Oxford University Press.
Fricker, Miranda. 2007. *Epistemic Injustice.* Oxford: Oxford University Press.
Friedrich, Carl. 1972. *Corruption Concepts in Historical Perspective.* In *Political Corruption,* 3rd ed., edited by Arnold Heidenheimer and Michael Johnston, 15–24. New Brunswick, NJ: Transaction.
Fukuyama, Francis. 2011. *The Origins of Political Order.* New York: Farrar, Straus, and Giroux.
Fuller, Lon. 1969. *The Morality of Law.* Rev. ed. New Haven, CT: Yale University Press.
Gardiner, John. 1993. "Defining Corruption." In *Political Corruption,* 3rd ed., edited by Arnold Heidenheimer and Michael Johnston, 25–40. New Brunswick, NJ: Transaction.
Gaus, Gerald. 2003. "Liberal Neutrality: A Compelling and Radical Principle." In *Perfectionism and Neutrality: Essays in Liberal Theory,* edited by Steven Wall and George Klosko, 137–166. Lanham, MD: Rowman and Littlefield.

———. 2009. "The Moral Foundations of Liberal Neutrality." In *Contemporary Debates in Political Philosophy,* edited by Thomas Christiano and John Christman, 81–98. Chichester, UK: Wiley-Blackwell.

———. 2011. *The Order of Public Reason: A Theory of Freedom and Morality in a Diverse and Bounded World.* Cambridge: Cambridge University Press.

———. 2014. "The Good, the Bad, and the Ugly: Three Agent-Type Challenges to *The Order of Public Reason.*" *Philosophical Studies* 170:563–577.

Gilens, Martin. 2012. *Affluence and Influence.* Princeton, NJ: Princeton University Press.

Gilens, Martin, and Benjamin Page. 2014. "Testing Theories of American Politics: Elites, Interest Groups, and Average Citizens." *Perspectives on Politics* 12: 564–581.

Goldman, Alan. 1979. "The Paradox of Punishment." *Philosophy and Public Affairs* 9:42–58.

Goldman, Alvin. 1999. "Why Citizens Should Vote: A Causal Responsibility Approach." *Social Philosophy and Policy* 16:201–217.

González-Ricoy, Iñigo. 2019. "Firm Authority and Workplace Democracy: A Reply to Jacob and Neuhäuser." *Ethical Theory and Moral Practice* 22:679–684.

González-Ricoy, Iñigo, and Jahel Queralt. 2021. "No Masters Above: Testing Five Arguments for Self-Employment." In *Wither Work? The Politics and Ethics of Contemporary Work,* edited by Keith Breen and Jean-Philippe Deranty, 87–101. New York: Routledge.

Gosepath, Stefan. 2015. "The Principles and the Presumption of Equality." In *Social Equality: Essays on What It Means to Be Equals,* edited by Carina Fourie, Fabian Schuppert, and Ivo Wallimann-Helmer, 167–185. Oxford: Oxford University Press.

Graeber, David and David Wengrow. 2021. *The Dawn of Everything.* New York: Farrar, Straus and Giroux.

Greenawalt, Kent. 1983. "How Empty Is the Idea of Equality?" *Columbia Law Review* 83:1167–1185.

Guerrero, Alex. 2014. "Against Elections: The Lottocratic Alternative." *Philosophy and Public Affairs* 42:135–178.

Guinier, Lani. 1994. *The Tyranny of the Majority.* New York: Free Press.

Habermas, Jürgen. 1996. *Between Facts and Norms.* Translated by William Rehg. Cambridge, MA: MIT Press.

Hacker, Jacob, and Paul Pierson. 2010. *Winner-Take-All Politics.* New York: Simon and Schuster.

———. 2016. *American Amnesia.* New York: Simon and Schuster.

Haksar, Vinit. 1976. "Coercive Proposals." *Political Theory* 4:65–79.

Hale, Robert. 1923. "Coercion and Distribution in a Supposedly Non-Coercive State." *Political Science Quarterly* 38:470–494.

Hart, H. L. A. 1963. *Law, Liberty, and Morality.* Stanford, CA: Stanford University Press.

———. 1968. "Prolegomenon to the Principles of Punishment." In *Punishment and Responsibility: Essays in the Philosophy of Law,* 1–27. Oxford: Oxford University Press.

———. 1992. *The Concept of Law.* 2nd ed. Oxford: Oxford University Press.

Hasen, Richard. 2016. *Plutocrats United.* New Haven, CT: Yale University Press.

Hayek, Friedrich. 1944. *The Road to Serfdom.* Chicago: University of Chicago Press.

———. 1960. *The Constitution of Liberty.* Chicago: University of Chicago Press.

Heidenheimer, Arnold, and Michael Johnston. 2002. *Political Corruption.* 3rd ed. New Brunswick, NJ: Transaction.

Hellman, Deborah. 2008. *When Is Discrimination Wrong?* Cambridge, MA: Harvard University Press.

Hellman, Deborah, and Sophia Moreau. 2013. *Philosophical Foundations of Discrimination Law.* Oxford: Oxford University Press.

Herzog, Lisa. 2018. *Reclaiming the System.* Oxford: Oxford University Press.

Hobbes, Thomas. (1651) 1994. *Leviathan.* Edited by Edwin Curley. Indianapolis, IN: Hackett.

Huang, Y. 2018. "Opinion: China's Economy Is Not Normal. It Doesn't Have to Be." *New York Times*, March 13, 2018.

Huemer, Michael. 2013. *The Problem of Political Authority.* London: Palgrave.

Huntington, Samuel. 1968. "Modernization and Corruption." In *Political Corruption,* 3rd ed., edited by Arnold Heidenheimer and Michael Johnston, 253–264. New Brunswick, NJ: Transaction.

Hurka, Thomas. 1993. *Perfectionism.* Oxford: Oxford University Press.

Husak, Douglas. 2005. "For the Legalization of Drugs." In *The Legalization of Drugs,* edited by Douglas Husak and Peter De Marneffe, 1–108. Cambridge: Cambridge University Press.

Husak, Douglas, and Peter De Marneffe. 2005. *The Legalization of Drugs.* Cambridge: Cambridge University Press.

Ingham, Sean. 2021. "Representative Democracy and Social Equality." *American Political Science Review* 116:689–701.

Jones, Peter. 1983. "Political Equality and Majority Rule." In *The Nature of Political Theory,* edited by David Miller and Larry Seidentrop, 155–182. Oxford: Oxford University Press.

Julius, A. J. 2013. "The Possibility of Exchange." *Politics, Philosophy, Economics* 12:361–374.

Kamm, Frances. 2006. *Intricate Ethics.* Oxford: Oxford University Press.

Kant, Immanuel. (1797) 2017. *The Metaphysics of Morals.* Translated by Mary Gregor. Cambridge: Cambridge University Press.

Kershnar, Stephen. 2002. "The Structure of Rights Forfeiture in the Context of Culpable Wrongdoing." *Philosophia* 29:57–88.

Kleiman, Mark. 2009. *When Brute Force Fails.* Princeton, NJ: Princeton University Press.
Klein, Ezra. 2020. *Why We're Polarized.* New York: Avid.
Klosko, George. 2005. *Political Obligations.* Oxford: Oxford University Press.
Kolodny, Niko. 2019. "Why Equality of Treatment and Opportunity Might Matter." *Philosophical Studies* 176:3357–3366.
———. 2022. "Saving Posterity from a Worse Fate." In *Essays in Honour of Derek Parfit: Population Ethics, edited by* Jeff McMahan, Tim Campbell, James Goodrich, and Ketan Ramakrishnan, 264–310. Oxford: Oxford University Press.
Kosinski, Michal, David Stillwell, and Thore Graepel. 2013. "Private Traits and Attributes Are Predictable from Digital Records of Human Behavior." *Proceedings of the National Academy of Sciences* 110:5802–5805.
Kramer, Matthew. 2008. "Liberty and Domination." In *Republicanism and Political Theory,* edited by Cécile Laborde and John Maynor, 31–57. Oxford: Blackwell.
Landemore, Hélène. 2013. *Democratic Reason.* Princeton, NJ: Princeton University Press.
———. 2020. *Open Democracy.* Princeton, NJ: Princeton University Press.
———. 2021. "Open Democracy and Digital Technologies." In *Digital Technology and Democratic Theory,* edited by Lucy Bernholz, Hélène Landemore, and Rob Reich, 62–89. Chicago: University of Chicago Press.
Larmore, Charles. 1999. "The Moral Basis of Political Liberalism." *Journal of Philosophy* 96:599–625.
———. 2008. *The Autonomy of Morality.* Cambridge: Cambridge University Press.
Lazar, Seth. Unpublished manuscript. "Legitimacy, Authority, and the Political Value of Explanations."
Lee, Steven. 2001. "Democracy and the Problem of Persistent Minorities." In *Groups and Group Rights,* edited by Christine Sistare, Larry May, and Leslie Francis, 124–136. Lawrence: University Press of Kansas.
Leff, Nathaniel. 1964. "Economic Development through Bureaucratic Corruption." In *Political Corruption,* 3rd ed., edited by Arnold Heidenheimer and Michael Johnston, 307–320. New Brunswick, NJ: Transaction.
Leiter, Brian. 2013. *Why Tolerate Religion?* Princeton, NJ: Princeton University Press.
Lelkes, Yphtach. 2016. "Mass Polarization: Manifestations and Measurements." *Public Opinion Quarterly* 80:392–410.
Lessig, Lawrence. 2011. *Republic Lost: How Money Corrupts Congress—and a Plan to Stop It.* New York: Hachette.
———. 2015. *Republic, Lost: The Corruption of Equality and the Steps to End It.* New York: Hachette.
Lewinsohn, Jed. 2020. "Paid on Both Sides: Quid Pro Quo Exchange and the Doctrine of Consideration." *Yale Law Journal* 129:690–772.

Lippert-Rasmussen, Kasper. 2014. *Born Free and Equal? A Philosophy Inquiry into the Nature of Discrimination.* Oxford: Oxford University Press.
———. 2018. *Relational Egalitarianism.* Cambridge: Cambridge University Press.
Locke, John. (1689) 1960. *Second Treatise of Government.* In *Locke: Two Treatises of Government,* edited by Peter Laslett, 265–428. Cambridge: Cambridge University Press.
López-Guerra, Claudio. 2014. *Democracy and Disenfranchisement.* Oxford: Oxford University Press.
Lovett, Adam. 2020. "Democratic Autonomy and the Shortcomings of Citizens." *Journal of Moral Philosophy* 18:363–386.
———. 2021. "Must Egalitarians Condemn Representative Democracy?" *Social Theory and Practice* 47:171–198.
Lovett, Frank. 2010. *A General Theory of Domination and Justice.* Oxford: Oxford University Press.
———. 2019. "Republicanism and Democracy Revisited." In *Republicanism and the Future of Democracy,* edited by Yiftah Elazar and Geneviève Rousselière, 117–129. Cambridge: Cambridge University Press.
Lovett, Frank, and Philip Pettit. 2019. "Preserving Republican Freedom: A Reply to Simpson." *Philosophy and Public Affairs* 46:363–383.
Lowenstein, D. H. 1985. "Political Bribery and the Intermediate Theory of Politics." *UCLA Law Review* 32:784–851.
———. 2004. "When Is a Campaign Contribution a Bribe?" In *Private and Public Corruption,* edited by William Heffernan and John Kleinig, 127–172. Lanham, MD: Rowman and Littlefield.
Manin, Bernard. 1997. *The Principles of Representative Government.* Cambridge: Cambridge University Press.
Mann, Thomas, and Norman Ornstein. 2016. *It's Even Worse than It ~~Looks~~ Was.* New and expanded ed. New York: Basic Books.
Manne, Kate. 2018. *Down Girl.* Oxford: Oxford University Press.
Mansbridge, Jane. 2009. "A 'Selection Model' of Political Representation." *Journal of Political Philosophy* 17:369–398.
Marx, Karl. (1849) 1978. *Wage Labor and Capital.* In *The Marx-Engels Reader,* edited by Robert Tucker, 203–217. New York: W.W. Norton and Company.
———. (1867) 1978. *Capital, Volume 1.* In *The Marx-Engels Reader,* edited by Robert Tucker, 294–438. New York: W.W. Norton and Company.
Mason, Lilliana. 2018. *Uncivil Agreement.* Chicago: University of Chicago Press.
May, Kenneth. 1952. "A Set of Independent Necessary and Sufficient Conditions for Simple Majority Decision." *Econometrica* 20:680–684.
McCarty, Nolan. 2019. *Polarization: What Everyone Needs to Know.* Oxford: Oxford University Press.
McGann, Anthony, Charles Anthony Smith, Michael Latner, and Alex Keena. 2016. *Gerrymandering in America.* Cambridge: Cambridge University Press.

McMahon, Christopher. 2009. *Public Capitalism.* Philadelphia: University of Pennsylvania Press.
Mill, John Stuart. (1859) 2015. *On Liberty.* In *On Liberty, Utilitarianism, and Other Essays,* 5–114. Oxford: Oxford University Press.
———. (1861) 2015. *Considerations on Representative Government.* In *On Liberty, Utilitarianism, and Other Essays,* 181–408. Oxford: Oxford University Press.
Miller, David. 1997. "Equality and Justice." *Ratio,* n.s., 10:223–237.
———. 2010. "Why Immigration Controls Are Not Coercive: A Reply to Arash Abizadeh." *Political Theory* 38:111–120.
Moreau, Sophia. 2010. "What Is Discrimination?" *Philosophy and Public Affairs* 38:143–179.
———. 2020. *Faces of Inequality.* Oxford: Oxford University Press.
Morris, Christopher. 1991. "Punishment and Loss of Moral Standing." *Canadian Journal of Philosophy* 21:53–79.
Motchoulski, Alexander. 2021. "Relational Egalitarianism and Democracy." *Journal of Moral Philosophy* 20:1–30.
Munoz-Dardé, Véronique. 2005. "Equality and Division: Values in Principle." Supplement, *Proceedings of the Aristotelian Society* 79:255–284.
———. 2018. "Fellow Feelings: Fraternity, Equality and the Origin and Stability of Justice." *Daimon: Revista Internacional de Filosofia* 7:107–123.
———. Forthcoming. "The Cost of Belonging: Universalism vs. the Political Appeal of Solidarity." In *Solidarity,* edited by Andrea Sangiovanni and Juri Viehoff. Oxford: Oxford University Press.
Murphy, Jeffrie. 1980. "Blackmail: A Preliminary Inquiry." *The Monist* 156:22–37.
Murphy, Liam. 2014. *What Makes Law.* Cambridge: Cambridge University Press.
Nagel, Thomas. 1973. "Rawls on Justice." *Philosophical Review* 82:220–234.
———. 1979. "Ruthlessness in Public Life." In *Mortal Questions,* 75–90. Cambridge: Cambridge University Press.
———. 1991. *Equality and Partiality.* Oxford: Oxford University Press.
———. 2002. *Concealment and Exposure.* Oxford: Oxford University Press.
———. 2005. "The Problem of Global Justice." *Philosophy and Public Affairs* 33:113–147.
Nagel, Thomas, and Liam Murphy. 2004. *The Myth of Ownership.* Oxford: Oxford University Press.
Narveson, Jan. 2010. "The Right to Liberty Is Incompatible with the Right to Equality." In *Are Liberty and Equality Compatible?,* edited by Jan Narveson and James Sterba, 123–250. Cambridge: Cambridge University Press.
Narveson, Jan, and James Sterba. 2010. *Are Liberty and Equality Compatible?* Cambridge: Cambridge University Press.
Norman, Richard. 1997. "The Social Basis of Equality." *Ratio,* n.s., 10:238–252.
Nozick, Robert. 1974. *Anarchy, State, and Utopia.* New York: Basic Books.

———. 1999. "Coercion." In *Socratic Puzzles,* 15–44. Cambridge, MA: Harvard University Press.

Nussbaum, Martha. 2011. "Perfectionist Liberalism and Political Liberalism." *Philosophy and Public Affairs* 39:3–45.

Nye, J. 1967. "Corruption and Political Development: A Cost-Benefit Analysis." In *Political Corruption,* 3rd ed., edited by Arnold Heidenheimer and Michael Johnston, 281–302. New Brunswick, NJ: Transaction.

Olsaretti, Serena. 2009. "Responsibility and the Consequences of Choice." *Proceedings of the Aristotelian Society* 109:165–188.

Olson, Mancur. 1965. *The Logic of Collective Action.* Cambridge, MA: Harvard University Press.

Orwell, George. (1949) 2017. *1984.* Boston: Mariner.

Otsuka, Michael. 2003. *Libertarianism without Equality.* Oxford: Oxford University Press.

Pallikkathayil, Japa. 2010. "Deriving Morality from Politics: Rethinking the Formula of Humanity." *Ethics* 121:116–147.

———. 2016. "Neither Perfectionism nor Political Liberalism." *Philosophy and Public Affairs* 44:171–196.

———. 2017. "Persons and Bodies." In *Freedom and Force: Essays on Kant's Legal Philosophy,* edited by Sari Kisilevsky and Martin Stone, 35–54. Oxford: Hart Publishing.

Patten, Alan. 2014. *Equal Recognition: The Moral Foundations of Minority Rights.* Princeton, NJ: Princeton University Press.

Pettit, Philip. 1997. *Republicanism: A Theory of Freedom and Government.* Oxford: Oxford University Press.

———. 2009. "Law and Liberty." In *Legal Republicanism: National and International Perspectives,* edited by Samantha Besson and José Luis Martí, 39–59. Oxford: Oxford University Press.

———. 2012. *On the People's Terms: A Republican Theory and Model of Democracy.* Cambridge: Cambridge University Press.

———. 2014. *Just Freedom: A Moral Compass for a Complex World.* New York: Norton.

Pevnick, Ryan. 2016. "Does the Egalitarian Rationale for Campaign Finance Succeed?" *Philosophy and Public Affairs* 44:46–76.

Philp, M. 2002. "Conceptualizing Political Corruption." In *Political Corruption,* edited by A. H. Johnston, 41–58. New Brunswick, NJ: Transaction.

Pildes, Richard. 2014. "Romanticizing Democracy, Political Fragmentation, and the Decline of American Government." *Yale Law Journal* 124:804–852.

Pitkin, Hannah Fenichel. 1967. *The Concept of Representation.* Berkeley: University of California Press.

Quinn, Warren. 1985. "The Right to Threaten and the Right to Punish." *Philosophy and Public Affairs* 14:327–373.

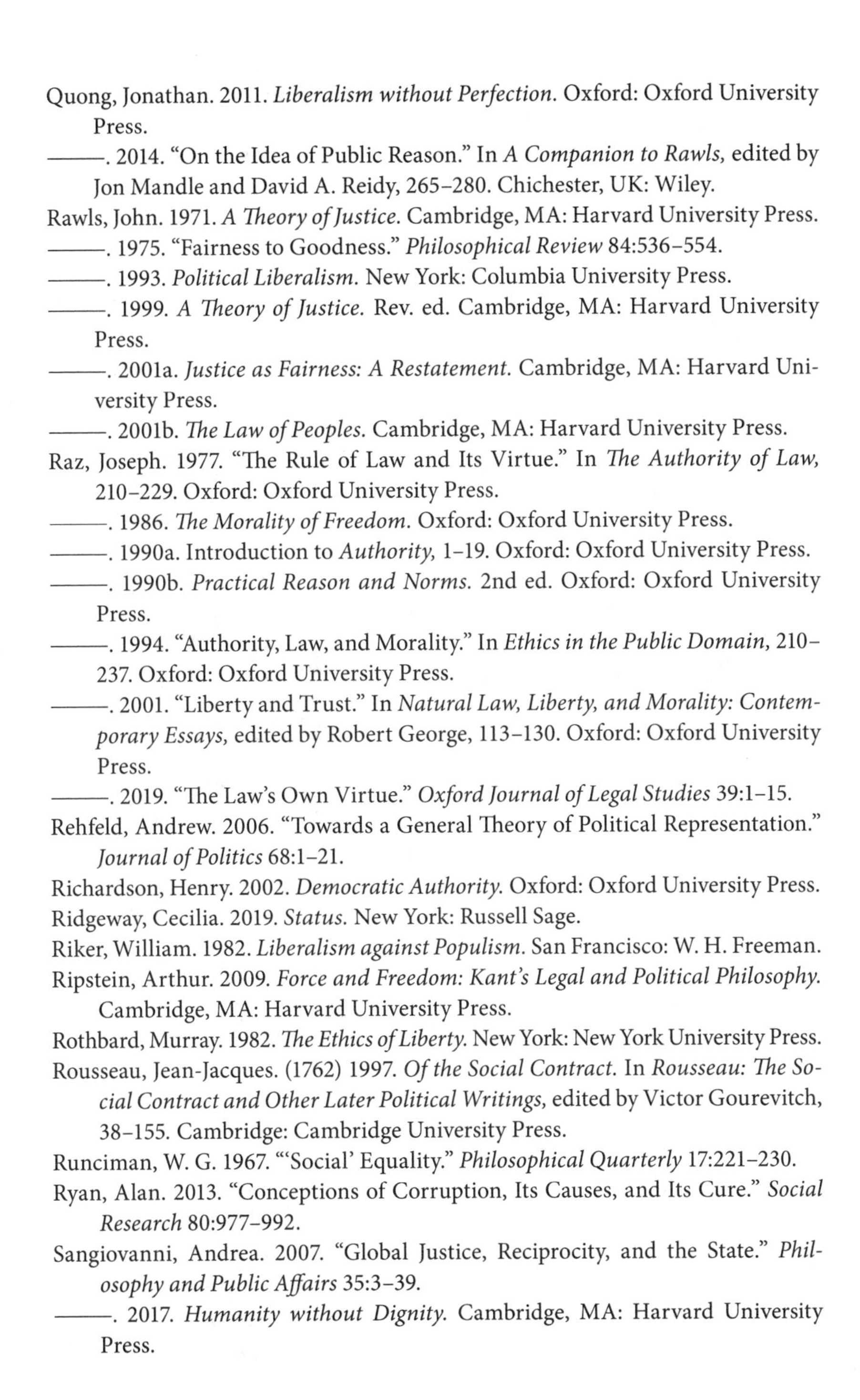

Quong, Jonathan. 2011. *Liberalism without Perfection.* Oxford: Oxford University Press.

———. 2014. "On the Idea of Public Reason." In *A Companion to Rawls,* edited by Jon Mandle and David A. Reidy, 265–280. Chichester, UK: Wiley.

Rawls, John. 1971. *A Theory of Justice.* Cambridge, MA: Harvard University Press.

———. 1975. "Fairness to Goodness." *Philosophical Review* 84:536–554.

———. 1993. *Political Liberalism.* New York: Columbia University Press.

———. 1999. *A Theory of Justice.* Rev. ed. Cambridge, MA: Harvard University Press.

———. 2001a. *Justice as Fairness: A Restatement.* Cambridge, MA: Harvard University Press.

———. 2001b. *The Law of Peoples.* Cambridge, MA: Harvard University Press.

Raz, Joseph. 1977. "The Rule of Law and Its Virtue." In *The Authority of Law,* 210–229. Oxford: Oxford University Press.

———. 1986. *The Morality of Freedom.* Oxford: Oxford University Press.

———. 1990a. Introduction to *Authority,* 1–19. Oxford: Oxford University Press.

———. 1990b. *Practical Reason and Norms.* 2nd ed. Oxford: Oxford University Press.

———. 1994. "Authority, Law, and Morality." In *Ethics in the Public Domain,* 210–237. Oxford: Oxford University Press.

———. 2001. "Liberty and Trust." In *Natural Law, Liberty, and Morality: Contemporary Essays,* edited by Robert George, 113–130. Oxford: Oxford University Press.

———. 2019. "The Law's Own Virtue." *Oxford Journal of Legal Studies* 39:1–15.

Rehfeld, Andrew. 2006. "Towards a General Theory of Political Representation." *Journal of Politics* 68:1–21.

Richardson, Henry. 2002. *Democratic Authority.* Oxford: Oxford University Press.

Ridgeway, Cecilia. 2019. *Status.* New York: Russell Sage.

Riker, William. 1982. *Liberalism against Populism.* San Francisco: W. H. Freeman.

Ripstein, Arthur. 2009. *Force and Freedom: Kant's Legal and Political Philosophy.* Cambridge, MA: Harvard University Press.

Rothbard, Murray. 1982. *The Ethics of Liberty.* New York: New York University Press.

Rousseau, Jean-Jacques. (1762) 1997. *Of the Social Contract.* In *Rousseau: The Social Contract and Other Later Political Writings,* edited by Victor Gourevitch, 38–155. Cambridge: Cambridge University Press.

Runciman, W. G. 1967. "'Social' Equality." *Philosophical Quarterly* 17:221–230.

Ryan, Alan. 2013. "Conceptions of Corruption, Its Causes, and Its Cure." *Social Research* 80:977–992.

Sangiovanni, Andrea. 2007. "Global Justice, Reciprocity, and the State." *Philosophy and Public Affairs* 35:3–39.

———. 2017. *Humanity without Dignity.* Cambridge, MA: Harvard University Press.

Satz, Debra. 2010. *Why Some Things Should Not Be for Sale: The Moral Limits of Markets*. Oxford: Oxford University Press.

———. 2017. "Some (Largely) Ignored Problems with Privatization." *NOMOS* 60:9–28.

Scanlon, T. M. 1998. *What We Owe to Each Other*. Cambridge, MA: Harvard University Press.

———. 1999. "Punishment and the Rule of Law." In *Deliberative Democracy and Human Rights,* edited by H. Hongju Koh and R. Slye, 257–271. New Haven, CT: Yale University Press.

———. 2008. *Moral Dimensions: Meaning, Permissibility, and Blame*. Cambridge, MA: Harvard University Press.

———. 2018. *Why Does Inequality Matter?* Oxford: Oxford University Press.

Schattschneider, E. E. 1960. *The Semisovereign People*. New York: Holt, Rinehart and Winston.

Scheffler, Samuel 2003. "What Is Egalitarianism?" *Philosophy and Public Affairs* 31:5–39.

———. 2005. "Choice, Circumstance, and the Value of Equality." *Politics, Philosophy and Economics* 4:5–28.

———. 2015. "The Practice of Equality." In *Social Equality: Essays on What It Means to Be Equals,* edited by Carina Fourie, Fabian Schuppert, and Ivo Wallimann-Helmer, 21–44. Oxford: Oxford University Press.

Schumpeter, Joseph. 1942. *Capitalism, Socialism, and Democracy*. New York: Harper and Brothers.

Shapiro, Scott. 2012. "Authority." In *The Oxford Handbook of Jurisprudence and Philosophy of Law,* edited by Jules Coleman, Kenneth Einar Himma, and Scott Shapiro, 382–439. Oxford: Oxford University Press.

Shapley, L. S., and Martin Shubik. 1954. "A Method for Evaluating the Distribution of Power in a Committee System." *American Political Science Review* 48:787–792.

Shaw, James. 2012. "The Morality of Blackmail." *Philosophy and Public Affairs* 40:165–196.

Shelby, Tommie. 2007. *We Who Are Dark*. Cambridge, MA: Harvard University Press.

Shiffrin, Seana. 2000. "Paternalism, Unconscionability Doctrine, and Accommodation." *Philosophy and Public Affairs* 29:205–250.

———. 2004a. "Egalitarianism, Choice-Sensitivity, and Accommodation." In *Reasons and Value: Themes from the Moral Philosophy of Joseph Raz,* edited by R. Jay Wallace, Philip Pettit, Michael Smith, and Samuel Scheffler, 270–302. Oxford: Oxford University Press.

———. 2004b. "Race, Labor, and the Fair Equality of Opportunity Principle." *Fordham Law Review* 72:1643.

Simmons, A. John. 1979. *Moral Principles and Political Obligations.* Princeton, NJ: Princeton University Press.
———. 1991. "Locke and the Right to Punish." *Philosophy and Public Affairs* 20: 311–349.
———. 2000. "Justification and Legitimacy." In *Justification and Legitimacy: Essays on Rights and Obligations,* 122–157. Cambridge: Cambridge University Press.
———. 2005. "The Duty to Obey and Our Natural Moral Duties." In *Is There a Duty to Obey the Law?,* edited by A. John Simmons and Christopher Heath Wellman, 93–196. Cambridge: Cambridge University Press.
Simmons, A. John, and Christopher Heath Wellman. 2005. *Is There a Duty to Obey the Law?* Cambridge: Cambridge University Press.
Simpson, Thomas. 2017. "The Impossibility of Republican Freedom." *Philosophy and Public Affairs* 45:27–53.
Singer, Peter. 1973. *Democracy and Disobedience.* Oxford: Oxford University Press.
Skinner, Quentin. 1998. *Liberty before Liberalism.* Cambridge: Cambridge University Press.
———. 2002. "A Third Concept of Liberty." *London Review of Books* 24:16–18.
———. 2008. "Freedom as the Absence of Arbitrary Power." In *Republicanism and Political Theory,* edited by Cécile Laborde and John Maynor, 83–101. Oxford: Blackwell.
Stephanopoulos, Nicholas, and Eric McGhee. 2015. "Partisan Gerrymandering and the Efficiency Gap." *University of Chicago Law Review* 82:831–900.
Sterba, James 2010. "Equality Is Compatible with and Required by Liberty." In *Are Liberty and Equality Compatible?,* edited by Jan Narveson and James Sterba, 7–119. Cambridge: Cambridge University Press.
Still, Jonathan. 1981. "Political Equality and Election Systems." *Ethics* 91:375–394.
Stilz, Anna. 2009. *Liberal Loyalty: Freedom, Obligation, and the State.* Princeton, NJ: Princeton University Press.
Stone, Peter. 2011 *The Luck of the Draw.* Oxford: Oxford University Press.
Strauss, David. 1995. "What Is the Goal of Campaign Finance Reform?" *University of Chicago Legal Forum* 1995:141–161.
Tadros, Victor. 2011. *The Ends of Harm.* Oxford: Oxford University Press.
———. 2016. *Wrongs and Crimes.* Oxford: Oxford University Press.
Tamanaha, Brian. 2004. *On the Rule of Law.* Cambridge: Cambridge University Press.
Tawney, R. H. (1912) 1972. *R. H. Tawney's Commonplace Book.* Cambridge: Cambridge University Press.
Teachout, Zephyr. 2014. *Corruption in America.* Cambridge, MA: Harvard University Press.
Temkin, Larry. 1993. *Inequality.* Oxford: Oxford University Press.

Thaler, Richard H., and Sunstein, Cass R. 2008. *Nudge: Improving Decisions about Health, Wealth, and Happiness.* New Haven, CT: Yale University Press.

Thomas, Alan. 2017. *Republic of Equals: Predistribution and Property-Owning Democracy.* Oxford: Oxford University Press.

Thompson, Dennis. 1995. *Ethics in Congress.* Washington, DC: Brookings Institution.

Thomson, Judith Jarvis. 1985. "The Trolley Problem." *Yale Law Journal* 94: 1395–1415.

Tilly, Charles. 1998. *Durable Inequality.* Berkeley: University of California Press.

Tomasello, Michael. 2016. *A Natural History of Human Morality.* Cambridge, MA: Harvard University Press.

Tomlin, Patrick. 2015. "What Is the Point of Egalitarian Social Relationships?" In *Distributive Justice and Access to Advantage: G.A. Cohen's Egalitarianism,* edited by Alexander Kaufman, 151–179. Cambridge: Cambridge University Press.

Tsuruda, Sabine. 2020. "Working as Equal Moral Agents." *Legal Theory* 26: 305–337.

Tuck, Richard. 2015. *The Sleeping Sovereign.* Cambridge: Cambridge University Press.

Valentini, Laura. 2013. "Justice, Disagreement, and Democracy." *British Journal of Political Science* 43:177–199.

Vallentyne, Peter. 2002. "Brute Luck, Option Luck, and Equality of Initial Opportunities." *Ethics* 112:529–557.

Van der Vossen, Bas. 2015. "Imposing Duties and Original Appropriation." *Journal of Political Philosophy* 23:64–85.

Van Klaveren, Jacob. 1957. "Corruption as a Historical Phenomenon." In *Political Corruption,* 3rd ed., edited by Arnold Heidenheimer and Michael Johnston, 83–94. New Brunswick, NJ: Transaction.

Van Parijs, Philippe. 2003. "Difference Principles." In *The Cambridge Companion to Rawls,* edited by Samuel Freeman, 200–240. Cambridge: Cambridge University Press.

Van Vugt, Mark, and Joshua Tybur. 2016. "The Evolutionary Foundations of Hierarchy: Status, Dominance, Prestige, and Leadership." In *The Handbook of Evolutionary Psychology,* 2nd ed., edited by David M. Buss, 788–809. Hoboken, NJ: Wiley.

Van Wietmarschen, Han. 2021. "What Is Social Hierarchy?" *Nous.* Early view.

Viehoff, Daniel. 2014. "Democratic Equality and Political Authority." *Philosophy and Public Affairs* 42:337–375.

———. 2017. "The Truth in Political Instrumentalism." *Proceedings of the Aristotelian Society* 117:273–294.

———. 2019. "Power and Equality." *Oxford Studies in Political Philosophy* 5:1–38.

Vredenburgh, Kate. 2021. “The Right to Explanation.” *Journal of Political Philosophy* 30:209–229.
Waldron, Jeremy. 1993. “Special Ties and Natural Duties.” *Philosophy and Public Affairs* 22:3–30.
———. 2001. *Law and Disagreement.* Cambridge: Cambridge University Press.
Wall, Steven. 2005. “Perfectionism, Public Reason, and Religious Accommodation.” *Social Theory and Practice* 31:281–304.
———. 2007. “Democracy and Equality.” *Philosophical Quarterly* 57:416–438.
———. 2013a. “Enforcing Morality.” *Criminal Law and Philosophy* 7:455–471.
———. 2013b. “Moral Environmentalism.” In *Paternalism: Theory and Practice,* edited by Christian Coons and Michael Weber, 93–114. Cambridge: Cambridge University Press.
———. 2013c. “Perfectionism.” In *Routledge Companion to Political and Social Philosophy,* edited by F. D’agostino and G. Gaus, 342–352. New York: Routledge.
Wall, Steven, and Klosko, George. 2003. *Perfectionism and Neutrality: Essays in Liberal Theory.* Lanham, MD: Rowman and Littlefield.
Wallace, R. Jay. 2010. “Hypocrisy, Moral Address, and the Equal Standing of Persons.” *Philosophy and Public Affairs* 38:307–341.
———. 2013. *The View from Here.* Oxford: Oxford University Press.
———. 2019. *The Moral Nexus.* Princeton, NJ: Princeton University Press.
Walzer, Michael. 1983. *Spheres of Justice.* New York: Basic Books.
Wang, Sam 2016. “Three Tests for Practical Evaluation of Partisan Gerrymandering.” *Stanford Law Review* 68:1263–1321.
Weber, Max 2019. *Economy and Society.* Translated by Keith Tribe. Cambridge, MA: Harvard University Press.
Wellman, Christopher Heath. 1996. “Liberalism, Samaritanism, and Political Legitimacy.” *Philosophy and Public Affairs*:211–237.
———. 2005. “Samaritanism and the Duty to Obey the Law.” In *Is There a Duty to Obey the Law?,* edited by A. John Simmons and Christopher Heath Wellman, 3–89. Cambridge: Cambridge University Press.
———. 2009. “Rights and State Punishment.” *Journal of Philosophy* 56:419–439.
———. 2012. “The Rights Forfeiture Theory of Punishment.” *Ethics* 122:371–393.
Westen, Peter. 1982. “The Empty Idea of Equality.” *Harvard Law Review* 95:537–596.
White, Stephen. 2017. “On the Moral Objection to Coercion.” *Philosophy and Public Affairs* 45:199–231.
Williams, Bernard. 1982. “Persons, Character, and Morality.” In *Moral Luck.* Cambridge: Cambridge University Press.
———. 2005. *In the Beginning Was the Deed.* Princeton, NJ: Princeton University Press.
Williamson, Oliver. 1973. “Markets and Hierarchies: Some Elementary Considerations.” *American Economic Review* 63:316–325.

———. 2010. "Transaction Cost Economics: The Natural Progression." *American Economic Review* 100:673–690.
Wilson, James. 2019. *Democratic Equality.* Princeton, NJ: Princeton University Press.
———. 2021. "An Autonomy-Based Argument for Democracy." *Oxford Studies in Political Philosophy* 7:194–226.
Wolff, Jonathan. 1998. "Fairness, Respect, and the Egalitarian Ethos." *Philosophy and Public Affairs* 27:97–122.
———. 2015. "Social Equality and Social Inequality." In *Social Equality: Essays on What It Means to Be Equals,* edited by Carina Fourie, Fabian Schuppert, and Ivo Wallimann-Helmer, 209–226. Oxford: Oxford University Press.
———. 2019. "Equality and Hierarchy." *Proceedings of the Aristotelian Society* 119:1–23.
Wolff, Robert Paul. 1970. *In Defense of Anarchism.* New York: Harper and Row.
Wollheim, Richard 1962. "A Paradox in the Theory of Democracy." In *Philosophy, Politics, and Society,* edited by Peter Laslett and W. G. Runciman, 71–87. New Haven, CT: Yale University Press.
Wu, Tim. 2018. *The Curse of Bigness.* New York: Columbia Global Reports.
Yancy, George. 2018. *Backlash.* Lanham, MD: Rowman and Littlefield.
Yankah, Ekow. 2008. "The Force of Law." *University of Richmond Law Review* 42:1195–1256.
Young, Iris Marion. 1990. *Justice and the Politics of Difference.* Princeton, NJ: Princeton University Press.
———. 2011. *Responsibility for Justice.* Oxford: Oxford University Press.
Zhao, Mike. 2019. "Solidarity, Fate-Sharing, and Community." *Philosophers' Imprint* 49:1–13.

Acknowledgments

My greatest intellectual debts are to Sam Scheffler and Jay Wallace, who brought me, as a graduate student, to appreciate the significance of many of the ideas on which this book is based. Looking back, I'm dumbstruck at my good fortune to have them as advisors and then to have, on top of that, the supererogatory mentoring of Seana Shiffrin in a year when she visited Berkeley. The influence of Joseph Raz and Tim Scanlon exceeds what my specific references to their work, as numerous as they are, might gauge. (I don't kid myself, though, that the aerial-castle-building in which so much of this book indulges is much to their taste.) I am grateful for the friendship, philosophical and otherwise, of Véronique Munoz-Dardé, whose judgment that anything I write is worth commenting on builds the confidence I need to withstand the comments. I am also grateful for the friendship of the literary theorist Kevin Ohi, a friendship that survives the occasional bafflement at, if ever-present admiration for, what the other is up to.

I have learned much from ongoing work on similar issues by Eric Beerbohm (2012), Sean Ingham (2021), Kathryn Joyce, Adam Lovett (2020, 2021), Sophia Moreau (2020), Han van Wietmarschen (2021), Daniel Viehoff (2014, 2019), James Wilson (2019, 2021), and Jake Zuehl. I hope that the appearance of my book won't contribute to a neglect of their work or, worse, that their work will be tarnished by association with my quirks and errors.

This book draws on several previously published papers. Portions of Chapters 2 and 4 were first published as "Political Rule and Its Discontents" in *Oxford Studies in Political Philosophy* 2 (2016). Portions of Chapter 3 were first published as "What Makes Threats Wrong?" in *Analytic Philosophy* 58 (2017): 87–118. Much of "Towards an Analysis of Social Hierarchy," published in the *Journal of Contemporary Legal Issues*, is reprinted in Chapters 5 and 6. Portions of Chapter 9 were first published by Oxford University Press in 2023 as "Is There an Objection to Workplace Hierarchy Itself?" in

Jonker and Rozenboom, eds., *Working as Equals.* Chapter 10 builds on ideas first discussed in, and Chapter 23 and the conclusion include portions of text first published by Cambridge University Press in 2019 as "Being Under the Power of Others" in Yiftah Elizar and Geneviève Rousselière, eds., *Republicanism and Democracy,* 94–114. Portions of Chapter 17 were first published as "Why Equality of Treatment and Opportunity Might Matter" in *Philosophical Studies* 176 (2019): 3357–3366. Portions of Chapters 19 and 20 were first published as "Standing and the Sources of Liberalism" in *Politics, Philosophy, Economics* 17 (2018): 169–191. Much of the text of "Rule over None I: What Justifies Democracy?" in *Philosophy and Public Affairs* 42 (2014): 195–229 is reprinted in Chapters 24 and 26. Portions of Chapters 29 and 30 were first published as "Rule over None II: Social Equality and the Justification of Democracy" in *Philosophy and Public Affairs* 42 (2014): 287–336. Chapters 5 and 27 also build on ideas first published in this article. Much of Chapter 30 was first published as "What, If Anything, Is Wrong with Gerrymandering?" in *University of San Diego Law Journal* 56 (2019): 1013–1038. Portions of Chapter 32 were first published on February 17, 2017, in *Boston Review* as "How People Vote," a review of Christopher H. Achen and Larry M. Bartels, *Democracy for Realists* (Princeton University Press, 2016) and Jason Brennan, *Against Democracy* (Princeton University Press, 2016).

In notes to those papers, I record debts to many reviewers, commenters, and interlocutors. This book inherits those debts, with renewed gratitude. I am also grateful to Dick Arneson, David Copp, Sophia Moreau, Paul Weithman, and Andrew Williams, who gave prepared comments on unpublished talks incorporated into this book.

I have had the privilege of discussing drafts or overviews of the manuscript as a whole on several occasions. I am grateful to Ariel Zylberman and Arthur Ripstein for their prepared comments on a summary of the book at the University of Toronto in the fall of 2019. Participants in my graduate seminar in the spring of 2020 worked through a manuscript even less forgiving than the present book; my thanks go to Valentin Beck, Jonas Blatter, Scott Casleton, Monika Chao, Jorge Cortes-Montoy, Joshua Freed, Jes Heppler, Dan Khokhar, Cherí Kruse, Véronique Munoz-Dardé, Christian Nakazawa, Tony Rook, Klaus Strelau, and Jay Wallace. Subsequent discussions with Christian and Tony, in particular, shaped ideas in the book. I was flattered when Jake Zuehl organized a virtual workshop on the manuscript in the fall of 2020, which was attended by Evan Behrle, Chuck Beitz, Clara Lingle, Adam Lovett, Aiden Penn, Sam Scheffler, Annie Stilz, Daniel Viehoff, Brad Weslake, and James Wilson. I was also likewise flattered when Jon Quong and Mark Schroeder organized another virtual workshop on the book in the spring of 2021, hosted by the Conceptual Foundations of Conflict Project at the University of Southern California, with a dream team of commentators: Kristi Olson, Sophia Moreau, Seana Shiffrin, Zofia Stemplowska, and Annie Stilz. I received helpful comments subsequently from Pablo Gilabert, Adriano Mannino, Rowan Mellor, and Merlin Wehrs. I owe a special debt of gratitude to Mannino and Wehrs, whose extensive comments, throughout the manuscript, were extraordinarily insightful and penetrating. There was not enough time before the manuscript was due at the press to attempt to answer all of Mannino's and Wehrs's many questions and objections. That remains a task for the future.

I was very fortunate that Harvard University Press was able to enlist Chuck Beitz and Arthur Ripstein as referees, whose comments prompted a substantial reworking of the manuscript and, insofar as I followed their advice, a substantial improvement. James Brandt, who was the primary reason I wanted to work with Harvard, sent similarly invaluable comments after punching his last time card with the press. It was a rare piece of good fortune to have an editor at once fluent in the academic debates and shrewd about matters of publishing. And the lucky streak only continued when Ian Malcolm and then Joseph Pomp adopted the project and saw it through to completion. I am indebted to Christian Nakazawa and Paula Durbin-Westby for preparing the index. Finally, I am grateful to the forbearance of my family during the countless hours that went into this project. I hope Colette and Eddie will take this book no more seriously than they took my early foray into science fiction, *Jim 3000*. This book is dedicated to Jessica.

Index